A FRA
YOUR

Code Fragn
Code Resou
and Macint

Joe Zobkiv

Foreword by

Addison-Wesley Publishing Company

Reading, Massachusetts • Menlo Park, California • New York
Don Mills, Ontario • Wokingham, England • Amsterdam
Bonn • Sydney • Singapore • Tokyo • Madrid • San Juan
Paris • Seoul • Milan • Mexico City • Taipei

Many of the designations used by manufacturers and sellers to distinguish their products are claimed as trademarks. Where those designations appear in this book, and Addison-Wesley was aware of a trademark claim, the designations have been printed in initial capital letters or all capital letters.

The author and publisher have taken care in preparation of this book, but make no expressed or implied warranty of any kind and assume no responsibility for errors or omissions. No liability is assumed for incidental or consequential damages in connection with or arising out of the use of the information or programs contained herein.

Library of Congress Cataloging-in-Publication Data

Zobkiw, Joe.
    A fragment of your imagination : code fragments and code resources
for Power Macintosh and Macintosh programmers / Joe Zobkiw.
        p.   cm.
    Includes bibliographical references and index.
    ISBN 0-201-48358-0
    1. Macintosh (Computer)—Programming.   2. PowerPC microprocessors—
Programming.   I. Title.
QA76.8.M3Z63   1995
005.26—dc20   95-17045
                                                                    CIP

The Tiger Slider used in Chapter Seven, "Control Definition" is © 1995 Tiger Technologies. It was written by Robert L. Mathews.

The Infinity Windoid WDEF used in Chapter Eight, "Window Definitions," is © 1991–95 by Infinity Systems and Troy Gaul.

The TV Tube Photoshop filter used in Chapter Ten, "Photoshop Filters," was written by Troy Gaul and was based on the Dissolve sample from Adobe.

The RefConLDEF is loosely based on an initial concept by Manoj Patwardhan called LDEF1, which is © 1995 Crystal Software Inc. All rights reserved. It was renamed and changed for use in this book.

All other code, unless otherwise noted, is © 1995 by Joe Zobkiw. All rights reserved.

Sponsoring Editor: Martha Steffen
Project Manager: John Fuller
Production Coordinator: Ellen Savett
Cover Design: Chris St. Cyr
Set in 10 point Palatino by Clarinda

1 2 3 4 5 6 7 8 9-MA-9998979695
First printing, July 1995

Addison-Wesley books are available for bulk purchases by corporations, institutions, and other organizations. For more information please contact the Corporate, Government, and Special Sales Department at (800) 238-9682.

This book is dedicated to the memory of my father,
Richard Zobkiw

Contents

Special Thanks

This being my first book, it is tempting to thank everyone with whom I've ever come into contact. However, because I only have a page to do it all, here I go . . .

Special thanks first and foremost to my wife, Reneé, for letting me spend the time away from her to write this book. I couldn't have done it without her support. Thanks to Sasha Doodles for not barking too loud. Thanks to my parents for supporting me. Thanks to David Mash for my first big break and his friendship. Thanks to Troy Gaul and Rob Mathews for the awesome code and the time they invested in preparing it for this book. Thanks to Marty Wachter, Ron Davis, Jim Luther, and Nitin Ganatra for reviewing the manuscript and keeping me in check. To Greg Galanos and Metrowerks, thanks for everything. Thanks to Scott Knaster for taking time out of his busy schedule of creating cool stuff to write the Foreword. Thanks to Mike Groh and Scott Crenshaw for being cool about stuff. Thanks to Kaethin Prizer, John Fuller, Ellen Savett, and everyone at Addison-Wesley for their assistance. And of course, thanks to Martha Steffen for believing in me enough to allow this to happen in the first place. Little did she know . . .

And how could I not mention all those who have helped shape my life in one way or another over the years: John "The Jingle Man" Hunter, "Funky" Chris Haynes, Jeff "Wheat Bread" Dopko, Steve "Rye Bread" Rossi, Chris Rose, Jim Lent, Rick Rainone, Dick "The

Howe" Howard, Ira "Adam Bomb" Horvitz, David Zobkiw, the Emmi family (all of them), the Lockett family, Chris Wysocki, Greg LaSalle, Dave Mark, everyone at TPS, everyone at Berklee, my SmartFriends™, and anyone else I may have missed (you know who you are), especially those who owe me money.

Foreword

I don't want to alarm you here, but your Macintosh is not so much a personal computer as it is a digital petri dish, an environment where tiny things live. You see, there are all sorts of wacky little programs running around inside there, helping make your Macintosh work better. (Of course, viruses work that way, too, but that's the way petri dishes are: you'll find lots of different things growing inside.) Joe Zobkiw is your expert tour guide through this densely populated world.

When you're using your favorite application, you may think that it's in control of what's going on, and you're right, sort of. Although the application is running the show, it has a lot of help. Every time it draws a window, it calls upon a crafty little specialist of a program that only draws windows. Apple supplies this small piece of code, but you can have lots of fun learning how to replace it with your own to make windows look and act just how you want them to. Controls, menus, and lists work the same way, and Joe tells you about all of them in this secret-spilling book.

While your application develops a close personal friendship with these code resources, there are various other programs (not applications) hanging out and doing their own thing. Among the most important of these are system extensions that are loaded when your Macintosh starts up. You'll find out how to make those, too.

Some applications are just so studly that they provide their own personal environment for code resources. The best-known example of these applications, HyperCard and its famous XCMD extensions, is covered in Chapter 9.

The Macintosh has always had zillions of little programs sharing the road, getting work done, but the platforms for code resources keep getting richer. When Apple's technology advanced to include QuickTime, Apple introduced the Component Manager, a fancy new playland for code resources. And when the Power Macintosh made its successful debut in 1994, Apple made sure that it could handle all the code resources hosted by its predecessor, while introducing new tricks of its own. With a taste for the latest technology, Joe tells you all about these goodies.

Both the original Macintosh (68000 family) and the extra-crispy (Power Mac), have gotten a lot of mileage out of using code resources to handle a wide variety of tasks. With code resources, clever programmers (hello, clever programmer!) can make their Macs behave more like they want them to. Joe Zobkiw has figured out this essential secret and has written a thorough and insightful guide to crafting code resources. Joe writes from his own experience and enthusiasm because he knows that these critters are everywhere. Hey—there's one crawling up your leg!

—Scott Knaster
Macintosh Semi-Geek

Introduction

So, you want to learn about code resources and fragments, huh?

By writing this book, I attempt to introduce code resources and fragments to the intermediate Macintosh programmer. I assume that you have experience writing applications or some other type of code on the Macintosh. I also assume that you are familiar, to some extent, with things like the Resource Manager, the File Manager, the Dialog Manager, QuickDraw, the Menu Manager, the Control Manager, and other Toolbox and operating system managers. If you have successfully completed just about any small Macintosh program, you can probably pick up the information in this book with little effort. Simply read it and absorb.

I do assume that you understand a bit about how the concepts work on the Macintosh. For example, before delving into the chapter on how to write a PowerPC native control panel, you should probably have read the *Inside Macintosh* chapter on control panels and maybe even have implemented a simple control panel for 680x0 Macintosh. Also, although the important bits of source code are displayed and discussed in each chapter, by reading through the actual source code for each individual project, available on the accompanying CD-ROM, you will obtain a greater understanding of the project as a whole. Read the book, look at the source code, compile the project, and experiment. This book is meant to augment the *Inside Macintosh* volumes by offering useful, extended examples of the concepts presented there.

I sincerely hope you enjoy this book and gain something from it. The information in it represents years of experience and experimentation. If something in this book saves you a day off your programming schedule, then I've done my job. Enjoy this book and use it well.

CHAPTER ONE

Introduction to Code Resources

"Regularly scheduled programming" is an oxymoron.

—Doug McKenna

Introduction

When the Macintosh was released in 1984, those who purchased the new machine knew it was a winner. The moment they put their hand to the mouse, users felt the ease of use that Macintosh promised. Programmers, on the other hand, saw a uniquely designed operating system that allowed total customization of the look and feel of the computer. The ability to customize was due to an ingenious approach of factoring the functionality of specific user interface elements into separate code pieces. An engineer working on the Macintosh decided that if most user interface elements were completely handled by drop-in pieces of code, it would make development simpler and would also be less stressful on the then-limited 128K of memory. The Macintosh code resource was born.

You probably already know that all radio buttons, check boxes, scroll bars, menus, lists of items, windows, and dialog boxes are drawn by code stored in resources of different types. For example, the Control Manager handles drawing buttons and scroll bars by executing code in resources of type CDEF. The Menu Manager executes code in resources of type MDEF to draw its menus. Programmers can even create custom lists of items by means of the List Manager resources of type LDEF. Resources of type INIT are loaded at startup and allow programmers to customize features of the system on a global scale.

> Eventually, Apple was forced to release strict guidelines about how a Macintosh application should look and feel to the user. These user interface guidelines are constantly being updated as new interface elements are being created. If you ever look at some of the programs that were released early on, you will see why Apple's decision to set up guidelines was a good one.

Anatomy of a Code Resource

As the name implies, code resources are standard Macintosh resources that just happen to contain executable code. Code stored in a resource can be accessed by any other code—whether it be in the operating system or in your application. If you are familiar with HyperCard, you know that it can access external commands and functions in your stacks if they are stored in resources of type XCMD and XFCN, respectively. These resources contain executable code originally written in C, Pascal, or some other language that is then compiled into code resource form. You can consider the resource as simply a container that houses the code. By storing the code in a resource-based container, HyperCard is able to use the Resource Manager functions to load it and eventually execute it. Later on in this book, we explore HyperCard externals in detail.

When your development environment compiles your source as a code resource it expects it to have a single, main entry point—also known simply as *main*. This entry point is used to assemble the code resource in such a way that, when it is called, the main function will be executed first (Figure 1-1). The main function can then call other functions in the code resource, as you are used to seeing when writing any other type of code.

Calling a Code Resource

In order for an application, or any other software, to execute code stored in a resource, it must know certain information about the code it is about to execute. First, it must know the type of resource in which

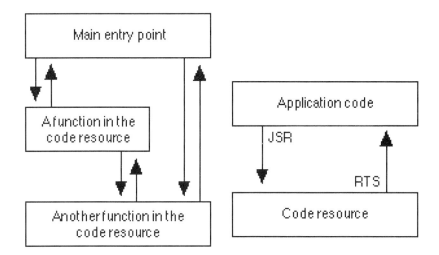

Figure 1-1. Main entry point calling other functions in a code resource

Figure 1-2. Calling a code resource—the details

the code is stored. Second, it must know the resource name or identification number (also known as the resource ID.) At this point, the application loads the code resource by using any of the standard Resource Manager functions. Once loaded, it locks the resource in memory and then calls the main entry point function of the resource, using its specific calling conventions, to perform its duty. You should note that a code resource can take any number of parameters and return any type. However, you must decide on this before you create your code resource. The calling code needs to know this information in order to properly execute the code resource (as in the following code).

```
typedef void (*VoidProc)(void);
OSErr CallCodeResource(void)
{
    Handle      hCode = Get1Resource(kResType, kResID);
    OSErr       err = noErr;


    if (hCode) {
        HLockHi(hCode);


    ((VoidProc)(*hCode))();

    HUnlock(hCode);
```

```
                ReleaseResource(hCode);
          } else err = ResError();


          return err;
          }
```

On a 680x0 Macintosh, you call the main entry point of a code resource by simply jumping to it via a JMP or JSR 680x0 assembly language instruction. This immediately begins execution of the code
stored in the code resource. When the code resource is finished, it performs an RTS 680x0 assembly language instruction, which returns control to the caller (Figure 1-2). Normally, in C, you will never see these
instructions, but it is good to understand what is happening behind
the scenes.

Real-world Example of Using Code Resources

As mentioned, code resources are used by system software-level services in order to implement many user interface elements. By taking
advantage of this fact, you can customize the look and feel of your application. You can add custom buttons, popup menus, colorful windows and controls, and more.

Another way you can take advantage of code resources is to write
them into your application design. Let's say you want to write a program that edits sound. You may want to display the sound waveform
in a window and then allow users to select portions of it to which they
could apply effects such as echo, flange, chorus, etc. Your program
might have a menu named Effect that would contain a list of all possible effects that are available to the program (Figure 1-3).

By storing the code to generate these effects in a specific resource
type, you can create your Effect menu simply by using the AddRes-
Menu function. This is a similar technique that programs use to add
desk accessories to the Apple menu. When the user selects an item
from your Effect menu, you can then load the resource by name, since
the name of the menu item is the same as the name of the resource.
After it is loaded, you simply call the code resource (discussed in detail in subsequent chapters) by passing it the raw sample data on
which the user has selected to act, and then wait for it to return. After
the code resource has completed its job, you simply call Release-
Resource to free the memory it is taking up. This is a very simple way
to implement modularity in your program.

In addition to this technique of loading, calling, and unloading
your code resources as they are needed, you can also load all of them

```
 Effect
  Delay...
  Echo...
  Flange...
  Reverb...
```

Figure 1-3. Menu containing options available via code resources

at application startup and keep them loaded until you quit the application. This may work better, depending on the type of application you are writing. In our example, the effect never takes place until the user explicitly selects the item from the menu, so a few ticks to load a resource might not be a big deal. However, if you have lots of memory available to your application and you need to muster all the speed you can out of your calling mechanism, you may elect to load all of the code resources first, then call them as needed, which saves any extra disk access time each time the resources are used.

Yet another technique for dealing with code resources is to store each one in a separate file, as opposed to storing the resource in your application. The files themselves would contain the code resource and any extra resources (such as dialog boxes or alerts) that they might use to do their job. When your application launches, you might peruse a folder called Effect folder, which would exist in the same folder as your application. Any files that contain your effect resources could then be listed in your menu. Now when a user selects an effect, you need to make sure to open the particular file in which the effect is stored, make it the current resource file, load the code resource, call it, and then, after it is finished, close the file and restore your application as the current resource file. This is a very popular way of implementing modular code in applications since it allows users to easily add and remove only those effects that they may want to use.

As you can imagine, there are numerous optimizations you can apply to this last technique. For example, you may load all effect code resources from each file and call DetachResource on each one of them. Although you would still have to open the resource file of each effect (if it used any resources within the file), this technique accelerates the process of calling each effect by avoiding the resource loading overhead. You may also include a configuration resource in each file that contains certain information about the particular effect. One of the flags in this resource might tell the calling application if the effect needs any resources in its file, so you know whether or not you even need to open it at all when you call the effect.

Each application you write may have different needs when it comes to code resources. As you explore the possibilities of each, you will find what works best for you and your particular situation. It's safe to say, however, that implementing portions of your application in this way will undoubtedly make your programming life easier.

Code Resource Limitations

Like all good things, there are some things to be aware of when dealing with code resources on a 680x0 Macintosh. Although they are very straightforward—after you've created a few—there are some limitations involved that may or may not impact your project. Let's take a look at some of them.

Globals in Code Resources

As you may know, the Macintosh keeps track of application global data based off of the 680x0 register named A5. Whenever an application attempts to access global data, it is always assumed that register A5 contains the proper value and then an offset is added to it to access the global data. Code resources have no such "A5 world" and, therefore, do not have access to any global data by default. Luckily, there is a simple way to allow access to global data from within your code resource.

> The Power Macintosh allows global data in code fragments, which are the equivalent of code resources on that platform. This is discussed fully in subsequent chapters, so please stay tuned.

Different development environments have different mechanisms for making global data usable in stand-alone code resources. Apple's Macintosh Programmers Workshop (MPW) has a scheme that creates a fake A5 world. Both Metrowerks' CodeWarrior and Symantec's THINK C make use of A4-relative global data. That is, all references to global data are referenced at an offset off of the value stored in register A4. It is up to programmers to include some simple calls in their code in order to ensure that register A4 contains the proper value when access to this global data is needed.

Because this book makes use of CodeWarrior, we will be showing an example of global data using that development environment. The THINK C environment is similar and MPW is totally different. You should consult the documentation that came with your particular environment in order to learn the specifics of using globals in code resources.

Before we learn how to access global data, let's take a look at what exactly global data consists of. Most of the time, you assume global data is simply a variable that is defined outside of any function. This is true. But in CodeWarrior, for example, other things in your code are considered global data and are, therefore, referenced off of the value in register A4. The following code snippet shows many types of global data in CodeWarrior.

```
long gVersionNumber;

void SetVersion(void);

void main(void)
{
    Point               p = {50,100};
    Str255              s;

    GetIndString(s, 128, 1);
    if (EqualString(s, "\pUtopia", true, true))
        return;

    SetVersion();
}

void SetVersion(void)
{
    gVersionNumber = 0L;
}
```

It is probably obvious to you that the gVersionNumber variable is a global variable. However, did you know that although the Point variable, p, is local, the way it is initialized makes use of global data? Sure enough, the values 50 and 100 are both referenced off of the value in register A4. The hard-coded string "\pUtopia" is also treated as global data. Take a look at the 680x0 assembly language version of this code, which follows. It shows us exactly what is happening.

```
Hunk:Kind=HUNK_LOCAL_IDATA Name="@"(2) Size=4
00000000: 00 32 00 64                                       '.2.d'

Hunk:Kind=HUNK_LOCAL_IDATA Name="@6"(6) Size=7
00000000: 06 55 74 6F 70 69 61                              '.Utopia'

Hunk:Kind=HUNK_GLOBAL_CODE Name="main"(7) Size=72
00000000: 4E56 FEFC           LINK     A6,#$FEFC
00000004: 2D6C 0000 FEFC      MOVE.L   @(A4),$FEFC(A6)
0000000A: 486E FF00           PEA      $FF00(A6)
0000000E: 2F3C 0001 0080      MOVE.L   #$00010080,-(A7)
00000014: 4EB9 0000 0000      JSR      GETINDSTRING
0000001A: 554F                SUBQ.W   #$2,A7
0000001C: 486E FF00           PEA      $FF00(A6)
00000020: 486C 0000           PEA      @6(A4)
00000024: 1F3C 0001           MOVE.B   #$01,-(A7)
00000028: 1F3C 0001           MOVE.B   #$01,-(A7)
0000002C: 4EB9 0000 0000      JSR      EQUALSTRING
00000032: 101F                MOVE.B   (A7)+,D0
00000034: 6606                BNE.S    *+$0008      ; 0000003C
00000036: 4EB9 0000 0000      JSR      SetVersion
0000003C: 4E5E                UNLK     A6
0000003E: 4E75                RTS

Hunk:Kind=HUNK_GLOBAL_CODE Name="SetVersion"(8) Size=26
00000000: 4E56 0000           LINK     A6,#$0000
00000004: 42AC 0000           CLR.L    gVersionNumber(A4)
00000008: 4E5E                UNLK     A6
0000000A: 4E75                RTS

XRef:Kind=HUNK_XREF_DATA16BIT Name="gVersionNumber"(3) #Pairs=1
        Offset=$00000010 Value=$00000000
```

You will also notice that the SetVersion function makes use of the global gVersionNumber. In an application, this would not be a problem and all would be well. However, in a code resource, the SetVersion function cannot be guaranteed access to the gVersionNumber

The code presented here, which is CodeWarrior's representation of the assembly language that it generates, has lots of information in it. The column to the left is the offset at which that line of code exists. The offset always begins at 0 and increments by the size of the previous instruction. Since the first instruction is 4 bytes in length, the second offset is 4. The second column is the hexadecimal representation of the instruction. The remaining information is the assembly language English representation of the instruction. Don't worry if you don't understand assembly language, we will still let you finish reading the book.

global, unless it sets up the value of the A4 register before attempting to access it. The following code snippet shows the extra code needed to make global data work in this example.

```
#include "A4Stuff.h"
#include "SetupA4.h"

long gVersionNumber;

void SetVersion(void);

void main(void)
{
    long    oldA4;
    Point   p;
    Str255  s;

    oldA4 = SetCurrentA4();
    RememberA4();

    p.h = 50; p.v = 100;

    GetIndString(s, 128, 1);
    if (EqualString(s, "\pUtopia", true, true))
        return;

    SetVersion();

    SetA4(oldA4);
}

void SetVersion(void)
{
```

```
long oldA4 = SetUpA4();
gVersionNumber = 0L;
RestoreA4(oldA4);
}
```

As you can see, by making use of the specialized A4 functions, you can ensure that your code has access to your global data. Assuming you've included the proper A4-related header files, as we have done here, the first thing that your main function does is to set the current A4 as the A4 that you use when you need access to globals. This is accomplished via the SetCurrentA4 and RememberA4 functions. After this is done, your other functions in this source file can access the proper A4 by calling SetUpA4 and RestoreA4, as the SetVersion function does. These simple utility functions (see the following code) make the difference between accessing the data you expect and accessing random data that will most likely make you crash deep into your debugger. So, if you notice a crash in your code resource, and it looks like you may be trying to access some data at an offset off of register A4, you may not have set things up properly.

```
Hunk:        Kind=HUNK_LOCAL_CODE Name="SetUpA4"(1) Size=32
00000000: 200C              MOVE.L     A4,D0
00000002: 49FA 0006         LEA        *+$0008,A4     ; 0000000A
00000006: 2854              MOVEA.L    (A4),A4
00000008: 4E75              RTS
0000000A: 0000 0000         ORI.B      #$00,D0
0000000E: 41FA FFFA         LEA        *-$0004,A0     ; 0000000A
00000012: 208C              MOVE.L     A4,(A0)
00000014: 4E75              RTS

Hunk:        Kind=HUNK_LOCAL_IDATA Name="@5"(4) Size=7
00000000: 06 55 74 6F 70 69 61                        '.Utopia'

Hunk:        Kind=HUNK_GLOBAL_CODE Name="main"(5) Size=100
00000000: 4E56 FEF8         LINK       A6,#$FEF8
00000004: 4EB9 0000 0000    JSR        SetCurrentA4
0000000A: 2D40 FEF8         MOVE.L     D0,$FEF8(A6)
0000000E: 4EB9 0000 0000    JSR        RememberA4
00000014: 3D7C 0032 FFFE    MOVE.W     #$0032,$FFFE(A6)
0000001A: 3D7C 0064 FFFC    MOVE.W     #$0064,$FFFC(A6)
00000020: 486E FEFC         PEA        $FEFC(A6)
00000024: 2F3C 0001 0080    MOVE.L     #$00010080,-(A7)
0000002A: 4EB9 0000 0000    JSR        GETINDSTRING
00000030: 554F              SUBQ.W     #$2,A7
00000032: 486E FEFC         PEA        $FEFC(A6)
00000036: 486C 0000         PEA        @5(A4)
0000003A: 1F3C 0001         MOVE.B     #$01,-(A7)
0000003E: 1F3C 0001         MOVE.B     #$01,-(A7)
```

```
00000042: 4EB9 0000 0000      JSR       EQUALSTRING
00000048: 101F                MOVE.B    (A7)+,D0
0000004A: 660C                BNE.S     *+$000E     ; 00000058
0000004C: 4EB9 0000 0000      JSR       SetVersion
00000052: 202E FEF8           MOVE.L    $FEF8(A6),D0
00000056: C18C                EXG       D0,A4
00000058: 4E5E                UNLK      A6
0000005A: 4E75                RTS

Hunk:               Kind=HUNK_GLOBAL_CODE Name="SetVersion"(6)  Size=42
00000000: 4E56 FFFC           LINK      A6,#$FFFC
00000004: 4EB9 0000 0000      JSR       SetUpA4
0000000A: 2D40 FFFC           MOVE.L    D0,$FFFC(A6)
0000000E: 42AC 0000           CLR.L     gVersionNumber(A4)
00000012: 202E FFFC           MOVE.L    $FFFC(A6),D0
00000016: C18C                EXG       D0,A4
00000018: 4E5E                UNLK      A6
0000001A: 4E75                RTS

XRef:               Kind=HUNK_XREF_DATA16BIT Name="gVersionNumber"(3)
                    #Pairs=1
                    Offset=$00000010 Value=$00000000
```

> In reality, the SetVersion function would have been able to access
> the global data without a problem in this particular case (even if
> it didn't set up A4 itself), since the main function had already set
> up A4. When SetVersion was called, A4 was set properly. How-
> ever, in some cases your SetVersion call may have been called
> from a function that did not set up A4 for global access. This
> might happen if you called it from a trap patch. We simply want
> to show you how the A4 functions work in relation to each other.
> You are expected to experiment with these functions and to learn
> when you may or may not need them.

What we've learned about global data is all well and good, assuming the source code of your code resource is contained in only one
text file. However, if the source code is spread across multiple text files
and you have functions in each that need access to the same global
data, you need to perform a few more tricks before continuing. You
see, the A4 functions that we just mentioned only work for a single
source file. When you #include the A4-related header files, you are actually including code that is self-modifying (as in the following code).
That is, when you execute the RememberA4 function, it actually

stashes the value of A4 within itself. Since it only #includes itself in the particular file that #includes it, other files will not have access to this much-needed information. Therefore, you must ensure they have access to the A4 value in some other way.

```
static void RememberA4(void);

static asm long SetUpA4(void)
{
    move.l      a4,d0
    lea         storage,a4
    move.l      (a4),a4
    rts

    // this storage is only referenced thru data cache
storage:    dc.l 0

    entry static RememberA4
    lea         storage, a0
    move.l      a4,(a0)
    rts
}
```

Luckily, there is an easy way around this problem. From your main function, after you have set up A4 completely, you should call a function in each file that may use globals. This function will set up A4 for each file individually. It simply needs to call RememberA4 in order to copy the current, proper value of A4 into its own, local A4 storage location (as in the following code). Then, whenever any function in the file needs access to any globals, it can do exactly what SetVersion does in the previous example. That's it!

```
#include "A4Stuff.h"
#include "SetupA4.h"

void SetUpGlobalsInFile(void)
{
    RememberA4();
}
```

32K Limit and Multisegment Code Resources

Because of the way things are, there is an inherent 32K limit to the size of code resources. You see, the 680x0 BRAnch instruction that allows you to jump from one part of your code to another takes only a 2-byte value as an offset. As you know, the largest signed number that can fit into 2 bytes is 32767. Therefore, you can not BRAnch more than about 32,000 bytes at a time. This limit has survived the evolution of the Macintosh and is just now being taken away with the advent of the Power Macintosh.

Because of this limit, developers have been forced to write code resources that are smaller than 32K in size. As with global data, different development environments have implemented different approaches to getting around this limit for those that need to get around it. MPW has implemented features such as branch islands that split a large branch into several smaller branches. If you needed to branch 40,000 bytes, you might first branch to an "island" that was 20,000 bytes away and then immediately branch the remaining 20,000 bytes. The island contains nothing but another BRAnch instruction. All 68020 or later CPUs contain the bsr.1 instruction that allows for 32-bit relative branches, doing away with the need for branch islands on those processors.

CodeWarrior and THINK have implemented multisegment code resources that allow the developer to have as many segments as are needed—all less than 32K each. In this mechanism, a stub of code is added to the beginning of the first code resource that automatically loads the other segments and updates any jump table information. So, the fact that multiple segments exist is totally transparent to the caller. In many cases, the caller can simply execute the code resource as if it were a single segment and all will work fine.

One case where this may not work is if the code resource is detached and the resource file in which it is stored is closed. In this case, since the stub code that the development environment adds does not detach the other segments (via a call to DetachResource), you will probably find yourself in your friendly, local debugger with an address error or similar unwanted crash. The workaround is to either have the calling code detach the segments (which would require it to know how many segments existed) or have the main code resource segment itself do the detaching. Either way, it can be tricky if you add a segment to your project but forget to change the code to detach it. It's problems like these that help build character and debugging skills.

Code Resource Tips

This chapter discusses techniques and problems that are explored further in chapters later in the book. Even if you don't fully understand some of the finer points now, you will soon be delving deep into code resources and how they interact with other parts of the operating system and your applications. In the meantime, here are some things to watch out for when dealing with code resources.

- Unless you explicitly detach a code resource using the Resource Manager DetachResource function when the file in which the resource is stored is closed, the code resource will be released from memory. Therefore, if you load your resource from a separate file, and that file is closed, your code will no longer be valid. Attempting to execute code that is in this state will most likely cause a crash.
- In many cases, even though code resources are limited to 32K in size, development environments like CodeWarrior allow you to create resources that are not affected by this limit. You can use the Multi-Segment and Link Single Segment options in CodeWarrior to create a code resource that is practically any size at all.
- Global data comes in many forms. Luckily, CodeWarrior displays (in the main project window) how much global data is used by a particular file. If you are writing a code resource and are not using the A4 functions for globals, yet CodeWarrior shows you have global data in a file, something is wrong. Make sure you find out exactly where you are using the globals and either remove them or use the A4 functions.
- Removing global data in a file can be easy in many cases. Instead of hard coding a string in place in your code, load it from a resource using the GetIndString function. Instead of initializing structure-based variables such as a Point in place as it is declared, set its fields individually in the code below it.
- If you have a multisegment code resource that you need to load and detach from the resource file in which it is contained, make sure you also detach any extra resources it may use. Obviously, multisegment resources have multiple code segments that will need detaching. You should also keep an eye out for extra resources that your development environment might create that are used by the multisegment code—these may also have to be detached.
- Make sure your code resources are locked down before you attempt to execute them. By calling HLock on the handle to your code, you will ensure that the code doesn't move out from under you if you happen to do something within the code resource that causes memory to move. Remember, your code resource is simply a handle to memory and is prone to moving just like other unlocked handles. If it moves in the middle of execution, you are toast.

C H A P T E R   T W O

Power Macintosh Code Fragments

What the @#$@#$#@ is wrong with this!?

—Andrew Welch

Introduction

The Power Macintosh is one heck of a computer. Apple took the time to design it right from the start in order to make it incredibly fast and very compatible with all the cool 680x0 Macintosh software that already exists. Anyone who knows any bit of history of the Macintosh operating system knows that, over its lifetime, hundreds of programmers have added to the code that is responsible for the daily goings on inside your Macintosh. Getting it all to work in the first place is a job of which many programmers would cringe at the thought. The amazing thing is that not only did the Power Macintosh engineers make a Macintosh that was faster than any other, using an entirely new type of computer chip, but they also made it entirely backward compatible with most 680x0-based software.

The first Power Macintosh was based on the Motorola PowerPC 601 reduced instruction set computer (RISC) chip. This chip is a 32-bit implementation of the 64-bit PowerPC architecture originally designed by IBM. The chip itself can execute up to three instructions in a single clock cycle and can even execute them out of order for increased performance. The chip houses enough power to handle many of the jobs that otherwise would have taken a computer that filled a small room. PowerPC-based Macintosh computers can be two or more times faster than the 680x0 variety—and they will only get faster.

As mentioned, just about any 680x0 software that runs under System 7, is 32-bit clean, is compatible with virtual memory, and understands how to be kind to the Process Manager (also known as MultiFinder in the days of old) should run fine on a Power Macintosh. The reason the PowerPC chip can run 680x0 software is because Apple provided a 680x0 emulator in the Power Macintosh system software. This emulator, in conjunction with the Mixed Mode Manager, ensures that 680x0 code and PowerPC code coexist peacefully on the same machine.

> The 680x0 emulator actually emulates the 68LC040 chip from Motorola. It does not support Paged Memory Management Unit (PMMU) instructions, however, and no Floating Point Unit (FPU) is present. In fact, the only difference between a 68LC040 and a 68040 is the missing FPU on the "LC" version. The emulator is basically a Centris (also known as a Quadra) 610 computer. Many developers use this machine as a guide when testing their software.

This chapter will introduce you to the new managers that make the Power Macintosh what it is today. We will discuss the Mixed Mode Manager, which helps to keep 680x0 and PowerPC code straight from one another. We will then delve into the Code Fragment Manager to explain how code is handled on the PowerPC as opposed to what we've learned about 680x0 Macintosh computers. What you learn in this chapter will pave the way for the projects in the rest of the book. So pay attention and let's begin.

The Mixed Mode Manager

The Mixed Mode Manager is responsible for managing mode switches between differing instruction set architectures. An instruction set architecture is the set of instructions that is recognized by a particular family of processors. The PowerPC chip is a processor, as is the 680x0 family of chips. A mode switch occurs when code from one instruction set architecture is currently running and is about to execute code written in another instruction set architecture. For example, your 680x0 program may attempt to execute a Toolbox function that is now written in the PowerPC native instruction set. The Mixed Mode Manager will intervene in order to switch execution contexts between the 680x0 emulator and the PowerPC native mode. After the function has completed execution, the Mixed Mode Manager will switch modes back to the original 680x0 emulator in order to return to your code. These switches are all carried on without your knowledge when running current 680x0 software on a Power Macintosh.

If you are writing code that will run on a Power Macintosh in native mode, you need to make some changes to the way you currently do things. The new universal header files force you to make some of them; others you need to be aware of or suffer the fate of a crash. You may not have to make any changes to your application to make it run in native mode on a Power Macintosh, but that chance is pretty slim. In most cases, you will need to sweep through your code and "fix" things here and there to make it compile and run properly. If you use your compilers "full warnings" option, it will find most of your potentially problematic code for you. This will make your job much easier when trying to figure out what needs to be changed. Let's take a look at some of the changes that you will most likely need to make.

Universal Procedure Pointers

As mentioned, the Mixed Mode Manager handles mode switches between instruction set architectures for you. But how does it know how to do it? All procedure pointers are now called universal procedure pointers. The definition of a universal procedure pointer varies depending on the instruction set architecture with which you are dealing. For the 680x0, a universal procedure pointer is simply defined as a procedure pointer, a pointer to a procedure—something with which you are probably already familiar. However, for the PowerPC a universal procedure pointer is defined as a pointer to a RoutineDescriptor—a special structure that helps the Mixed Mode Manager perform its magic. Whenever your application is going to call code that may require a mode switch, you actually execute a universal procedure pointer instead of an old-fashioned procedure pointer. A universal procedure pointer is defined as follows:

```
#if    GENERATINGCFM
    typedef struct RoutineDescriptor UniversalProcPtr,
        **UniversalProcHandle;
```

```
#else
    typedef ProcPtr UniversalProcPtr, *UniversalProcHandle;
#endif

struct RoutineDescriptor {
    unsigned short      goMixedModeTrap;
    SInt8               version;
    RDFlagsType         routineDescriptorFlags;
    unsigned long       reserved1;
    UInt8               reserved2;
    UInt8               selectorInfo;
    short               routineCount;
    RoutineRecord       routineRecords[1];
};
typedef struct RoutineDescriptor RoutineDescriptor;

typedef RoutineDescriptor *RoutineDescriptorPtr,
    **RoutineDescriptorHandle;

struct RoutineRecord {
    ProcInfoType        procInfo;
    SInt8               reserved1;
    ISAType             ISA;
    RoutineFlagsType    routineFlags;
    ProcPtr             procDescriptor;
    unsigned long       reserved2;
    unsigned long       selector;
};
typedef struct RoutineRecord RoutineRecord;

typedef RoutineRecord *RoutineRecordPtr, **RoutineRecordHandle;
```

You may have just reread the last sentence of the previous paragraph, where I mention executing a universal procedure pointer instead of an old-fashioned procedure pointer. Furthermore, you may be asking yourself, since a universal procedure pointer actually points to a RoutineDescriptor structure, how is it possible to execute a structure? This is a very good question, with an ingenious answer provided by the good folks on the PowerPC development team.

Let's take a look at the fields of the RoutineDescriptor. The first field is a short that is the value of the _MixedModeMagic trap. Because the first thing in a RoutineDescriptor is a trap word, if you were to execute a pointer to a RoutineDescriptor you would be actually executing the trap represented by the trap word stored in that location. In this case, this value should always be _MixedModeMagic, which is defined as 0xAAFE (see page 19). After the RoutineDescriptor, also known as the universal procedure pointer, is executed, the _MixedModeMagic trap is called and it analyzes the rest of the information in the structure to decide if a mode switch is needed. This is just a portion of the magic that is performed by the Mixed Mode Manager.

```
/* MixedModeMagic Magic Cookie/Trap number */
enum {
    _MixedModeMagic                        = 0xAAFE
};
```

The version field contains the version of the RoutineDescriptor structure. This allows the structure to be changed later on, while maintaining compatibility with older versions. The routineDescriptorFlags field contains flags that describe the routine that the RoutineDescriptor represents. The reserved1 and reserved2 fields are reserved and should always be set to 0. The selectorInfo field contains information concerning the use of selector-based routines such as _HFSDispatch, which in most cases should be set to 0. The routineCount field contains the index of the last RoutineRecord, which follows as an array. Every RoutineDescriptor must have at least one RoutineRecord. Therefore, a value of 0 in the routineCount field actually means that one RoutineRecord is present.

Each RoutineRecord describes the routine that this RoutineDescriptor represents. The reason there is an array of RoutineRecords available is because you may choose to have a PowerPC native routine and a 680x0 routine available for use, while letting the Mixed Mode Manager decide which one should execute based on the current instruction set architecture. Using this technique, you can ensure that the best, fastest-executing code for the current situation will be run.

When you allow the Mixed Mode Manager to choose which code to execute, you can ask it to always execute the PowerPC code on a Power Macintosh. You can also ask it to execute the code that will not require a mode switch. Depending on what the code that will be executed actually does, it may be faster to run the 680x0 version and skip a mode switch than to put up with the overhead of the mode switch and execute the PowerPC version. This is an unlikely scenario, since PowerPC code can be blazingly fast, but the fact remains that this is an option.

Looking at the RoutineRecord, the procInfo field is a value that describes the calling conventions of the routine in question. You create this procedure information by using macros provided in the universal header files. The macros allow you to specify totally the size, order, and number of parameters; the size of the result; any specific usage of registers; and more. The Mixed Mode Manager uses this information to properly execute your routine. Some of the macros, and the constant values that they use, follow for your reading enjoyment and intellectual stimulation.

```
enum {
/* Calling Convention Offsets */
    kCallingConventionWidth             = 4,
    kCallingConventionPhase             = 0,
    kCallingConventionMask              = 0xF,

/* Result Offsets */
    kResultSizeWidth                    = 2,
    kResultSizePhase                    = kCallingConventionWidth,
    kResultSizeMask                     = 0x30,

/* Parameter offsets & widths */
    kStackParameterWidth                = 2,
    kStackParameterPhase                = (kCallingConventionWidth +
                                        kResultSizeWidth),
    kStackParameterMask                 = 0xFFFFFFC0,

/* Register Result Location offsets & widths */
    kRegisterResultLocationWidth        = 5,
    kRegisterResultLocationPhase        = (kCallingConventionWidth +
                                        kResultSizeWidth),

/* Register Parameter offsets & widths */
    kRegisterParameterWidth             = 5,
    kRegisterParameterPhase             = (kCallingConventionWidth +
                                        kResultSizeWidth +
                                        kRegisterResultLocationWidth),
    kRegisterParameterSizePhase         = 0,
    kRegisterParameterSizeWidth         = 2,
    kRegisterParameterWhichPhase        = kRegisterParameterSizeWidth,
    kRegisterParameterWhichWidth        = 3,

/* Dispatched Stack Routine Selector offsets & widths */
    kDispatchedSelectorSizeWidth        = 2,
    kDispatchedSelectorSizePhase        = (kCallingConventionWidth +
                                        kResultSizeWidth),

/* Dispatched Stack Routine Parameter offsets */
    kDispatchedParameterPhase           = (kCallingConventionWidth +
                                        kResultSizeWidth +
                                        kDispatchedSelectorSizeWidth),
```

```
/* Special Case offsets & widths */
    kSpecialCaseSelectorWidth          = 6,
    kSpecialCaseSelectorPhase          = kCallingConventionWidth,
    kSpecialCaseSelectorMask           = 0x3F0,

/* Component Manager Special Case offsets & widths */
    kComponentMgrResultSizeWidth       = 2,
    kComponentMgrResultSizePhase       = kCallingConventionWidth +
                                         kSpecialCaseSelectorWidth,
                                         /* 4 + 6 = 10 */
    kComponentMgrParameterWidth        = 2,
    kComponentMgrParameterPhase        = kComponentMgrResultSizePhase +
                                         kComponentMgrResultSizeWidth
                                         /* 10 + 2 = 12 */
};

#define SIZE_CODE(size)           \
    (((size) == 4) ? kFourByteCode : (((size) == 2) ? kTwoByteCode :
(((size) == 1) ? kOneByteCode : 0)))


#define RESULT_SIZE(sizeCode)     \
    ((ProcInfoType)(sizeCode) << kResultSizePhase)

#define STACK_ROUTINE_PARAMETER(whichParam, sizeCode) \
    ((ProcInfoType)(sizeCode) << (kStackParameterPhase +
(((whichParam) - 1) * kStackParameterWidth)))
```

```
#define DISPATCHED_STACK_ROUTINE_PARAMETER(whichParam, sizeCode) \
    ((ProcInfoType)(sizeCode) << (kDispatchedParameterPhase +
(((whichParam) - 1) * kStackParameterWidth)))

#define DISPATCHED_STACK_ROUTINE_SELECTOR_SIZE(sizeCode) \
    ((ProcInfoType)(sizeCode) << kDispatchedSelectorSizePhase)

#define REGISTER_RESULT_LOCATION(whichReg) \
    ((ProcInfoType)(whichReg) << kRegisterResultLocationPhase)

#define REGISTER_ROUTINE_PARAMETER(whichParam, whichReg, sizeCode) \
    ((((ProcInfoType)(sizeCode) << kRegisterParameterSizePhase) |
((ProcInfoType)(whichReg) << kRegisterParameterWhichPhase)) << \
    (kRegisterParameterPhase + (((whichParam) - 1) *
kRegisterParameterWidth)))

#define COMPONENT_MGR_RESULT_SIZE(sizeCode) \
    ((ProcInfoType)(sizeCode) << kComponentMgrResultSizePhase)

#define COMPONENT_MGR_PARAMETER(whichParam, sizeCode) \
    ((ProcInfoType)(sizeCode) < (kComponentMgrParameterPhase +
(((whichParam) - 1) * kComponentMgrParameterWidth)))
```

```
#define SPECIAL_CASE_PROCINFO(specialCaseCode) \
    (kSpecialCase | ((ProcInfoType)(specialCaseCode) << 4))
enum {
    kSpecialCase              =
(CallingConventionType)0x0000000F
};

enum {
/* all of the special cases enumerated.
   The selector field is 6 bits wide */
    kSpecialCaseHighHook          = 0,
    kSpecialCaseCaretHook         = 0,

    /* same as kSpecialCaseHighHook */
    kSpecialCaseEOLHook           = 1,
    kSpecialCaseWidthHook         = 2,
    kSpecialCaseTextWidthHook     = 2,

    /* same as kSpecialCaseWidthHook */
    kSpecialCaseNWidthHook        = 3,
    kSpecialCaseDrawHook          = 4,
    kSpecialCaseHitTestHook       = 5,
    kSpecialCaseTEFindWord        = 6,
    kSpecialCaseProtocolHandler = 7,
    kSpecialCaseSocketListener  = 8,
    kSpecialCaseTERecalc          = 9,
    kSpecialCaseTEDoText          = 10,
    kSpecialCaseGNEFilterProc   = 11,
    kSpecialCaseMBarHook          = 12,
    kSpecialCaseComponentMgr    = 13
};
```

Continuing with the RoutineRecord structure, the reserved1 field (and the reserved2 field, while we are here) are both reserved for use by Apple and should be set to 0. The ISA field describes the instruction set architecture of the routine in question—currently either 680x0 or PowerPC, but open for growth. The routineFlags field describes routine-specific information such as how the location of the routine is related to the structure in memory, whether or not the code fragment needs to be prepared (which we will discuss shortly), whether we always want to use the fastest code or the one that won't require a mode switch, and other information. The procDescriptor field is a pointer to the routine code we are actually calling. This may be a pointer to a function inside our program or to a resource that contains code. Lastly, the selector field is used for dispatched calls, which don't concern us here.

As you can see, the RoutineDescriptor is a pretty advanced structure. It allows for future expansion by containing an array of possible routines to be called depending on the current instruction set architecture and other factors. In reality, this could even support a Pentium processor being put inside a Macintosh. You could easily execute code for a Pentium, PowerPC, or 680x0 all on the same machine and from any other instruction set architecture!

Using Universal Procedure Pointers

Now that you know a bit about the definition of a universal procedure pointer, let's take a look at how you make use of them in your programs. In order to call functions in your program that you know are PowerPC code, you can simply treat them as you always have. However, there are some exceptions. Whenever you would normally pass a procedure pointer to an operating system function, you now need to pass a universal procedure pointer. Functions such as grow-zone functions, control action procedures, Dialog Manager event filters, vertical blanking "VBL" tasks, trap patches, and any other functions you may encounter now require you to use universal procedure pointers. The reason for this is because you cannot be sure if the code in the Toolbox or operating system is 680x0 or PowerPC. Therefore, you need to pass the universal procedure pointers so the Mixed Mode Manager can always do the right thing—no matter what the calling code instruction set architecture.

For most of these standard types of procedures, their specific header files contain macros that you can use in your code to make everything work fine under 680x0 and PowerPC compilers. For example, if you had a user item in a dialog box and you wanted the user item to automatically draw whenever it received an update event, you would use the GetDItem and SetDItem functions to associate a user item drawing procedure with the user item itself, assuming you had a drawing function similar to the following code.

```
pascal void MyUserItemDrawProc(DialogPtr d, short theItem)
{
    short       iKind;
    Handle      iHandle;
    Rect        iRect;
    GrafPtr     savePort;

    GetPort(&savePort);
    SetPort(d);
```

```
GetDItem(d, theItem, &iKind, &iHandle, &iRect);
FrameRect(&iRect);

SetPort(savePort);
}
```

In the old days, you would have used code like the following.

```
short        iKind;
Handle       iHandle;
Rect         iRect;

GetDItem(d, kMyUserItem, &iKind, &iHandle, &iRect);
SetDItem(d, kMyUserItem, iKind,
     (Handle)MyUserItemDrawProc, &iRect);

// Do dialog box stuff here
```

The previous code snippet shows that all you really needed to do was call GetDItem and SetDItem in order to set the drawing procedure to be activated when the user item in question needed to be drawn. The function would be called automatically by the Dialog Manager. In the days of universal procedure pointers, you need to do things a bit differently, as in the following code.

```
short        iKind;
Handle       iHandle;
Rect         iRect;
UserItemUPP  MyUserItemDrawProcUPP = nil;

MyUserItemDrawProcUPP =
NewUserItemProc(MyUserItemDrawProc);

GetDItem(d, kMyUserItem, &iKind, &iHandle, &iRect);
SetDItem(d, kMyUserItem, iKind,
     (Handle)MyUserItemDrawProcUPP, &iRect);

// Do dialog box stuff here

DisposeRoutineDescriptor(MyUserItemDrawProcUPP)
```

Because the Dialog Manager may or may not be native code, it needs to handle the calling of your drawing function in a special way. By passing a universal procedure pointer to the Dialog Manager, it can easily call the drawing procedure as it likes and the Mixed Mode Manager will take care of any needed mode switches, if required. The NewUserItemProc macro is defined in the standard Dialogs.h universal header file and automatically creates the proper RoutineDescriptor when being compiled for PowerPC. (See the following code.) In this way, the same source code can be used for both 680x0 and PowerPC versions of your program, since the header file handles dealing with any differences for you.

```
#if GENERATINGCFM
    #define NewUserItemProc(userRoutine)                    \
        (UserItemUPP) NewRoutineDescriptor((ProcPtr)(userRoutine),
        uppUserItemProcInfo, GetCurrentArchitecture())
#else
    #define NewUserItemProc(userRoutine)                    \
        ((UserItemUPP) (userRoutine))
#endif
```

The NewRoutineDescriptor function actually allocates a pointer by calling the Memory Manager NewPtr function. In reality, you should check to make sure that the pointer is allocated before continuing. It is worth noting that you can allocate a RoutineDescriptor as a local variable if you so desire, in order to avoid heap storage of the RoutineDescriptor. This has the added advantage that it automatically gets deallocated when execution leaves its scope, so it is good for RoutineDescriptors that will be used only temporarily. Another advantage of using this macro is that it does not call the Memory Manager so it is both faster and doesn't move memory. You can take advantage of this by using the BUILD_ROUTINE_DESCRIPTOR macro in the file Mixed-Mode.h.

Many of the universal header files contain definitions such as this that automatically equate to the proper code, depending on if you are compiling for the 680x0 or the PowerPC. This can make your source files much easier to read, as you can avoid a bunch of #ifdef statements in your code. It's normally easy to convert your existing code to include the required changes. It's also quite easy to know what to change. If your program crashes on a PowerPC as soon as a dialog appears, you probably forgot to convert a drawing or event filter function to use universal procedure pointers.

> Header files are a great place to learn some interesting informa-
> tion. By perusing them you can sometimes find references to un-
> documented function calls. You may also find definitions of
> low-memory globals that you didn't know existed. I would like
> to be the first to recommend taking a good hard look at what is
> in the header files used by your development environment.

The Code Fragment Manager

On the Power Macintosh all code and its data are stored as fragments.
These fragments are all manipulated and tracked by the Code Fragment Manager. Whether the code be an application, code resource, or
extension, it is organized in this way. Because all code types are
treated the same, they all share the same benefits, such as

- a simplified and uniform set of calling conventions
- the ability to store code that is used by numerous entities in an import library
- the use of global data (also known as global variables)
- the ability to execute special initialization and termination routines when a fragment is loaded and unloaded from memory

Although fragments share the same structure and are treated the
same by the Code Fragment Manager, they can take many different
forms—all of which you may be familiar with including

- an application that can be launched from the Finder by double-
  clicking the files icon. The application has a user interface and is
  based on an event-driven architecture.
- an import library, which is a fragment that contains code and data
  that are used by other entities, such as an application. The Code
  Fragment Manager can automatically resolve references to symbols in any import libraries that may be used. Because an import
  library can share its routines among many different clients, you
  may hear it being called a shared library.
- an extension, which is a fragment that extends the capabilities of
  another entity. Application extensions are used by a single application and include HyperCard externals such as XCMDs. System
  extensions are used by multiple applications and possibly the system software, and include INIT and cdev resources. Because a system extension can be shared among many different clients, you
  may hear it also being called a shared library.

Code fragments can be stored in any of a variety of ways, but the most common container in which to find them depends on the type of code you are writing. For example, the code and data of a PowerPC native application are usually stored in the data fork of the application, as opposed to storing them in resources of type CODE, as is done in 680x0-based Macintosh operating systems. There are numerous reasons for this, but the most important is the use of virtual memory. By placing the entire code and data fragment in the data fork, the virtual memory mechanism in the Power Macintosh can use that data fork as a paging file. In other words, whenever memory is needed, it can dump the code from RAM. Rest assured that it can be loaded again quickly from the data fork of the file. Mind you, this also means that you cannot use any self-modifying code, but that really isn't much of a limitation any more and is frowned on in most cases.

Another place you will find code fragments stored is in resources. As you are aware, many different types of code are stored in resources. Looking through any large application you will find control definitions (CDEF resources), list definitions (LDEF resources), window definitions (WDEF resources), and menu definitions (MDEF resources). Many system extensions also contain initialization resources (INIT resources), control panel resources (cdev resources), and possibly even drivers (DRVR resources). All of these resource types contain code under the 680x0 environment. In turn, they can also contain code fragments under the PowerPC environment.

Always Be Prepared

Before a code fragment can be used it must be prepared. Preparing a code fragment basically consists of resolving any references to routines in any import libraries that it may use. For example, assume you write a code fragment that calls some standard operating system functions. When your code fragment is prepared, the Code Fragment Manager will automatically search for any other import libraries that it uses and attempt to resolve the names of the routines or data that your code fragment references. If a required import library cannot be found, an error will occur, your fragment will not be prepared, and, furthermore, cannot be used.

One interesting thing to note is that a code fragment may make use of multiple import libraries and an import library that it uses may use another import library. In this case the Code Fragment Manager must prepare the fragments in reverse order, since a fragment that uses another fragment cannot be prepared until the other fragment is prepared first. You also have to be aware that circular references may occur, which can really confuse things. That is, your code fragment uses another fragment, which uses your code fragment. In most cases this will not be a problem, but it can happen and you should be aware of it, as it may point to a poor design decision on your part.

After a fragment is prepared, the preparer can make use of its unique connection ID in order to access information about the fragment. This number is returned after the fragment is prepared. You can use this number whenever you need to refer to that specific fragment. Using this number and Code Fragment Manager routines, you can locate symbols for code or data within the fragment and modify them if you so desire. The connection ID is your ticket to information about the fragment for as long as the fragment is loaded. You also use it to close your connection to the fragment when you are done using the fragment.

> Don't try to prepare a code fragment that contains a RoutineDescriptor attached to it by using the Code Fragment Manager function GetMemFragment. GetMemFragment expects the PowerPC Preferred Executable Format (PEF) information to begin immediately at the start of the resource. If a RoutineDescriptor is in this location instead, the Code Fragment Manager will crash. The Mixed Mode Manager and Code Fragment Manager, however, are able to prepare code that contains a RoutineDescriptor when it is called, without first trying to prepare it explicitly. You'll remember that one of the flags in the RoutineDescriptor is whether or not the fragment needs preparation. This flag tells the Mixed Mode Manager and Code Fragment Manager to implicitly prepare the fragment properly.

Code Fragment Structure

As mentioned before, a fragment contains both code and data sections. Although when loaded into memory these sections may not be contiguous, your code need not be concerned with their locations. Because there is no practical limit to the size of the code or data, a fragment can be just about any size and store just about any amount of information, assuming there is enough RAM to do so.

You may recall that in the 680x0 environment, code resources are limited to 32K—unless you make use of special functions in your compilers. This limitation was created by the Segment Manager and the segmentation of an application into multiple CODE resources. Also, an application could only have up to 32K of global variables. These two major limitations are history with the advent of the Power Macintosh. Although now you don't have to worry about how much code and data you use, this should not be an excuse to write sloppy programs. You should still take the time to optimize and reoptimize to get the best performance out of the machine on which you are running.

Because code in a code fragment must execute no matter where it is located in memory, it cannot contain any absolute branches to other code. It must branch based on offsets from its current position. By containing no absolute addresses, it is considered position independent and is referred to as pure code. Fragments make use of a special table of contents in order to locate code and data within itself and other fragments. Each fragment contains its own table of contents.

The data in a fragment is also unique by nature. It can be loaded into the system heap or the application heap depending on the use of the fragment. It also can be loaded into memory more than once in order to create multiple copies of itself. This can be useful if more than one entity is going to be using your fragment. Since the code itself never changes, all clients can share one copy of it, but still have their own copies of the data section of the fragment.

Although code and data sections of fragments can be loaded anywhere in memory, they cannot be moved in memory while they are loaded. When a fragment is prepared, part of what happens is that internal pointers, in the table of contents, are updated to point to other code and data in other fragments. If those fragments were to move in memory, these pointers would be no longer valid. In order to not have to constantly update these pointers in any of a number of fragments that may be loaded at any time, all fragments must be locked in memory while they are being used.

Each fragment contains a table of contents (TOC) that contains pointers to all code and data that are used by the fragment. This TOC is initialized when the fragment is prepared by the Code Fragment Manager. This mechanism allows a fragment to address data easily that it has imported from another fragment, without worrying about where that fragment may be in memory at runtime. The fragment can simply reference the TOC entry for a particular code or data item and be sure it will be led to the correct thing.

Fragment-specific Routines

Fragments can define three special routines that are separate from any of their other exported symbols. These routines are

- the initialization routine, which is called when a fragment is loaded and prepared. This routine can be used to perform any actions that should be done before the fragment is otherwise accessed. This function is passed a pointer to a fragment initialization block that contains information on where the fragment is stored. This routine is automatically called by the Code Fragment Manager after preparation, but before any other execution of the fragment takes place.
- the main routine, which is called if the fragment is an application. Other types of fragments such as control definitions, list definitions, etc., can also define the main routine. The main routine is also known as the main entry point. This routine can be called by anyone using the fragment.
- the termination routine, which is called when the fragment is unloaded. It can be used to clean up any memory or resource allocations performed by the initialization routine. This routine is automatically called by the Code Fragment Manager.

The main symbol of a code fragment (and just about any other symbol as well) need not contain code. It may contain a pointer to a block of data. This can make important information about the fragment easily accessible to any potential caller of the fragment. Any symbol can be exported—whether it be code or data.

The Code Fragment Resource

As mentioned, code fragments can be stored in a variety of ways—as data in the data fork of a file or as a resource in the resource fork. Although it is not required by all fragments, some applications contain a resource of type cfrg and ID 0 that is used to define whether or not a PowerPC native fragment exists and to determine where it is located in the file. This is actually how the Process Manager decides if an application is PowerPC native or not—by seeing if this resource exists. The code fragment resource contains the instruction set architecture of the fragment, its version number, size of its default stack, and information about where it is located. Using this information, the Process Manager can ask the Code Fragment Manager to prepare the fragment and begin its execution as an application.

Application fragments must contain a main entry point so the Process Manager can execute them. Also, even though most application fragments are stored in the data fork in order to facilitate the use of virtual memory as mentioned earlier, they can also be stored in resources if need be. It should also be noted that more than one code fragment may be stored in a single data fork. In fact, you can have any number of fragments stored in a single container such as a data fork or resource.

You have probably heard the term fat used to refer to an application. A fat application is one that contains both 680x0 CODE resources as well as a code fragment resource and application fragment, usually in the data fork. In this way, the application can be run on 680x0 Macintosh computers as usual, since these computers ignore the existence of the code fragment resource. In turn, the Power Macintosh can first check for the existence of the code fragment resource and, if it does exist, can execute the PowerPC native code. If no code fragment resource exists, the Power Macintosh will simply alert the 680x0 emulator that a 680x0 application needs to be executed and it will be done. Fat applications can be launched successfully no matter what Macintosh they are running on.

Resources

One of the main focuses of this book is accelerated and private resources. Private resources are those that are used by your application. Accelerated resources are those that are defined by the system software. Both contain PowerPC code and can dramatically improve the performance of your programs.

Accelerated resources are those such as control definitions (CDEF resources), list definitions (LDEF resources), window definitions (WDEF resources), and menu definitions (MDEF resources). Others include initialization resources (INIT resources), control panel resources (cdev resources), and drivers (DRVR resources). By compiling a fragment as a resource and using the same calling conventions as any of these predefined code resource types, you can make use of PowerPC code even in a 680x0 application running on a Power Macintosh. All accelerated resources should begin with a RoutineDescriptor, since they are called by the operating system, that may still contain 680x0 code. Using this mechanism, you need not do anything special (other than build your accelerated resource correctly) for it to work properly and run with enhanced speed.

Accelerated resources have some restrictions, however, that stem from the fact that they are backward compatible. Because the operating system doesn't know that they are accelerated (and doesn't really care), the following rules apply

- No termination routine is allowed. Since the operating system doesn't know when the resource will no longer be needed, it cannot call it.
- The accelerated resource must contain a main symbol, since the resources it replaces all use a single main entry point.
- You cannot call any Code Fragment Manager routine that requires a connection ID, since that information is stored internally by the operating system and is not available to your accelerated resource or application.
- The fragments data section is instantiated in place (i.e., within the block of memory used to store the resource itself). This requires that the data section not be compressed—an option you can set in your compiler. In Metrowerks' CodeWarrior, this is called Expand Uninitialized Data.

Because an accelerated resource may move in memory between it being called, but while it is still prepared, there is the chance that some pointers to its data may be no longer valid. Because of this, the Code Fragment Manager and Mixed Mode Manager work together to ensure that the fragment is always prepared before use—especially if it has moved since the last call. Because of this, your accelerated resource cannot use global pointers (declared as static or extern) that are initialized at runtime or contained in a dynamically allocated data structure to point to code or data contained in the resource itself. You can use uninitialized global data to point to heap objects, such as a pointer or handle, and you can initialize global pointers at compile time, but they cannot be changed at run time.

Private resources, on the other hand, are those that are completely defined by your application. You define the parameters and calling conventions, the use of the resources, and what they do. HyperCard XCMDs are a perfect example of a private resource. They are called private because they are only used by one particular program. Private resources need not contain a RoutineDescriptor, depending on how they will be called from your program. There are numerous different ways to handle their use. The one you use will depend on your needs.

Fat and Safe Fat Resources

So far we've discussed how to create 680x0 code resources and PowerPC native fragments. We've mentioned how you can place a PowerPC fragment in a resource to create a private or accelerated resource. But did you know that you can also create a hybrid of these 680x0 and PowerPC code fragments?

There may be times when you want to create one resource that contains both 680x0 code and PowerPC code. It would be nice if this resource would execute the best code when running on a Power Macintosh, depending on the instruction set architecture from which it is called. A fat resource is one that contains both types of code in the same container. The resource also contains a RoutineDescriptor that defines all the information needed to let the Mixed Mode Manager choose which code should be executed when the resource is called. Fat resources allow you to include more than one instruction set architecture in the same resource and have the proper one executed at runtime.

Fat resources are fine and dandy, but they only work on Macintosh computers that have the Mixed Mode Manager implemented. With this limitation, they will only work on the Power Macintosh as of this writing. The safe fat resource, on the other hand, will work without incident on both Power Macintosh and 680x0 Macintosh computers. The safe fat resource is essentially the same format as a fat resource, except it is preceded by a snippet of 680x0 code that checks for the existence of the Mixed Mode Manager. If it exists, it ensures that the RoutineDescriptor is moved to the top of the resource itself, using the Memory Manager BlockMove routine. Each subsequent time the resource is called, the RoutineDescriptor is executed first, which will function just as it would in a fat resource. On Macintosh computers without the Mixed Mode Manager, the 680x0 snippet ensures that only the 680x0 code is called and the RoutineDescriptor and PowerPC code are ignored. It does this by using BlockMove to move the 680x0 code to the top of the resource.

For complete information on how to create fat and safe fat resources see Chapter Twelve, "Advanced and Undocumented Techniques." They are also used and explained in detail in Chapter Three, "Application Extensions."

Code Fragment and Mixed Mode Tips

It might take some trial and error to learn some of the finer points of the Mixed Mode Manager and Code Fragment Manager. You should note that you don't need to understand them too deeply in order to make your 680x0 code work on the PowerPC, but it helps. Also, if you really want to take advantage of some of the new features that the Power Macintosh offers, you will need to spend some time learning about them. Here are some tips to keep in mind when dealing with these two new managers.

- Fragments can be any size and enforce no practical limit on the size of the data and code they contain.
- Fragments can be stored anywhere—in a resource or in the data fork of a file.
- If you find your code is crashing and you can't seem to figure out why, check and double-check your ProcInfo values and also your macros that you use to call your functions. If one tiny thing is wrong with your RoutineDescriptor, it could cause your program to not work at all.
- Watch for the use of int in code that you are converting to PowerPC native. Using short or long is safer, since int can be of different sizes (depending on environment options) and may prove confusing.
- When sharing data structures between 680x0 and PowerPC code, make sure the PowerPC compiler treats the structures with the alignment rules of the 680x0 chip. If you don't, you may find yourself accessing parts of the structure that you weren't expecting to access due to misalignment. Your compiler provides #pragma statements to accomplish this.

- In general, if you have to choose between creating a plug-in architecture that uses accelerated resources or data-fork based Code Fragment Manager plug-ins, use the latter. Data-fork-based plug-ins get all the advantages of the Code Fragment Manager including file mapping, read-only code, no worries about floating handles, and more. They are also much faster in many cases.
- Something to keep a look-out for is the Code Fragment Manager for the 680x0-based Macintosh. Soon—maybe even by the time you read this—the functionality of the Code Fragment Manager will not be limited to Power Macintosh. This will change some of the rules for the better. Watch for it!

We covered a lot of material in this chapter. If you found it to be a bit overwhelming, take a break for a day and read it again. Read it slowly. Understand each point before moving on. This is an entirely new way of looking at code and only a few people pick it all up the first time through. As you move through the rest of the book and see the examples, your understanding will begin to solidify. You're doing great—keep it up!

CHAPTER THREE

Application Extensions

If I don't have an icon and a really cool about box, I sometimes have trouble finding the enthusiasm to write the program in the first place.

—Anonymous

Introduction

If you've ever used a program like HyperCard or Adobe Photoshop, then you may be familiar with the concept (and maybe even the development) of plug-in components and external tools (known today as application extensions). HyperCard, for example, allows you to write external code resources, known as XCMDs and XFCNs, that allow you to extend the functionality of the program itself. Since version 2, you can call special functions within HyperCard (known as callback functions) that give even more power to your externals. HyperCard also allows you to access its own internal data via these callback functions. This model allows programmers to easily extend the functionality and usefulness of the program, without requiring its source code.

Since the release of the Power Macintosh, it is now possible to create even more powerful application extensions. In HyperCard, for example, you can create an accelerated XCMD. By doing this, you are able to run your XCMD code in native mode on a Power Macintosh, even though HyperCard may still be running under the 680x0 emulator. This flexibility allows you to accelerate applications that otherwise may not be optimized for the PowerPC processor.

This chapter discusses how you can make use of application extensions with your own application. Whether you are writing for a 680x0 or the PowerPC, this chapter shows you how to write your extensions to take best advantage of the platform on which your code will be running.

Private Resources

One type of application extension is the private resource. There are many reasons to package certain functionalities of your software as private resources. First and foremost, your design may warrant an object-oriented approach, whereby you wish to access many types of tools from within your application. Assuming that all the tools are called in a similar fashion, but each performs specific manipulation of data, it makes sense to keep the architecture extensible. By packaging each tool as a separate code resource, either within your application or in a separate file, you allow your program to have additional functionality simply by writing another tool and making that tool available to the application.

For instance, your application may look for special files in a folder called Tools folder that would be found in the same folder as the application itself. When your application launches, it enumerates the files in the Tools folder and gathers information about each one. Each of these files may contain a specific code resource or fragment that your application loads and executes when requested by the user. The files may also contain any resources needed by the tool, such as dialog boxes and pictures. In Figures 3-1 and 3-2, if programmers want to

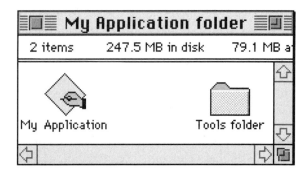

Figure 3-1. Application folder contents

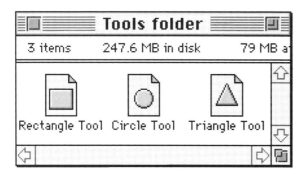

Figure 3-2. Tools folder contents

add the ability to draw a rhombus, they merely need to create a rhombus tool and place it in the Tools folder. The application would not need to be recompiled, because it would automatically load the tool and its newly created functionality.

When your application is about to execute the code from one of the tools, it might open the tools resource fork (using the Resource Manager function FSpOpenResFile) and make it the current resource file (using the Resource Manager function UseResFile). Then, when the code for the tool is executed, it can count on being able to load any of its resources by simply calling the Resource Manager function Get1Resource or other similar resource-loading routine. After the tool completes its job, it returns control to the application, which closes the tools resource fork and continues about its business.

Beyond Private Resources

Storing application extensions as private resources is one mechanism that has been very popular since the introduction of the Macintosh. Whenever a programmer needed to separate functionality from the main application, the private resource was the only logical choice available. However, with the advent of the Power Macintosh, there are now many other ways to factor your code into separate entities without having to rely on a resource-based storage mechanism.

As previously mentioned, PowerPC fragments can be stored not only in resources, but also in the data fork of any file. In fact, you can store multiple fragments in a single data fork, much like you can store multiple resources in a single resource fork. The code fragment resource, stored as a resource of type cfrg, provides the Code Fragment Manager with a map of the code fragments available in the data fork of that particular file or wherever else they may be. Storing a code fragment in the data fork is sometimes known as a shared library or, simply, a library, depending on how it is used and how you feel that day.

> The code fragment resource can represent the location of any number of fragments in any number of locations. It can very easily describe a single fragment in a data fork or multiple fragments stored in various resources or any combination of these.

There is actually a good reason to store your application extension code in the data fork of a file, and it's not simply to be different. By storing your fragment in the data fork, you are able to take advantage of file-mapped virtual memory on the Power Macintosh. This allows your application to use far less memory than it otherwise might require, since your fragment can be dismissed from RAM and read in from disk (mapped into memory) whenever it is needed. The data fork of your application extension becomes the virtual memory paging file. This option also offers you the side benefit of making your fragment read-only in nature—a simple form of memory protection. That is, you cannot write to your code or data without causing an error—no more self-modifying code. If you were to stick with resource-based storage, you would have to write your own file-mapped virtual memory scheme. You don't want to have to do that, so Power Macintosh gives you the option.

Calling the Code

The example program in this chapter shows you how to call many different types of application extensions, including a shared library, a 680x0 private resource, a PowerPC accelerated private resource, and a fat private resource. Many of these types of code can be called from 680x0 or PowerPC code. For example, you might call a PowerPC application extension from your 680x0 application code when running on a Power Macintosh. This options allows you to write native tools for your currently nonnative (and not-easy-to-update-because-someone-else-owns-the-source code) application. The example program in this chapter doesn't necessarily do anything practical, but it should give you the building blocks you need to create your own application extensions.

Test your PowerPC native applications with and without virtual memory turned on to catch bugs early! Because your PowerPC code is treated differently, in very subtle ways, when virtual memory is turned on, you should test your PowerPC code with both virtual memory on and off. If you make any use of self-modifying code, which Apple has warned us against in the past, you may have problems when your application is run with virtual memory turned on. Remember, your code is considered read-only in nature when it is loaded from the data fork and may be dumped from memory at any time. You may make a self-modification, then your code is dumped, then loaded from the disk again when it is needed. Guess what? Your modification is now no longer with you. Who knows what might happen next? Most likely your code will cause an error to occur and you'll end up in a place called MacsBug.

The first portion of the program we will discuss is how we execute private resources. All of our private resources are stored in separate files of type xMOD and contain either a resource of type 68k or one of type PPC. One of these resources contains code written especially for the 680x0 processor and the other for the PowerPC processor. We also have a resource of type Fat that contains a fat private resource—a marriage of the previously mentioned types. Using the Preferences... item in the Edit menu of our application, we choose which type of code we want to execute (Figure 3-3). When running on a Power Macintosh, we can execute any type of code, no matter what version (680x0 emulated or PowerPC native) of the application is running.

Figure 3-3 describes the different options available to us when executing our private resources. The options are 680x0 code, PowerPC code, and code that won't require a mode switch.

680x0 Code

No matter what the current ISA, we will always execute the 680x0 code. When running on a Power Macintosh, this code will be executed via the 680x0 emulator. This executes our 68k resource.

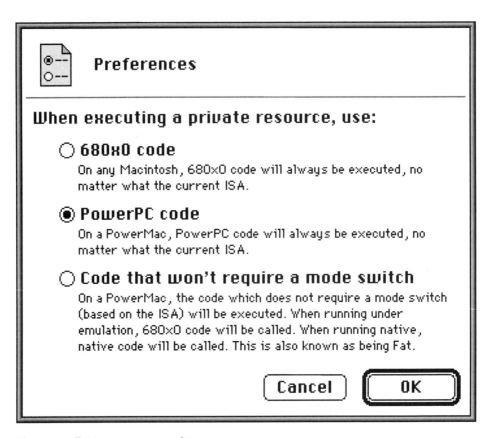

Figure 3-3. Private resource preferences

PowerPC Code

No matter what the current ISA, if we are running on a Power Macintosh, we will always execute the PowerPC code. Even if the emulated version of the application is running, we will switch modes to execute the native private resource. This executes our PPC resource.

Code That Won't Require a Mode Switch

Also known as a fat private resource, whichever code will avoid a mode switch will be executed. Therefore, if the emulated version of the application is running, the 680x0 code in the fat private resource will be executed. If the native version of the application is running, the

Figure 3-4. Code menu

PowerPC code in the fat private resource will be executed. This executes our Fat resource.

To actually execute the code, we select Execute Private Resource... from the Code menu (Figure 3-4). After we choose one of our xMOD files, we attempt to open the file using FSpOpenResFile, look for a resource of the required type based on the selected preferences, and execute it. Depending on the type, we handle the execution in a variety of ways. This is the first climax of this chapter, so stay awake through this section.

Calling 680x0 Code

If we are executing 680x0 code, we generate the following code.

```
OSErr Call68k(void)
{
    long                  moduleResult;
    ModuleEntryProcUPP    mepUPP;
    Handle                hCode = Get1Resource(kModule68kResType,
                                     kModuleResID);
    OSErr                 err = noErr;

    if (hCode) {
        HLockHi(hCode);

        mepUPP = NewModuleEntryProc68k(*hCode);
        moduleResult = CallModuleEntryProc(mepUPP, 0L);
        DisposeRoutineDescriptor(mepUPP);

        HUnlock(hCode);
        ReleaseResource(hCode);
    } else err = ResError();

    return err;
}
```

This function first loads the 680x0 code-containing resource. After it's loaded, we move the resource high in memory and lock it into position. We must then create a UniversalProcPtr for the code. To do this, we use a handy macro that is defined two different ways, depending on if we are using the 680x0 or the PowerPC compiler. The macros are defined in the following code.

```c
typedef long (*ModuleProc)(long inData);

enum {
    uppModuleEntryProcInfo = kCStackBased
            | RESULT_SIZE(SIZE_CODE(sizeof(long)))
            | STACK_ROUTINE_PARAMETER(1,
                    SIZE_CODE(sizeof(long)))
};

#if USESROUTINEDESCRIPTORS

typedef UniversalProcPtr    ModuleEntryProcUPP;

#define CallModuleEntryProc(userRoutine, params)        \
    CallUniversalProc((UniversalProcPtr)(userRoutine),  \
            ppModuleEntryProcInfo, params)

#define NewModuleEntryProc(userRoutine)                 \
    (ModuleEntryProcUPP) NewRoutineDescriptor(          \
                (ProcPtr)(userRoutine),                 \
                uppModuleEntryProcInfo, GetCurrentISA())

#define NewModuleEntryProc68k(userRoutine)              \
    (ModuleEntryProcUPP) NewRoutineDescriptor(          \
                (ProcPtr)(userRoutine),                 \
                uppModuleEntryProcInfo, (ISAType) kM68kISA)

#else

typedef ModuleProc          ModuleEntryProcUPP;

#define CallModuleEntryProc(userRoutine, params)        \
    (*(userRoutine))(params)

#define NewModuleEntryProc(userRoutine)                 \
    (ModuleEntryProcUPP)(userRoutine)

#define NewModuleEntryProc68k(userRoutine)              \
    (ModuleEntryProcUPP)(userRoutine)

#endif
```

A macro is a simple way that your development environment allows you to turn a potentially long statement of code into a much more manageable "minifunction." The difference between a macro and a real function is that the macro is compiled inline. That is, when your macro is called, the compiler will not generate a JSR instruction to execute it. It will, instead, directly insert the contents of the macro into your code. Macros are an important step in coding for PowerPC compatibility. Look through the universal header files for many examples of conditional compilation using macros.

As you can see, when we call the NewModuleEntryProc68k macro when compiled under the 680x0 compiler, we are returned a UniversalProcPtr, (which is really a ProcPtr), to the address of our private code resource. However, when compiled under the PowerPC compiler, USESROUTINEDESCRIPTORS is #defined. Therefore, the macro equates to a function call to NewRoutineDescriptor. Under the PowerPC, we are actually allocating memory for a RoutineDescriptor and initializing it to describe and point to the 680x0 code resource. The macro then returns a UniversalProcPtr that points to our newly created RoutineDescriptor.

Now that we have the code in the proper form to be executed, we call the CallModuleEntryProc macro, which when compiled under the 680x0 compiler simply de-references the UniversalProcPtr and JSRs to the code. However, when compiled under the PowerPC compiler, the macro equates to a function call to CallUniversalProc. Under the PowerPC, the call invokes the Mixed Mode Manager to examine the RoutineDescriptor and decide whether or not a mode switch is necessary. The Mixed Mode Manager sees that the code is of a different instruction set and changes modes. When the code resource finishes execution, the Mixed Mode Manager restores the previous instruction set and returns control to our application.

Lastly, we must dispose of any RoutineDescriptors that we may have allocated. When compiled under the 680x0 compiler, the DisposeRoutineDescriptor call does nothing. However, when compiled under the PowerPC compiler, the function call releases the memory allocated earlier by NewRoutineDescriptor call. We can then release the code resource and be on our way.

Our 680x0 code resource follows.

```
┌─────────────────────────────┐
│                             │
│         680x0 code          │
│                             │
└─────────────────────────────┘
```

Figure 3-5. 680x0 private resource format

Calling PowerPC Code

If we are executing PowerPC code, we generate the following code.

```
OSErr CallPPC(void)
{
    long    moduleResult;
    Handle  hCode = Get1Resource(kModulePPCResType, kModuleResID);
    OSErr   err = noErr;

    if (hCode) {
        HLockHi(hCode);

        moduleResult = CallModuleEntryProc((ModuleEntryProcUPP)
                                                 *hCode, 0L);

        HUnlock(hCode);
        ReleaseResource(hCode);
    } else err = ResError();

    return err;
```

Because our PowerPC private code resource (Figure 3-6) is compiled with a RoutineDescriptor automatically preceding it, we have a very easy time of calling this code from either 680x0 or PowerPC in-

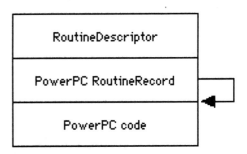

Figure 3-6. PowerPC private resource format

struction set architectures. Simply enough, after loading the resource, we call the CallModuleEntryProc macro as described earlier in calling 680x0 code. Since the code already has a RoutineDescriptor attached to it, there is no need for us to create one. All mode switches occur automatically for us by CallUniversalProc and the Mixed Mode Manager.

Calling Code That Won't Require a Mode Switch

Now that we've looked at private resources that contain code specific for one platform, let's talk about the fat private resource. A fat private resource contains code for both the 680x0 and the PowerPC, all in one convenient package. If you plan on having your code called from PowerPC code or 680x0 code while running on a Power Macintosh, this may be the best choice for you. The fat resource begins with a RoutineDescriptor that contains two RoutineRecords that describe the 680x0 and the PowerPC code. The code itself follows the two RoutineRecords.

When this code is called from your application, the Mixed Mode Manager is invoked (via the first field of the RoutineDescriptor, which, you may remember, happens to be filled in with the trap word _MixedModeMagic). The Mixed Mode Manager looks at the RoutineRecords that follow, sees that there is one for PowerPC code and one for 680x0 code, then looks at the current instruction set architecture. The Mixed Mode Manager then makes a decision (based on a flag in each RoutineRecord) to execute the code in the private resource that will not require a mode switch. Therefore, if you are calling a fat private resource from 680x0 code, the 680x0 code in the resource will be executed. If you are calling it from PowerPC code, the PowerPC code in the resource will be executed. The main reason for having fat private resources (Figure 3-7) is to help optimize your calls to them. Since a mode switch can take the same amount of time as 50–100 680x0 instructions, if you can get rid of a few, you can effectively speed up your application.

It should be noted that the routineFlags field of each RoutineRecord actually indicates how the code should be called. By "ORing" in kUseCurrentISA or kUseNativeISA, the Mixed Mode Manager will choose the proper code to execute based on the current ISA and the native ISA of the hardware. In this case, we assume that we are using kUseCurrentISA. This will execute the code that has the same ISA as the current ISA—avoiding a mode switch.

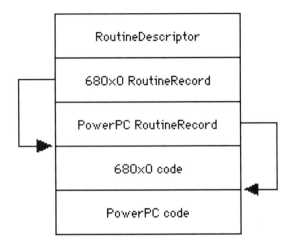

Figure 3-7. Fat private resource format

Remember, there is twice the code to test when you are using a fat resource, since your 68k code may be executing on 680x0 machines and PowerPC machines. Unless you know for sure that your fat resource will only execute its PowerPC code when on a Power Macintosh, you must remember to test both your 680x0 and your PowerPC code when running on the Power Macintosh. This is twice as much testing as otherwise required, so be sure to include enough time for it in your schedule.

The Resource Code

Before we go much further, we should at least take a quick look at the code that we are actually calling in this case. The code resource we are dealing with here has a single entry point and is very simple in nature. Let's take a look at the following code.

```
#ifndef __powerc
#include <SetUpA4.h>
#include <A4Stuff.h>
#else
ProcInfoType __procinfo = uppModuleEntryProcInfo;
#endif
```

```
long main(long inData)
{
#ifndef __powerc
    long oldA4;
    oldA4 = SetCurrentA4();
    RememberA4();
#endif

#ifdef __powerc
    ParamText("\pPowerPC", "\p", "\p", "\p");
#else
    ParamText("\p68k", "\p", "\p", "\p");
#endif

    NoteAlert(128, nil);
    ParamText("\p", "\p", "\p", "\p");

#ifndef __powerc
    SetA4(oldA4);
#endif

    return 0L;
}
```

The code you see is what you get. That's it. This code resource first sets up A4 for global access, if we are compiling for 680x0. We then use the ParamText function to display the text 68k or PowerPC in our alert, so we can quickly tell, for which platform the currently running code was compiled. When complete, restore A4 if needed and exit. Quick and easy.

Other Types of Private Resources

Thus far we've discussed 680x0-code-only application extensions, PowerPC-code-only application extensions, and the fat resource that, when run on a PowerPC, will yield the best performance by not forcing a mode switch. These three mechanisms cover a lot of ground, but it is possible that you have different needs.

If your application is going to be run on 680x0-based Macintosh computers, and you want to keep your application extension in one fat resource, you will have some problems. As soon as your application loads the extension and attempts to execute it, it will encounter the _MixedModeMagic trap word that begins all RoutineDescriptors. One hundred percent of the time, you will crash with an unimplemented instruction error, since the _MixedModeMagic trap is only implemented on the Power Macintosh, as of this writing. What is a poor programmer to do?

Apple foresaw this problem and created something called the safe fat resource. The safe fat resource is exactly the same as a fat resource except for one important difference—it is preceded by a stub of 680x0 code.

The 680x0 code stub is executed the first time the safe fat resource is called. The code determines if the Mixed Mode Manager is present by checking for the existence of system software version 7.0 or later and also the _MixedModeMagic trap in the trap tables. If _Mixed-ModeMagic is unimplemented (doesn't exist), then a 680x0 BRAnch instruction is placed at the beginning of the resource. Then, each time the code is called, it immediately branches to the 680x0-only code. If _MixedModeMagic is implemented, a RoutineDescriptor is moved to the beginning of the resource. This RoutineDescriptor exists just below the 680x0 code stub and is essentially BlockMoved to the beginning of the resource.

This template cannot currently be used for resources containing code with register-based calling conventions, because the 68k code at the beginning of the resource uses D0, A0, and A1. But *you* can change the code stub that precedes the safe fat resource. You can also optimize memory usage by effectively deleting italicized areas of the following figures with some well-placed BlockMoves, since these areas are considered "dead" code and are not used after the first time the resource is executed.

Figures 3-8, 3-9, and 3-10 show what the private resource looks like, in memory, before and after the initial execution on each platform. Note that the italicized items represent portions of the resource that are never accessed in that particular scenario. You should note that this is self-modifying code—something you shouldn't normally do. But in this case, we must. Look at the actual code (in Mixed-Mode.r) to see the precautions that are taken to ensure that it is as safe as possible.

As you will see in later chapters, we will make great use of fat and safe fat resources. This is how we will create a cdev (control panel) resource that executes in native mode on the PowerPC. We will also make CDEF (control definition), LDEF (list definition), Photoshop filters, and other resources that take advantage of this same functionality. You could even create HyperCard XCMDs in this manner. Any

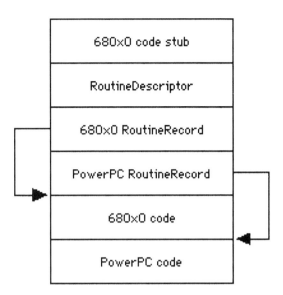

Figure 3-8. Safe fat private resource format before initial execution

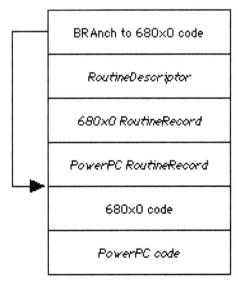

Figure 3-9. Safe fat private resource format after initial execution on a 680x0-based Macintosh

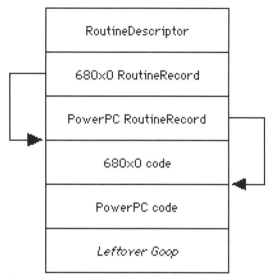

Figure 3-10. Safe fat private resource format after initial execution on a Power Macintosh (note that 680x0 code stub is overwritten)

code resource can become a safe fat code resource with little hassle on the part of the programmer. Think of the possibilities.

Working with Shared Libraries

My mother always told me to share, so now that we have discussed how to deal with resource-based application extensions, what about shared libraries? Shared libraries are files of type shlb that contain a code fragment resource and a data fork filled with PowerPC code. Although the file type and code location aren't set in stone, this is how shared libraries are normally created. Shared libraries export functions and global variables to other fragments, including your application. A shared library can also be considered an import library, which is loaded automatically at runtime by the Code Fragment Manager, for use in your application. Many of the native PowerPC system software routines are in this type of library.

There are many advantages to using a shared library over a private resource if your application will be running on a Power Macintosh. For one, you can share your code with other applications—either written by you or someone else. This way, if you have multiple applications that use many of the same functions, you can separate those functions into a shared library and access them from all of your applications. This will save disk space and possibly memory as well, depending on how you choose to load the shared library.

Another advantage is the fact that if your users have virtual memory enabled on their Power Macintosh, the data fork of the shared library acts as the virtual memory paging file. This effectively makes your code read-only and doesn't allow you to perform any self-modification. The reason your code becomes read-only is because the Virtual Memory Manager works off of disk-based files, as you know. Normally, virtual memory would write out the data from memory into a disk file when it needed to be purged, then read it back in when it needed to be executed. This disk thrashing would take valuable time. However, with a shared library (or any data fork container for PowerPC code) the Virtual Memory Manager can read the code from disk and, if it must be purged from RAM, can simply "nuke" it. When it needs to execute the code again, it reads it from the file again. You can see that any changes you make to your code may be destroyed at any time, due to the Virtual Memory Manager disposing of your memory-resident copy.

Calling Our Shared Library

To execute the code in a shared library, we select Execute Shared Library... from the Code menu (Figure 3-11). When we do this, we execute a function in our application called ExecuteSharedLib. This function performs the following tasks:

1. Locates our shared library by name by calling the Code Fragment Manager function GetSharedLibrary. This function locates and loads the shared library and prepares it for execution by resolving any references to other shared libraries that it uses. The most important parameter that this function returns to us is a connection ID to our shared library. We use this connection ID to communi-

Figure 3-11. Code menu

cate with the Code Fragment Manager when we want to refer to our shared library. NOTE: If our shared library has an initialization routine, it is called now.

2. We then call the Code Fragment Manager function FindSymbol to locate the address of our exported function BeepThreeTimes.

3. After we have the address of our BeepThreeTimes function, we call the Mixed Mode Manager function NewRoutineDescriptor to create a UniversalProcPtr to the function.

4. We then call the Mixed Mode Manager function CallUniversalProc to execute the function in the shared library.

5. After CallUniversalProc returns, the function has completed execution and we call the Mixed Mode Manager function DisposeRoutineDescriptor to deallocate the UniversalProcPtr.

6. Repeat steps 2 through 5 to execute other functions.

7. Call the Code Fragment Manager function CloseConnection to deallocate memory associated with our shared library connection and sever the connection itself. NOTE: If our shared library has a termination routine, it is called now.

> Using FindSymbol doesn't actually return the address of the function. It really returns a pointer to a TOC entry in the code fragment. You may remember a discussion of this in Chapter 2.

```
OSErr ExecuteSharedLib(Str255 errName)
{
    OSErr          err = noErr, err2 = noErr;
    ConnectionID   connID = kNoConnectionID;
    Ptr            mainAddr = nil;

    //
    // attempt to locate and prepare the shared library
    //

    err = GetSharedLibrary("\pCustom Shared Lib", kPowerPCArch,
                        kLoadNewCopy, &connID, &mainAddr,
                        errName);
    if (err == noErr) {
        Ptr         symAddr = nil;
        SymClass    symClass;

        //
```

```
// look up the symbol (in this case, a function)
// that we are interested in
//

        err = FindSymbol(connID, "\pBeepThreeTimes",
                         &symAddr, &symClass);
        if (err == noErr) {

        //
        // create a routine descriptor for the function, call it,
        // then dispose the routine descriptor.
        //

                UniversalProcPtr upp = NewRoutineDescriptor(
                                        (ProcPtr)symAddr,
                                        kCStackBased,
                                        GetCurrentISA());
                if (upp) {
                    SetCursor(*GetCursor(watchCursor));
                    CallUniversalProc(upp, kCStackBased);
                    InitCursor();
                    DisposeRoutineDescriptor(upp);
                } else err = memFullErr;
        }


//
// look up another symbol, just for fun.
//

if (err == noErr) {
        err = FindSymbol(connID, "\pShowLibAlert",
                         &symAddr, &symClass);
        if (err == noErr) {

        //
        // create a routine descriptor for the function, call
        // it, then dispose the routine descriptor.
        //

                UniversalProcPtr upp = NewRoutineDescriptor(
                                        (ProcPtr)symAddr,
                                        kCStackBased,
                                        GetCurrentISA());
                if (upp) {
                    CallUniversalProc(upp, kCStackBased);
                    DisposeRoutineDescriptor(upp);
                } else err = memFullErr;
        }
}
```

```
    //
    // close the connection
    //

    err2 = CloseConnection(&connID);
    if (err == noErr) err = err2;
  }

  return err;
}
```

In our example, we use the FindSymbol function to locate functions to execute. You will see in our system extension example (in Chapter Four) that we use the FindSymbol function to locate global variables. After you have the address of a global variable, you can edit it as if it were your very own.

Our Shared Library Code

Now that you know how to call a shared library from within an application, let's take a look at the shared library code itself. It is very simple in our case, since we only supply two functions that were exported for use by our application. Before we take a look at those functions, let's look at the initialization and termination routines of which we mentioned fragments could take advantage.

```
OSErr __initialize(InitBlockPtr ibp)
{
    OSErr    err = noErr;

    gFileRefNum = -1;

    if (ibp->fragLocator.where == kDataForkCFragLocator) {
        gFileRefNum =
            FSpOpenResFile(ibp->fragLocator.u.onDisk.fileSpec,
                fsRdPerm);
        if (gFileRefNum == -1)
            err = ResError();
    }

    return err;
}
```

The initialization routine that is used by our shared library is called automatically by the Code Fragment Manager before our shared library is accessed by the caller. This gives us a chance to initialize any internal variables we may need to initialize. The initialization routine is passed a pointer to a block of memory containing information about the location of our fragment. In our case we simply open the resource file of the shared library in order to access our resources. We then save the reference number of our file in a global variable. You should note that even though the shared library code is in the data fork of the file, the resource fork is available for our use.

```
void __terminate(void)
{
    if (gFileRefNum != -1)
        CloseResFile(gFileRefNum);
}
```

The termination routine couldn't be much simpler without breaking a law or two. This routine is called when the caller attempts to close the connection to the shared library. The termination routine gives us a chance to clean up any messes we may have made in the initialization routine. In our case, we simply close our resource file.

The two exported functions that our shared library has made available to calling programs are very simple. One beeps three times while displaying a dialog box; the other displays an alert. The following code shows how to access the private resources of the shared library by simply making the resource file current, using the resources, and restoring the previously current resource file. In your experimentation, you should add more functions and other globals to the shared library, then attempt to access them from your programs.

```
void BeepThreeTimes(void)
{
    short       saveResFile = CurResFile();
    DialogPtr   d;

    UseResFile(gFileRefNum);

    d = GetNewDialog(256, nil, (WindowPtr)-1);
    if (d) {
        ShowWindow(d);
        DrawDialog(d);
    }
```

```
        SysBeep(0);
        SysBeep(0);
        SysBeep(0);

        if (d)
                DisposeDialog(d);

        UseResFile(saveResFile);
}

void ShowLibAlert(void)
{
        short   saveResFile = CurResFile();
        UseResFile(gFileRefNum);
        NoteAlert(128, nil);
        UseResFile(saveResFile);
}
```

Compiling Our Code

This project makes use of many project files (Figures 3-12, 3-13, and 3-14) that take many different forms. We compile an application, a shared library, and custom code-bearing resources. This book makes no attempt to teach you how to use CodeWarrior or your development environment. You should read the documentation that came with your compiler to learn how to build these different types of projects. You should also note that each code example on the CD contains a file of build instructions to help you build the programs. Experiment with the source we have provided—that's why it's here.

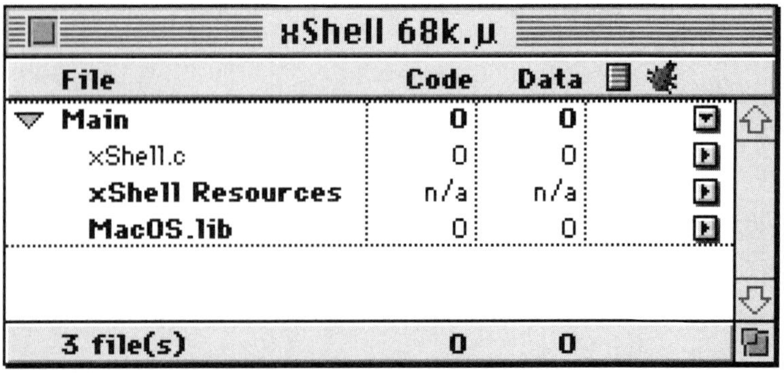

Figure 3-12. 680x0 private resource project file

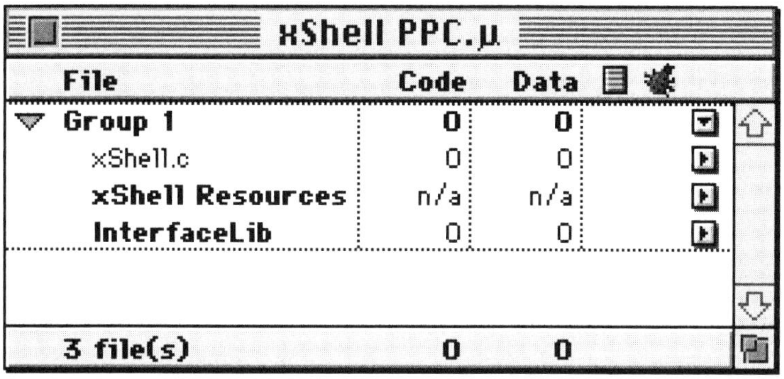

Figure 3-13. PowerPC private resource project file

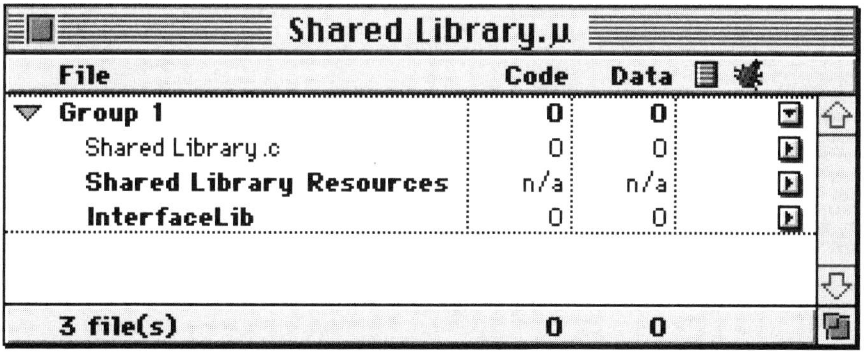

Figure 3-14. PowerPC shared library project file

Private Resource Tips

You can easily extend the capabilities of your application by designing it in a modular fashion. The Power Macintosh and the Code Fragment Manager have made this even more important to consider when writing your technical specification. The following tidbits are some things to keep in mind.

• If your application makes use of many "tools" that perform different functions on the same data, you should think about making those tools external to the application. This allows your users (and other developers) to extend or limit the functionality easily of your application based on their custom requirements and/or limitations.

- Writing your application in a modular fashion that supports application extensions can dramatically reduce the memory footprint of your application. You only need to load the tools that the user is currently using, which frees up valuable RAM for other applications or your own application extensions.
- When writing external tools, you need not consider them islands of code that only your application can access. You can easily allow your tools to call back into the application for services (such as AppleEvent) communication with other applications.
- Remember that your external tools will not have access to globals in your application. However, you can pass these globals to the tools in a variety of ways. Consider storing all application globals in a structure and passing a pointer to that structure to each external tool when it is called. In this manner, your tools can access just about any information your application can.
- Don't forget to register the file types of your application and external tool files with Apple. Doing this will prevent you from crashing. How? If you register your file types, this will ensure that no other company can use those types. This, in turn, will shield you from ever opening a file that looks like one of your tools but is really something completely different. Mind you, you shouldn't crash anyway, but you just never know.

CHAPTER FOUR

System Extensions

All is fair in love and war and patching traps.

—Anonymous

Introduction

System extensions have been around since the beginning of Macintosh time. Originally known as INITs, short for initialization programs, system extensions were renamed when System 7 was released in order to make the Macintosh even less intimidating to new computer users. The name INIT sounded a bit too technical for most users, whereas system extension was much more palatable.

System extensions perform all sorts of functions, but mostly you find them in the form of useful utility programs that handle such things as disk compression, RAM doubling, network functions, and other system-level tasks. Examples of system extensions from Apple Computer include QuickTime^{TM}, PowerTalk Manager, Apple Photo Access, and ColorSync^{TM}.

System extensions come in many forms, but are mostly seen as files of type INIT or appe. Files of type INIT contain one or more resources also of type INIT. These resources are executed by the system software at boot time. Boot time is from the time you see the "Welcome To Macintosh" message until the Finder launches and the desktop appears. Files of type INIT almost always perform tasks that alter the way the computer and system software operate. This is accomplished, in most cases, by patching traps (discussed later) or by installing a device driver during boot time.

Before System 7, system extensions were called INITs—short for initialization programs. These INITs were loaded by what is known as the INIT31 mechanism. It was called INIT31 because the code that loaded the INITs was stored in a resource in the system file of type INIT with an ID of 31. Today the system startup code is responsible for this feat.

On the other hand, files of type appe are actually applications with a few special considerations. These files are also known as faceless-background or daemon applications. They are written just as a normal application is written. However, they cannot make use of any Quick-Draw functionality—including the Random() function. These faceless-background applications are just that. They have no user interface at all and always execute in the background. Because they were designed to not have a user interface, they have no A5 QuickDraw world. The File Sharing Extension is an example of a faceless-background application. Files such as this can also contain resources of type INIT. These INIT resources are executed at startup as previously described.

Depending on the functionality you have in mind for your program, either an APPE or an INIT may be the proper choice. If you only need periodic time and the ability to send and receive AppleEvents, a faceless-background application might be the best way to go. However, if you need to interact with the machine based on user actions and other criteria, or need to intercept traps on a global scale, an INIT might be for you.

Anatomy of a System Extension

Now that you've had a brief overview of the system extension and how it works, let's take a look at one in particular. In this chapter we develop a system extension called MenuScript. This system extension is a file of type INIT and contains one INIT resource. It also contains other code in order to support the Power Macintosh. This chapter will show you how to write an INIT resource, patch traps to alter the functionality of the computer, execute PowerPC native code when running on a Power Macintosh, and more.

As mentioned in previous chapters, most pre-Power Macintosh code resources have a single entry point. An entry point is the place to which the caller jumps in order to execute the code. For example, an application might load a resource that contains code, lock the resource using the Memory Manager function HLock, dereference the handle to the resource to obtain a ProcPtr, and perform a 680x0 JSR instruction to begin execution of the code. Parameters may be passed to the code on the stack or in registers, if any are needed. When the code is finished doing its job, it will execute a 680x0 RTS instruction, returning any values that are required, and the application will be back in control (Figure 4-1). On the Power Macintosh, on the other hand, a code fragment can have as many entry points as it needs and each can accept different parameters and return a unique value as well.

At startup, the system software loads system extensions in a similar manner. The system extension's INIT resources will be loaded one by one and then executed in the fashion described earlier. During the time your INIT resources execute, you can do just about anything you may have a need to do. You should note that, during this time, the computer is not in the most pristine of states. There is a limit to what you can perform during boot time. However, this boundary is a bit blurry at times. For example, you cannot always draw to the screen without first setting up QuickDraw globals. (See "Creating Your Own A5 Word" in Chapter Twelve for more information on setting up QuickDraw globals within a code resource.) In any case, what INIT resources usually need to do is patch traps, initialize variables, read and/or write preference files, allocate memory, etc. All of this can be done safely during boot time.

The simplest INIT resource looks like the following code:

```
void main(void)
{
    SysBeep(0);
}
```

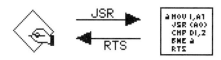

Application   Code Resource

Figure 4-1. A 680x0 application calling a
680x0 code resource

This particular INIT does absolutely nothing except beep. It simply executes, beeps once, and immediately exits. Unlike some other code resources, INIT resources are passed no parameters and return no values.

Introduction to MenuScript and Patching Traps

The system extension we will be developing in this chapter is called MenuScript. The concept for it is very simple, with the advent of AppleScript (Apple's systemwide scripting language). I thought it would be interesting if users could replace any menu item in any application with an AppleScript. Because I do not have access to the source code for all known Macintosh applications, this problem needed to be solved at the system level in a much more generic way. I decided that a system extension of file type INIT would be the perfect choice to solve this problem.

When thinking through the idea, the first step was to figure out how to make any application execute an AppleScript instead of doing the task it was supposed to do when the user selected one of its menu items. The Menu Manager documentation (see *Inside Macintosh*) states that in order for an application to receive a user's menu choices, it must call the MenuSelect and/or MenuKey toolbox functions. MenuSelect is called by the application when the user clicks the mouse in the menu bar. When the mouse button is released, MenuSelect returns the menu ID and the menu item that the user chose, if any. Similarly MenuKey is called when the user types a command key combination. MenuKey compares that command key combination to those in the current menu bar and returns the corresponding menu ID and menu item, if any. By patching these two toolbox functions (also known as traps), I can intercept the return values before the calling application gets to examine them.

In our system extension, we also patch the function System-Menu. This function is called internally by the Menu Manager when a "DA" (Desk Accessory) is selected. We patch this trap also in order to ensure that we receive all menu selections, including those in the Apple menu and other system-managed menus.

Patching traps can be a difficult task at times, depending on which traps you are patching. The MenuSelect and MenuKey traps are relatively straightforward to patch, however. In order to patch a trap, the first thing you must do is understand the calling convention of the trap you want to patch. You will need to structure your patch to mimic this convention in order to have it work properly. For instance, MenuSelect is defined in the universal header file Menus.h as the following code.

```
pascal long MenuSelect(Point startPt);
```

Therefore, our patch's function prototype (for the 680x0, anyway) will look like the following code.

```
pascal long MenuSelect68k(Point startPt);
```

Now that we know what our patch needs to look like for the compiler, we need to actually apply the patch. Applying a patch to a trap is very easy, but first you need to know with which type of trap you are dealing—a ToolTrap or an OSTrap. A ToolTrap is a trap that is implemented via the Toolbox. An OSTrap is an operating system-level trap. There are subtle differences in the way these two types of traps are handled by the system. By checking bit 11 of the trap word, you can tell the difference. If bit 11 is set, then the trap is a ToolTrap. Otherwise, it is an OSTrap. Since the trap word for MenuSelect is 0xA938 (which in binary is displayed as 1010 1001 0011 1000), it is a ToolTrap. Note that bit 11 (the underlined bit) is turned on, or set, in the trap word. Tool Traps are Pascal-based and accept their parameters on the stack. OS Traps are register-based and accept their parameters in registers. CodeWarrior makes it very easy to write 680x0 operating system patches. You can use register parameters to specify which parameters in your function prototype come from which registers, and in which register any results should be placed. This net feature is documented, for those of you who want to take advantage of it, in the *Metrowerks C/C++ & Assembly Language Manual* that is available with CodeWarrior.

Because MenuSelect is a ToolTrap, we will use the functions GetToolTrapAddress and SetToolTrapAddress to patch the trap. If it were an OSTrap we would have used GetOSTrapAddress and SetOSTrapAddress, respectively. Patching MenuSelect might look something like the following code.

```
oldMenuSelectAddr = GetToolTrapAddress(_MenuSelect);
SetToolTrapAddress(newMenuSelectCode, _MenuSelect);
```

The basic premise behind patching traps is that you save the previous address of the trap and put your new address in its place. Then, when your code is called, you can choose whether or not to call the previous address before or after you execute your own code. If you perform an operation before you call the previous address it is called a head patch. If you perform an operation after you call the previous address it is called a tail patch. Sometimes you will perform operations before and after you call the previous address—this can be called anything you like.

More MenuScript Features

Executing an AppleScript is an interesting thing to do, but we need some type of control over which AppleScripts we execute when users select specific menu items in their applications. In order to do this, I have adopted a simple approach. The idea is this: In the System Folder we create a folder called MenuScripts folder. Within it, we create a folder called Any Application. Users may also create folders within the MenuScripts folder named after their favorite applications. For example, we might create a folder named Finder. Whenever the user selects a menu item, we look for a folder in the MenuScripts folder that has the same name as the currently running application. If one exists, we look in that folder for an item with the same name as the selected menu item. If one exists, we tell the Finder to open it, instead of having the application execute the real menu item. If no folder or item exists, we then look in the Any Application folder for an item of the same name as the selected menu item. This allows users to have default actions occur across all applications, yet have specific control over some applications.

For example, in Figure 4-2, if the user selected Show Clipboard from within the Finder, the item named Show Clipboard in the Finder folder would be opened. In this case, it happens to be a stand-alone AppleScript application, but it could be an alias to anything—a document, another folder, a network server, etc. By the same token, if the user selected Quit from within any application, the item in the Any Application folder named Quit would be opened.

Whenever an item exists and is opened, it overrides the menu selection. We are able to override the menu selection by altering the return value from MenuSelect and MenuKey before the application gets a chance to look at it. If MenuSelect returns that the user selected item 10 from menu ID 129, we can use that information to locate the item to open and then change it so the application thinks the user didn't select any menu item at all. Are you beginning to see the power of patching a trap?

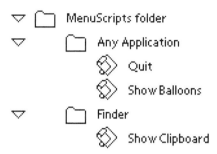

Figure 4-2. MenuScripts folder
hierarchy in the System folder

MenuScript Code

Now that we've discussed a bit about what our system extension needs to do and how we plan on doing it, let's dive in and look at the code. The first thing we need to consider is our INIT resource. This code gets executed by the system and applies all of our patches, which basically puts us in business to handle menu selections later on. The INIT resource's attributes should be marked sysHeap and may be optionally marked as locked. This ensures that our code is loaded into the system heap and not any other heap at startup. The locked bit would see to it that our code is locked in memory, without us needing to do it ourselves from within code, as in the following code.

```
void main(void)
{
    FSSpec      menuScriptsFolderFSSpec;
    FSSpec      anyApplicationFolderFSSpec;
    Str32       menuScriptsFolderName;
    Str32       anyApplicationFolderName;
    Handle      hINIT = nil;
    THz         savedZone;
    long        oldA4;
    long        response;
    long        foundDirID;
    short       foundVRefNum;
    OSErr       err = noErr;
```

The first thing we do is define our main entry point and allocate our local variables for this function. We also initialize some of these variables here. Remember, INIT resources take no parameters and return no values.

```
savedZone = GetZone();
SetZone(SystemZone());
```

We then want to ensure that the current heap is set to the system heap. Because we must allocate memory and load resources, we want to make sure they are in a heap that stays valid throughout the entire time the computer is turned on. If we didn't perform this step, it is possible that some other system extension that loaded before ours may have inadvertently left us in a very small heap that it created, which could cause us to not load due to low memory. The previous code is simply a precaution, but it is a good one to take.

```
oldA4 = SetCurrentA4();
RememberA4();
```

Because we are using Metrowerks' CodeWarrior, we can make use of global data within our 680x0 code resources. In order to do this, we must make a few simple calls to set this up and maintain it, as in the previous code. CodeWarrior references global data off of 680x0 register A4. (You should refer to your CodeWarrior manual for more information on how to use these functions.) Other development environments support register A4 and A5 referencing of global data. The documentation for your environment will explain how to make use of it.

```
err = Gestalt(gestaltSystemVersion, &response);
if ((err != noErr) || (response < kMinimumSystemVersion)
goto fail;
```

We can only run under System 7 or later, so we check that in the previous code.

```
gGlobalsPtr = (GlobalsPtr)NewPtrSysClear(sizeof(Globals));
if (gGlobalsPtr == nil) {
    err = MemError() ? MemError() : memFullErr;
    goto fail;
}
```

Because we are able to allocate global data in our code resource, we do that here. Note that we allocate the memory in the system heap using the Memory Manager NewPtrSysClear function. We have defined a structure called Globals that contains all of the information our patches need to perform their functions. It looks like the following code.

```
typedef struct {
    long                menuScriptsFolderDirID;
    long                anyApplicationFolderDirID;
    UniversalProcPtr    oldMenuSelectAddr;
    UniversalProcPtr    oldMenuKeyAddr;
    UniversalProcPtr    oldSystemMenuAddr;
    FSSpec              ourFSSpec;
} Globals, *GlobalsPtr, **GlobalsHdl;
```

The menuScriptsFolderDirID and anyApplicationFolderDirID
fields contain the directory IDs of our custom folders that we are
about to create. This makes it easier and faster for us to locate specific
files during our patches. The three UniversalProcPtr fields are the
original addresses (returned from GetToolTrapAddress) of the Toolbox
traps that we patch. This allows us to call through to the original traps
easily. The ourFSSpec field is a standard File Manager specification
record that points to our system extension file. This is handy to keep
around if we ever need to open our system extension file from one of
our patches, which we do in the case of an error. See the ShowError-
Alert function in the source code for an example of this.

```
err = RememberMe(&gGlobalsPtr->ourFSSpec);
if (err != noErr) goto fail;
```

We then fill in the FSSpec mentioned previously. This is done by
calling a simple utility function called RememberMe. It is defined in
the following code.

```
OSErr RememberMe(FSSpecPtr fsp)
{
    FCBPBRec    pb;
    OSErr       err = noErr;

    pb.ioCompletion = nil;
    pb.ioNamePtr = fsp->name;
    pb.ioVRefNum = 0;
    pb.ioRefNum = CurResFile();
    pb.ioFCBIndx = 0;

    err = PBGetFCBInfoSync(&pb);

    fsp->vRefNum = pb.ioFCBVRefNum;
    fsp->parID = pb.ioFCBParID;

    return err;
}
```

RememberMe fills in a File Manager FCBPB record and calls the low-level function PBGetFCBInfoSync. This returns the volume reference number, directory ID, and name of our file (which also happens to be, thanks to the system, the current resource file). As mentioned, having this information around allows us to access resources in our file at a later time.

```
GetIndString(menuScriptsFolderName, rStringListID,
iMenuScriptsFolderName);
if (menuScriptsFolderName[0] == 0) {
    err = resNotFound;
    goto fail;
}

err = FindFolder(kOnSystemDisk, kSystemFolderType,
kDontCreateFolder, &foundVRefNum, &foundDirID);
if (err != noErr) goto fail;

err = FSMakeFSSpec(foundVRefNum, foundDirID,
menuScriptsFolderName, &menuScriptsFolderFSSpec);

if (err == fnfErr) {

    err = FSpDirCreate(&menuScriptsFolderFSSpec, smSystemScript,
        &gGlobalsPtr->menuScriptsFolderDirID);

} else if (err == noErr) {

    err = GetDirectoryID(&menuScriptsFolderFSSpec,
        &gGlobalsPtr->menuScriptsFolderDirID);
}

if (err != noErr) goto fail;
```

The next step is to find (or create if it does not exist) our MenuScripts folder in the System folder. The first thing we do is load a string resource that defines the name of the folder. We then use Find-Folder to get the volume reference number and directory ID of the System folder. After we have this information, we can attempt to create an FSSpec for the MenuScripts folder. If the File Manager's FS-MakeFSSpec function returns a file not found error (fnfErr), then we must create the directory ourselves, as it does not exist. We call the FSpDirCreate function to create the directory and get its directory ID, which we then save in the menuScriptsFolderDirID field of our global data. If the folder already exists, we simply call our own GetDirectoryID function to ascertain the menuScriptsFolderDirID field. The GetDirectoryID function looks like the following code.

```
OSErr GetDirectoryID(FSSpec *spec, long *dirID)
{
    OSErr          err = noErr;
    CInfoPBRec     pb;

    pb.hFileInfo.ioNamePtr = spec->name;
    pb.hFileInfo.ioVRefNum = spec->vRefNum;
    pb.hFileInfo.ioFDirIndex = 0;
    pb.hFileInfo.ioDirID = spec->parID;

    err = PBGetCatInfoSync(&pb);

    *dirID = pb.hFileInfo.ioDirID;

    return err;
}
```

GetDirectoryID is another useful utility function from our arsenal of useful utility functions. By passing in the FSSpec of a directory, GETDirectoryID will return the directory ID of that directory. We can then use the directory ID to look for files within the directory.

Many programmers become confused when dealing with FSSpecs and trying to access the contents of a directory. When you have an FSSpec that describes a directory, you cannot use it to access the contents of that directory. That is, you need to obtain the directory ID of the directory itself, first. You can use the function PBGetCatInfo to obtain this information. The function GetDirectoryID in this chapter's project shows you exactly what you need to know to access the contents of the directory.

```
GetIndString(anyApplicationFolderName, rStringListID,
    iAnyApplicationFolderName);
if (anyApplicationFolderName[0] == 0) {
    err = resNotFound;
    goto fail;
}

err = FSMakeFSSpec(foundVRefNum,
    gGlobalsPtr->menuScriptsFolderDirID,
    anyApplicationFolderName, &anyApplicationFolderFSSpec);

if (err == fnfErr) {
```

```
                        err = FSpDirCreate(&anyApplicationFolderFSSpec,
                            smSystemScript,
                            &gGlobalsPtr->anyApplicationFolderDirID);

            } else if (err == noErr) {

                    err = GetDirectoryID(&anyApplicationFolderFSSpec,
                        &gGlobalsPtr->anyApplicationFolderDirID);
            }

            if (err != noErr) goto fail;
```

The next step is to find (or create if it does not exist) our Any Application folder in the MenuScripts folder. We take similar steps to that of creating the MenuScripts folder described previously. Ultimately, the goal of the previous code snippet is to fill in the anyApplication-FolderDirID field of our global data with the directory ID of the Any Application folder.

```
        hINIT = Get1Resource(kINITResourceType, kINITResourceID);
        if (hINIT == nil) {
                err = ResError() ? ResError() : resNotFound;
                goto fail;
        }
```

Eventually, we will need to detach our INIT resource. The system loads our INIT resource for us. However, the problem arises that after the system closes our system extension file, the INIT resource will be released automatically. We do not want this to happen, since it contains code that we need to use during our patches. Therefore, we need to detach the INIT resource using the Resource Manager's DetachResource function. To do this, we call Get1Resource to obtain a handle to our already loaded INIT resource. At the end of the INIT resource code (after our patches are applied successfully), we will detach the resource handle, which will allow it to survive in the system heap for the entire time the machine is turned on. When you detach a resource handle, it turns into a standard Memory Manager-type handle with no attachment to any resource file. Therefore, when the system closes our resource file, the memory will not be deallocated.

```
        err = Gestalt(gestaltSysArchitecture, &response);
        if (err != noErr) goto fail;
```

```
    if (response == gestalt68k)
        ApplyPatches(MenuSelect68k, MenuKey68k, SystemMenu68k);
    else if (response == gestaltPowerPC)
        err = PatchPPC();
    else err = gestaltUnknownErr;    // who knows what might be next?
    if (err != noErr) goto fail;
```

It's finally time to patch our traps. The previous code will be explained later in more detail. Basically, we see if we are running on a Power Macintosh or not. If not, we simply call our ApplyPatches routine, shown below, passing in pointers to the patches we wish to apply (say that three times fast). If we are running on a Power Macintosh, we call our PatchPPC routine (which is explained in the next section, "Patching Traps for PowerPC") to apply our native PowerPC patches.

> The gestaltSysArchitecture, which is used to see which platform we are executing on, is only available with PowerPC System 7.1.2 and 680x0 7.5 or later. If the selector is not available you may opt to assume 680x0 as opposed to returning an error as we have done here. To each his own.

```
void ApplyPatches(void * menuSelectCode, void * menuKeyCode,
                  void * systemMenuCode)
    {
        gGlobalsPtr->oldMenuSelectAddr = GetToolTrapAddress(_MenuSelect);
        SetToolTrapAddress((UniversalProcPtr)menuSelectCode, _MenuSelect);

        gGlobalsPtr->oldMenuKeyAddr = GetToolTrapAddress(_MenuKey);
        SetToolTrapAddress((UniversalProcPtr)menuKeyCode, _MenuKey);

        gGlobalsPtr->oldSystemMenuAddr = GetToolTrapAddress(_SystemMenu);
        SetToolTrapAddress((UniversalProcPtr)systemMenuCode, _SystemMenu);
    }
```

The ApplyPatches function simply fills in our global data with the previous trap addresses and applies the new patches to allow us to intercept the toolbox calls in which we are interested, as in the previous code. These functions alone (GetToolTrapAddress and SetToolTrapAddress) are responsible for some of the coolest programs available for the Macintosh.

```
    DetachResource(hINIT);
```

As previously mentioned, before our INIT resource exits, we must detach it, as in the previous code. This ensures it will stay resident in memory throughout the time the machine is turned on.

```
        goto exit;

fail:
    if (gGlobalsPtr) {
        DisposePtr((Ptr)gGlobalsPtr);
        gGlobalsPtr = nil;
    }

    if (hINIT) {
        ReleaseResource(hINIT);
        hINIT = nil;
    }

    if (err != noErr) {
        SysBeep(0);
    }

exit:

    SetA4(oldA4);

    SetZone(savedZone);
}
```

This last bit of code is just to make sure we clean things up in case of an error. At the very end, we need to restore our A4 world (remember, we use A4 to access globals) and restore the heap zone that was active when our INIT resource was called. Note the use of the goto statement in C—it comes in very handy for the end of functions like this one. We enter the fail label of code if we ever failed earlier. Otherwise, we goto the exit label directly. Although others don't like using the goto statement in C, I think it is very useful for handling failure cases such as this one.

In this project, we have made our INIT resource 680x0 code only. You will learn, in subsequent chapters, that you can make any resource (even an INIT resource) contain both 680x0 and PowerPC code simply by making it fat. We could have taken this approach in this chapter, but then we wouldn't have anything to keep your interest later on.

Patching Traps for PowerPC

As previously mentioned, MenuScript is a system extension that installs 680x0 trap patches when running on a non-Power Macintosh. However, in order to take advantage of the speed of a Power Macintosh, we install native PowerPC code when running on that processor. The function PatchPPC, called from main, performs this task. You should read *Inside Macintosh—PowerPC System Software* for complete information about the capabilities of these new Toolbox functions. But in the meantime, let's take a look at the code:

```
OSErr PatchPPC(void)
{
    OSErr               err = noErr;
    Handle              ppcCodeH = nil;
    SymClass            symClass;
    Ptr                 symAddr;
    ConnectionID        connID = kNoConnectionID;
    Str255              errStr;
    Ptr                 mainAddr;
    UniversalProcPtr    menuSelectUPP = nil, menuKeyUPP = nil,
                        systemMenuUPP = nil;
```

The first thing we do is allocate and initialize our local variables, as always.

```
    ppcCodeH = Get1Resource(kPPCResourceType, kPPCResourceID);
    if (ppcCodeH == nil) return ResError() ? ResError() :resNotFound;
    DetachResource(ppcCodeH);
    HLock(ppcCodeH);
```

We then want to load our resource that contains our PowerPC code fragment. We compiled our PowerPC code as a shared library and then copied that data (using Resorcerer, a resource editor) into a resource. There are other ways to accomplish this, but we found this mechanism quite easy to deal with. We also make sure we detach the code and lock it down in memory, as in the previous code. The resource's attributes should be marked sysHeap and may be optionally marked as being locked, in which case we wouldn't have had to call HLock. In fact, marking a resource as locked is a better thing to do if you are going to end up locking it anyway, since doing so alerts the Resource Manager to call the ReservMem function to ultimately load the resource as low in the heap as possible. This helps to prevent unnecessary heap fragmentation.

Both ToolServer and the Rez Tool, which can also be used to copy code from the data fork to a resource, are very advanced programs and allow you to perform a wide variety of tasks. You should read the documentation that came on your CodeWarrior CD for full instructions on how to make use of them.

```
errStr[0] = 0;
err = GetMemFragment(*ppcCodeH, GetHandleSize(ppcCodeH),
     kPPCFragmentName, kLoadNewCopy, &connID, &mainAddr, errStr);
if (err != noErr) goto fail;
```

We must then open a connection to the code fragment, as in the previous code. This allows the Code Fragment Manager to initialize the fragment and resolve any external references within it. We tell the Code Fragment Manager to load an entirely new copy of the code and its data by passing the constant kLoadNewCopy. The connection ID is returned in the connID parameter. The address of the code is returned in the mainAddr parameter. Any error is returned as a human-text message in the errStr parameter, which we can use during debugging or to display to the user.

```
err = FindSymbol(connID, kGlobalsSymbolName, &symAddr, &symClass);
if (err != noErr) goto fail;
```

After the fragment is prepared, we can request the address of symbols that we told our compiler to export. In our case, we exported a global variable symbol and also the symbols for our native patches. In the previous code, we request the address of our global data.

```
*(Globals**)symAddr = gGlobalsPtr;
```

After we obtain the address of the native globals, we update it (see the previous code) to point to the global data that we have already allocated in our main function of our 680x0 INIT. This allows all of our code to share the same global data.

```
err = FindSymbol(connID, kMenuSelectFunctionName,
     &symAddr, &symClass);
if (err != noErr) goto fail;
```

```
#if  1
     menuSelectUPP = (UniversalProcPtr) NewRoutineDescriptor(
          (ProcPtr)symAddr, kMenuSelectProcInfo, kPowerPCISA);
#else
     menuSelectUPP = (UniversalProcPtr) NewFatRoutineDescriptor(
          MenuSelect68k, symAddr, kMenuKeyProcInfo);
#endif
     if (menuSelectUPP == nil) goto fail;
```

We now request the address of the native patch to MenuSelect. After we get the address of our native code, we can build a routine descriptor to represent it. You can build either a standard routine descriptor, which contains only PowerPC code, or a fat routine descriptor, which contains both 680x0 and PowerPC code. A fat routine descriptor allows the Mixed Mode Manager to automatically execute the code that will yield the best overall throughput, depending on the mode from which the code is being called. In our case, since we want to test the PowerPC code only, we choose to create a PowerPC code routine descriptor. The kMenuKeyProcInfo parameter is a Mixed Mode procedure information definition of the calling conventions of this function. It is defined in the following code.

```
kMenuSelectProcInfo = kPascalStackBased
        | RESULT_SIZE(SIZE_CODE(sizeof(long)))
        | REGISTER_RESULT_LOCATION(kRegisterD0)
        | STACK_ROUTINE_PARAMETER(1,SIZE_CODE(sizeof(Point))),

CallUniversalProc(gGlobalsPtr->oldMenuSelectAddr,
        kMenuSelectProcInfo, pt)
```

Apple has devised this mechanism in order to call PowerPC code easily from our programs. On the PowerPC, you must use the Call-UniversalProc function (or CallOSTrapUniversalProc) to execute a function such as ours. One of the parameters to CallUniversalProc is a ProcInfoType. This information tells the Mixed Mode Manager the calling conventions of the code, as in the previous code. The Call-OSTrapUniversalProc function differs from CallUniversalProc in that it saves and restores certain registers before and after the call to the function. It is mostly used when calling OSTrap patches, for example.

```
     err = FindSymbol(connID, kMenuKeyFunctionName,
          &symAddr, &symClass);
     if (err != noErr) goto fail;
#if  1
     menuKeyUPP = (UniversalProcPtr) NewRoutineDescriptor(
```

```
            (ProcPtr)symAddr, kMenuKeyProcInfo, kPowerPCISA);
#else
        menuKeyUPP = (UniversalProcPtr) NewFatRoutineDescriptor(
            MenuKey68k, symAddr, kMenuKeyProcInfo);
#endif
        if (menuKeyUPP == nil) goto fail;

        err = FindSymbol(connID, kSystemMenuFunctionName,
            &symAddr, &symClass);
        if (err != noErr) goto fail;
#if 1
        systemMenuUPP = (UniversalProcPtr) NewRoutineDescriptor(
            (ProcPtr)symAddr, kSystemMenuProcInfo, kPowerPCISA);
#else
        systemMenuUPP = (UniversalProcPtr) NewFatRoutineDescriptor(
            SystemMenu68k, symAddr, kSystemMenuProcInfo);
#endif
        if (systemMenuUPP == nil) goto fail;
```

We then perform the same thing (as in the previous code) for the MenuKey and SystemMenu native patches.

```
    ApplyPatches(menuSelectUPP, menuKeyUPP, systemMenuUPP);
```

After we have all of the native code in the form of routine descriptors, we pass them to our ApplyPatches routine described earlier, as in the previous code. The patches are applied and we are ready to intercept the Menu Manager!

```
        goto exit;
fail:
    if (menuSelectUPP) {
            DisposeRoutineDescriptor(menuSelectUPP);
            menuSelectUPP = nil;
    }
    if (menuKeyUPP) {
            DisposeRoutineDescriptor(menuKeyUPP);
            menuKeyUPP = nil;
    }
    if (connID != kNoConnectionID) {
            CloseConnection(&connID);
            connID = kNoConnectionID;
    }
    if (ppcCodeH) {
            DisposeHandle(ppcCodeH);
            ppcCodeH = nil;
    }
```

```
        if (errStr[0] != 0)
              DebugStr(errStr);
exit:
    return err;
}
```

Lastly, we have our cleanup code. If errors occur, we dispose any allocated routine descriptors, close our Code Fragment Manager connection, and dispose of our native code resource (that has since been detached).

Inside the Patches

Now that you know how to set up and apply the 680x0 and PowerPC trap patches, let's take a look at the patches themselves. The 680x0 and PowerPC versions are very similar when you look at the C code. However, when compiled, they are quite different.

```
pascal long MenuSelect68k(Point startPt)
{
    long              result;
    long              oldA4;
    OSErr             err = noErr;

    oldA4 = SetUpA4();

    result = ((MenuSelectProc)
          gGlobalsPtr->oldMenuSelectAddr)(startPt);

    if (result != 0L) {
          err = DoMenuPatchStuff(result, gGlobalsPtr);
          if (err == noErr)
                result = 0L;
    }

    RestoreA4(oldA4);
    return result;
}

pascal long MenuSelectPPC(Point startPt)
{
    long      result;
    OSErr     err = noErr;

    result = CallMenuSelect(startPt);
```

```
                         if (result != 0L) {
                             err = DoMenuPatchStuff(result, gGlobalsPtr);
                             if (err == noErr)
                                     result = 0L;
                         }

                         return result;
                     }
```

As you can see in the previous code, the only differences in the 680x0 and PowerPC versions of the MenuSelect patch are the way in which we call the previous MenuSelect trap address and the fact that the PowerPC version need not set up A4 to access global data. PowerPC code fragments are able to use global data automatically, without any additional code. The patches to MenuKey and SystemMenu share the same similarities.

In the 680x0 code, we take the previous trap address and treat it as if it were a function pointer. We can simply call it as if it were a regular function. In the PowerPC code, however, we must use the CallUniversalProc routine, as described earlier.

Both patches call the previous trap addresses first and then handle themselves according to the returned result. This allows us to let the Menu Manager obtain the user's selection before we do anything. Our routine DoMenuPatchStuff is then called to handle the main functionality of the system extension. Let's look at that function in the following code.

```
        OSErr  DoMenuPatchStuff(long menuResult, GlobalsPtr  gp)
        {
            FSSpec          appFolderSpec;
            OSErr           err = noErr;
            short           menuID = HiWord(menuResult);
            short           menuItem = LoWord(menuResult);
            MenuHandle      hMenu = GetMHandle(menuID);
            FSSpec          menuItemSpec;
            Str255          itemString;
```

The first thing DoMenuPatchStuff must do is obtain the menu ID and menu item from the result returned by the Menu Manager. After we have this information, we can get the menu handle associated with that menu ID, as in the previous code.

```
    if (hMenu) {
            GetItem(hMenu, menuItem, itemString);
    } else {
            return -1;
    }
}
```

Assuming we were able to get the menu handle, we can then attempt to get the name of the item that was selected from that menu, as in the previous code.

```
err = FSMakeFSSpec(-1, gp->menuScriptsFolderDirID,
    (unsigned char *)LMGetCurApName(), &appFolderSpec);
```

We then see if a folder exists for the currently running application. If a folder does exist, then we must look within it (as in the following code) to find an item to launch based on the name of the menu item selected.

```
if (err == noErr) {
    long    appFolderDirID;

    err = GetDirectoryID(&appFolderSpec, &appFolderDirID);
    if (err == noErr) {

            err = FSMakeFSSpec(-1, appFolderDirID,
                itemString, &menuItemSpec);
            if (err == noErr) {
                err = OpenSelection(&menuItemSpec, kOpenItem);
                if (err != noErr) {
                        ShowErrorAlert(&gp->ourFSpec,
                            aOpenSelection, err);
                        return err;
                } else goto exit;
            } // fnfErr
    } else { ShowErrorAlert(&gp->ourFSpec,
            aGetAppDirID, err); return err; }
} // fnfErr
```

If we are able to get the directory ID of the folder for the current application, we can search it for an item with the same name as the currently selected menu item. We do this by calling FSMakeFSSpec. If this function returns noErr, we know the item exists and we call our OpenSelection function, passing it as the item to open. This function simply sends an AppleEvent to the Finder, asking it to open the newly found item. At this point, the item is opened and our patch sets the result to 0L which tells the calling application that the user selected nothing from the menu. In effect, we have just overridden the menu selection.

> You may notice that we are sending the Finder an AppleEvent from within our INIT code. You may ask yourself, how is this possible? Well, the AppleEvent Manager is nice enough to allow anyone to send AppleEvents. However, since our INIT does not have a main event loop, we cannot receive any replies to them. In our case, this is not a major problem, since all we want to do is attempt to launch a document. The AppleEvents we are using return no useful information anyway.

```
        err = FSMakeFSSpec(-1, gp->anyApplicationFolderDirID,
            itemString, &menuItemSpec);
    if (err == noErr) {
            err = OpenSelection(&menuItemSpec, kOpenItem);
            if (err != noErr)
                ShowErrorAlert(&gp->ourFSpec, aOpenSelection, err);
            else goto exit;
    } // fnfErr

exit:
    return err;
}
```

If we get to this point, we either did not have a folder named after the current application or no item existed in the current application's folder with the same name as the selected menu item. Therefore, it is now time to search in the Any Application folder. We use the same technique to find an item to open. We use FSMakeFSSpec, if the item exists, and call OpenSelection to send an AppleEvent to the Finder. Once again, our patch sets the result to 0L and we have successfully overridden the menu selection.

Compiling Our Code

Although we discuss the source code in this chapter in quite a bit of detail, there are still some things to consider. There are actually two Code-Warrior projects that we use to compile the 680x0 code and the PowerPC code. Each project and source files have special compiler directives that tell the compiler to do certain things in certain ways. In order to make all of this come together, it's important to understand your compiler as much as you understand the *Inside Macintosh* chapters that explain the different managers we have used in this example. I recommend opening the projects and exploring the preferences dialog boxes yourself in order to see how the different options are used in this chapter. Also, look at the relationship of the source files and note which functions are in which files. Some files are compiled in both projects, as PowerPC and 680x0 code (Figures 4-3 and 4-4). Once again, experiment with the code we have provided. That is why it is here.

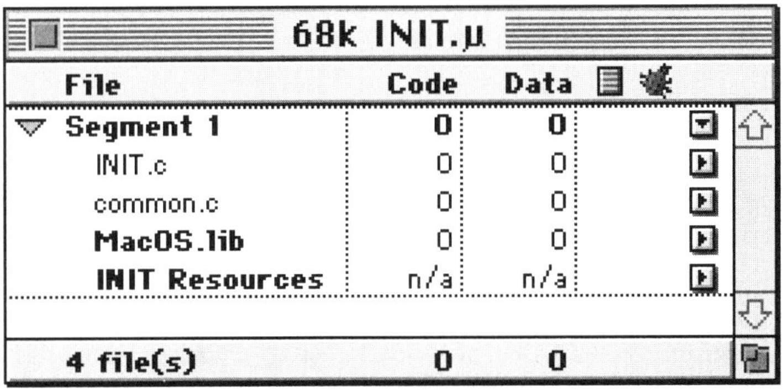

File	Code	Data		
▽ **Segment 1**	**0**	**0**		▾
INIT.c	0	0		▸
common.c	0	0		▸
MacOS.lib	0	0		▸
INIT Resources	n/a	n/a		▸
4 file(s)	**0**	**0**		

68k INIT.µ

Figure 4-3. 680x0 project file

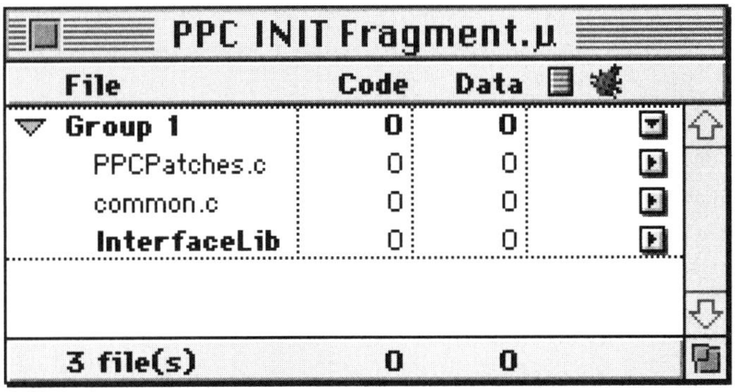

File	Code	Data		
▽ **Group 1**	**0**	**0**		▾
PPCPatches.c	0	0		▸
common.c	0	0		▸
InterfaceLib	0	0		▸
3 file(s)	**0**	**0**		

PPC INIT Fragment.µ

Figure 4-4. PowerPC project file

System Extension Tips

There are many things to keep in mind when writing a system extension. This section reviews and outlines some of the key issues.

- In most cases, you will want to make sure your INIT resource's attributes are marked sysHeap. This ensures that the resource will be loaded into the system heap when it is executed by the system.
- Any resources that your system extension uses should also be marked sysHeap. If, during a patch, you open your system extension file and access resources (via the RememberMe function), you should be sure they are all loaded into the system heap. Otherwise, there may not be enough memory to load them, depending on which applications are currently running, for example.
- You will also want to set your INIT resource to be locked if you plan to detach it. By setting the locked attribute of the resource, the Resource Manager will load it as low in the system heap as possible, which will ease memory fragmentation as you (and other system extensions) allocate memory, load other resources, etc.
- System extensions have gotten a bad rap for being incompatible with each other in a good number of cases. System extensions are like parasites. They all live off of the system software and other applications—not always with their permission. If two system extensions are in need of a particular resource (whether it be memory, an actual resource, or something else) a conflict may occur. There is no way to tell if you will be 100 percent compatible with other system extensions unless you test yours with all the others. One good rule of thumb is to code defensively, don't make assumptions, and don't try to do too much in your system extension. Remember, you must share the playground.
- System extensions of type INIT can send AppleEvents, but cannot receive them and, therefore, cannot receive a reply.
- System extensions of type APPE can send and receive Apple-Events because they have a main event loop. However, they cannot use QuickDraw and they have a smaller stack than most applications, only 2K by default.
- You can increase the stack size of your faceless-background application by using the SetApplLimit function as documented in Inside Macintosh: Memory. You should note, however, that the minimum you can increase the stack to is 16K so make sure your application heap is large enough to contain it. Also, your faceless-background application should call InitGraf, but shouldn't use

QuickDraw (with the exception of the Random function) since some other pieces of the system software depend on a valid A5 world for some operations.

* If you are writing an INIT that uses a large amount of system heap space, you should make use of the sysz resource. That is, by adding a resource of type sysz with an ID of 0 to your INIT file, you are telling the System that you want it to do what it needs to do to ensure that you have that much memory available to run. This can be a helpful thing, not only for yourself but for your users.

C H A P T E R   F I V E

Control Panels

When are you coming to bed?

—Significant other of a certain Macintosh programmer

Introduction

Control panels are files of type cdev that provide a user interface for your system extensions and other systemwide software. Control panels live within the constraints of the Finder. The Finder launches the control panel when the user double-clicks its icon and then feeds it a steady stream of events to keep it busy. The control panel handles these events much like any application would—by drawing the contents of its windows, managing clicks on its controls, and returning information about itself and the environment in which it can operate.

Programmers mostly use control panels (Figure 5-1) to allow easy editing of preferences associated with a system extension. The control panel file contains a code-bearing resource of type cdev that is executed by the Finder when the control panel is launched. The file also contains other resources that assist the Finder in knowing how large to make the control panel window, where to place the window on the screen, on which computers it can operate, and the list goes on and on.

Of these extra resources, the nrct resource contains a list of rectangles that tell the Finder to draw bold rectangular outlines within the

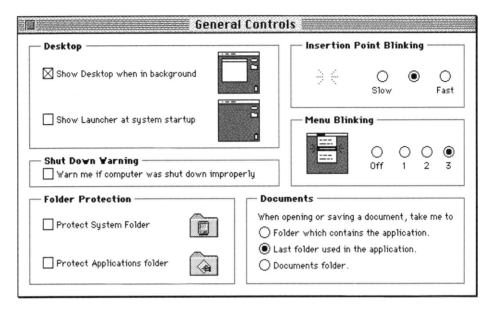

Figure 5-1. The System 7.5 General Controls control panel

control panel window. The Finder also sizes the window based on the union of these rectangles. (See Figures 5-2 and 5-3.)

The fwst resource is created by the Finder and is added to the control panel file the first time it is launched. This resource contains information so the Finder knows the last location at which the window

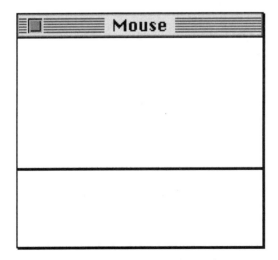

Figure 5-2. Graphical representation of an nrct resource containing two rectangles

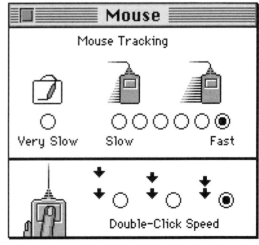

Figure 5-3. Control panel with nrct rectangles automatically outlined by the Finder

was positioned on the screen. Each time the control panel is opened, if this resource exists, its window is placed in the saved position. When the control panel is closed, the Finder updates this resource to represent the new position.

Don't forget to remove the fwst before you ship! When you first launch your control panel by double-clicking it in the Finder, the Finder places the window in a default location. However, when the window is closed, the Finder stores its current position in a resource of type fwst inside your control panel. This allows the Finder to open the window in the same position as when it was last closed. So, if users like to position the control panel in the lower right corner of their screen, each time they open it, it will appear there. Your control panel need not know anything about the location and will work fine no matter where it is. One thing to remember, however, is that you should remove this fwst resource before you ship your control panel. If you don't, it may appear in a location that is undesirable (or inaccessible) to the first users who launch it. Remember, not everyone has two 27-inch monitors; some are constrained to nine inches of desk top.

The mach resource contains flags telling the Finder on which computers your control panel can operate. There is also a setting in these flags that tells the Finder to ask your control panel (via the macDev message) if it can run on the current machine. When your control panel is first loaded, it is called with this message. You can then determine if you can run in the current configuration and return true or false to the Finder.

Anatomy of a Control Panel

Now that you've had a brief overview of how a control panel works (see *Inside Macintosh*, "More Macintosh Toolbox" for a complete introduction), let's take a look at one in particular. In this chapter, we add a control panel user interface to our system extension created in the previous chapter. Our control panel simply allows the user to turn the MenuScript INIT on and off. Changes to the control panel take effect immediately, with no need to restart the computer. Because we are

The mach resource, also known as the machine resource, tells the Finder what hardware and software your control panel requires to run or tells the Finder to ask your control panel to decide for itself. The mach resource contains two word-sized masks—a soft mask followed by a hard mask. The settings in Table 1-1 are valid.

Table 1-1. Valid mach settings

Soft mask	Hard mask	Action
$0000	$FFFF	Finder asks the control panel, via the macDev message, to decide for itself
$3FFF	$0000	Control panel runs on Macintosh II systems only
$7FFF	$0400	Control panel runs on all systems with an Apple Desktop Bus (ADB)
$FFFF	$0000	Control panel runs on all systems

In the majority of cases, you will want the Finder to send your control panel a macDev message, since the other mask values are quite limited and outdated.

creating a safe fat version of our cdev resource, at the bottom of the control panel window we display some text to indicate which version we are running. This makes it easier to debug our code, since we always know which version is running (Figure 5-4).

System Extension Changes

In order to implement the control panel version of MenuScript, we made a few minor changes to our system extension source code. Mainly, we added a new field containing our preferences information in our global data structure. We also implemented a function named GestaltGetGlobals that we install as a custom Gestalt selector, using the NewGestalt function, in order to allow access to this data (as in the following code). These changes allow our control panel to access the global data in the system extension and alter it in real time.

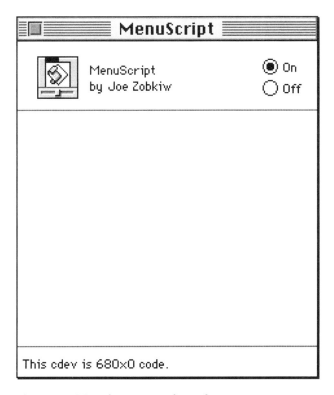

Figure 5-4. MenuScript control panel

```
pascal OSErr GestaltGetGlobals(OSType selector, long *response)
{
    long oldA4 = SetUpA4();      // set up access to our globals
                                 // return pointer to our globals
    *response = (long)&(gGlobalsPtr->preferences);
    RestoreA4(oldA4);            // restore access to our globals
    return noErr;                // return no error
}
```

Our control panel calls the UpdateINIT function to set the preferences in the system extension to the current values in the control panel itself. For example, when the user clicks the on or off radio button, the control panel fills in its PreferencesHdl structure and then passes it to the UpdateINIT function. UpdateINIT calls the Gestalt Manager function Gestalt to access the system extension's global data.

The system extension function GestaltGetGlobals is then called by the Gestalt Manager and fills in the response parameter with a pointer to its globals. Our control panel can then edit any value in the preferences and those changes will take effect immediately in the system extension (as in the following code).

```
#define kGestaltSelector      'Menu'

typedef struct {
    short                  fEnabled;
} Preferences, *PreferencesPtr, **PreferencesHdl;

void UpdateINIT(PreferencesHdl ph)
{
    OSErr              err = noErr;
    PreferencesPtr     pp;

    // get pointer to current system extension globals
    err = Gestalt(kGestaltSelector, (long*)&pp);
    if (err == noErr) {
          // either enable or disable it
          pp->fEnabled = (*ph)->fEnabled;
    } else SysBeep(0);       // INIT is not loaded, most likely
}
```

This method of communication is used by many different types of programs and is a valid way for your control panel to "talk" to your system extension and vice versa. You can also have applications and other types of code resources communicate with your system extension in this manner. Many commercial products allow programmers to change the way they function or obtain useful information about them via calls to Gestalt.

Using Gestalt, as previously described, is a great way to request information from an entity and have something returned. Most of the time you will use Gestalt to return a value or a pointer or handle to data. However, you can also use Gestalt for two-way communication. You can use Gestalt to pass information to the Gestalt selector you are calling. Simply fill in the response variable with the information you like and call Gestalt. When the selector is invoked, it can extract any data from the response parameter and use it as it sees fit. You could easily pass a UniversalProcPtr in this way and allow your system extension, for example, to be the initiator of communication with your control panel—instead of the other way around. When your control panel closes, don't forget to tell the system extension that the UniversalProcPtr is no longer valid by passing a value of nil. And remember, your control panel might move in memory, so make sure you lock it in place if you use this trick.

Control Panel Code

Now that we understand what has changed in order to allow our control panel to access the globals in our system extension, let's look at the structure of the control panel itself. All of our code is stored in the cdev resource. Ultimately, we will create a safe fat version of this resource so it will run on a 680x0 Macintosh as well as a Power Macintosh in the most optimized form.

> Remember, you can safely create a fat or safe fat resource of just about any code-bearing resource. It might make them bigger, but it is better for your users.

Like most code resources that are supported by the system software, each has a strict calling convention. Control panels are no different in this requirement. The main entry point of the control panel code resource is defined in the following code.

```
pascal long main(    short          message,
                     short          item,
                     short          numItems,
                     short          CPanelID,
                     EventRecord    *theEvent,
                     Handle         cdevStorage,
                     DialogPtr      CPDialog)
```

The control panel returns a long that varies depending on the message received. This value may be a Boolean value (true or false), an error code, or a handle to the private storage of the control panel.

The parameters to the control panel function include the message we are sending, the item that was clicked in the item list, the number of items before your first item in the item list, the ID number of the control panel item list, the current event, a handle to private storage that you allocate and deallocate, and the pointer to your control panels window. The following code represents the main control panel function.

```
{
    long    result = 0L;

#ifndef __powerc
    long    oldA4;
```

```
        oldA4 = SetCurrentA4();
        RememberA4();
#endif

    if (message == macDev) {        /* check our configuration */
            result = CanRun();
            goto exit;
    } else if (cdevStorage != nil) {

            switch(message) {

                    /* init ourselves */
                    case initDev:
                        cdevStorage = InitControlPanel(CPDialog,
                            numItems);
                        if (cdevStorage == nil) {
                            result = (long)cdevMemErr;
                            goto exit;
                        }
                        break;

                    /* close ourselves down */
                    case closeDev:
                        if (cdevStorage != nil) {
                            CloseControlPanel(cdevStorage);
                            cdevStorage = nil;
                        }
                        break;

            /* handle hit on item & update cdevStorage each time since
            we can not trust the item list during a closeDev msg */
                case hitDev:
                        HitControlPanel(CPDialog, item,
                            numItems, cdevStorage);
                        break;

                case nulDev:        /* null event */
                        break;

                case cursorDev:     /* adjust our cursor */
                        break;

                case updateDev:     /* handle any update drawing */
                        UpdatePanel(CPDialog, cdevStorage, numItems);
                        break;
```

```
            case activDev:   /* activate any needed items */
            case deactivDev: /* deactivate any needed items */
            case keyEvtDev:  /* respond to keydown */

                break;
            case undoDev:    /* undo event */
            case cutDev:     /* cut event */
            case copyDev:    /* copy event */
            case pasteDev:        /* paste event */
            case clearDev:        /* clear event */
                break;
        }

        result = (long)cdevStorage;
        goto exit;

    } else {

        /*
        **    if cdevStorage = NIL then ControlPanel
        ** will put up memory error
        */

        result = nil; /* cdevStorage == nil */
        goto exit;
    }

exit:

#ifndef __powerc
    SetA4(oldA4);
#endif

    return result;
}
```

The control panel function simply handles each message as it is received in the appropriate manner. For example, if we receive a hitDev
message, we examine the item and numItems parameters to conclude
which item in our window was clicked. If we receive an updateDev
message, we know to draw any items in our window that are not
drawn automatically.

```
long CanRun(void)
{
    long    response;
    OSErr   err = noErr;

    err = Gestalt(gestaltSystemVersion, &response);
    if ((err != noErr) || (response < 0x00000700)) {
        return (long)false;
    } else {
        return (long)true;
    }
}
```

When the control panel is called with the macDev message, it is the Finder's way of asking us if we can operate in the given environment. At this point, we could easily check for a specific hardware configuration or ensure that other software is loaded. In the previous code, we simply check the system software version.

```
Handle InitControlPanel(DialogPtr d, short numItems)
{
    Handle      cdevStorage = nil;
    short       iType;
    Rect        iRect;
    Handle      iHandle;

    cdevStorage = Get1Resource(kPreferencesResType,
            kPreferencesResID);
    if (cdevStorage != nil) {
        DoRadioGroup(d, itemOnRadio + numItems,
                itemOffRadio + numItems,
                (*(PreferencesHdl)cdevStorage)->fEnabled ?
                itemOnRadio : itemOffRadio + numItems);
        GetDItem(d, numItems + itemStaticText,
                &iType, &iHandle, &iRect);
#ifdef __powerc
        SetIText(iHandle, "\pThis cdev is native PowerPC code.");
#else
        SetIText(iHandle, "\pThis cdev is 680x0 code.");
#endif
    }
    return cdevStorage;
}
```

Assuming we can run in the given environment, we will then be asked to initialize and return a handle to our private storage. The Finder then maintains this handle for us and passes it to us as a parameter each time it is called. In our case, we simply load our preferences resource and set the radio buttons properly. We also fill in the

static text item at the bottom of the control panel window with text describing the type of code that is currently running.

```
void HitControlPanel(DialogPtr d, short item,
  short numItems, Handle cdevStorage)
{
    short myItem = item - numItems;
    switch (myItem) {
        case itemIcon:
            Alert(129, nil);
            break;
        case itemOnRadio:
        case itemOffRadio:
            DoRadioGroup(d, itemOnRadio + numItems,
                itemOffRadio + numItems, item);
            (*(PreferencesHdl)cdevStorage)->fEnabled =
                (GetRadioFromGroup(d, itemOnRadio + numItems, ...
                itemOffRadio + numItems) ==
                (itemOnRadio + numItems)); ...
            UpdateINIT((PreferencesHdl)cdevStorage);
            break;
    }
}
```

When the user clicks on an item in our control panel window, we are
sent the hitDev message. When we receive this message, we check to
see which item was hit and act appropriately. In our case, we simply
toggle the radio buttons if one was hit and call the UpdateINIT routine
to either enable or disable the INIT as in the previous code.

```
void CloseControlPanel(Handle cdevStorage)
{
    ChangedResource(cdevStorage);
    WriteResource(cdevStorage);
    ReleaseResource(cdevStorage);
}
```

When the user clicks the close box of our control panel window, the
Finder sends us a closeDev message. This is where we clean up any
messes we may have made and write our preferences. Since we loaded
the preferences resource earlier and never detached it from the resource file, we can simply call ChangedResource and WriteResource in
order to update the resource itself. We then call ReleaseResource to release the memory that it occupies, as in the previous code.

One thing to note is that during the closeDev message, you cannot depend on the existence of any editable text items that may be in your control panel window. These editable text items may be destroyed before your control panel is called with the closeDev message. Therefore, you need to keep track of any changes while they occur. The best way to do this is to always watch the values of any editable text item during the hitDev message. Assuming the editable text items are enabled, you will receive hitDev messages whenever the user types a character in them, so you can call GetIText to keep current with the text. I would suggest that you simply avoid editable text items in the main control panel window and use a dialog box triggered from a button in the control panel window instead.

By handling the messages that the Finder sends us, we are, in effect, a mini-application—only our event loop is really in the Finder itself.

Compiling Our Code

Although we discuss the source code in this chapter in quite a bit of detail, there are still some things to consider. As mentioned, we have created both a 680x0 and a PowerPC version of our control panel cdev resource. We have two projects that we can simply build and merge into our control panel that will work fine. One of these projects compiles the 680x0 code, the other compiles the PowerPC code (Figures 5-5 and 5-6). However, if we want to build a fat or safe fat control panel, we have to perform an extra step.

As you remember from Chapter Three and our discussion of private resources, a fat and safe fat resource contains both 680x0 and PowerPC code in the same convenient package. With the addition of a RoutineDescriptor and possibly a 680x0 code stub, we ensure that our code will run in the most optimized form on either platform. Although this makes our cdev resource a bit larger than it would be if it contained 680x0 code only, it will improve the performance of the control panel, to a degree, depending on what your control panel does.

Say, for instance, that your control panel is as simple as ours—just a group of two radio buttons that allow the user to turn your system extension on and off. You may elect to write it only as 680x0 code, today. You see, since your control panel code is so minimal, and hardly does anything, it might not be worth the time to make it PowerPC native. However, if your control panel does any time-consuming work or has a fancy user interface, you may elect to optimize the control panel on the Power Macintosh by specifically compiling the code for it. You will have to make this decision based on the functionality and the performance requirements of your control panel.

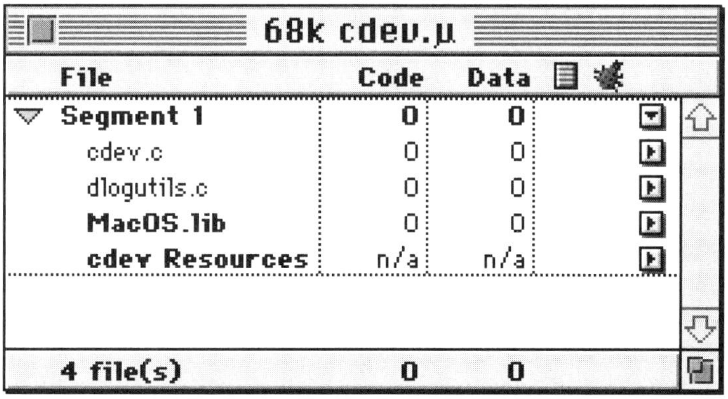

File	Code	Data	📄	🍁
▽ **Segment 1**	**0**	**0**	▾	
cdev.c	0	0	▶	
dlogutils.c	0	0	▶	
MacOS.lib	0	0	▶	
cdev Resources	n/a	n/a	▶	
4 file(s)	**0**	**0**		

68k cdev.µ

Figure 5-5. 680x0 project file

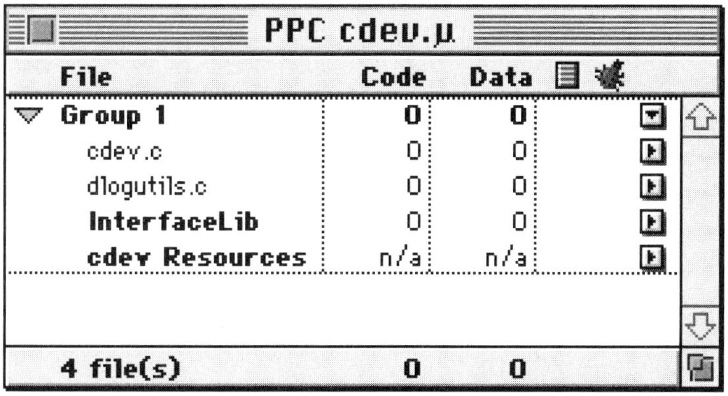

File	Code	Data	📄	🍁
▽ **Group 1**	**0**	**0**	▾	
cdev.c	0	0	▶	
dlogutils.c	0	0	▶	
InterfaceLib	0	0	▶	
cdev Resources	n/a	n/a	▶	
4 file(s)	**0**	**0**		

PPC cdev.µ

Figure 5-6. PowerPC project file

Control Panel Tips

There are many things to keep in mind when writing a control panel. This section reviews and outlines some of the key issues.

- Those of you familiar with the Dialog Manager will know that you make use of user item procedures to automatically draw items in your dialogs whenever an update event occurs. Although, technically, you can do this in your control panel window as well, there are some things of which to be aware. For example, your control panel code may move in memory between calls to itself. Therefore, if you set the user item procedure during the initDev message, your pointer to the user item procedure that you pass to the Dialog Manager routine SetDItem may become invalid if your code resource moves. If you must use this technique, either set the user item procedure each time you receive a message (not recommended) or make sure your code is locked at all times by setting the lock resource bit of your cdev resource. Mind you, you could just use the updateDev message to do your drawing like you should.
- In order to figure out which of your items was clicked on in a hitDev message, you must subtract the numItems parameter from the item parameter. The numItems parameter is left over from System 6, when your control panel window was a mere portion of the main control panel desk accessory window—a window that happened to contain other items. Under System 7, the majority of the time the value of numItems will be 0, since your control panel window is stand-alone, so to speak. However, some utilities that "run" control panels still use the parameter. Therefore, to be compatible, do the subtraction.
- Control panels can be a great way to add a window to the Finder. Even if your control panel doesn't contain any INIT code, it can be a nice way to integrate functionality into the Finder. Control panels can even take advantage of features such as the Drag Manager to allow dragging of Finder items into and out of your control panel window. Think of the possibilities.
- If you find your control panel getting very large, maybe you should rethink your approach. Should your control panel really be an application? Depending on exactly what tasks it performs, it might be better suited as one.
- Even though a control panel is like a mini-application, in that it receives lots of different types of events, it does not receive AppleEvents. Mind you, your control panel can still send AppleEvents, but don't expect a reply.

- You can use the Drag Manager with a control panel. For those of you who aren't familiar with it, the Drag Manager allows you to drag items, such as files or folders, into and out of different windows between applications. If you choose to use the Drag Manager (for which documentation exists elsewhere) in a control panel, you should make sure your control panel is locked down at all times so your drag handler functions can be called properly. To do this, use the locked resource attribute for your cdev resource. You see, the Finder calls HGetState and then HLocks your cdev down when it calls it. It then restores the cdev handles state with HSetState when the cdev returns control. This seems to indicate that you cannot lock yourself down from within your own cdev code without being set back to whatever you were before. Therefore, use the locked resource attribute in this case.

- Sometimes a control panel isn't the best choice for implementing your program. When a control panel is opened, the Finder calls WaitNextEvent with a very small sleep value—even if the Finder is not the front most application—so that it can give the control panel events on a regular basis. This can really affect system performance. If you intend to have your control panel left open for a long period of time, consider writing an application instead.

C H A P T E R S I X

List Definitions

Computer Science is the name of a course, not a fact.

—C.J.S.

Introduction

What's a program without a list? Not all programs need to have lists of items, but sometimes it makes sense to organize your data in that form. A list allows users to see all possible choices and make their selection or selections by clicking on items in the list. The List Manager gives the programmer control over the look of the items in the list, how many rows and columns are in the list, and whether or not multiple items or only a single item can be selected from the list.

To customize the look of a list, the List Manager uses a list definition procedure. This code is stored as a resource of type LDEF and is usually in the same file as the application or control panel that creates the list. By default, the List Manager includes a list definition procedure known as LDEF 0 (zero) that draws only text using the default font of the window—normally Chicago 12 point. By creating your own list definition procedure, you can customize the data and the way it is drawn in the cells of your list. You can draw in different fonts, draw icons, pictures, just about anything you desire.

The point of a list is to display numerous items and allow the user to select one or more of those items. After a selection is made in the list, the programmer can query the List Manager to find out which item or items are selected and what data they contain. For example, in Figure 6-1 we see the default list definition procedure in action. If we were to query the List Manager to return the data in the selected cell by calling the LGetCell function, it would tell us that an 11-byte stream of data is within that cell. Since we know the data stream is really text, we can convert it simply to a Pascal string for use in our program. The List Manager also allows us to set the contents of a cell, add cells, and remove cells. We have total control over the size and contents of our lists.

What happens if you need to display more than just simple strings? As mentioned, the list definition procedure is available for your use when that need arises. The LGetCell and LSetCell routines that allow you to get and set the cell data don't really care what that data is. In the default case, it may be a stream of characters. In your case, it may be a pointer to a custom data structure. As long as the List Manager knows the proper size of the data, all is well. When your list

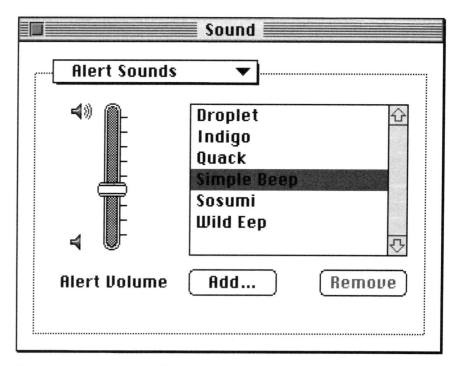

Figure 6-1. An example of a list of text strings

definition procedure is called to draw a particular cell, it extracts the data from the cell and uses the data to draw the cell contents. For example, you may store a pointer to a custom data structure in each cell that contains a handle to an icon family and a string of text that defines a name. Figure 6-2 displays a list of icons with names.

a The List Manager has a 32K limit to the data that can be in any list. Therefore, no matter what your cell data is, it must not exceed 32K for the entire list. If each cell contains a pointer to a structure, then each cell takes up 4 bytes. Remember, a pointer is basically a long integer that is 4 bytes in size. If you divide 32,000 bytes per list by 4 bytes per cell, you can see that the list can store approximately 8,000 cells.

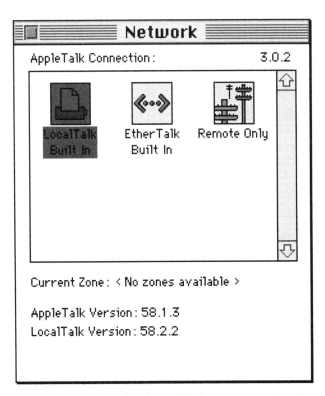

Figure 6-2. An example of a multicolumn custom list of icons

List Definition Code

In this chapter, we create a custom list definition procedure and tester application that displays a hierarchical list of the contents of your startup disk. You've all seen this type of list structure in the Finder, if you've ever used the View By Name option. Therefore, we call this the ViewByName LDEF.

As you can see in Figure 6-3, folders are represented by a folder icon and have an icon flag to their left that can be used to open and close the contents of the folder. Double-clicking a folder icon or name also opens and closes it. Single-clicking on an item simply selects it. Only one item can be selected at a time in our list—for no real reason, we just decided to do it that way. We also attempt to use the real icon of the item we are listing if it is available from the Desktop Database. Otherwise, we will draw a generic icon.

In order to implement the ViewByName LDEF, we need to create an LDEF resource that contains all the code to parse the data struc-

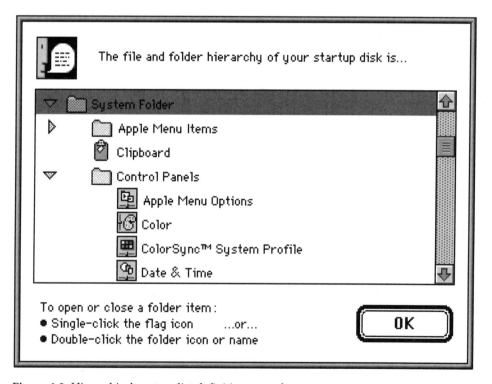

Figure 6-3. Hierarchical custom list definition procedure

tures of and draw each individual cell. We've decided to take another approach instead and use something called the RefConLDEF. The RefConLDEF is a list definition procedure that doesn't really know how to draw anything. What it does know how to do, however, is call a drawing function and pass a reference constant to it. The RefConLDEF gets this information from the cell that is about to be drawn. You see, the data for each cell contains a reference constant that can be anything we desire and a universal procedure pointer that points to a drawing function. When a cell needs to be drawn, the RefConLDEF calls the drawing function and passes to it the rectangle of the cell, the cell coordinates, the handle to the list in which the cell is located, and the reference constant (as in the following code). Our drawing function then does the right thing and draws the contents of the cell based on whatever data is stored in the reference constant (e.g., a handle to another data structure that is customized to our list and program).

```
typedef struct RefconLDEFCell {
    long                    refCon;
    RefconLDEFDrawProcUPP   drawProc;
} RefconLDEFCell, *RefconLDEFCellPtr, **RefconLDEFCellHdl;
```

Using the RefConLDEF has several advantages.

- We can use the same LDEF resource for any list in our program.
- We can have a different drawing procedure for every single cell in our list, if needed.
- Our drawing procedure can be inside our application, which allows for access to application global variables and also makes source-level debugging easier.
- There is no need for numerous LDEF projects floating around, which ultimately simplifies the build process for our application.

The RefConLDEF is also discussed in a bit more detail in Chapter Twelve's "Multiple Cell Formats in a List" section.

Now that you understand how we will be dealing with the use of our custom list definition procedure, let's look at the data structure (in the following code) that will be hanging off the reference constant field of each RefConLDEF cell. The value of the reference constant (which is a handle to a structure of type ListItem) is passed to our drawing function, which we will discuss in a moment.

```
typedef struct ListItem {
    FSSpec              spec;
    short               iconID;
    unsigned char       indentLevel;
    unsigned char       isOpen;
} ListItem, *ListItemPtr, **ListItemHdl;
```

Each ListItem structure contains the information needed to draw and track the status of each cell in our list. The spec field contains an FSSpec structure of the item in question, a folder, or a file. The iconID field is the resource ID of the icon to draw for the item if it does not have an icon available via the Desktop Database. For example, folders do not have icons stored in the Desktop Database, so we use the value in this field to know what to draw in its absence—namely, the little folder icon. The indentLevel field starts at 0 to designate an item on the root of the startup disk and is incremented by one for each level we open. The isOpen field is only valid for folders and is used to designate in the display whether or not a folder is currently open.

Now that we've looked at the data that we store for each cell, let's ponder the function that is called whenever one of our cells needs to be drawn. The ListElementProc function is called to do just that (as in the following code). The function doesn't do anything all that special, but it is one of the main parts of our program. Normally this function would be inside your LDEF, but because of our RefConLDEF, we are able to write it as part of our application code, making it much simpler to write and debug.

```
void ListElementProc(Rect *cellRect, Cell lCell,
                ListHandle theList, long refCon)
{
    ListItemHdl        lih;
    GrafPtr            savePort;
    Rect               iconRect;
    short              width;
    FInfo              fndrInfo;

    lih = (ListItemHdl)refCon;

    GetPort(&savePort);
    SetPort((**theList).port);
    PenNormal();

    MoveTo(cellRect->left + (44 + (20 * (*lih)->indentLevel)),
        cellRect->bottom - 4);
```

```
if (FSpGetFInfo(&((*lih)->spec), &fndrInfo) == noErr) {
      if (fndrInfo.fdFlags & 0x8000)
            TextFace(italic);
      DrawString((*lih)->spec.name);
      TextFace(0);
} else
      DrawString((*lih)->spec.name);
width = StringWidth((*lih)->spec.name);

if ((*lih)->iconID == rFolderIcon) {
      iconRect = *cellRect;
      iconRect.left += 4;
      iconRect.right = iconRect.left + 16;
      iconRect.top += 1;
      iconRect.bottom = iconRect.top + 16;
      PlotIconID(&iconRect, atNone, ttNone,
            (*lih)->isOpen ? rArrowOpenedIcon : rArrowClosedIcon);
}

iconRect = *cellRect;
iconRect.left += (24 + (20 * (*lih)->indentLevel));
iconRect.right = iconRect.left + 16;
iconRect.top += 1;
iconRect.bottom = iconRect.top + 16;

if ((*lih)->iconID == rFolderIcon) {
      PlotIconID(&iconRect, atNone, ttNone, (*lih)->iconID);
} else {
      if (DrawFileIcon(&((*lih)->spec), &iconRect) != noErr)
            PlotIconID(&iconRect, atNone, ttNone, (*lih)->iconID);
}

SetPort(savePort);
}
```

The first thing our drawing function does is typecast the refCon parameter to the proper type, to make it easier to access the data stored within. After we set up the port properly, we can then parse the data and draw. The first portion of the cell that is drawn is the file name. You will note that we first see if the item is an alias or not and draw the text in italics, if this is so. Then we draw the proper open or close flag icon, if the item is a folder. Lastly we draw the icon of the item—a generic folder icon if the item is a folder. Otherwise, we call the DrawFileIcon routine to draw the Finder icon of the item. The DrawFileIcon routine simply accesses the Desktop Database in order to find the icon that belongs to the file. If it can be found, it will be drawn. Otherwise, a generic icon will be drawn.

> Even though our drawing function may be relatively speedy, the List Manager can slow down when it contains lots of cells. Remember, the List Manager is not a spreadsheet. It is very useful for short lists of items, but if you find yourself listing more than a few thousand items, you may elect to write your own List Manager replacement. It isn't as hard as it sounds and it may prove to increase the responsiveness of your program.

When the list is first created, we must fill it with items to draw. This is done via the FillList function, as demonstrated in the following code. This function is passed a volume reference number and a directory ID, and then it fills in the list with the items in that directory. We also pass other parameters to it to allow us to use the same function to insert items when the user opens a folder item in the list.

```c
void FillList(short vRefNum, long dirID, ListHandle theList,
             short beforeThisRow, short indentLevel)
{
    short           index;
    OSErr           err = noErr;
    CInfoPBRec      pb;
    ListItemHdl     lih = nil;
    RefconLDEFCell  cellData;
    Cell            cell = {0,0};
    short           maxItems = 32000 / sizeof(RefconLDEFCell);

    LDoDraw(false, theList);

    index = 0;
    do {

        lih = (ListItemHdl)NewHandleClear(sizeof(ListItem));
        if (lih == nil) goto exit;
        HLock((Handle)lih);

        ++index;
        pb.hFileInfo.ioNamePtr = (*lih)->spec.name;
        pb.hFileInfo.ioVRefNum = vRefNum;
        pb.hFileInfo.ioFDirIndex = index;
        pb.hFileInfo.ioDirID = dirID;
        err = PBGetCatInfoSync(&pb);
```

```
                    if (err == noErr) {
                        if (pb.hFileInfo.ioFlAttrib & ioDirMask)
                            (*lih)->iconID = rFolderIcon;
                        else
                            (*lih)->iconID = GetIconID
                                (pb.hFileInfo.ioFlFndrInfo.fdType);

                        cell.v = LAddRow(1, beforeThisRow++, theList);

                        (*lih)->spec.parID = dirID;
                        (*lih)->spec.vRefNum = vRefNum;
                        (*lih)->indentLevel = indentLevel;
                        (*lih)->isOpen = false;

                        cellData.refCon = (long)lih;
                        cellData.drawProc = gListElementProcUPP;

                        LSetCell(&cellData, sizeof(RefconLDEFCell),
                            cell, theList);
                    }

                    HUnlock((Handle)lih);
                    if (err != noErr) DisposeHandle((Handle)lih);

            } while ((err == noErr) && ((**theList).dataBounds.bottom
                <= maxItems));

    exit:
        LDoDraw(true, theList);
    }
```

The first time the FillList function is called, it is told to fill the entire list by passing kAddToEnd as the beforeThisRow parameter and 0 as the indentLevel. At subsequent times, these values depend on the position and indent level of the folder item that is about to be opened. FillList first calculates the maximum number of cells that can be in the list by dividing the approximate maximum list data size of 32000 bytes by the size of the data stored in one cell. This ensures that we do not try to add more data than the list can handle. We then tell the List Manager to not draw the cells while we are adding them to the list by calling the LDoDraw function and passing false. This makes our list manipulation occur faster, because we aren't drawing the changes as they occur. We draw them all at once at the end.

After we've prepared the list itself, we are ready to begin adding items. By using the File Manager function PBGetCatInfoSync, we can easily peruse the items in the chosen directory by index. We first allocate a handle for the cell data and then fill it with information about the first item in the directory. We then decide which icon the item should use (in case the real icon cannot be found), add the cell row, fill in our other variable fields, and, ultimately, set the cell data. When the cell is being drawn, this is the data that will be accessed by the drawing function. This process is repeated for each item in the directory until each item has been processed. At the end, list drawing is turned back on and the list is updated on the screen.

Lastly, the list must react when the user clicks on it. The function HandleClickOnList does just that by being called whenever the user clicks on the user item that is used to represent the list (as in the following code). This function is responsible for adding and deleting rows from the list when the user opens or closes a folder item, respectively. It also tracks the clicking on one of the flag icons and can be used to track the selection of other items as well.

```
void HandleClickOnList(DialogPtr d, ListHandle theList)
{
        Point                localPt = {0,0};
        Boolean              doubleClick = false;
        Rect                 cellRect = {0,0,0,0};
        ListItemHdl          lih = nil;
        RefconLDEFCell       cellData;
        short                dataLen = sizeof(RefconLDEFCell);
        Cell                 theCell = {0,0};
        Rect                 iconRect, trackRect;
        Boolean              found = false;

        GetMouse(&localPt);

        if (localPt.h < (**theList).rView.left + 20) {

                theCell.h = theCell.v = 0;
                do {
                        LRect(&cellRect, theCell, theList);
                        if (PtInRect(localPt, &cellRect))
                                found = true;
                } while (!found && LNextCell(false, true,
                        &theCell,  theList));

                if (found) {
                        LGetCell(&cellData, &dataLen, theCell, theList);
                        lih = (ListItemHdl)cellData.refCon;
                        if ((*lih)->iconID == rFolderIcon) {
                                iconRect = cellRect;
                                iconRect.left += 4;
                                iconRect.right = iconRect.left + 16;
                                iconRect.top += 1;
```

```
                            iconRect.bottom = iconRect.top + 16;
                            trackRect = cellRect;
                            trackRect.right = trackRect.left + 20;

                            doubleClick = TrackIconByRect(&iconRect,
                                    &trackRect, (*lih)->isOpen ?
                                    rArrowOpenedIcon : rArrowClosedIcon);

                            if (doubleClick) {
                                    Cell theTCell;

                                    if (AnyCellsSelected(theList, &theTCell))
                                            LSetSelect(false, theTCell,
                                                    theList);
                                    LSetSelect(true, theCell, theList);
                            }
                    } else {
                            doubleClick = LClick(localPt, 0, theList);
                    }
            }
    } else {
            doubleClick = LClick(localPt, 0, theList);
    }

    if (doubleClick) {

            if (AnyCellsSelected(theList, &theCell)) {
                LGetCell(&cellData, &dataLen, theCell, theList);
                lih = (ListItemHdl)cellData.refCon;

                if ((*lih)->iconID == rFolderIcon) {
                        if ((*lih)->isOpen == false) {
                                long dirID =
                                        GetDirectoryID(&((*lih)->spec));
                                if (dirID != 0L) {
                                        Boolean listFilled =
                                                FillList((*lih)->spec.vRefNum,
                                                dirID, theList, theCell.v + 1,
                                                (*lih)->indentLevel + 1);
                                        if (listFilled) {
                                                (*lih)->isOpen = true;
                                                LSetCell(&cellData,
                                                        sizeof(RefconLDEFCell),
                                                        theCell, theList);
                                                LUpdate(gd->visRgn, glh);
                                        }
                                }
                        } else {
                                short  indentLevelToDelete =
                                        (*lih)->indentLevel + 1;
                                short  numRowsToDelete = 0;
                                short  firstRowToDelete = theCell.v + 1;
```

```
                                  (*lih)->isOpen = false;
                                  LSetCell(&cellData,
                                          sizeof(RefconLDEFCell), theCell,
                                          theList);

                          checkNextCell:
                                  theCell.v++;
                                  if (theCell.v <
                                          (**theList).dataBounds.bottom) {
                                          dataLen = sizeof(RefconLDEFCell);
                                          LGetCell(&cellData, &dataLen,
                                              theCell, theList);
                                          lih = (ListItemHdl)cellData.refCon;
                                          if ((*lih)->indentLevel >=
                                              indentLevelToDelete) {
                                              numRowsToDelete++;
                                              DisposeHandle((Handle)lih);
                                              lih = nil;
                                              goto checkNextCell;
                                          }
                                  }

                                  if (numRowsToDelete > 0L)
                                          LDelRow(numRowsToDelete,
                                              firstRowToDelete, theList);
                              }
                          }
                      }
                  }
              }
```

The HandleClickOnList function is a bit large, but is relatively
straightforward. First it uses the GetMouse function to get the local coordinates of the location that was clicked. Assuming we clicked in the
column that contains the folder flag icons, we then attempt to find out
exactly which cell we clicked on by looping and calling LNextCell. If
we actually did click on a cell, then we get the data for that cell and
see if it is a folder item. Assuming it is a folder item, we call our utility function TrackIconByRect to track the user's mouse movement
over the flag icon. If the user releases the mouse while still within the
flag icon, we treat it as if the user double-clicked on that item. Before
continuing, we select the cell that we just "double-clicked." If it ends
up that the item was not a folder item, or we clicked somewhere other
than in the column that displays the flag icons, we simply call LClick
to handle the click and select the cell for us. LClick will also return a
double-click on other portions of the cell.

Now that we know what, if anything, was double-clicked, we can
attempt to open any folder items. First we get the cell data for the cell

that was double-clicked and examine its type. If it is a folder item and is currently closed, we call FillList in order to insert the contents of the directory to which it pertains below the selected cell. The FillList function is passed the incremented indentation level to set all the newly added cells properly. This is how we tell how far to indent when we draw the cells and how deep in the hierarchy any particular cell is located. We then set the isOpen flag and update the data for the cell before redrawing the list items.

If the folder item was already opened, we need to close it. Closing a folder item is accomplished by deleting all rows below the current row that have an indentation level higher than the folder we are closing. After looping to count how many rows to actually delete and disposing of the handle stored in each cell, we delete them all at once by using the LDelRow function. We finish the function off with a lovely feature known as a quintuple brace.

> You may notice while looking at the code that we do not dispose of the handles in each cell when the program quits. We could do this very easily, but in our simple test program the list is destroyed seconds before the program quits. Therefore, because of the way memory works on the Macintosh, all handles allocated in the applications heap are disposed of automatically. You could easily write a function called DisposeAllHandles that would loop through all items in the list and dispose of any memory in the cells that remain. This is left as an exercise for the reader.

Compiling Our Code

The code in this chapter consists of our small RefConLDEF project (Figure 6-4), which is compiled as a resource of type LDEF. After it is compiled, we add it to our application, which contains the rest of the code. Using this technique dramatically increases the debug ability of our list definition drawing function and makes it easier to maintain in the future.

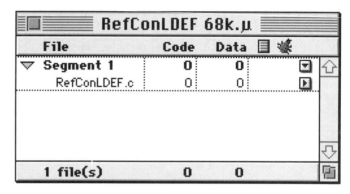

Figure 6-4. 680x0 RefConLDEF project file

File	Code	Data		
▽ **Segment 1**	**0**	**0**		▾
RefConLDEF.c	0	0		▸
1 file(s)	**0**	**0**		

Figure 6-4. 680x0 RefConLDEF project file

ViewByNameLDEF 68k.µ

File	Code	Data		
▽ **Sources**	**0**	**0**		▾
ViewByNameLDEF.c	0	0		▸
▽ **Resources**	**0**	**0**		▾
RefConLDEF 68k	n/a	n/a		▸
ViewByNameLDEF.rsrc	n/a	n/a		▸
▽ **Libraries**	**0**	**0**		▾
MacOS.lib	0	0		▸
4 file(s)	**0**	**0**		

Figure 6-5. 680x0 ViewByName LDEF application project file

RefConLDEF PPC.µ

File	Code	Data			
▽ **Group 1**	**0**	**0**		•	▾
RefConLDEF.c	0	0		•	▸
InterfaceLib	0	0			▸
2 file(s)	**0**	**0**			

Figure 6-6. PowerPC RefConLDEF project file

ViewByNameLDEF PPC.µ				
File	**Code**	**Data**	▤	🍂
▽ **Sources**	0	0	•	▾
ViewByNameLDEF.c	0	0	•	▶
▽ **Resources**	0	0		▾
RefConLDEF PPC	n/a	n/a		▶
ViewByNameLDEF.rsrc	n/a	n/a		▶
▽ **Libraries**	0	0		▾
InterfaceLib	0	0		▶
MWCRuntime.lib	0	0		▶
5 file(s)	**0**	**0**		

Figure 6-7. PowerPC ViewByName LDEF application project file

Modifying the List Definition

As you can see, the List Manager can be very useful for displaying lists of data to your users. It can also really spice up your programs if you use it wisely and make your lists look nice by using custom list definition procedures. Be careful not to overdo it, though. Too many useless icons in a list can be confusing to look at but if you have data to display that is in list form, consider the List Manager. Figures 6-8

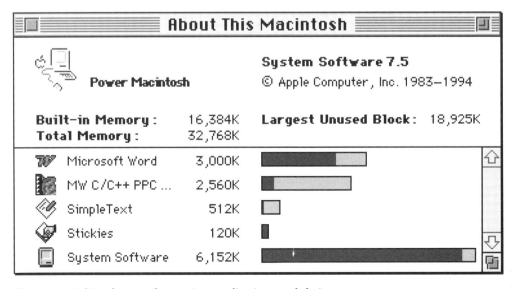

Figure 6-8. A list of currently running applications and their memory usage

and 6-9 are some more examples of types of lists that you may consider implementing in your programs.

List Definition Tips

Writing a list definition can be a great deal of fun and can really add some pizzazz to your application. Here are some tips to keep in mind when creating your LDEFs.

- The List Manager is limited to 32K of data per list. Therefore, you may want to store as little data as possible in each cell. If the data in each cell is going to be more than 8 bytes or so, you may elect to allocate a handle or pointer for each cell's data instead. On the other hand, if you only plan on displaying a few items in your list, using a large data structure per cell may not be that much of a drawback.
- In our example, we allocate a handle that is stored in the data for each cell. You may have noticed that we never actually dispose of that memory. Fortunately, since our application quits when the list itself is destroyed, the memory (which is allocated in the applications heap) is disposed of automatically. However, if your list is created and destroyed while your application is still running, you will need to deallocate the memory for each cell when you delete each cell, which you will have to do individually. Don't use LDel-Row without first deleting all the data in those cells. Otherwise, you will have a major memory leak.
- Lists can add a real flair to your program. Look at commercial programs to get ideas about how the pros use lists. In fact, do that for all of your user interface elements. Watching how another programmer uses a specific element can give you ideas on how to improve your own programs.
- The List Manager can slow down when thousands of cells exist in a list. If you find yourself displaying large amounts of data, you may want to write your own simple list management scheme. Remember, the List Manager is not a spreadsheet.
- The List Manager can be a tricky thing to learn the first time through, but stick with it. Over time, you will learn its quirks and how to make it work for you.

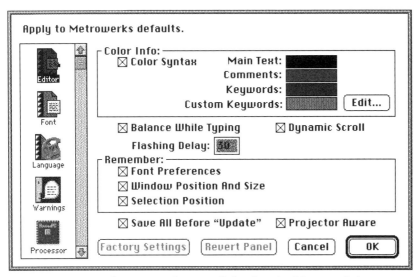

Figure 6-9. An icon list in a preferences dialog box for Metrowerks'
CodeWarrior

CHAPTER SEVEN

Control Definitions

There are some things that C is good for . . .
but programming is not one of them!

—Joey Gray

Introduction

Like list definitions, control definitions (Figure 7-1) are one of the building blocks of the Macintosh graphical user interface. Whenever you click on a button, a popup menu, a scroll bar, a check box, or a radio button, you are calling the Control Manager and a control definition to handle the interaction. The code of a control definition is stored in a resource of type CDEF.

The Control Manager handles tracking your clicks and mouse movements, and relays this information to a control definition in the form of a message and parameters. For instance, when a control needs to be drawn, it receives a drawCntl message. When it needs to test if the user has clicked in an important area of itself, it receives a testCntl message. By handling these messages, as well as others, the control definition works in harmony with the Control Manager to give users the visual, and maybe auditory, feedback they expect.

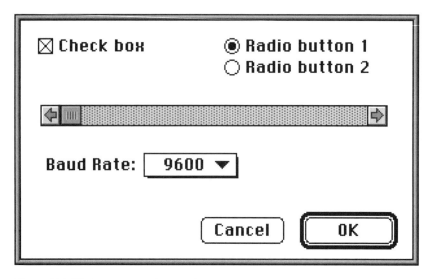

Figure 7.1. Various types of controls

Auditory feedback? Well, sure, why not? Your custom controls can make use of other resources that might exist in the same file as the control itself, or another file for that matter. These resources might be pictures, icons, or even sounds. It is not inconceivable that you may write a control that plays sounds or a short riff of music when it is clicked. New user interface ideas will be explored in the future, especially with the extra processing power that the Power Macintosh provides. Enhanced controls will, most definitely, be one of them.

If you are at all familiar with the Macintosh, you will recognize the standard types of controls displayed in Figure 7-1. What might be surprising to you is that the check box, radio button, and button controls are all handled by the same control definition. Because these three controls generally function in the same way, we decided to package them all as one control definition. When the control definition is called, it examines the variation code parameter to decide as which control it should function. You can use this variation code in your own CDEF for any purpose you like—it might specify the color in which to draw, the style of text to draw, or any other options you may decide.

Writing a control definition might take you only a few minutes if you are creating a simple button control (like our Icon Family control, discussed in the following section), or several days, if you are writing a specialized popup color palette or slider control. Either way, if you code it properly, it will be quite easy for you to create a PowerPC native version with minimal effort.

Icon Family Control

One of the controls we develop in this chapter is one that functions similar to the standard button control in the system software. The user clicks on it, it tracks mouse movements, and, when the mouse button is released, springs back to its normal position. It draws an icon family within its rectangle using the PlotIconID function. This function takes the resource ID of an icon family and other parameters that automatically draw the icons in question in the proper colors and modes (Figures 7-2 and 7-3). By using this function, our control definition need not worry about monitor bit depth, graphics devices, and other code-consuming features—PlotIconID does it all for us. This drastically reduces the size of our control definition and also makes it less prone to bugs and incompatibilities in the future by using system-level services to perform the majority of its work. It also makes our code much easier to read and understand.

Control Definition Code

The code for our icon family control definition is quite straightforward and should give you a very usable base from which to work. After you understand the code that I describe here, duplicate the project and source files, and extend it to suit your needs. I will give you some

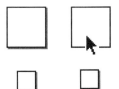

Figure 7-2. An example of our icon family buttons, slightly depressed, in black and white

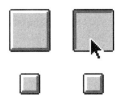

Figure 7-3. An example of our icon family buttons, slightly depressed, in color

ideas to modify this control later in the chapter. For now, let's take a walk through the code.

Main

```
pascal long    main(    short varCode, ControlHandle control,
                        short message, long param)
```

The main entry point of a control definition accepts four parameters and returns a long-integer result. The result varies depending on the message. In short, the parameters are the variation code that we discussed earlier, the handle to the control itself (normally within a window or dialog box), the message that we are currently receiving, and a long parameter that varies from message to message.

```
{
    long result = 0L;

    switch(message) {

        case drawCntl:
                Draw(varCode, control, param);
                break;

        case testCntl:
                result = Test(control, param);
                break;

        case calcCntlRgn:
                CalcRegions(control, param);
                break;

        case initCntl:
        case dispCntl:
        case calcThumbRgn:
        case posCntl:
        case thumbCntl:
        case dragCntl:
        case autoTrack:
        default:
                break;
    }

    return result;
}
```

Next, we simply implement a switch statement to handle each message in the proper way. You will note that this particular control doesn't handle a large number of the messages that are implemented by the Control Manager. Some of these messages we will never receive in our type of control, such as the thumbCntl message, and others we simply do not care about, such as the initCntl message, in our case.

If we were interested in making use of global variables in our control definition, we might use the initCntl and dispCntl messages to allocate and dispose of any global data, respectively. To see how to use global data in CodeWarrior, see Chapter Four "System Extensions," which makes use of this technique. If you are not using CodeWarrior, consult the documentation for your compiler.

Draw

```
void Draw(short varCode, ControlHandle control, long param)
{
    Rect    r = (*control)->contrlRect;
    short   id, transform = ttNone;
    OSErr   whoCares = noErr;

    if ((*control)->contrlVis == 0xFF) {
        id = (*control)->contrlMin;
        if ((*control)->contrlHilite == 255) {
            transform = ttDisabled;
        } else {
            if ((*control)->contrlHilite == 0) {
                id = (*control)->contrlMin;
            } else {
                if (varCode == 0) {
                    id = (*control)->contrlMax;
                } else {
                    id = (*control)->contrlMin;
                    transform = ttSelected;
                }
            }
        }
        whoCares = PlotIconID(&r, atAbsoluteCenter, transform, id);
    }
}
```

When our control receives the drawCntl message, we call our Draw function. This function handles checking the state of the control and then drawing it appropriately. If the control is invisible, it is not drawn at all. If the control is disabled, it is drawn in ttDisabled mode, which shades the icon. If the control is not depressed, the icon ID stored in the contrlMin field of the control record is drawn. If the control is depressed, we examine the variation code parameter to see how we should draw the depressed state. Our control handles two variation codes. A varCode of 0 means we draw the icon family represented by the ID stored in the contrlMax field of the control record. If the varCode is 1, or anything other than 0 in our code, we draw the contrlMin icon ID in ttSelected mode. This allows us to use our buttons as if they were actual buttons that physically moved when depressed or, like icons in the Finder, that "dim" when selected (Figure 7-4).

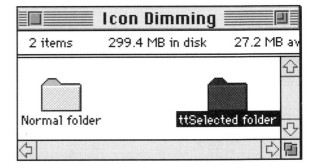

Figure 7-4. Finder-like ttSelected icon dimming

Test

```
long Test(ControlHandle control, long param)
{
    Rect    r = (*control)->contrlRect;
    Point   hitPt;
    long    result;

    hitPt.h = LoWord(param);
    hitPt.v = HiWord(param);
    if ((*control)->contrlHilite == 255) {
        result = 0L;
```

```
    } else {
            if (PtInRect(hitPt, &r))
                    result = inButton;
            else
                    result = 0L;
    }

    return result;
}
```

When our control receives the testCntl message, we call our Test function. This function returns a value indicating if the user is currently clicking inside the rectangle of our control. In our case, if the hit point is inside our rectangle, we return the constant inButton, which lets the Control Manager know the status of the click. When the mouse moves out of our rectangle, the Control Manager knows to call us with a drawCntl message so we can draw our new state properly. It is conceivable that your control definition will receive repeated testCntl and drawCntl messages as the user moves his mouse around your control.

CalcRegions

```
void CalcRegions(ControlHandle control, long param)
{
    Rect r = (*control)->contrlRect;
    param = param & 0x7FFFFFFF;
    RectRgn((RgnHandle)param, &r);
}
```

When our control receives the calcCntlRgn message, we call our CalcRegions function. This function calculates the region that our control occupies based on its rectangle. Although we could get fancy and return the region of the actual pixels of the icon we are drawing for each button, we simply return the rectangle of the control in the form of a region. The Control Manager uses this information when calculating, for example, which controls need to be updated when the contents of a dialog box are drawn.

Compiling Our Code

Control definitions, depending on what they do, can definitely benefit from being PowerPC native. For instance, if your control draws a 24-bit color image of itself or performs some type of real-time calculation, it might make sense to compile it for the PowerPC processor. As mentioned in previous chapters, it is relatively easy to do this and then create a fat or safe fat version for use on all platforms. You should examine the PowerPC project file to see how we created a native version of our icon family control definition (Figures 7-5 and 7-6). Then create a fat or safe fat version of your control for use in your programs.

Modifying the Icon Family Control

There are many ways for you to modify the icon family control definition to make it more exciting and usable in your programs. This section outlines a few things to try. You are encouraged to duplicate the project and source files for each project in the book and experiment with your own ideas.

Icon Family CDEF 68k.π				
File	**Code**	**Data**	📄 ✹	
▽ **Segment 1**	0	0	▾	⇧
Icon Family CDEF.c	0	0	▸	
Icon Family Button Resources	n/a	n/a	▸	
2 file(s)	0	0		⇩

Figure 7-5. 680x0 icon family CDEF project window

Icon Family CDEF PPC.π				
File	**Code**	**Data**	📄 ✹	
▽ **Group 1**	0	0	• ▾	⇧
Icon Family CDEF.c	0	0	• ▸	
Icon Family Button Resources	n/a	n/a	▸	
InterfaceLib	0	0	▸	
3 file(s)	0	0		⇩

Figure 7-6. PowerPC icon family CDEF project window

Figure 7-7. Double icon drawing

Figure 7-7 shows how you can use double icon drawing to draw your buttons. That is, you have one template icon that you use for the background of all of your buttons. The actual symbol displayed within each icon is drawn on top of the template. In your code, you will call PlotIconID twice when you want to draw an icon—once for the template icon, then again for the symbol. This can make it easier for you to change the look of your buttons by making it so you only have to edit your template icon and not every single icon in your application. Other benefits may also apply, except where prohibited by law.

Slider Control

The second control that we will be looking at in this chapter is a slider-type control given to us by Robert L. Mathews of Tiger Technologies. The Tiger Slider, as Rob calls it, uses a PICT resource as a background, another PICT resource as the indicator, and a custom resource of type Sinf to specify picture ID numbers, indicator position, indicator values, and other information (Figure 7-8). Before we get into the Tiger Slider, let's talk about how a slider is used today and why the Tiger Slider is a useful addition to your source code arsenal.

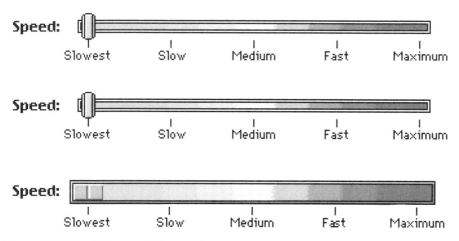

Figure 7-8. Tiger Slider control examples

Sliders are used in many places throughout the Macintosh user interface. The Sound control panel uses sliders to set the current volume of the Macintosh speaker (Figure 7-9). The color picker dialog box uses a slider to help choose your favorite hue (Figure 7-10), Sliders can be found throughout the Macintosh user interface serving many different uses. The one thing that intrigues me the most, though, is how some people use the scroll bar control instead of a more sliderlike control. Scroll bars are great for showing you how much you've scrolled through an unknown amount of data. As the thumb moves up and down the scroll bar, you are constantly given a visual clue as to where you are within the document. However, in cases where there is a finite choice of values, a slider control—not a scroll bar—can be much more effective.

The Tiger Slider gives us the power we need to display a horizontal slider control with a custom background and custom indicator. It is designed for use under System 7 and assumes that your pictures will look adequate in black and white, and in color, since the same pictures are used for both. The indicator moves smoothly over the background

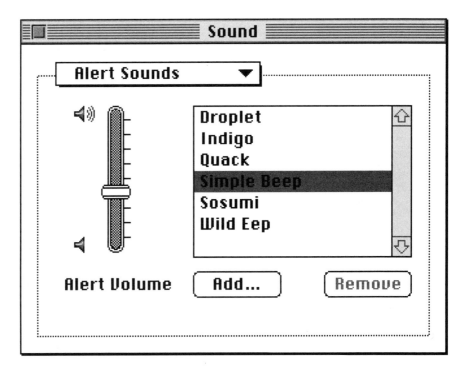

Figure 7-9. The Sound control panel making use of a slider control

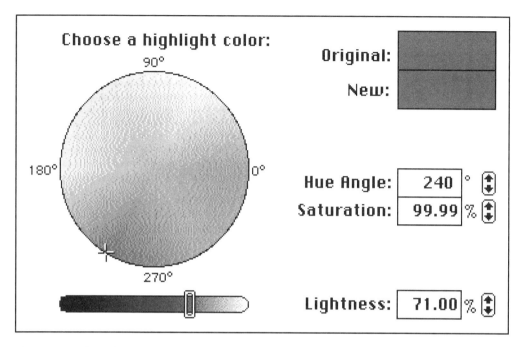

Figure 7-10. The color picker dialog box and horizontal slider

to give the sliding effect. An added feature is that you can click anywhere in the groove that the indicator follows and it will jump to that
location or the location as close to it as possible. You should also note
that the code uses Color QuickDraw GWorlds to maintain the smooth
animation of the scrolling indicator.

Even though GWorlds are a Color QuickDraw feature, they exist
on any Macintosh that is running System 7. So black-and-white
Macintosh computers can make use of GWorlds while running
System 7, since Color QuickDraw is built into the system software itself. Although this book does not go into how to use
GWorlds, you can read *Inside Macintosh* to learn all about how
they work and the benefits they can bring to your drawing code.

The Tiger Slider uses double-buffered animation. This technique prevents any flicker that you would otherwise see if you were to erase the indicator in its old position, redraw the background picture, and redraw the indicator in its new position each time it moved. If you were to try this, you would see that no matter how quickly you erased and redrew, the screen would display a momentary, distracting white flash. We avoid this by performing the erasing and redrawing in an off-screen buffer, known as a GWorld. After the new image has been drawn into the GWorld, we copy the GWorld to the screen using CopyBits, which plasters the new image onto the screen all at once. This erases the old image and draws the new image over it—all in one lightning-fast step. There is never a moment when the old indicator is invisible and the new one has yet to be drawn.

To do this, the Tiger Slider actually uses three different GWorlds— the background world (which stores a copy of the background of the slider with no indicator on it), the indicator world (which stores the indicator), and the composite world (which is the size of the controls rectangle and is used for temporarily merging the two other worlds). So, whenever we need to draw a piece of the slider to the screen, here is what we do:

1. Figure out the part that needs to be drawn, such as the rectangle enclosing both the old and new locations of the indicator.
2. Copy that rectangle from the background world to the composite world. This section of the composite world now looks just the same as the portion of the background world that we copied.
3. Draw the indicator in the appropriate, new position in the composite world. This section of the composite world now looks just the same as it should on the screen when the indicator is in its new position.
4. Copy the entire rectangle, old and new, from the composite world to the screen all at once. The screen has now been updated, with the old location of the indicator being erased at exactly the same time the new location is drawn.

This technique gives flicker-free drawing, as we had hoped. Now let's take a look at the code that makes it all happen.

This technique is flicker free to a point, but there is a case that still may cause a slight amount of flicker. Known to some as "tearing," this occurs when the electron beam of the screen passes through the copied rectangle while it is being drawn to the screen. Believe it or not, there is a way to prevent this by waiting for the electron beam to disappear as it moves from the bottom of the screen back to the top and then drawing, very quickly, during this time. By syncing to the vertical blanking interrupt, you can make your drawing as flicker free as possible.

Control Definition Code

By nature, slider controls are a bit more advanced than simple button controls. In our case, the Tiger Slider is even more complicated due to its use of GWorlds for off-screen drawing. However, don't let this scare you away. You should be able to understand the flow of the code quite easily, even if you are unsure as to how some of the advanced drawing functions work. We will explain them to a point here, but if you would like more information on using GWorlds and off-screen drawing, you should consult your local copy of *Inside Macintosh.*

Main

```
pascal long main (short varCode, ControlHandle theControl,
    short theMessage, long theParam)
{
    long    result = 0;

    switch (theMessage)
    {
        case    initCntl:
                InitTheControl (theControl);
                break;

        case    dispCntl:
                DisposeTheControl (theControl);
                break;

        case    drawCntl:
                DrawTheControl (theControl);
                break;
```

```
            case   testCntl:
                   if (PtInRect ((*(Point*) &theParam),
                        &(*theControl) -> contrlRect)) {
                        result = 130;
                   }
                   break;

            case   dragCntl:
                   if (theParam) {
                        DragTheControl (theControl);
                        result = 1;
                   }
                   break;

        case calcCntlRgn:
        case calcThumbRgn:
                   RectRgn ((RgnHandle) (theParam),
                        &(*theControl) -> contrlRect);
                   break;

        case calcCRgns:
                   RgnHandle tempRgn = (RgnHandle)
                        StripAddress ((Ptr) theParam);
                   RectRgn (tempRgn, &(*theControl) -> contrlRect);
            break;
    }

    return (result);
}
```

As with our previous control definition, the main entry point is a standard switch statement that allows us to easily handle each of the possible messages we will receive. Because we will use a slider, we need to handle a few of the other messages, such as dragCntl and calcThumbRgn, that our simple button control did not.

Init

```
void InitTheControl (ControlHandle theControl)
{
    OSErr           err;
    SliderInfoH     resHandle;


    (*theControl) -> contrlData = nil;
    resHandle = (SliderInfoH)
        GetResource (kSliderInfoType, (*theControl) -> contrlRfCon);
    if (!resHandle)
    {
```

```
      (*theControl) -> contrlData = nil;
}
else
{
      (*theControl) -> contrlData = (Handle) resHandle;
      HNoPurge ((*theControl) -> contrlData);
      DetachResource ((*theControl) -> contrlData);
      HLock ((*theControl) -> contrlData);
      Rect compositeRect = (*theControl) -> contrlRect;
      OffsetRect (&compositeRect, -compositeRect.left,
            -compositeRect.top);

      err = NewGWorld (&(*resHandle) -> indicatorWorld,
            (*resHandle) -> bitDepth,
            &(*resHandle) -> indicatorRect, nil, nil, 0);
      if (err)
      {
            err = NewGWorld (&(*resHandle) -> indicatorWorld,
                  (*resHandle) -> bitDepth,
                  &(*resHandle) -> indicatorRect,
                  nil, nil, useTempMem);
      }

      if (!err)
      {
            GWorldPtr        currPort;
            GDHandle         currDev;

            GetGWorld (&currPort, &currDev);
            SetGWorld ((*resHandle) -> indicatorWorld, nil);
            PixMapHandle pixMap = GetGWorldPixMap (
                  (*resHandle) -> indicatorWorld);
            LockPixels (pixMap);

            PicHandle picture =
                  GetPicture ((*resHandle) -> indicatorPictResID);
            if (picture)
            {
                  DrawPicture (picture, &(*resHandle) ->
                        indicatorWorld->portRect);
            }

            UnlockPixels (pixMap);
            SetGWorld (currPort, currDev);
      }

      err = NewGWorld (&(*resHandle) -> backgroundWorld,
            (*resHandle) -> bitDepth, &compositeRect,
            nil, nil, 0);
      if (err)
      {
```

```
        err = NewGWorld (&(*resHandle) -> backgroundWorld,
        (*resHandle) -> bitDepth, &compositeRect,
        nil, nil, useTempMem);
    }

    if (!err)
    {
        GWorldPtr        currPort;
        GDHandle         currDev;

        GetGWorld (&currPort, &currDev);
        SetGWorld ((*resHandle) -> backgroundWorld, nil);
        PixMapHandle pixMap = GetGWorldPixMap (
            (*resHandle) -> backgroundWorld);
        LockPixels (pixMap);

        PicHandle picture = GetPicture (
            (*resHandle) -> backgroundPictResID);
        if (picture)
        {
            DrawPicture (picture, &compositeRect);
        }

        UnlockPixels (pixMap);
        SetGWorld (currPort, currDev);
    }

    err = NewGWorld (&(*resHandle) -> compositeWorld,
        (*resHandle) -> bitDepth, &compositeRect,
        nil, nil, 0);
    if (err)
    {
        NewGWorld (&(*resHandle) -> compositeWorld,
            (*resHandle) -> bitDepth, &compositeRect,
            nil, nil, useTempMem);
    }

    HUnlock ((*theControl) -> contrlData);
    }
}
```

The InitControl routine is called to allocate the GWorlds and prepare them by filling them with the pictures we will use for the background and the indicator. It should be noted that the information
about this control, including some of its options, is stored in a resource
of type Sinf, which has the same ID as the value of the refCon for the
control. Therefore, we call GetResource to obtain this information during initialization and store it for the lifetime of the control in the contrl-
Data field.

After we have loaded the Sinf resource, we allocate the GWorlds based on the bit depth stored in the Sinf. First we call GetPicture to load the indicator and then draw it into the GWorld itself using the DrawPicture function. Then we allocate the GWorld for the background and draw it using the same method. These two GWorlds will never change from this point on, they are read-only in nature. You should note that, in reality, you could do without these two GWorlds and then, instead of using CopyBits later in the draw routine, simply use DrawPicture. It would be a bit slower to do it this way, but it would still work adequately. If your slider is tight on memory, you may opt for this method. We then, lastly, allocate the GWorld used for the composite image. This GWorld is constantly being drawn to and CopyBits'd to the screen as the indicator is moved along the background.

Dispose

```
void DisposeTheControl (ControlHandle theControl)
{
    SliderInfoH    sHandle = (SliderInfoH) (*theControl) -> contrlData;

    if (sHandle)
    {
        if ((*sHandle) -> indicatorWorld)
        {
            DisposeGWorld ((*sHandle) -> indicatorWorld);
        }

        if ((*sHandle) -> backgroundWorld)
        {
            DisposeGWorld ((*sHandle) -> backgroundWorld);
        }

        if ((*sHandle) -> compositeWorld)
        {
            DisposeGWorld ((*sHandle) -> compositeWorld);
        }

        DisposeHandle ((Handle) sHandle);
    }
}
```

The Dispose routine is pretty straightforward. It simply disposes of our three GWorlds and then disposes of the handle to the detached Sinf resource. You always have to clean up your messes—for which this routine is responsible.

Draw

```
void DrawTheControl (ControlHandle theControl)
{
    if ((*theControl) -> contrlData)
    {
        HLock ((*theControl) -> contrlData);
        SliderInfoP    infoPtr = (*(SliderInfoH)
            (*theControl) -> contrlData);

        if ((*theControl) -> contrlVis && infoPtr -> indicatorWorld
            && infoPtr -> backgroundWorld
            && infoPtr -> compositeWorld)
        {
            GWorldPtr        currPort;
            GDHandle         currDev;

            GetGWorld (&currPort, &currDev);
            SetGWorld (infoPtr -> compositeWorld, nil);

            PixMapHandle compositePixMap =
                GetGWorldPixMap (infoPtr -> compositeWorld);
            LockPixels (compositePixMap);

            PixMapHandle backgroundPixMap =
                GetGWorldPixMap (infoPtr -> backgroundWorld);
            LockPixels (backgroundPixMap);

            CopyBits ((BitMap*) *backgroundPixMap,
                (BitMap*) *compositePixMap,
                &infoPtr -> backgroundWorld -> portRect,
                &infoPtr -> compositeWorld -> portRect,
                srcCopy, nil);

            UnlockPixels (backgroundPixMap);


            PixMapHandle indicatorPixMap =
                GetGWorldPixMap (infoPtr -> indicatorWorld);
            LockPixels (indicatorPixMap);

            Rect    destinationRect = infoPtr -> indicatorRect;
            short   offsetUnits = (*theControl) -> contrlValue -
                (*theControl) -> contrlMin;
            OffsetRect (&destinationRect,
                (infoPtr -> pixelsPerValue * offsetUnits), 0);
```

```
            CopyBits ((BitMap*) *indicatorPixMap,
                (BitMap*) *compositePixMap,
                &infoPtr -> indicatorWorld -> portRect,
                &destinationRect, srcCopy, nil);

            UnlockPixels (indicatorPixMap);

            SetGWorld (currPort, currDev);

            ForeColor (blackColor);
            BackColor (whiteColor);

            CopyBits ((BitMap*) *compositePixMap,
            &((GrafPtr) (*theControl) -> contrlOwner) -> portBits,
                &infoPtr -> compositeWorld -> portRect,
                &(*theControl) -> contrlRect, srcCopy, nil);

            UnlockPixels (compositePixMap);
        }
        HUnlock ((*theControl) -> contrlData);
    }
}
```

The Draw routine is probably the most important routine of all. When you have an idea for a control, this is the routine that actually produces what your control looks like on the screen. Because we use a double-buffering mechanism to draw, we decided to simply draw the entire control each time. Using CopyBits, this is extremely fast. Technically, it is possible to figure out which part of the control needs to be drawn and draw only that portion, but to keep this example clear, we've decided not to implement it that way.

Assuming the control itself is visible, we first copy the background GWorld to the composite GWorld. We then draw the indicator in the proper position in the composite GWorld as well. Then, in one fell swoop, we can CopyBits the composite GWorld to the screen using the CopyBits routine. That's it!

You may note that this function sets the ForeColor to blackColor and the BackColor to whiteColor before calling CopyBits. This is done to avoid unwanted coloring of the blitted pixels by Copy-Bits. If you don't do this, and if the colors were set to some other value than to what we are setting them, strange things can happen. Experiment with the code and see for yourself.

Test

```
case testCntl:
    if (PtInRect ((*(Point*) &theParam),
        &(*theControl) -> contrlRect))
    {
        result = 130;
    }
    break;
```

Our testCntl message is handled directly in our main entry point function. It simply tests the current mouse location to see if it is within the rectangle of the control. If it is, it returns a value, of no particular importance, that simply tells the Control Manager that a custom part of our control was clicked. At this point, the Control Manager will call us with a dragCntl message.

Drag

```
void DragTheControl (ControlHandle theControl)
{
    if ((*theControl) -> contrlData)
    {
        HLock ((*theControl) -> contrlData);
        SliderInfoP    infoPtr =
            (*(SliderInfoH) (*theControl) -> contrlData);

        Point            mousePt,
                         topLeftPt;
        short            leftEdgeOffset,
                         leftLoc,
                         rightLoc,
                         oldMouseHoriz,
                         oldValue,
                         newValue;
        GWorldPtr        currPort;
        GDHandle         currDev;
        Rect             oldThumb,
                         newThumb,
                         unionOfRects,
                         tempRect;

        GetGWorld (&currPort, &currDev);

        PixMapHandle compositePixMap =
            GetGWorldPixMap (infoPtr -> compositeWorld);
        LockPixels (compositePixMap);
```

```
PixMapHandle backgroundPixMap =
      GetGWorldPixMap (infoPtr -> backgroundWorld);
LockPixels (backgroundPixMap);

PixMapHandle indicatorPixMap =
      GetGWorldPixMap (infoPtr -> indicatorWorld);
LockPixels (indicatorPixMap);

ForeColor (blackColor);
BackColor (whiteColor);

oldThumb = infoPtr -> indicatorRect;
short    offsetUnits = (*theControl) -> contrlValue -
      (*theControl) -> contrlMin;
OffsetRect (&oldThumb, (infoPtr -> pixelsPerValue *
      offsetUnits), 0);

SetPt (&topLeftPt, (*theControl) -> contrlRect.left,
      (*theControl) -> contrlRect.top);
oldMouseHoriz = -1; // make sure we draw at least once

leftEdgeOffset = (infoPtr -> indicatorRect.right -
      infoPtr -> indicatorRect.left) / 2;
leftLoc = infoPtr -> indicatorRect.left + leftEdgeOffset;
rightLoc = leftLoc + (infoPtr -> pixelsPerValue *
      ((*theControl) -> contrlMax -
      (*theControl) -> contrlMin));

oldValue = (*theControl) -> contrlValue,
newValue = oldValue;

do {
      GetMouse (&mousePt);
      mousePt.h -= topLeftPt.h;
      mousePt.v -= topLeftPt.v;

      mousePt.h = min (mousePt.h, rightLoc);
      mousePt.h = max (mousePt.h, leftLoc);

      if (mousePt.h != oldMouseHoriz)
      {
            newThumb = oldThumb;
            newThumb.left = mousePt.h - leftEdgeOffset;
            newThumb.right = newThumb.left +
                  (infoPtr -> indicatorRect.right -
                  infoPtr -> indicatorRect.left);

            UnionRect (&oldThumb, &newThumb, &unionOfRects);
            SetGWorld (infoPtr -> compositeWorld, nil);
```

```
                        CopyBits ((BitMap*) *backgroundPixMap,
                                (BitMap*) *compositePixMap,
                                &unionOfRects, &unionOfRects,
                                srcCopy, nil);

                        CopyBits ((BitMap*) *indicatorPixMap,
                                (BitMap*) *compositePixMap,
                                &infoPtr -> indicatorWorld -> portRect,
                                &newThumb, srcCopy, nil);

                        SetGWorld (currPort, currDev);
                        tempRect = unionOfRects;
                        OffsetRect (&tempRect, topLeftPt.h,
                                topLeftPt.v);
                        CopyBits ((BitMap*) *compositePixMap,
                                &((GrafPtr)
                                (*theControl) -> contrlOwner) -> portBits,
                                &unionOfRects, &tempRect, srcCopy, nil);

                        oldThumb = newThumb;
                        oldMouseHoriz = mousePt.h;

                        short rawValue = newThumb.left -
                                infoPtr -> indicatorRect.left;
                        newValue = rawValue / infoPtr -> pixelsPerValue;
                        if ((rawValue % infoPtr -> pixelsPerValue) >
                                (infoPtr -> pixelsPerValue / 2))
                        {
                        // it's more than halfway to the next "stop"
                                newValue ++;
                        }
                }
        }   while (StillDown ());

        UnlockPixels (indicatorPixMap);
        UnlockPixels (backgroundPixMap);
        UnlockPixels (compositePixMap);
        SetGWorld (currPort, currDev);

        HUnlock ((*theControl) -> contrlData);

        (*theControl) -> contrlValue = newValue;
        DrawTheControl (theControl);
    }
}
```

Dragging a control can be a real job and this function shows that fact. It may look intimidating at first, but it really isn't that bad once you sit down and think about what it is doing. The object of the routine is to change the value of the control while the user drags the indicator across it. After allocating what seems like an endless list of local variables, we prepare the GWorlds for drawing by locking down all the pixels in them. We then calculate where the indicator is to start. We then enter a loop that is called during the entire time the mouse is down. Note that we will always enter the loop at least once, so even the fastest mouse clicker in the East will not be able to sneak past us.

Our do loop is constantly redrawing our control, much like our draw function does. In fact, we could have used the same code by separating it into its own function. You should feel free to make that optimization. As the user moves the mouse along the control, we recalculate the new position of the indicator and redraw it using our double-buffering mechanism mentioned earlier. This gives us a nice, smooth drag of which a certain camel would be proud.

Calculating Regions

```
case calcCntlRgn:
case calcThumbRgn:
    RectRgn ((RgnHandle) (theParam),
        &(*theControl) -> contrlRect);
    break;

case calcCRgns:
    RgnHandle tempRgn = (RgnHandle)
        StripAddress ((Ptr) theParam);
    RectRgn (tempRgn, &(*theControl) -> contrlRect);
```

Because the Control Manager has no idea what your control looks like on the screen or how much of its rectangle it actually uses to draw, the control definition itself is asked to calculate specific regions that represent itself. These regions include the entire control region and the region that represents the thumb (if one exists). For these two messages in particular, we simply return the region that represents the entire control, since we draw in the entire rectangle of the control. This aids us in supporting our "jump to" effect when the user clicks on an area of our control and the slider jumps to that point. The calcCRgns message is an old mechanism for returning region information and is only received in 24-bit mode. We simply return the region of our entire rectangle, once again. You can read *Inside Macintosh* to learn more about QuickDraw regions.

Compiling Our Code

As with most of the projects in this book, this one also contains multiple project files. With these, you can build the control for the 680x0 or the Power Macintosh (Figures 7-11 and 7-12). You will also note that the slider is compiled using the C++ compiler, as opposed to the standard C compiler used elsewhere. The reason for this is simply because Rob wanted to take advantage of some of the features of C++, such as inline variable declarations. If you convert the code to be straight C, which you probably don't need to do, you will need to move all of the variable declarations to the top of each function. Other than that, play with the projects and experiment with the background and indicator pictures to create your own custom slider.

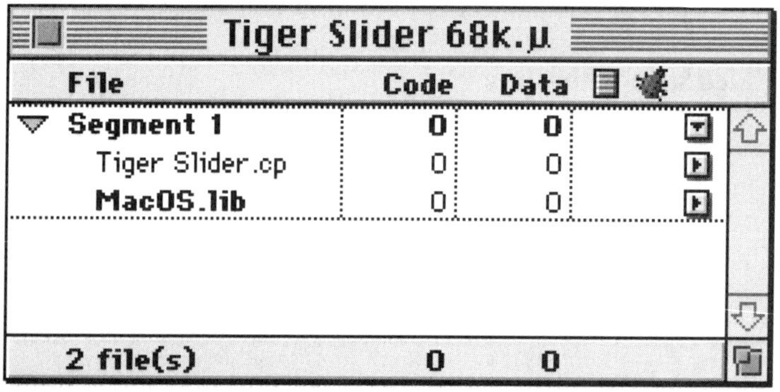

Tiger Slider 68k.μ				
File	Code	Data		
▽ Segment 1	0	0		▾
Tiger Slider.cp	0	0		▸
MacOS.lib	0	0		▸
2 file(s)	0	0		

Figure 7-11. 680x0 Tiger Slider project

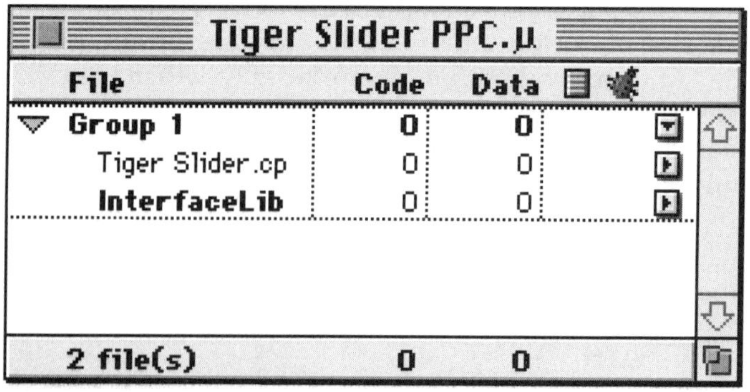

Tiger Slider PPC.μ				
File	Code	Data		
▽ Group 1	0	0		▾
Tiger Slider.cp	0	0		▸
InterfaceLib	0	0		▸
2 file(s)	0	0		

Figure 7-12. PowerPC Tiger Slider project

Modifying the Slider Control

There are many ways to improve and customize the Tiger Slider control. One thing I would consider is allowing for a black-and-white, and a color, set of pictures to be used for the same control. You may choose to use the DeviceLoop QuickDraw function in order to draw the pictures properly, if they were to span multiple monitors. This will give you much more flexibility in choosing your art. You will not have to limit yourself to colors that work well in color or black and white, since the control will draw properly both ways.

You may also elect to update the slider to support vertical positions. Currently, the Tiger Slider is a horizontal-only slider. Rob made a conscious decision to write it that way, since that was what he needed at the time. He may have already converted it by the time you read this, but that doesn't mean that you shouldn't try to do it yourself. Don't compromise your user interface for a horizontal slider. If you need a vertical slider, make it vertical.

Control Definition Tips

Control definitions are a great way to spruce up your application's user interface. You can create all sorts of different types of custom controls using these short stubs of code. Here are some tips and ideas to keep in mind while writing your control.

- Make your CDEFs safe fat. Depending on the size of your controls and what they do on the inside, you may wish to make them native for the PowerPC. The best way to ensure that one control works on just about any Macintosh you throw at it is to make it safe fat in nature.
- The Tiger Slider uses other resources, such as PICT and Sinf, in order to do its job. You can also take advantage of sound resources in the file that contains the CDEF or any other file on the Macintosh for that matter. Write a cool control and make it available for others to use.
- Make sure you deallocate any memory your control uses before it is disposed. The Tiger Slider shows you how this can be done by handling the dispCntl message.
- Write a next-generation control. Add sound and 3D-rendered graphics to your controls. It will make them the coolest around and will take advantage of some of the power in the Power Macintosh.
- Invent a new control style. Radio buttons, check boxes, and popup menus are great, but they have been around forever. Brainstorm and invent a new control. Who knows, it might end up in the next version of the system software if it is really useful.

CHAPTER EIGHT

Window Definitions

If it's too easy, you're doing something wrong.

—Philip Cummins

Introduction

Every window you see on the Macintosh is drawn by a window definition procedure. These snippets of code, which are usually stored in resources of type WDEF, are called by the Window Manager in order to give a window its familiar look and feel. Window definitions handle many different tasks, but the most evident is to draw the window using the proper colors, style, and other criteria.

The standard window definition is stored in the system file as a resource of type WDEF with an ID of 0. This WDEF is used to draw many of the windows you see on the Macintosh, including dialog boxes, alert boxes, and document windows. Other types of windows, such as floating palettes, movable modal dialogs, and help balloons, are drawn by other window definition resources (Figures 8-1, 8-2, and 8-3).

When a window is created, the Window Manager calls the proper window definition resource based on the type of window the programmer specifies. The window type can be specified in the WIND or DLOG resource, or in a call to the toolbox routines NewDialog or NewWindow. The window definition resource then handles drawing the window, returning information such as where the user clicked within it,

147

Figure 8-1. Dialog box as drawn by the standard system window definition

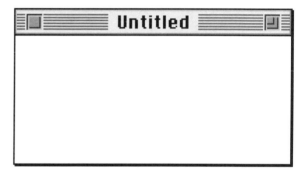

Figure 8-2. Document window as drawn by the standard system window definition

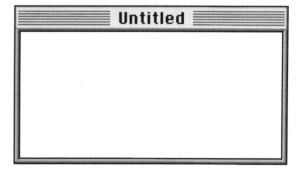

Figure 8-3. Movable, modal dialog box

and performs other tasks requested by the Window Manager. Your program never actually calls the window definition resource directly; this is all handled transparently by the Window Manager.

In System 7.0, the standard WDEF added color tinges that are capable of being via the Color control panel. These tinges make the windows look puffy and three dimensional. You might notice that the choices for window color in the Color control panel are limited to just a few selections. The reason for this is that the Macintosh, by default, has a standard, 256-color palette. Since most Macintosh computers operate in 8-bit mode, using 256 colors, the engineers at Apple had to choose color schemes that would work well with the available colors. Therefore, there are only a few from which to choose. In the future, when all Macintosh computers run in 24-bit color, you may be able to set the window colors to anything you like!

In this chapter, we discuss how you can customize the look of your application's windows by creating your own window definition resource. Window definition expert Troy Gaul has been kind enough to offer the source code of his very popular Infinity Windoid window definition. This window definition is used by numerous developers to add an attractive looking "floating" window to their programs. You can see this style used for floating tool and pattern palettes in many paint programs as well as some word processors. Odds are good that you own a program that uses the Infinity Windoid (Figures 8-4 and 8-5).

Figure 8-4. One variation of the Infinity Windoid by Troy Gaul

Figure 8-5. Infinity Windoid as used in CodeWarrior

Window Definition Code

The Infinity Windoid is one of the most advanced window definitions you will find. Mind you, source code in general for these types of code resources is very difficult to locate, in many cases, and this is a top-notch example.

Main

```
pascal long main(    short varCode, WindowPeek window,
                     short message, long param)
```

The main entry point of the window definition is very similar to that of a control panel, list definition, or control definition. The function is declared as Pascal, returns a long integer, and takes four parameters. The first parameter is the variation code, which has the same meaning as it does when used in a control definition. This is how the window definition knows which variation of itself to draw and maintain. The second parameter is a pointer to the window record with which the definition is about to be dealing. The third parameter is the message that the definition is being called to handle. Lastly, the fourth parameter varies depending on the message.

Now that you know the calling convention and parameters of the window definition itself, let's take a look at the code that makes it all happen.

```
pascal long main(    short varCode, WindowPeek window,
                     short message, long param)
{
    long        result = 0;
    GrafPtr     savePort;
    Boolean     needSyncPorts;

    needSyncPorts = (message == wDraw
                        || message == wHit
                        || message == wGrow
                        || message == wDrawGIcon) && HasCQDraw();
```

```
    if (needSyncPorts) {
        GetPort(&savePort);
        SyncPorts();
    }

    switch (message) {
        case wNew:          DoWInit(window, param, varCode);
                            break;

        case wDispose:      DoWDispose(window, param);
                            break;

        case wDraw:         DoWDraw(window, param & 0xFFFF);
                            break;

        case wHit:          result = DoWHit(window, param);
                            break;

        case wCalcRgns:     DoWCalcRgns(window, param);
                            break;

        case wGrow:         DoWGrow(window, param);
                            break;

        case wDrawGIcon:    DoWDrawGIcon(window, param);
                            break;
    }

    if (needSyncPorts)
        SetPort(savePort);

    return result;
}
```

As usual, when dealing with single-entry point code resources, our main function consists of a switch statement that dispatches each message to the appropriate function that handles that message. We will discuss each of these functions in turn. One thing to note in our main function is the needSyncPorts flag. For any message that requires us to draw, we set the needSyncPorts flag accordingly. Once set, we then call the function SyncPorts (straight from *Macintosh Programming Secrets,* 2nd Edition, by Knaster and Rollin) to ensure that the color drawing environment is set up properly on a color machine.

New

```
typedef struct {
    WStateData      wState;
    unsigned char   closeToggle;
    unsigned char   zoomToggle;
    unsigned char   isHoriz;
    unsigned char   ignoreHilite;
    unsigned char   hasGrow;
} WindoidData, *WindoidDataPtr, **WindoidDataHandle;

void DoWInit(WindowPeek window, long param, short varCode)
{
    Handle zoomDataHndl = NewHandleClear(sizeof(WindoidData));

    if (zoomDataHndl != nil) {
        WindoidDataPtr wdata = (WindoidDataPtr) *zoomDataHndl;

        wdata->closeToggle = 0;
        wdata->zoomToggle    = 0;

        wdata->ignoreHilite = (varCode & kSystem75_toggleTBar) == 0;
        wdata->hasGrow = (varCode & kSystem75_hasGrow) != 0;
        window->spareFlag    = (varCode & kSystem75_hasZoom) != 0;
        wdata->isHoriz = (varCode & kSystem75_vertTBar) == 0;

        window->dataHandle = zoomDataHndl;
        SetZoomRects(window);
    }
}
```

When our window definition receives a wNew message, we call the function DoWInit to allocate and initialize our private data structures. After this is done, we stash the handle in the dataHandle field of the window itself. This allows us to access the information each time we are called and gives us a handy storage mechanism for just about any information we may need to track. This technique is used in many ways throughout the Macintosh Toolbox.

Draw

```
void DoWDraw(WindowPeek window, long param)
{
    WDLDataRec userData;
```

```
        if (window->visible) {
            userData.wdlWindow = window;
            userData.wdlParam = param;

            if (SystemSevenOrLater || HasSystem7()) {
#if USESROUTINEDESCRIPTORS
                RoutineDescriptor drawProc
                    = BUILD_ROUTINE_DESCRIPTOR(
                    uppDeviceLoopDrawingProcInfo, WindoidDrawLoop);
                DeviceLoopDrawingUPP uppDrawProc = &drawProcRD;
#else
                DeviceLoopDrawingUPP uppDrawProc
                    = (DeviceLoopDrawingUPP) &WindoidDrawLoop;
#endif

                DeviceLoop(window->strucRgn, uppDrawProc,
                    (long) &userData, (DeviceLoopFlags) 0);
            } else {
                WindoidDrawLoop(1, 0, nil, &userData);
            }

            switch (param) {
                case wInGoAway:
                    WindData.closeToggle = !WindData.closeToggle;
                    break;

                case wInZoomIn:
                case wInZoomOut:
                    WindData.zoomToggle = !WindData.zoomToggle;
                    break;
            }
        }
    }
```

What good is a window definition if it doesn't draw a window? When we receive the wDraw message we need to do what we do best—draw. Assuming the window is visible, we check our system software version to see how to draw. If we are running under System 6, we simply draw in black and white; under System 7, we use the DeviceLoop function to draw in color or black and white, depending on the monitors our window spans at the time.

DeviceLoop is one of those functions that not too many people know about. Yet after you discover it, you will wonder how you ever programmed without it. Here's how it works. DeviceLoop accepts a few straightforward parameters including the region into which you will be drawing, a universal procedure pointer to your drawing function, a userData field that can be used to hold private data, and some flags. DeviceLoop then calls your drawing function, passing it the bit depth of the monitor on which to draw, device flags, a handle to the device, and your custom data. Your function simply looks at the bit depth parameter and draws accordingly. The neat part is that if the object you are drawing happens to span more than one monitor, DeviceLoop will call your drawing function once for each possible bit depth or graphics device. For example, if your window spanned two monitors, your drawing function would be called twice. You simply draw it the right way for each bit depth, while DeviceLoop handles setting up your clipping regions to make sure that what shows up on the screen is what should show up in that particular bit depth (Figure 8-6). Once complete, your object will show up in beautiful color on the color monitor and in black and white on the 1-bit monitor.

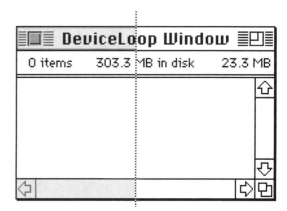

Figure 8-6. A window being drawn across two monitors with different bit depths

```
typedef struct {
    WindowPeek    wdlWindow;
    long          wdlParam;
} WDLDataRec;

static pascal void
WindoidDrawLoop(   short depth, short deviceFlags,
                        GDHandle targetDevice, WDLDataRec *userData)
{
    WindowPeek window = userData->wdlWindow;
    Boolean isColor =
        CheckDisplay(depth, deviceFlags, targetDevice, window);

    switch (userData->wdlParam) {
        case wNoHit:
            DrawTitleBar(window, isColor);
            DrawWindowFrame(window, isColor);
            break;

        case wInGoAway:
            ToggleCloseBox(window, isColor);
            break;

        case wInZoomIn:
        case wInZoomOut:
            if (window->spareFlag)
                ToggleZoomBox(window, isColor);
            break;
    }
    ColorsNormal();
}
```

DeviceLoop causes our WindoidDrawLoop function to be called
to do the actual drawing of our window. When this function is called,
it, in turn, calls special functions to draw specific portions of the window. Since the functions use straightforward QuickDraw techniques
to draw, we will not go into them too deeply here. This chapter's
source code contains full comments if you wish to explore these functions further. Suffice it to say that this function is responsible for drawing the entire windoid and does a good job at that.

Hit

```
long DoWHit(WindowPeek window, long param)
{
  Rect theRect;
  Point hitPt;
  long result = wNoHit;

  hitPt.v = HiWord(param);
  hitPt.h = LoWord(param);

  if (PtInRgn(hitPt, window->strucRgn)) {
        result = wInContent;

        if (PtInRgn(hitPt, window->contRgn)) {
              // Look for a hit in the grow box.
              if (WindData.hasGrow) {
                  GetGrowBox(window, &theRect);
                  InsetRect(&theRect, -1, -1);
                  if (PtInRect(hitPt, &theRect))
                        result = wInGrow;
              }

        } else {
              // Look for a hit in the titlebar.
              Rect titleRect;
              GetTitleBarRect(window, &titleRect);

              if (PtInRect(hitPt, &titleRect))
              {
                    Boolean isActive = window->hilited ||
                                      WindData.ignoreHilite;
                    result = wInDrag;

                    if (isActive) {
                          if (window->goAwayFlag) {
                                GetCloseBox(window, &theRect);
                                InsetRect(&theRect,
                                      -kGadgetHitFudge,
                                      -kGadgetHitFudge);
                                if (PtInRect(hitPt, &theRect))
                                      result = wInGoAway;
                          }

                          if (window->spareFlag) {
                                GetZoomBox(window, &theRect);
                                InsetRect(&theRect,
                                      -kGadgetHitFudge,
                                      -kGadgetHitFudge);
```

```
                                   if (PtInRect(hitPt, &theRect))
                                       result =
                                             GetZoomHitType(window);
                                }
                            }
                        }
                    }
                }

        return result;
    }
```

When the user clicks in our window (when your program calls FindWindow), the Window Manager sends us a wHit message. This message tells us to find out where the user clicked, if anywhere, in our window. After extracting the hit point from the long param field, we use a series of PtInRgn and PtInRect calls to narrow down the click and return the location where the user clicked. The value that we return at this point is passed on to FindWindow, which returns the same value to the calling program. The program then handles the click accordingly by calling DragWindow, GrowWindow, HideWindow, or any other Window Manager call it deems appropriate.

CalcRegions

```
void DoWCalcRgns(WindowPeek window, long param)
{
    Rect theRect;

    // Calculate the content Rect in global coordinates.
    GetGlobalContentRect(window, &theRect);
    RectRgn(window->contRgn, &theRect);

    // Start off with the structure equal to the content
    // and make it include the window frame and titlebar.
    InsetRect(&theRect, -1, -1);
    if (WindData.isHoriz)
        theRect.top -= kTitleHeight - 1;
    else
        theRect.left -= kTitleHeight - 1;

    RectRgn(window->strucRgn, &theRect);

    // Add the shadow to the structure.
```

```
    {
        RgnHandle tempRgn = NewRgn();

        OffsetRect(&theRect, 1, 1);
        RectRgn(tempRgn, &theRect);
        UnionRgn(tempRgn, window->strucRgn, window->strucRgn);

        DisposeRgn(tempRgn);
    }
}
```

The Window Manager needs to know certain things about our
window that only we can calculate, such as the region that describes
the entire window. The wCalcRgns message asks for the region that
describes our window entirely, similar to the messages with which our
CDEFs have dealt in previous chapters. This function calculates that
region by first converting the rectangle of the window to a region, then
adding the drop shadow and title bar. Regions are a really neat concept that you may wish to explore further by reading about Quick-
Draw in *Inside Macintosh*.

Grow and Grow Icon

```
void DoWGrow(WindowPeek window, long param)
{
    Rect growingRect = *(Rect*) param;

    if (WindData.isHoriz)
        growingRect.top -= kTitleHeight - 1;
        // Add room for the titlebar.
    else
        growingRect.left -= kTitleHeight - 1;
        // Add room for the titlebar.
    InsetRect(&growingRect, -1, -1);

    // Draw the window frame.
    FrameRect(&growingRect);

    if (WindData.isHoriz)
        growingRect.top += kTitleHeight - 1;
    else
        growingRect.left += kTitleHeight - 1;

    // Now mark the titlebar area.
    MoveTo(growingRect.left, growingRect.top);
    if (WindData.isHoriz)
```

```
                LineTo(growingRect.right - 2, growingRect.top);
        else
                LineTo(growingRect.left, growingRect.bottom - 2);

        // Mark the scroll bars too.
        MoveTo(growingRect.right - kScrollBarPixels,
                growingRect.top + 1);
        LineTo(growingRect.right - kScrollBarPixels,
                growingRect.bottom - 2);

        MoveTo(growingRect.left,
                growingRect.bottom - kScrollBarPixels);
        LineTo(growingRect.right - 2,
                growingRect.bottom - kScrollBarPixels);
    }
```

The wGrow message tells us to draw the growing outline of the window—that is, the outline that is drawn when our window is being resized. We are called repeatedly during a window resizing to draw this in order to give users feedback as to how large or how small the window will be when they release the mouse (Figure 8-7).

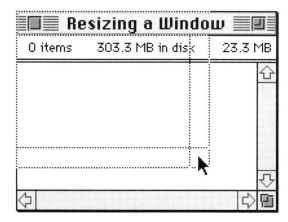

Figure 8-7. Drawing the growing outline while resizing a window

```
void DoWDrawGIcon(WindowPeek window, long param)
{
    if (window->visible && WindData.hasGrow) {
        WDLDataRec userData;
        RgnHandle saveClip = NewRgn();
        RgnHandle tempRgn = NewRgn();
        Point mappingPoint;

        SectRgn(window->port.visRgn, window->port.clipRgn, tempRgn);

        GetClip(saveClip);

        GetGlobalMappingPoint(window, &mappingPoint);
        OffsetRgn(tempRgn, mappingPoint.h, mappingPoint.v);

        SetClip(tempRgn);

        userData.wdlWindow = window;

        if (SystemSevenOrLater || HasSystem7()) {
#if USESROUTINEDESCRIPTORS
            RoutineDescriptor drawProcRD
                = BUILD_ROUTINE_DESCRIPTOR(
                uppDeviceLoopDrawingProcInfo,
                GrowBoxDrawLoop);
            DeviceLoopDrawingUPP uppDrawProc = &drawProcRD;
#else
            DeviceLoopDrawingUPP uppDrawProc
                = (DeviceLoopDrawingUPP) &GrowBoxDrawLoop;
#endif

            DeviceLoop(window->strucRgn, uppDrawProc,
                        (long) &userData, (DeviceLoopFlags) 0);
        } else {
            GrowBoxDrawLoop(1, 0, nil, &userData);
        }

        SetClip(saveClip);

        DisposeRgn(saveClip);
        DisposeRgn(tempRgn);
    }
}

static pascal void
GrowBoxDrawLoop(short depth, short deviceFlags,
                GDHandle targetDevice, WDLDataRec *userData)
{
    WindowPeek window = userData->wdlWindow;
    Boolean isColor = CheckDisplay(depth, deviceFlags,
                        targetDevice, window);
```

```
        DrawGrowBox(window, isColor);
        ColorsNormal();
    }
```

The wDrawGIcon message tells us to draw the grow icon in the lower right corner of the window. As in our wDraw message, we make use of DeviceLoop to ensure our drawing is done at its best in any possible bit depth.

In reality, we need not draw the grow icon in the lower right corner of our window. Although there are standards for the locations of items like the grow icon, our window definition totally defines the look and feel of our window. Therefore, we can place items anywhere within it that we choose. Mind you, you wouldn't want to draw your grow icon in the middle of the window, but you should understand that you do have some flexibility when it comes to custom window definitions.

Dispose

```
    void DoWDispose(WindowPeek window, long param)
    {
        if (window->dataHandle)
            DisposeHandle(window->dataHandle);
    }
```

Finally, when our window is being destroyed, we are called with a wDispose message that gives us a chance to dispose of our private data and clean up any other messes we may have created. In our case, we simply dispose of our dataHandle field, which we allocated earlier.

Compiling Our Code

The window definition projects that we have included allow you to compile both a 680x0 and a PowerPC version (Figures 8-8 and 8-9). As mentioned in previous chapters, it is relatively easy to do this and then create a fat or safe fat version for use on all platforms. You should experiment with the provided code and make your own custom window definitions by editing the drawing functions. You can make your custom window look like anything you like, with just a few simple changes to the Infinity Windoid.

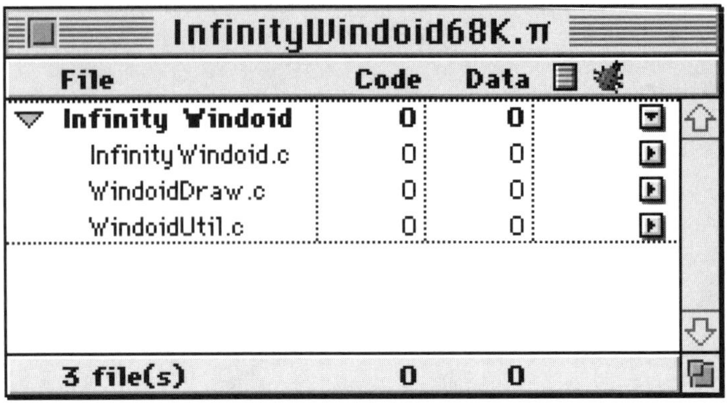

Figure 8-8. 680x0 Infinity Windoid project

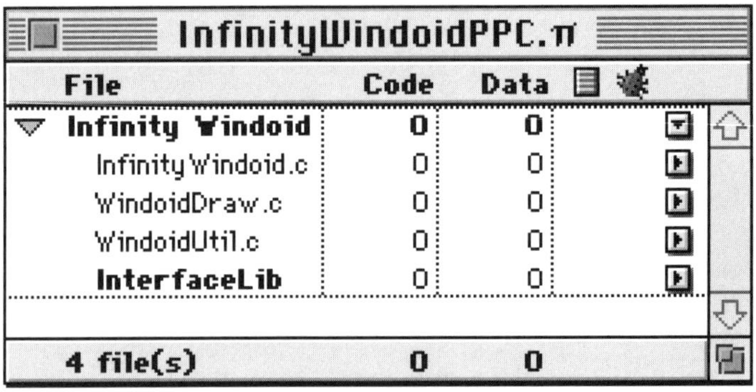

Figure 8-9. PowerPC Infinity Windoid project

Window Definition Tips

Window definitions are a great way to spruce up your application's user interface. By writing your own window definition, you can add a look to your program that is unique and eye-catching. You should be careful not to stray too far from the Macintosh user interface guidelines, however. Change is good, but too much change can be ugly. Here are some tips and tricks for which to watch when writing your own window definitions.

- The standard system window definition handles many different styles of windows. Although this is neat, it may be better to package your code in separate window definitions if you plan on supporting many variations. Not only can separate window definitions make your code easier to debug, it can also make your memory footprint smaller, depending on how the definitions are used in your program.

- Just because you have a floating palette-looking window definition doesn't mean you will be automatically able to create windows that "float." There are plenty of good articles in Macintosh technical journals that explain how to make windows float. Although it is not easy, it can be done without too much hassle. Just remember, the WDEF just makes it look like a floating palette, it doesn't make it float.

- WDEF resources should not have their purgeable resource bit set. The problem lies in the fact that if the WDEF resource is needed while another application is the current one, the current resource chain doesn't have the WDEF when the Toolbox tries to call Load-Resource. It punts and throws up a System Error 87 (couldn't load WDEF). By making sure your WDEF is not able to be purged, you will not need to worry about this problem.

- An even more interesting problem to track down is when the current application *does* have a WDEF of the ID that the Toolbox wants. In this case, as you might imagine, really strange things can occur. This can cause a window in your program to draw in a way that you did not expect, since the wrong WDEF is being used to do the drawing.

- Window definitions do not have to be so square. That is, make a round window definition or one with a really funky shape. You can define any region to be your window. One thing to keep in mind, however, is that it may slow down some Macintosh computers if they have to calculate a really difficult region whenever the window moves. Depending on the circumstances, it might look really cool.

CHAPTER NINE

HyperCard Externals

I didn't get where I am today by being wise!

—Lawrence D'Oliveiro

Introduction

Any HyperCard users out there? If so, this chapter is for you. As you probably already know, HyperCard allows you to write external commands and functions, known as XCMDs and XFCNs, to extend the built-in capabilities of the program. These externals are called from HyperTalk, HyperCard's built-in scripting language. Externals can return information to HyperTalk, accept parameters from HyperTalk, and allow access to every last Macintosh function.

> XCMDs and XFCNs are similar, yet different. Both allow you to access HyperCard's internal data and do things you otherwise wouldn't be able to do in HyperCard. The difference is in the way they are called by HyperCard. An XCMD normally doesn't return a value, yet acts on parameters passed to it. An XFCN, on the other hand, usually returns a value that you store in a HyperTalk variable. In reality, you can probably write your code as either an XCMD or XFCN. It is just up to you to decide how you want it to be used in HyperTalk.

Externals can be written in just about any high-level language, assuming you follow the proper calling conventions for them. Most development environments come with a header file, called HyperX-Cmd.h in CodeWarrior, for use with HyperCard. This header file contains all the constants, structures, and function prototypes to interface with HyperCard. By using this header file and its associated library, called HyperXLib, you can access the magic of HyperCard from your C code.

One advanced feature of HyperCard and HyperTalk is that your code can call back into functions that exist in HyperCard itself. By making use of these functions, you can alert HyperCard to the fact that you are about to play some sound, that you want to create a new window, that you want to hide all of HyperCards palettes, and more. These callbacks give you control over some of HyperCard's internal data structures and give you more overall flexibility when writing your external. You can even execute HyperTalk code from within your XCMD.

> Many externals can also be called from other environments, including AppleScript and other programs. Developers found the HyperCard XCMD and XFCN API (Application Programming Interface) to be so useful and popular that they decided to implement support for it in their own programs. By using Apple-Script, you can call XCMDs from the Finder to perform all types of actions. Mind you, any XCMD that takes advantage of custom callbacks that are available only in HyperCard will probably not work properly in other environments.

Externals are stored in resources inside the stack that uses them or in any other stack in the hierarchy. External commands are stored in resources of type XCMD and external functions are stored in resources of type XFCN. Externals are referenced by name and not by ID number, so you must be sure that the names you use are unique. For example, if you have an XCMD named BeepLoud and you wanted to call it from HyperTalk code in a button, you might use the following script:

```
on mouseup
    BeepLoud 3
end mouseup
```

This HyperTalk code would pass the parameter 3 to the XCMD resource named BeepLoud. The BeepLoud XCMD would then do whatever it did best. In our case, this might be to set the volume to the maximum, beep three times, and then reset the volume. Mind you, this example is relatively simple and doesn't really do much that HyperTalk can't already do by itself. Let's look at another example.

Pretend you have a formula that you want to execute very fast. Your front end is HyperCard, but you don't want to type your formula in HyperTalk; you would rather use C. You may create an XFCN in order to return the result of your processing in a HyperTalk variable. Your HyperTalk code might look like the following code.

```
on mouseup
      put ProprietaryFormula(field "fluid value",
            field "fluid level")
end mouseup
```

In this case, you would have a resource of type XFCN named ProprietaryFormula. HyperTalk would automatically load the resource by name and call it, passing the contents of the two fields as parameters. The XFCN can then do the math and return the result. Not only will a compiled external make your formula execute faster in most cases, but it will also keep the formula in a more protected form than if it were in HyperTalk code. It is harder to disassemble assembly language code than it is to look at HyperTalk code.

> Metrowerks' CodeWarrior also allows you to create your externals using C++, as opposed to straight C. This can be an advantage to those of you who want to code in that style using the features that C++ offers. You should note that there are some difficulties in doing this, but the good folks at Metrowerks have worked them out for you. See the examples that come on your CodeWarrior CD for more information on this.

PowerPC Support

If you've made it this far through the book, you probably have a pretty good handle on how code resources work. You may also have determined that it really isn't that hard to write a HyperCard external, assuming you follow all the rules set up by HyperCard's API. One thing that is lacking, however, is native externals for HyperCard. As of this writing, Apple has yet to produce an interface to the callbacks in HyperCard that can be used from PowerPC code. Luckily, Metrowerks provides a library, and source, called PowerHyperXLib by Robert Coie from Intrigue Corporation. These can be used until Apple provides their own solution.

> By the time you read this, HyperCard 2.3 (or later) should have been released. It is scheduled for release in mid-to-late 1995 and is supposed to include support for PowerPC native XCMDs and XFCNs. You should be able to replace the PowerHyperXLib easily with whatever is provided with this brand new version.

XCMD Development

In this chapter, we will be writing two externals for HyperCard—both of them XCMDs (Figure 9-1). The first will record audio to disk in the form of an AIFF file. The second will play back that AIFF

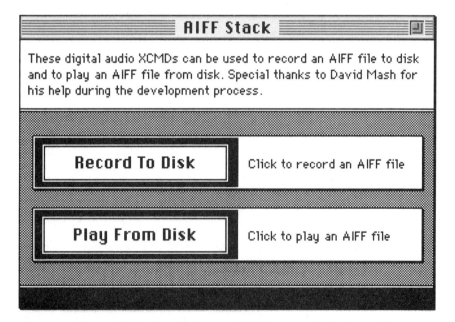

Figure 9-1. The stack that houses the two XCMDs we will develop in this chapter

audio from disk, asynchronously. That is, while the audio is playing back, you can continue to work in HyperCard, or launch another application, or go back to the Finder. Any amount of audio will be played in the background while you do other things. Let's look at the code for each.

RecordToDisk XCMD Code

The RecordToDisk XCMD uses the Sound Manager function SndRecordToFile to record sound data directly to your hard disk. The data that is recorded is stored as an AIFF file—a standard audio file format. You can read more about this format and the functions we are using in *Inside Macintosh*, "Sound." When the XCMD is invoked, it first asks the user where to save the file using the StandardPutFile function. After the user selects a directory and presses the Save button, the standard recording dialog box (Figure 9-2) is displayed to allow recording of audio. After the user records the audio and presses the Save button, the AIFF data is written to the file.

The RecordToDisk XCMD takes two parameters that are not required. If you would like to pass them in, you can, but if you do not, default values will be used. Those parameters are the top and left coordinates of the standard recording dialog box. If you pass in values, the dialog box will be positioned at that location. If you choose not to pass these values then the XCMD will automatically place the dialog box in a location relative to the frontmost window in HyperCard.

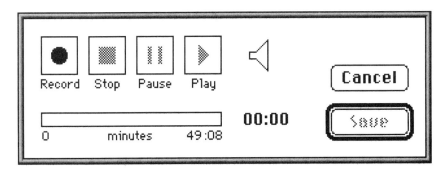

Figure 9-2. The standard recording dialog box as displayed by the RecordToDisk XCMD

```
struct XCmdBlock {
    short       paramCount;
    Handle      params[16];
    Handle      returnValue;
    Boolean     passFlag;
    Ptr         entryPoint;
    short       request;
    short       result;
    long        inArgs[8];
    long        outArgs[4];
};

#define kMinParamCount      0
#define kMaxParamCount      2
#define kErrorFlag          (short)-1

pascal void main(XCmdPtr xp)
{
    StandardFileReply   reply;
    Point               corner;
    OSErr               err = noErr;
    short               refNum = -1;
    Boolean             cancelled = false;
    Boolean             fileCreated = false;
    Str32               tempStr;

#ifndef powerc
    long    oldA4 = SetCurrentA4();
    RememberA4();
#endif
```

The first thing we want to do is declare our XCMD function the proper way. HyperCard defines that the format is a Pascal function that returns no value and takes a pointer to a data structure. This data structure contains all the information we need to do our job. You will note that if we are not running on a PowerPC, we make use of A4-based globals.

```
if ((xp->paramCount != kMinParamCount) &&
    (xp->paramCount != kMaxParamCount)) {
    SetError(xp, "Error: Form = RecordToDisk [h, v]. ", 0);
    goto fail;
}

if (xp->paramCount == 2) {
    corner.h = (short)HandleToNum(xp, xp->params[0]);
    corner.v = (short)HandleToNum(xp, xp->params[1]);
} else {
```

```
        err = GetLocOfCardWindow(xp, &corner);
    if (err == kErrorFlag) {
        SetError(xp,
            "Error: Couldn't get location of card window. ",
            0);
        goto fail;
    }
}
```

We then verify the number of parameters that were passed in to our XCMD. If the parameter count is wrong, it should either be 0 or 2, we send a message back to HyperCard to alert the user of the proper form. If the parameter count is 2, we use the values to represent the location of the standard recording dialog box. Otherwise, we get the location of the card window and use that as the location for the standard recording dialog box.

```
StandardPutFile("\pSave AIFF file as:", "\pAIFF Audio", &reply);
if (!reply.sfGood) {
    SetError(xp, "cancel", 0);
    goto exit;
}

ZeroToPas(xp, "Go to this card", tempStr);
SendHCMessage(xp, tempStr);
```

We must then ask the user where to save the file using the StandardPutFile function. After this function has been called, we attempt to update the screen by executing the HyperTalk script "Go to this card." This will get rid of any "white erased space" the standard file dialog box put on the screen after it disappeared.

```
if (reply.sfReplacing) {
    err = FSpDelete(&reply.sfFile);
    if (err != noErr) {
        SetError(xp, "Error: Couldn't replace file. ", err);
        goto fail;
    }
}

err = FSpCreate(&reply.sfFile, '????', 'AIFF', smRoman);
if (err != noErr) {
    SetError(xp, "Error: Couldn't create sound file. ", err);
    goto fail;
}
fileCreated = true;
```

```
err = FSpOpenDF(&reply.sfFile, fsRdWrPerm, &refNum);
if ((err != noErr) || (refNum == -1)) {
    SetError(xp, "Error: Couldn't open sound file. ", err);
    goto fail;
}
```

Now that we know the user wants to record a sound, we first must delete any previous file that might exist, create the new file with the proper type and creator, and then open the data fork of the file for recording.

```
BeginXSound(xp, nil);
err = SndRecordToFile(nil, corner, siBestQuality, refNum);
EndXSound(xp);
cancelled = (err == userCanceledErr);
if (cancelled) {
    SetError(xp, "cancel", 0);
    goto fail;
}
if (err != noErr) {
    SetError(xp, "Error: Couldn't record to sound file. ", err);
    goto fail;
}
```

Just before we call the Sound Manager to do the actual dirty work, we need to tell HyperCard that we are about to do something with sound. The BeginXSound callback function alerts HyperCard that our XCMD is about to allocate sound channels and use them. After we are through recording, we call EndXSound to tell HyperCard that it can reallocate any sound channels of which it may have temporarily disposed for us.

```
        goto exit;
    fail:
        if (refNum != -1)
            FSClose(refNum);
        refNum = -1;
        if (fileCreated)
            FSpDelete(&reply.sfFile);
    exit:

        if (refNum != -1) {
            FSClose(refNum);
            FlushVol(nil, reply.sfFile.vRefNum);
            if (cancelled)
                FSpDelete(&reply.sfFile);
        }
```

```
#ifndef powerc
     SetA4(oldA4);
#endif

     return;
}
```

Lastly, we clean up any messes in case of an error. Otherwise, close the file, flush the volume, and restore the value of A4. The XCMD is now completely through executing and has recorded an AIFF file to disk.

Some of the functions that are called from our main routine are in our code, but others are callback functions to HyperCard. Functions that send HyperCard a message, such as BeginXSound and EndXSound, are examples of callbacks.

In order to make this XCMD compile as native PowerPC code, we can simply add the PowerXLib to a PowerPC project that creates the XCMD resource. The resource needs to have a native header on it by default. This can be easily selected as an option in CodeWarrior. After this is done, you have a native XCMD using the exact same source code as the previous code.

PlayFromDisk XCMD Code

The PlayFromDisk XCMD plays back an AIFF file that was recorded using the RecordToDisk XCMD. In reality, it can play back any AIFF or AIFC file no matter how it was recorded. AIFC files are compressed versions of AIFF files that, ultimately, take less space on disk and are decompressed on the fly by the Sound Manager. The neat thing about this XCMD is that it makes use of the asynchronous Sound Manager and plays back the file, direct from disk, while still allowing the user to continue to use HyperCard or switch to another application and do other work. Using this XCMD, you could make HyperCard play background music for the entire time you use your Macintosh.

In order to make use of this asynchronous sound playback, we must take advantage of several features that are new to HyperCard 2.0. These include the ability for an external to contain interrupt code (i.e., code that is called at interrupt time). We also make use of the ability to create windows within HyperCard from our XCMD. Let's take a look at the following code and see just how all this works.

```
#define kMinParamCount          0
#define kMaxParamCount          1
#define kErrorFlag              (short)-1
```

```
#define  kDefaultBufferSize      (1024*100L)
#define  kBufferDecrement        (1024*5L)
#define  kSmallestBuffer         (1024*20L)

#define  kGlobalIsPlayingFlag    "\pZobkiwIsPlaying"
#define  kWindowName             "\pZobkiw"
#define  kIdleTime               1

Boolean                          gCloseFile;
short                            gFileRefNum;
long                             gSoundChannel;
FilePlayCompletionUPP            gFPCupp;


pascal void main(XCmdPtr xp)
{
#ifndef powerc
    long    oldA4 = SetCurrentA4();
    RememberA4();
#endif

    if (xp->paramCount == -1) {
        HandleWindowMessage(xp);
    } else {
        HandleXCMDMessage(xp);
    }

#ifndef powerc
    SetA4(oldA4);
#endif
}
```

Our main entry point is very straightforward. First it sets up our
A4 world for global access. It then checks the paramCount field of the
XCmdBlock to see if this is a message for the XCMD or for the window that is later created by the XCMD. Depending on who the message is for, one of two routines is called. In the order the messages are
received, while the XCMD is executing, we will look at the HandleX-
CMDMessage function first.

```
void HandleXCMDMessage(XCmdPtr xp)
{
    Str255              fileName;
    Str32               tempStr;
    StandardFileReply   reply;
    FSSpec              fileSpec;
    SFTypeList          typeList;
    long                bufferSize = kDefaultBufferSize;
    OSErr               err = noErr;
```

```
short                   refNum = -1;
WindowPtr               w = nil;
Rect                    boundsRect = {0,0,33,33};
SndChannelPtr           chan = nil;
```

The HandleXCMDMessage function exists mainly to begin the playing of an AIFF file. We start out by declaring a host of local variables that will assist with our main goal.

```
XWHasInterruptCode(xp, w, true);

if ((xp->paramCount != kMinParamCount) &&
        (xp->paramCount != kMaxParamCount)) {
        SetError(xp, "Error: Form = PlayFromDisk [fullPathName]. ",
            0);
        goto fail;
}
```

We need to make sure that HyperCard does not allow our XCMD to be moved in memory, so we call the XWHasInterruptCode function so HyperCard is made aware of that fact. With that in mind, we can then check our parameters to make sure that we have the proper number of them. This particular XCMD accepts either the full path name of the AIFF file to play or nothing at all (in which case it will ask the user to choose which file to play).

```
{
    Handle    hGlob;
    Str32     tempStr;
    hGlob = GetGlobal(xp, kGlobalIsPlayingFlag);
    HandleToPStr(tempStr, hGlob);
    if (StrToBool(xp, tempStr)) {
        MyCompletionRoutine((SndChannelPtr)gSoundChannel);
        return;
    }
}
```

Next we must see if we are already playing a sound. When we begin playing a sound, as you will see in the following code, we create and set a global variable in HyperCard to true. If this variable exists and is set to true at this point, we know that a sound is currently being played. In this case, we call our completion routine directly to begin the steps needed to stop the sound from playing. This way, calling the XCMD while a sound is playing will automatically stop that sound from playing.

```
gCloseFile = false;
gFileRefNum = -1;
gSoundChannel = 0L;
gFPCupp = NewFilePlayCompletionProc(MyCompletionRoutine);

if (xp->paramCount == 0) {
    typeList[0] = 'AIFF';
    typeList[1] = 'AIFC';
    StandardGetFile(nil, 2, typeList, &reply);
    if (!reply.sfGood) {
        SetError(xp, "cancel", 0);
        goto fail;
    }

    fileSpec = reply.sfFile;

    ZeroToPas(xp, "Go to this card", tempStr);
    SendHCMessage(xp, tempStr);
} else {
    HandleToPStr(fileName, xp->params[0]);
    err = FSMakeFSSpec(0, 0, fileName, &fileSpec);
    if (err != noErr) {
        SetError(xp, "Error: Couldn't locate file. ", err);
        goto fail;
    }
}
```

At this point we know that no sound is currently being played, so we begin the work to make it play. After initializing our global variables, we check the parameter count. If the count is 0, then we know we need to ask the user to choose which AIFF or AIFC file to play. Otherwise, the parameter count will be 1 and we can use that to create an FSSpec to point to the audio file. You will note that we use our "Go to this card" trick after we display the standard file dialog box in order to update the contents of the screen properly.

```
w = NewXWindow(xp, &boundsRect, kWindowName,
    false, documentProc, false, false);
if (w == nil) {
    SetError(xp, "Error: Couldn't create window. ", 0);
    goto fail;
}
```

When we know we have a file to play, we need to create a HyperCard window. The creation of this window is the key to our asynchronous operation. You see, we need to check periodically to see if the sound has completed playing. Normally, XCMDs cannot obtain periodic time from HyperCard. But, luckily, HyperCard's external window mechanism allows windows created by XCMDs to receive idle time. By creating a bogus window that we always leave invisible, we ensure that we will receive idle time to allow us to check if the sound is done playing.

```
err = FSpOpenDF(&fileSpec, fsRdPerm, &refNum);
if ((err != noErr) || (refNum == -1)) {
    SetError(xp, "Error: Couldn't open sound file. ", err);
    goto fail;
}

SetCursor(*GetCursor(watchCursor));

SetXWIdleTime(xp, w, kIdleTime);

BeginXSound(xp, nil);

err = SndNewChannel(&chan, sampledSynth, 0, nil);
if (err != noErr) {
    SetError(xp, "Error: Couldn't allocate sound channel. ",
            err);
    goto fail;
}

gFileRefNum = refNum;
gSoundChannel = (long)chan;
```

We now open the audio file, tell HyperCard that our window wants idle time every 1 tick, and alert HyperCard that we will be dealing with sound. We now allocate our own sound channel to be used when playing the sound. When it is allocated, we remember the reference number of the open file and the handle to the sound channel in global variables. These will be important to keep around, because when the sound is finished playing we need to close the file and dispose of the sound channel.

```
tryAgain:
    err = SndStartFilePlay(chan, refNum, 0, bufferSize,
        nil, nil, gFPCupp, true);
    if ((err == notEnoughBufferSpace) &&
      (bufferSize > kSmallestBuffer)) {
      bufferSize -= kBufferDecrement;
      goto tryAgain;
    }

    if (err != noErr) {
      SetError(xp, "Error: Couldn't play the sound file. ", err);
      goto fail;
    }
```

We now attempt to play the file using a specific buffer size. If the buffer cannot be allocated, we loop, decrementing the buffer size by 5K each time, until it can be accommodated or until we reach a minimum buffer size. In most cases, the sound will begin playing at this point, unless HyperCard is really tight on memory.

```
SetGlobal(xp, kGlobalIsPlayingFlag, CopyStrToHand("true"));
```

Assuming the sound begins playing, we set our custom global variable to true. Remember, this is the variable we tested earlier in this function to see if a sound was playing at all.

```
        goto exit;
    fail:
        gCloseFile = false;
        gFileRefNum = -1;
        gSoundChannel = 0L;
        if (gFPCupp) {
                DisposeRoutineDescriptor(gFPCupp);
                gFPCupp = nil;
        }
        SetXWIdleTime(xp, w, 0);
        XWHasInterruptCode(xp, w, false);
        EndXSound(xp);
        if (w)
            CloseXWindow(xp, w);
    exit:
        InitCursor();
        return;
    }
```

At this point, if we failed anywhere in the routine we would have entered the fail label and cleaned up after ourselves. Otherwise, we simply return and exit our XCMD.

```
    pascal void MyCompletionRoutine(SndChannelPtr chan)
    {
    #ifndef powerc
        long oldA4 = SetUpA4();
    #endif

        gCloseFile = true;

    #ifndef powerc
        RestoreA4(oldA4);
    #endif
    }
```

Remember, we have requested that the SndStartFilePlay function play asynchronously and have passed a universal procedure pointer to it that describes our MyCompletionRoutine function. Therefore, this function will be called as soon as the file has completed being played by the Sound Manager. When it is called, it will set the gCloseFile variable to true, which means it is now okay to close the audio file, as the sound is no longer playing.

The reason we set a flag at this point rather than actually closing the file is because this function is executing at interrupt time. Interrupt time is when the Macintosh is in a state of disrepair—the Memory Manager may be in the middle of moving blocks of memory or the File Manager may be in the middle of performing a read or write. When you have a completion routine, such as ours, that is called at interrupt time; you cannot move memory or do much of anything except set a flag. Therefore we follow the rules and do just that.

Now, because we created a window and requested that it receive idle time, our XCMD will be called with the paramCount field of the XCmdBlock set to -1 every tick or so. When this happens, our main entry point calls our HandleWindowMessage function. This function is responsible for checking to see if the sound has completed playing or not by looking at the value of the gCloseFile variable, among other things.

```
void HandleWindowMessage(XCmdPtr xp)
{
    XWEventInfoPtr   xw = (XWEventInfoPtr)(xp->params[0]);
    WindowPtr        w = xw->eventWindow;
    OSErr            err = noErr;

    if (xw->event.what == xOpenEvt) {
        ;       // ignore this message
    } else if (xw->event.what == xCloseEvt) {

        if (gFileRefNum != -1) {
            FSClose(gFileRefNum);
            gFileRefNum = -1;
        }

        if (gSoundChannel != nil) {
            err = SndDisposeChannel((SndChannelPtr)gSoundChannel,
                true);
            if (err != noErr)
                SetError(xp, "Error: Disposing sound channel. ",
                    err);
            gSoundChannel = 0L;
        }
```

```
                    SetXWIdleTime(xp, w, 0);
                    XWHasInterruptCode(xp, w, false);
                    EndXSound(xp);
                    SetGlobal(xp, kGlobalIsPlayingFlag, CopyStrToHand("false"));
                    xp->passFlag = true;

                    if (gFPCupp) {
                            DisposeRoutineDescriptor(gFPCupp);
                            gFPCupp = nil;
                    }

            }else  if ((gCloseFile == true) && (gSoundChannel != nil)) {
                    gCloseFile = false;
                    CloseXWindow(xp, w);
            }
    }
```

When this function is called, if the gCloseFile flag is set to true, we immediately set it to false and then call the HyperCard callback function CloseXWindow to close our invisible window. The XCMD is then called with the XCloseEvt message, which forces us to enter this function again. This time we will take the xCloseEvt path. The first thing we will do is close the audio file. Next, we dispose of the sound channel that we were using to play the audio, and alert HyperCard that we no longer need idle time, that we no longer have interrupt code being used, and that we are done using the Sound Manager. We also set our own HyperTalk global flag to false so we can begin playing another sound if needed. After this function exits, the XCMD has completed its job and will, most probably, be totally unloaded from memory. The next time it is called, it will start from scratch.

This XCMD performs some pretty advanced stuff. If you didn't quite understand it the first time through, take a break and then read through this section again. Believe it or not, everything it does is legal; it's just a bit tricky.

Compiling Our Code

The XCMDs in this chapter each have two projects. One project builds a 680x0 version of the XCMD and the other builds a PowerPC version (Figures 9-3, 9-4, 9-5, and 9-6). Our version builds them into two separate HyperCard stacks, but there is no reason why you couldn't build a fat or safe fat XCMD resource, as we have done in the past with other code resources. You can build it in any form you so desire and, as always, this will vary with your specific needs.

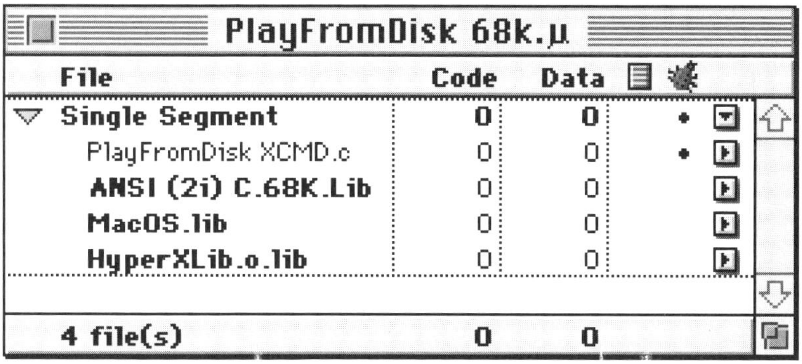

Figure 9-3. 680x0 project file for the PlayFromDisk XCMD

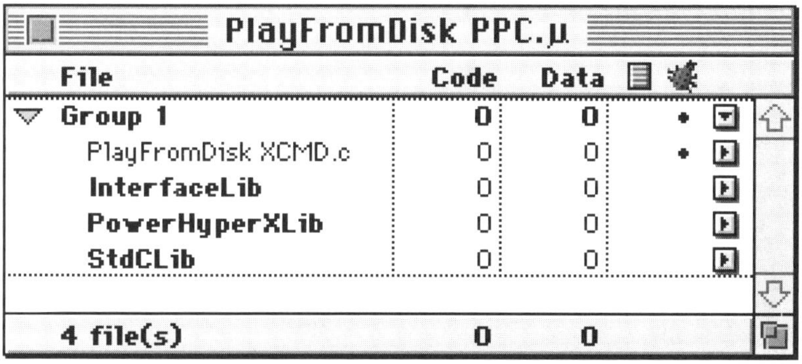

Figure 9-4. PowerPC project file for the PlayFromDisk XCMD

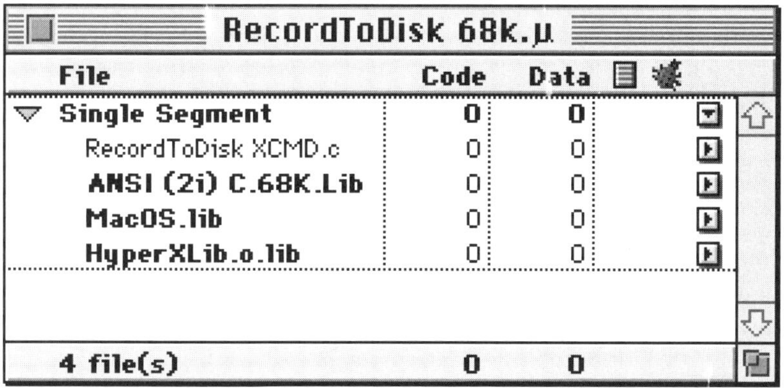

Figure 9-5. 680x0 project file for the RecordToDisk XCMD

RecordToDisk PPC.μ				
File	**Code**	**Data**	🗏	🐝
▽ **Group 1**	0	0		▾
RecordToDisk XCMD.c	0	0		▸
InterfaceLib	0	0		▸
PowerHyperXLib	0	0		▸
StdCLib	0	0		▸
4 file(s)	**0**	**0**		

Figure 9-6. PowerPC project file for the RecordToDisk XCMD

HyperCard External Tips

HyperCard externals offer many advantages. They allow you to concentrate on your algorithms and leave all of the user interface issues to HyperCard. This, alone, is a reason so many programmers like to program for HyperCard. Keep in mind the following tips and ideas when building your HyperCard externals.

- HyperCard can be a nice front end for your programming projects. You can easily hide your proprietary algorithms in the form of XCMDs and XFCNs. You will also gain speed increases in this manner as well.
- As with most code resources, the choice to make them PowerPC native or not will depend on what they actually do inside. If the XCMDs perform a very simple task, depending on the task, PowerPC code may not make a substantial speed difference. Given this, it may not be worth the extra memory that the PowerPC code will take up or the time invested in developing and testing the XCMD. The decision is yours.
- If you create a window in HyperCard—one that is visible—you can make it use any window definition you like. So, write a really cool window definition like we've discussed in Chapter Eight, include the WDEF in the HyperCard stack on which you are working, and then create your HyperCard window from within your external. You can have PowerPC code in any code resource to really make your stack fly.
- There are hundreds of externals for HyperCard available on online services for you to download. Many of them include source code as well. Even if you don't have an idea for an external,

download one and convert it to be PowerPC native. Think of the speed increase the XCMD will exhibit. Others may thank you and it will be good practice.

- Push it. Who would have thought that you could make Hyper-Card play an asynchronous AIFF file? Until I actually figured it out, I never really thought about how useful it would be. No idea is too crazy. I built off a concept that HyperCard had already im-plemented—play sounds. I took it to the next level and it worked! Experiment and explore the possibilities!

C H A P T E R   T E N

Photoshop Filters

Please don't crash!

(Who *hasn't* said this?)

Introduction

Adobe Photoshop is an amazing application. As of this writing, it is the world's leading photo design and production tool. It allows you to create your own images, edit scanned images, and even import images in a variety of formats. Photoshop also allows artists, photographers, and graphic design professionals to perform color-correction and other high-end tasks easily and directly on their Macintosh. Anyone who has used Photoshop agrees that it is one of the most powerful applications of its kind.

Photoshop contains many standard tools that allow users to grasp the power of the program quickly and easily. The tool palette in Figure 10-1 will most likely look familiar to you if you've ever used a paint program on the Macintosh. You have your standard selection and editing tools available, as well as other tools that allow you to manipulate your images in new and exciting ways. For example, Photoshop supports a magic wand tool, airbrush tool, smudge tool, blur tool, and a sponge tool, to name a few.

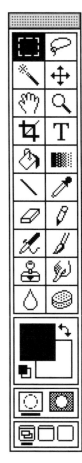

Figure 10-1. Photoshop's main tool palette

Along with the obvious tools that are available in the palette, there are numerous menu items that can be used to adjust your images. These options include the ability to adjust brightness, contrast, hue, saturation, color levels, and curves. Curves, for example, shown in Figure 10-2, allows you to adjust the tonal range of an image to your exact specifications. Photoshop gives you complete control over every aspect of your images.

Not that all of this power isn't enough, but one of the things that makes Photoshop so popular and useful is the fact that it supports Plug-in filters. These filters allow third-party developers, and Adobe, to create new functionality that can be added to the program simply

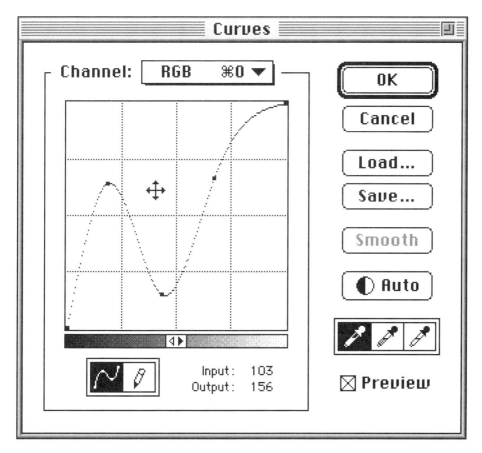

Figure 10-2. Editing curves

by dragging a file into the Plug-ins folder. Whenever Photoshop is launched, it scans this folder and all of its subdirectories and makes these filters available to the user (Figure 10-3). You may remember that this mechanism is similar to what we discussed in Chapter Three, "Application Extensions."

Photoshop actually supports a number of Plug-in filter types. These include

• acquisition modules, which open an image in a new window. Acquisition modules can be used to interface to scanners, read images in proprietary formats, or produce synthetic images. These modules are accessed via the Acquire hierarchical menu in the File menu.

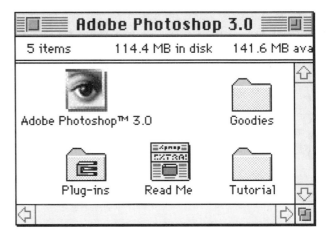

Figure 10-3. Photoshop folder hierarchy showing Plug-ins folder

- export modules, which output an existing image. Export modules can be used to send an image to a printer that is not accessible via the Chooser, or to save files in proprietary formats. These modules are accessed via the Export hierarchical menu in the File menu.
- file format modules, which provide support for additional image formats. These modules are accessed via popup menus in the Open—, Save As—, and Save a Copy— dialog boxes.
- filter modules, which modify a selected area of an image. These modules are accessed via the Filter menu and all of its submenus.

All of these filter types are discussed in detail in the Adobe Photoshop 3.0 Software Development Kit (SDK). This SDK is available directly from the Adobe Developers Association (ADA). You can contact them by sending email to devsupperson@adobe.com or by calling 415–961–4111. You can also download the SDK via "FTP" (File Transfer Protocol) by accessing ftp.adobe.com or ftp.mv.us.adobe.com. You should note that Adobe cannot offer technical support unless you join the ADA.

In this chapter, we will be discussing Photoshop Filter Plug-ins. These are undoubtedly the most popular type of Plug-in to write for Photoshop. Filters allow you to manipulate totally an entire image or the current selection. If you've ever used Kai's Power Tools from HSC Software, then you know what filters are capable of doing. Kai, and the entire team at HSC, are the masters of Photoshop filters and have created some exciting ones with incredible user interfaces. I think it is safe to say that they single-handedly pushed the envelope of filter design in Photoshop.

Filters can do just about anything you like to an image. When a filter is called, it is passed the image data, along with other information that describes specifics about the image and its environment. The filter can optionally display a dialog box to users to allow them to configure it and ultimately apply the changes to the image itself. Photoshop provides a long list of routines that are available to the filter in order to allow it to display dialog boxes, about boxes, and progress meters easily.

The Gaussian Blur filter displays the dialog box shown in Figure 10-4. The image preview area allows the user to view a portion of the image to see what it will look like after the blur takes effect. The + and − buttons allow the user to zoom in and out of the preview. The Preview check box makes the current settings apply to the entire image in real time, so you can move the dialog box off to the side and

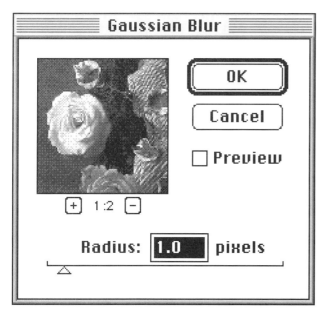

Figure 10-4. Gaussian Blur movable, modal options dialog box

see what your actual image will look like with the filter applied. The editable text area and the triangle slider allow you to change the level of the blur you want to apply. The dialog box in your filter can be as simple or complex as you like.

Technically speaking, filters are stored in files of type 8BFM with a creator of 8BIM. When writing your filter, you normally store your 680x0 code in a resource of type 8BFM in this file. Your PowerPC code is stored in the data fork of the filter. Most developers will also add an about box to their filter in the form of a DLOG resource. The only other required information in the filter file itself is a resource of type PiPL, affectionately called a Pipple resource. This Plug-in property list resource contains all of the information needed by Photoshop to allow it to use your filter.

> The PiPL resource is the new replacement for the old PiMI, pronounced "Pimmy," resource. The PiMI resource was very limited and contained only limited information. The PiPL resource is extensible and flexible, and allows for Plug-ins with code for multiple platforms as well as many other options. You can still include a PiMI resource in your Plug-in files if you want to support versions of Photoshop previous to 3.0. However, you will need to make sure you don't take advantage of any 3.0-specific features when running under an older version, unless of course you want to crash.

The PiPL resource is a very advanced data structure and contains lots of information. The basic structure begins as displayed in the following code.

```
typedef struct PIPropertyList {
    int32  version;
    int32  count;
    PIProperty  properties[1];
} PIPropertyList;
```

The version field contains the version of the PiPL resource format. The current version, as of this writing, is 0. The count field contains the number of properties in the PiPL. This field can be 0, meaning the PiPL contains no properties. The properties field is a variable-length array of PIProperty structures. The PIProperty structure is defined as presented in the following code.

```
typedef struct PIProperty {
    OSType        vendorID;
    OSType        propertyKey;
    int32         propertyID;
    int32         propertyLength;
    char          propertyData[1];
} PIProperty;
```

The vendorID field identifies the vendor defining this particular property type. This allows vendors to define types that do not interfere with Adobe or other vendors. The default vendorID for Adobe is 8BIM. The propertyKey field specifies the type of property. Each type of property contains specifically formatted data that follows in the propertyData field. The propertyID field allows developers to store more than one property of the same type, much like the Resource Manager allows more than one resource of the same type. Using this mechanism, each property has a unique type and ID for each vendorID. The propertyLength field contains the length of the propertyData field. This allows manufacturers who support the Plug-in architecture, but not a particular property, to skip over it without any ill effects. Lastly, the propertyData field contains the data specific to this property. Figure 10-5 displays an example portion of a PiPL.

You should note that we will see types such as int32 and others throughout the Plug-in SDK. The reason for this is because the entire Plug-in architecture is cross-platform. That is, it can be used to run under Windows, Macintosh, and Power Macintosh. By using types such as int32, they can be specified and defined for each platform to ensure that programmers know the exact type they are using. It takes some getting used to, but it shouldn't be much trouble. However, since we are writing code that we never intend to run on anything but a Macintosh, I have taken some liberties and have continued to use short, long, and other types with which I am familiar.

There are numerous different property keys available. Table 10-1 presents a partial list of some of the property keys you will see most often.

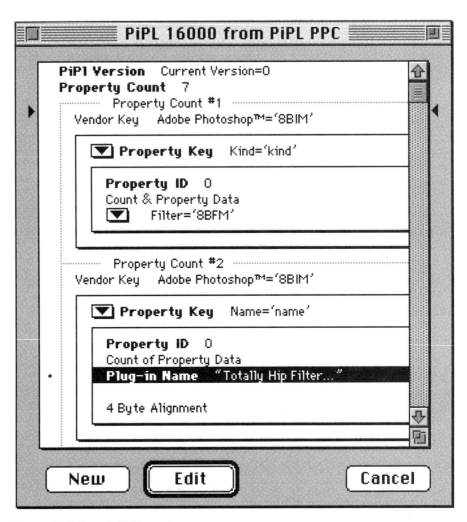

Figure 10-5. Sample PiPL portion

Table 10-1.   Property Keys

Property Key	What it Is Used For (propertyData Contents)
Kind	The type of Plug-in (filter, acquire, etc.)
Name	The name of the Plug-in
Category	Category of the type (For filters, this specifies the name of the hierarchical menu in the Filter menu within which the filter will appear.)
Version	The version of the Plug-in interface that the Plug-in supports
Code68k	Resource type and ID used to store the 680x0 code for the Plug-in
Code68kFPUOnly	Resource type and ID used to store the 680x0 code for the Plug-in that requires a floating point unit
CodePowerPC	Information on where in the data fork to find the PowerPC code for the Plug-in
SupportedModes	Flags describing which image modes the Plug-in supports
FilterCaseInfo	Flags controlling the filtering process and presentation of data to the Plug-in
RequiredHost	The creator of a specific host application (such as 8BIM for Photoshop) if the Plug-in requires a feature of that host to work properly

The vendorID exists because companies other than Adobe have adopted the Photoshop Plug-in architecture and use it in their own applications. When a program uses the architecture, it may decide to add a feature to the way it is implemented. By using a unique vendorID, these programs can know when they are dealing with one of their specific features or one that was created by Adobe. This addition shows forethought by the writers of the SDK and is good development practice: Think of the future.

You must fill in your PiPL resource properly in order for your Plug-in to work. There are numerous options and they can be overwhelming if you are new to advanced graphics terminology. However, this shouldn't stop you from experimenting. The filters developed in this chapter are relatively simple and should give you a starting point from which to jump if you decide to plug yourself in to Photoshop. Let's take a look at our filters!

As we developed our filters, we found some problems with version 3.0 of the SDK that we used when trying to compile with CodeWarrior. Here is a short list of the changes we made to the SDK. You may choose to implement these changes in another way, but we decided to take the brute force method.

1. Photoshop.h needs to check for *__MWERKS__* as well as all the other symbols it checks for before #including all of the standard Photoshop header files.
2. In MacStd.h, the *#define SystemSixOrLater 1* definition is a duplicate. We commented it out.
3. In MacStd.h, the *#include <FCntl.h>* does not exist and should be commented out.
4. In the sample code, the *#pragma unused* is not supported and was removed.
5. In MacStd.h, the *#include <SANE.h>* does not need to be included if __powerc is defined.
6. I added the following code to the sample:

```
#ifdef __powerc
enum {
    uppPhotoshopFilterProcInfo = kPascalStackBased
            | STACK_ROUTINE_PARAMETER(1, SIZE_CODE(sizeof(short)))
            | STACK_ROUTINE_PARAMETER(2, SIZE_CODE(sizeof(Ptr)))
            | STACK_ROUTINE_PARAMETER(3, SIZE_CODE(sizeof(Ptr)))
            | STACK_ROUTINE_PARAMETER(4, SIZE_CODE(sizeof(Ptr)))
};
ProcInfoType __procinfo = uppPhotoshopFilterProcInfo;
#endif
```

After these changes were made, all compiled smoothly.

ColorFill Filter

The first filter we develop in this chapter is called the ColorFill filter. It is really nothing more than a shell that can be used to start you off on your own filter excursions. The ColorFill filter allows you to select an area of the image, using any of the selection tools, and fills it with the foreground or background color (Figure 10-6). For our testing purposes, we also added the option for the filter to display timer results so we can compare the speed of our 680x0 and PowerPC code.

Filter Code

The code for our ColorFill filter is about the minimum of what a filter will need to do its job. This code is based off the Dissolve sample that comes with the Photoshop SDK. I changed portions of it to make it clearer and easier to understand. Let's take a look at the following code.

```
#define itemForegroundColor      3
#define itemBackgroundColor      4
#define itemShowTimer            6

typedef struct TParameters {
    short               whichColor;
    Boolean             fShowTimer;
    unsigned long       startTicks;
    unsigned long       endTicks;
} TParameters, *PParameters, **HParameters;
```

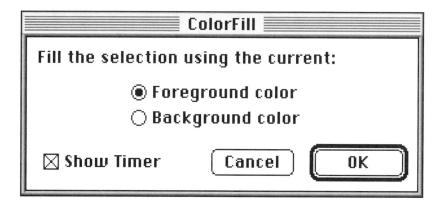

Figure 10-6. ColorFill movable, modal options dialog box

```
typedef struct Globals {
    short            result;
    FilterRecord     *stuff;
} Globals, *GPtr, **GHdl;

#define gResult ((*globals).result)
#define gStuff  ((*globals).stuff)
```

Before we can begin, we make a few simple #defines and type definitions. We #define the items in our options dialog box to make them easier to access in the code. We also define structures for the parameters that our dialog box uses as well as our global data. Photoshop filters are similar to control panels in the way they deal with globals. Most of the time, you will allocate your globals first and pass them back to Photoshop. Each subsequent time Photoshop calls your filter, it will pass you the global data that you previously allocated. When you are all through, you can deallocate the memory.

```
pascal void main (short selector, FilterRecord *stuff,
                  long *data, short *result)
```

Our main entry point is defined as being Pascal, much like almost all of the other code resources in this book. It returns no result. The first parameter is the selector that our filter uses to see what Photoshop wants us to do. Selectors tell a filter to display its about box, query the user for options, prepare for a filter process, begin a filter process, continue a filter process, and finish a filter process. The stuff parameter, which is a pointer to a FilterRecord structure, contains more information than you care to know about right now. Suffice it to say that everything you ever wanted to know about an image is stored there. You should read the SDK for the specifics of the structure. The data parameter is used to return your global data back to Photoshop. Photoshop maintains the value of this parameter across calls to the filter. It is set to 0 the first time the filter is called. The last parameter, result, is used to return a result code to Photoshop. If the filter returns 0, it means no error has occurred. If the filter returns a positive value, it means an error has occurred, but the filter has already alerted the user. If the filter returns a negative number, it means an error has occurred and the host application, in our case Photoshop, should alert the user.

```
{
    Globals    globalValues;
    GPtr       globals = &globalValues;

    if (!*data) {
            InitGlobals(globals);
            *data = (long)NewHandle(sizeof(Globals));
            if (!*data) {
                    *result = memFullErr;
                    return;
            }
            **(GHdl)*data = globalValues;
    }

    globalValues = **(GHdl)*data;

    gStuff = stuff;
    gResult = noErr;

    switch(selector) {

            case filterSelectorAbout:
                    DoAbout(globals);
                    break;

            case filterSelectorParameters:
                    DoParameters(globals);
                    break;

            case filterSelectorPrepare:
                    DoPrepare(globals);
                    break;

            case filterSelectorStart:
                    DoStart(globals);
                    break;

            case filterSelectorContinue:
                    DoContinue(globals);
                    break;

            case filterSelectorFinish:
                    DoFinish(globals);
                    break;

            default:
                    gResult = filterBadParameters;

    }

    *result = gResult;
    **(GHdl)*data = globalValues;
}
```

Our main function is not too difficult to understand. We first allocate and initialize our global data if the data parameter currently does not contain them. After we take care of making sure we can access the global data, we go into a switch statement that is used to call the proper routine, depending on the selector being passed in. After the routine returns, we fill in the result parameter, update the pointer to our global data, and exit back to the host application.

```
void InitGlobals(GPtr globals)
{

}
```

The InitGlobals function is simply a stub in this project. This function is called to initialize any global data we may need to initialize. In our case, we do not need to do this here, so we don't. The function is included here to be complete and to maintain similarity to the Dissolve sample.

```
void DoAbout(GPtr globals)
{
    ShowAbout(16000);
}
```

The DoAbout function is called when the selector is filterSelectorAbout. We pass our global data to this function, but do not use it in our simple case. We simply call the SDK-supplied function ShowAbout to display our about dialog box. This function takes the ID of a DLOG resource and displays it (Figure 10-7). Our dialog box must follow the rules set up by Adobe in that a Return or Enter key, or a click in the dialog box, disposes of it. We do this by hiding an OK

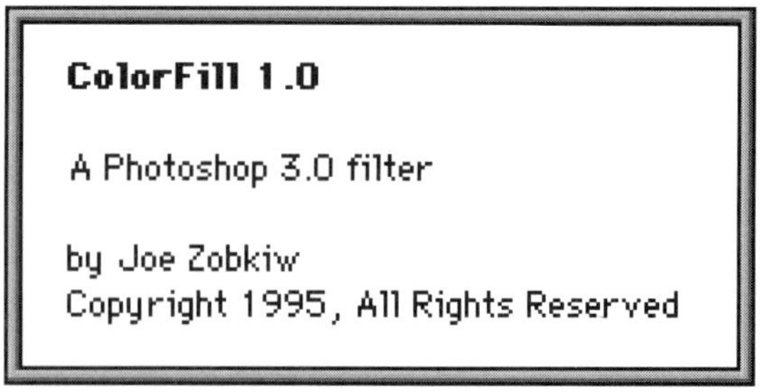

ColorFill 1.0

A Photoshop 3.0 filter

by Joe Zobkiw
Copyright 1995, All Rights Reserved

Figure 10-7. ColorFill about box as displayed to the user

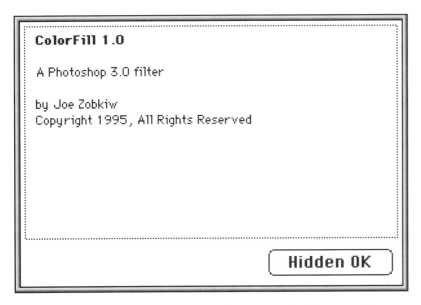

Figure 10-8. ColorFill about box as it really exists with a large user item

button in the dialog box, out of its content rectangle, and also have an enabled user item covering the entire dialog contents, as shown in Figure 10-8. The OK button is item number 1 and the user item is item number 2.

```
#define kOptionsDialogID 16001

void DoParameters(GPtr globals)
{
    short       item, whichColor;
    DialogPtr   dp;
    DialogTHndl dt;
    Boolean     done = false, fShowTimer;

    if (!gStuff->parameters) {
        gStuff->parameters = NewHandle((long)sizeof(TParameters));
        if (!gStuff->parameters) {
            gResult = memFullErr;
            return;
        }
        ((PParameters)*gStuff->parameters)->whichColor
            = itemForegroundColor;
        ((PParameters)*gStuff->parameters)->fShowTimer = false;
    }

    dt = (DialogTHndl)GetResource('DLOG', kOptionsDialogID);
```

```
HNoPurge((Handle)dt);
CenterDialog(dt);
SetUpMoveableModal(dt, gStuff->hostSig);

dp = GetNewDialog(kOptionsDialogID, nil, (WindowPtr) -1);

SetDialogDefaultItem(dp, ok);
SetDialogCancelItem(dp, cancel);
SetDialogTracksCursor(dp, true);
SetRadioGroupState(dp, itemForegroundColor, itemBackgroundColor,
        ((PParameters)*gStuff->parameters)->whichColor);
SetCheckBoxState(dp, itemShowTimer,
        ((PParameters)*gStuff->parameters)->fShowTimer);
SetArrowCursor();

while (!done) {
        MoveableModalDialog(dp, gStuff->processEvent, nil, &item);
        switch (item) {
                case ok:
                        whichColor = GetRadioGroupState(dp,
                                itemForegroundColor, itemBackgroundColor);
                        ((PParameters)*gStuff->parameters)->whichColor
                                = whichColor;
                        fShowTimer = GetCheckBoxState(dp,
                                itemShowTimer);
                        ((PParameters)*gStuff->parameters)->fShowTimer
                                = fShowTimer;
                        done = true;
                        break;

                case cancel:
                        done = true;
                        gResult = 1;
                        break;

                case itemForegroundColor:
                case itemBackgroundColor:
                case itemShowTimer:
                        PerformStandardDialogItemHandling(dp, item);
                        break;

                default:
                        break;
        }
}

DisposDialog(dp);
HPurge((Handle) dt);
}
```

When our filter receives the filterSelectorParameters selector we must display our options dialog box and allow the user to configure our filter. You should note that not all filters need to have options dialog boxes, but ours do. You will note that this is pretty standard-looking code. The only major difference is that we call some SDK-supplied functions to handle such things as toggling our radio buttons and check boxes, and handling a movable, modal dialog box. After making sure we have our parameters available, or allocating them, we use that information to prepare the dialog box, initialize it, and alert Photoshop to the fact that we are about to use a movable modal. Then we simply loop, much like you would when calling ModalDialog, only we call the SDK-supplied function MovableModalDialog. When the user clicks OK, we grab the newly chosen values and return.

```
void DoPrepare(GPtr globals)
{
     gStuff->bufferSpace = 0;
}
```

We are called with the filterSelectorPrepare selector just before our filter is going to be called to filter the image. This is where your filter can allocate memory needed for filtering or performing other tasks. In our case, we simply set the bufferSpace field in the FilterRecord to 0, which tells Photoshop that we do not plan on using any great amount of memory during our filtering. If we were to use lots of memory, we would fill this in with a number to allow Photoshop to preflight that memory for us.

```
void DoStart(GPtr globals)
{
    int16       row;
    int32       totalLines = gStuff->filterRect.bottom -
                    gStuff->filterRect.top;

    if (!WarnAdvanceStateAvailable()) {
        gResult = 1;
        goto done;
    }

    if (gResult != noErr)
        goto done;

    gStuff->inLoPlane = gStuff->outLoPlane = 0;
    gStuff->inHiPlane = gStuff->outHiPlane = gStuff->planes - 1;
```

```
        gStuff->inRect.left = gStuff->outRect.left =
            gStuff->filterRect.left;
        gStuff->inRect.right = gStuff->outRect.right =
            gStuff->filterRect.right;

        if (((PParameters)*gStuff->parameters)->fShowTimer)
            ((PParameters)*gStuff->parameters)->startTicks =
            TickCount();

        for (row = gStuff->filterRect.top;
            row < gStuff->filterRect.bottom; ++row) {

            UpdateProgress(row - gStuff->filterRect.top, totalLines);

            if (TestAbort()) {
                gResult = userCanceledErr;
                goto done;
            }

            gStuff->inRect.top = gStuff->outRect.top = row;
            gStuff->inRect.bottom = gStuff->outRect.bottom = row + 1;

            gResult = AdvanceState();
            if (gResult != noErr)
                goto done;

            DoFilterRect(globals);
        }

done:
    if (((PParameters)*gStuff->parameters)->fShowTimer)
        ((PParameters)*gStuff->parameters)->endTicks = TickCount();

    SetRect(&gStuff->inRect, 0, 0, 0, 0);
    SetRect(&gStuff->outRect, 0, 0, 0, 0);
}
```

Our DoStart function is actually the function in our filter that does all the work. This function begins by calculating the total number of rows in the selected portion of the image. We loop for each row that we must filter. We then check to see if the Advance State feature is available in the host application that we will use later. We then fill in fields in the FilterRecord to specify which planes of the image we want to filter. In our case, we will handle all available planes. Since we handle one row of the image at a time, we set the right and left boundaries next—these will never change. If the user wants this filter timed, we start the timer here. Now we are ready to loop.

For each row of the image, we loop and perform the following. The UpdateProgress SDK-supplied function is called to increment the watch cursor and possibly display a movable, modal progress meter dialog box. The TestAbort SDK-supplied function is called to check if the user has typed command-period or escape. This function also handles tracking the Cancel button if the progress meter is being displayed. Assuming the user hasn't canceled, we set the rectangle to encompass the first row of the selection. We then call the AdvanceState SDK-supplied function, which updates the buffers used for communication between Photoshop and the filter. Lastly, we call our DoFilterRect function, which actually does the filtering. After we loop for each row and filter, we set the inRect and outRect fields of the FilterRecord to be empty in order to alert Photoshop that we have completed our filtering process.

> You should note that the filter only need deal with the rectangle that describes the selection. If, for example, the user selected a region using a lasso tool, the filter would filter each pixel within the larger rectangle's bounds of the region. Photoshop automatically clips the filtered data before it blits it back to the document window. Therefore, your filter need not know about the strange shape of the selection—it does its work based on the encompassing rectangle.

```c
void DoFilterRect(GPtr globals)
{
    register short          width = gStuff->filterRect.right -
                                    gStuff->filterRect.left;
    register short          whichColor =
                        ((PParameters)*gStuff->parameters)->whichColor;
    register unsigned8      *srcPtr = (unsigned8 *)gStuff->inData;
    register unsigned8      *dstPtr = (unsigned8 *)gStuff->outData;
    register short          plane;

    while (--width >= 0) {

        for (plane = gStuff->planes - 1; plane >= 4; --plane)
            ;

        for (; plane >= 0; --plane)
            dstPtr[plane] = (whichColor == itemForegroundColor) ?
                gStuff->foreColor[plane] :
                gStuff->backColor[plane];

        srcPtr += gStuff->inHiPlane - gStuff->inLoPlane + 1;
        dstPtr += gStuff->planes;
    }
}
```

Our DoFilterRect function is called to filter one row of the selection. This function simply loops for each pixel in the row and for each plane, and sets the value of that pixel to the foreground or background color of the same plane. When it is completed with the row, it returns to the outer loop and is called again, for the next row.

A plane can be considered an element of a particular image mode. That is, if an image is in RGB mode, the red, green, and blue information for that mode would each be in their own plane. Each pixel of Red would be a byte containing a value from 0–255. Our DoFilterRect function edits the pixel values in this way. One composite pixel, therefore, is spread across n number of planes. That is why we must edit the pixel value on all planes in order to end up with the proper result.

```
void DoContinue(GPtr globals)
{
    SetRect(&gStuff->inRect, 0, 0, 0, 0);
    SetRect(&gStuff->outRect, 0, 0, 0, 0);
}
```

The DoContinue function is normally called repeatedly by Photoshop while your filter is processing. The way it works is, you might do the first step of work in the DoStart function and then subsequent steps each time DoContinue is called until all the work is done. In our case, we do all of our work in DoStart, since it makes it easier to understand. After DoStart is done, it sets the inRect and outRect fields of the FilterRecord to be empty, and DoContinue is never actually called in our filter. However, to be complete, we left it here so you could see the relationship and maybe even alter the filter to use it.

```
void DoFinish(GPtr globals)
{
    if (((PParameters)*gStuff->parameters)->fShowTimer) {
        unsigned long      totalTicks;
        Str32              totalTicksStr;

        totalTicks = ((PParameters)*gStuff->parameters)->endTicks -
                     ((PParameters)*gStuff->parameters)->startTicks;
        NumToString(totalTicks, totalTicksStr);
        ParamText(totalTicksStr, "\p", "\p", "\p");
        InitCursor();
```

```
                NoteAlert(16500, nil);
                ParamText("\p", "\p", "\p", "\p");
        }
    }
```

Our DoFinish routine is called when the filter is completely done
processing. Photoshop knows the filter is complete by examining the
inRect and outRect fields of the FilterRecord mentioned earlier. When
these are empty rectangles, Photoshop knows to call us with the
filterSelectorFinish selector. Our DoFinish routine simply displays the
alert that shows the timing information if the user requested it.

So you see, your first Photoshop filter isn't all that bad after all.

Compiling Our Filter

The ColorFill filter can be compiled as a 680x0 filter (Figure 10-9), a
PowerPC filter (Figure 10-10), or a fat filter. This allows us to time
and test the different versions of the code easily, and build our final
fat version last. The PIUtilities.c and the DialogUtilities.c files come
with the Photoshop SDK. These files contain routines that are used to
perform standard functions that many filters require. The projects
have been laid out in such a way to make them easy to understand
and change.

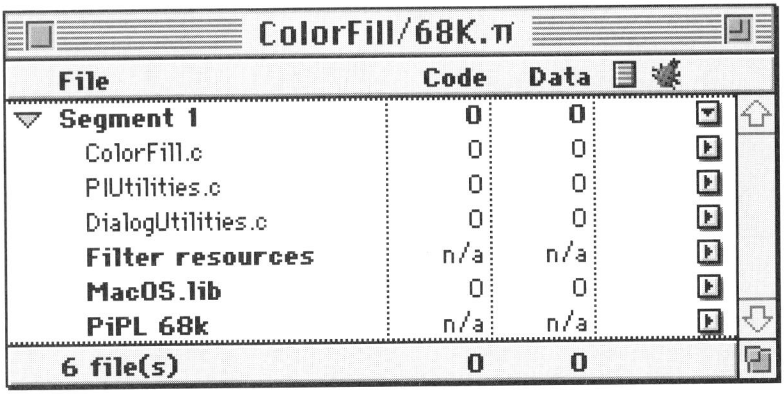

File	Code	Data		
▽ **Segment 1**	0	0	▼	⇧
ColorFill.c	0	0	▶	
PIUtilities.c	0	0	▶	
DialogUtilities.c	0	0	▶	
Filter resources	n/a	n/a	▶	
MacOS.lib	0	0	▶	
PiPL 68k	n/a	n/a	▶	⇩
6 file(s)	**0**	**0**		

Figure 10-9. ColorFill 680x0 project file

File	Code	Data		
▽ **Sources**	**0**	**0**	▼	⇧
ColorFill.c	0	0	▶	
DialogUtilities.c	0	0	▶	
PIUtilities.c	0	0	▶	
▽ **Libraries**	**0**	**0**	▼	
InterfaceLib	0	0	▶	
MathLib	0	0	▶	
MWCRuntime.Lib	0	0	▶	
▽ **Group 3**	**0**	**0**	▼	
PiPL PPC	n/a	n/a	▶	
Filter resources	n/a	n/a	▶	⇩
8 file(s)	**0**	**0**		

Figure 10-10. ColorFill PowerPC project file

If you would like to be able to support the Photoshop plug-in architecture in your programs, the first thing you need to do is to get hold of the Photoshop SDK. Then you need to learn it inside and out. This may take some time, but it will be well worth it. Depending on how many of the different types of plug-ins you want to support, this may be a large or even larger job. Basically, learn the specification and then work on implementing it, backward. If you are even thinking about this in any serious way, you don't need me to tell you what you're getting into. It will be no small task, but it can be done.

TV Tube Filter

The second filter we develop in this chapter is called TV Tube (Figure 10-11) and was written by Troy Gaul. Troy based this filter on the Dissolve sample, as we did with the ColorFill filter. Because TV Tube is structurally similar to ColorFill, we will only discuss the differences in this section.

The most obvious difference is the fact that the filter does a different type of filtering. TV Tube gives images a look as if you were looking at them with a magnifying glass on a television screen or

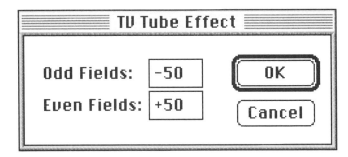

Figure 10-11. TV Tube movable, modal options dialog box

computer monitor. The value of each pixel in each plane of each odd row is increased or decreased by a specific amount. The same is done for each even row. If you use values such as –50 and +50 for the two rows, you get the TV Tube effect.

Troy made TV Tube compatible with Photoshop 2.5 and previous versions by making sure he did not use any 3.0-specific features in his filter, unless they were implemented. This would prevent any crashes from trying to use a 3.0 feature while running Photoshop 2.5. He also added a PiMI resource into his filter to accompany his PiPL. The PiMI resource is the precursor to the PiPL and allows Photoshop 2.5 and previous versions to use the filter.

Lastly, Troy added warning alerts to his filter's resource file (Figure 10-12). This is to ensure that 2.5 compatibility is kept. Older versions of the SDK contain these alerts, but version 3.0 does not. By adding them to his resource file, if Photoshop 2.5 attempts to access the alerts, they will be where it thinks they should be. Photoshop 3.0 will essentially ignore these extra resources.

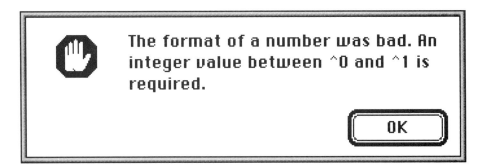

Figure 10-12. Example of a warning alert

Compiling Our Filter

Except for the few changes mentioned earlier, the TV Tube filter is compiled in, more or less, the same way as the ColorFill filter. You can choose to go 680x0 only (Figure 10-13), PowerPC only (Figure 10-14), or fat by simply building different versions of the projects.

Ideas For Other Filters

I have no shortage of ideas for Photoshop filters. I only wish I had the time to write them all. Here is a partial list that you may consider implementing yourself. Some of these can be done in Photoshop today by using numerous steps. The nice thing about filters is that you can take all those steps and roll them into a filter that performs them all at once. If you end up creating any of these, please don't forget to send me a copy to play with.

Oil Spill. This filter will invert the pixels around the edge of the selection to make it look as if an oil spill has just occurred. Watch out for the wildlife.

MultiFilter. This filter would simply call other filters from within itself. When it is called, it would allow you to preconfigure other filters and then run them sequentially all in one step. For example,

File	Code	Data	📄	🐛
▽ TV Tube	0	0		▼
TVTube.c	0	0		▶
PIUtilities.c	0	0		▶
DialogUtilities.c	0	0		▶
MacOS.lib	0	0		▶
▽ **Resources**	**0**	**0**		▼
PiMI	n/a	n/a		▶
PiPL 68k	n/a	n/a		▶
WarningAlerts	n/a	n/a		▶
Filter Resources	n/a	n/a		▶
8 file(s)	**0**	**0**		

TVTube/68K.π

Figure 10-13. TV Tube 680x0 project file

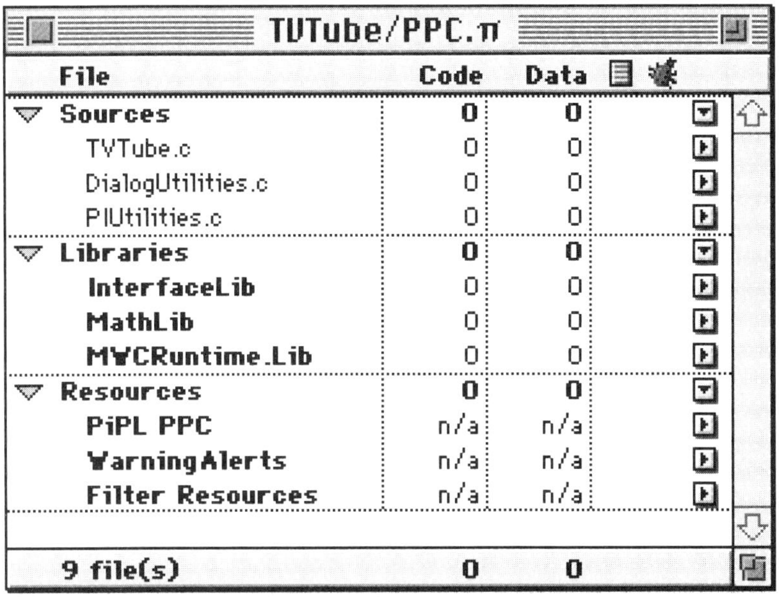

File	Code	Data	目 🐝
▽ **Sources**	**0**	**0**	▼
TVTube.c	0	0	▶
DialogUtilities.c	0	0	▶
PIUtilities.c	0	0	▶
▽ **Libraries**	**0**	**0**	▼
InterfaceLib	0	0	▶
MathLib	0	0	▶
MWCRuntime.Lib	0	0	▶
▽ **Resources**	**0**	**0**	▼
PiPL PPC	n/a	n/a	▶
WarningAlerts	n/a	n/a	▶
Filter Resources	n/a	n/a	▶
9 file(s)	**0**	**0**	

Window title: TVTube/PPC.π

Figure 10-14. TV Tube PowerPC project file

one MultiFilter setup might preconfigure a Blur and then a Crystallize with a cell size of 10. You could save this configuration with a specific name and then automatically perform the work all in one simple step. This might also be called FilterMacros. Kai, are you listening?

Fade. This filter would fade an image out to any color and in any direction. Using this filter you could take an image and fade it to black, or white, or red, or blue. . . .

Filter Tips

Photoshop filters are exciting things on which to work. The Photoshop SDK is very intense and can be confusing at times. But if you stick with it, and watch the code in action, you will be developing cool filters in no time. Here is a list of things to keep in mind while developing your Photoshop filters.

• When you create a fat Photoshop filter, you don't do it the same way we have learned in the rest of the book. Photoshop makes special provisions for the location of the 680x0 and the PowerPC code. Simply, you store the 680x0 code in a code resource and the PowerPC code in the data fork of the Plug-in. This allows your plug-in to be compatible with previous versions of Photoshop while being able to take advantage of native power in Photoshop 3.0 or later. Using techniques you've learned throughout the book, however, you should be able to write a PowerPC native filter easily that worked under versions of Photoshop previous to version 3.0.

- For the sake of time and energy, our filters in this chapter support only RGB and CMYK image modes. Your filter may support other image modes including Grayscale, Bitmap, Indexed Color, and more. Make sure you test your filter in all of these modes to ensure that it works properly and as expected. Flags for the modes your filter supports are stored in the PiPL resource.

- Watch for issues relating to compatibility if you want to make your filter work with version 3.0 and earlier versions such as 2.0 or 2.5 of Photoshop. The SDK has changed drastically with 3.0. Make sure you obtain older versions of the SDK in order to know the differences.

- Make sure you compile your code as native on the PowerPC and do your best to optimize inner loops. Photoshop filters can take a lot of horse power, but can really scream when they are optimized. Most users will prefer a filter optimized for speed, as opposed to size, when it comes to working on their large images.

- The Photoshop 3.0 SDK gives you lots of features for free. Make sure you look at all the available functions in the header files supplied with the SDK. These simple utilities will save you hours of programming time.

CHAPTER ELEVEN

Components

In the beginning there was the bit, and it was Clear.

—Doug McKenna

Introduction

With the advent of QuickTime, Apple developed the Component Manager to help handle many of the different pieces or components of the QuickTime architecture. Things like movie controllers, compression algorithms, and other features were implemented as components. A component is simply a code resource that has a fixed yet expandable programming interface. In a way, Apple took the concept of the generic code resource and put a few restraints on it—not to limit its usefulness, but to increase its ability to be used by many different programs and in many different environments.

Components are pieces of code that provide a specific service to one or more clients. These clients can consist of system extensions, applications, or even other components. Components are designed in such a way that a particular component usually offers a specific type of service. That is, a component may provide image compression or decompression services. An application could call the component to compress or decompress an image. The application need not know anything about the algorithm used, but only how to interface with the specific type of component itself. The Component Manager makes this interfacing simple and standard for all components of the same type.

The Component Manager keeps track of what components are currently available and handles routing requests from clients to the proper one. Components are identified by three main criteria—the type of service provided, the level of service provided, and the manufacturer of the component. This allows many different manufacturers to create components of the same type (like an image compressor), while also allowing different levels of service (30 percent compression or 50 percent compression). The Component Manager keeps it all straight and allows the client to simply request a 50 percent compression component without caring who the manufacturer is or how many other components may exist of that type. The client can be as specific or as general as need be when requesting the services of a particular type of component.

Components themselves respond to a variety of messages that the client or Component Manager send to them. Many of these are standard, such as the open, close, can do, and version messages. Along with these standard messages, your component can also define its own custom messages. Along with your custom messages, you also define your own custom parameters for each. This allows you to provide to your clients just about any service in any way you see fit. They need only know the proper calling conventions, which you provide in a header file. When you ship your component, you ship the component file itself, which is normally placed in the Extensions folder, and a header file that contains any information needed by the client to use the services of your component.

Component Code

In this chapter, we will be creating a very simple component in order to show you how it all fits together. Our component provides two simple services—a beeping service and a menu bar flashing service. We can tell our component to beep a specific number of times and/or flash the menu bar a specific number of times. Not too exciting, you say? The nice thing about our component is that it is simple and gives us the building blocks to edit our code to create a component to do whatever we like. Another good thing about our component is that it takes advantage of the Component Manager version 3.0. That is, we create a PowerPC native component to squeeze every last possible bit of power out of the Power Macintosh.

One thing to note is that even though we are creating a PowerPC native component, which is basically a code fragment, it still must be compatible with the 680x0 Macintosh and, therefore, has a single entry point—much like other code resources we have looked at previously. However, because we also want to support the PowerPC in native mode, we need to perform some pretty strange magic throughout this code. Strap yourself in; here we go.

```
pascal ComponentResult main (ComponentParameters *params,
                             Handle storage);


#ifdef __powerc
    INSTANTIATE_ROUTINE_DESCRIPTOR(FatCanDo);
    INSTANTIATE_ROUTINE_DESCRIPTOR(FatOpen);
    INSTANTIATE_ROUTINE_DESCRIPTOR(FatClose);
    INSTANTIATE_ROUTINE_DESCRIPTOR(FatVersion);

    INSTANTIATE_ROUTINE_DESCRIPTOR(FatDoBeep);
    INSTANTIATE_ROUTINE_DESCRIPTOR(FatDoFlash);

    RoutineDescriptor MainRD = BUILD_ROUTINE_DESCRIPTOR
            (uppComponentRoutineProcInfo, main);
    ProcInfoType __procinfo = uppComponentRoutineProcInfo;
#endif

pascal ComponentResult main(ComponentParameters *params,
                            Handle storage)
```

The first thing we need to do is to define our function prototype for the main entry point. A component takes two parameters and returns a ComponentResult, which is a long. The first parameter is a pointer to a structure that contains information that the component uses to determine the message with which it is being called and to determine the parameters to that message. There are also flags and other information in this structure that we will look at later. The second parameter is a handle to our private data storage. Our component can allocate this memory and have the Component Manager automatically pass it to us each time, as a parameter, whenever it is called—much like a control panel cdev code resource. Because there may be multiple instances of your component running at any time, you should use this mechanism to store any state data for your component, as opposed to using global variables in your code.

You'll notice that if we are running on a PowerPC, we need to do some special things right away in order to make things work properly. The INSTANTIATE_ROUTINE_DESCRIPTOR macro is a really neat trick that allows us to create routine descriptors easily for all of our functions for use on the PowerPC.

```
#define INSTANTIATE_ROUTINE_DESCRIPTOR(funcName) \
    RoutineDescriptor funcName##RD = \
    BUILD_ROUTINE_DESCRIPTOR (upp##funcName##ProcInfo, funcName)
```

Since components normally use the CallComponentFunction or Call-ComponentFunctionWithStorage functions to dispatch to their routines, and since the Component Manager is currently 680x0 code, we must be sure to pass a universal procedure pointer to these functions when we call them. The INSTANTIATE_ROUTINE_DESCRIPTOR macro allows us to create a global routine descriptor easily that can be used to access all of our component routines. For example,

```
INSTANTIATE_ROUTINE_DESCRIPTOR(FatCanDo);
```

equates to

```
RoutineDescriptor FatCanDoRD = BUILD_ROUTINE_DESCRIPTOR
    (uppFatCanDoProcInfo, FatCanDo);
```

So, assuming we've defined uppFatCanDoProcInfo elsewhere, which we have, we end up with a global variable in our PowerPC code called FatCanDoRD that can be used with the following macros to make our source code as similar as possible for both the 680x0 and the PowerPC. If you study each macro, you will see that the PowerPC versions make use of the ## operator to recreate the proper global variable name in order to call the component routine that we care about. When we call the CallComponentFunctionUniv macro under the 680x0, it calls the function name we pass in the funcName parameter. When we call the CallComponentFunctionUniv macro under the PowerPC, it tacks on the RD characters to the funcName parameter and executes our instantiated global variable of the same name. All in all, it is a really slick trick.

```
#ifdef __powerc

#define CallComponentFunctionWithStorageUniv \
    (storage, params, funcName) \
    CallComponentFunctionWithStorage(storage, params, &funcName##RD)
#define CallComponentFunctionUniv(params, funcName) \
    CallComponentFunction(params, &funcName##RD)

#else
```

```
#define CallComponentFunctionWithStorageUniv \
    (storage, params, funcName) \
    CallComponentFunctionWithStorage(storage, params, \
    (ComponentFunctionUPP)funcName)
#define CallComponentFunctionUniv(params, funcName) \
    CallComponentFunction(params, (ComponentFunctionUPP)funcName)

#endif
```

The ## preprocessor operator provides a way to concatenate actual arguments during the expansion of a macro. If a parameter name is adjacent to the ##, the parameter itself is inserted at that position. The ## and any surrounding white space are removed. Therefore, the macro

```
#define concat(first, second) first ## second
```

when called as

```
concat(Mac, intosh)
```

would yield

```
Macintosh
```

The word Macintosh would then attempt to be compiled by the compiler, which probably wouldn't get too far. But you can see how this can be a useful feature of which to take advantage, as we have done here.

```
{
    ComponentResult    result = noErr;

#ifndef __powerc
    long oldA4;
    oldA4 = SetCurrentA4();
#endif

    if (params->what < 0) {
        switch (params->what) {
            case kComponentOpenSelect:
                result = CallComponentFunctionUniv
                    (params, FatOpen);
```

```
                                break;

                        case kComponentCloseSelect:
                                result = CallComponentFunctionWithStorageUniv
                                        (storage, params, FatClose);
                                break;

                        case kComponentCanDoSelect:
                                result = CallComponentFunctionUniv
                                        (params, FatCanDo);
                                break;

                        case kComponentVersionSelect:
                                result = CallComponentFunctionUniv
                                        (params, FatVersion);
                                break;

                        case kComponentTargetSelect:
                                result = CallComponentFunctionWithStorageUniv
                                        (storage, params, FatTarget);
                                break;

                        case kComponentRegisterSelect:
                        default:
                                result = paramErr;
                                break;
                }
        } else {
                switch (params->what) {
                        case kDoBeepSelect:
                                result = CallComponentFunctionUniv
                                        (params, FatDoBeep);
                                break;

                        case kDoFlashSelect:
                                result = CallComponentFunctionUniv
                                        (params, FatDoFlash);
                                break;

                        default:
                                result = paramErr;
                                break;
                }
        }

#ifndef __powerc
        SetA4(oldA4);
#endif

        return result;
}
```

Our main function is nothing more than a big, old dispatcher. It simply looks at the message that is being passed and calls the proper function using our macros described earlier. The only thing to note is that under 680x0 we use the A4 routines mentioned previously to give us access to global variables and data. This is more for ease of our programming than anything else. It saves us having to worry about if we are using any globals or not, since sometimes you are using globals when you don't even think you are, such as when hard coding a string in your code under CodeWarrior. The other interesting thing is that this code actually contains two switch statements. The first is included to check for Apple-defined component messages—those that are less than 0. The other is included to handle our own messages—those that are greater than or equal to 0. This really doesn't need to be implemented this way, but it can make it easier to see how the messages are broken down.

Open Message

The open message is a required message that the component receives when a client requests it to be opened via the OpenComponent or OpenDefaultComponent call. This is your chance to initialize the component, allocate any needed global memory, and load any needed resources. Your component must support this request, although it need not do anything during it.

You will note that in our component's open function, we allocate and initialize a structure called PrivateGlobals, as in the following code. We use this structure to keep track of instance-specific information in our component. Remember, there may be any number of instances of our component running at one time, so this is the recommended way to maintain global variables within the component.

```
typedef    struct    PrivateGlobals
{
    Component           self;
}
PrivateGlobals, *PrivateGlobalsPtr, **PrivateGlobalsHdl;

pascal ComponentResult FatOpen(ComponentInstance self)
{
    ComponentResult    result = noErr;
    PrivateGlobals**   globals;
```

```
        globals = (PrivateGlobals**)NewHandleClear
            (sizeof(PrivateGlobals));
    if (globals != nil) {
        (*globals)->self = (Component)self;
        SetComponentInstanceStorage(self, (Handle)globals);
    } else result = MemError() ? MemError() : memFullErr;

    return result;
}
```

Our open function is very straightforward. We first allocate our private global data using the NewHandleClear function to allocate our memory in the current heap. Note that we do not use NewHandle-SysClear, which is a common mistake when writing components. If we were to use NewHandleSysClear, the memory would be allocated in the system heap, which is not what we want in this case. Assuming the memory allocation is successful, we can fill in the values of our globals and ultimately alert the Component Manager that we are using some global data by calling the SetComponentInstanceStorage. This will ensure that each time this is called, each individual instance will receive the proper global storage handle as a parameter to the call.

> If we thought our component was going to be registered globally (as opposed to our test bed, which only registers the component as available locally to our test application), we would need to set the A5 world of the instance during our open call. We would have simply called the SetComponentInstanceA5 function to ensure that when the component is called, the proper A5 world is current. In our case, the component is only used in one A5 world, which belongs to our test application. In reality, it doesn't hurt to call the A5 functions even if you don't think the component will be used globally at all.

Close Message

When a client calls CloseComponent, your component receives a close message. This is your chance to deallocate any global memory you may have allocated during your open call. Your component must support this request although it need not do anything during it.

```pascal
pascal ComponentResult FatClose(Handle storage,
                                ComponentInstance self)
{
    ComponentResult   result = noErr;
    PrivateGlobals**  globals = (PrivateGlobals**) storage;

    if (globals != nil) {
        DisposeHandle((Handle)globals);
        globals = nil;
    }

    return result;
}
```

When our component is called with the close message, it simply disposes of the global data if it exists. You may wonder why we have to check to see if it exists. Well, it seems that the Component Manager will send your component a close message even if the open message fails. Therefore, we do the check to avoid any crashing effect, which may or may not be enjoyed by the user, if our open failed before the memory was allocated.

Can Do Message

Clients sometimes want to find out if a component supports a particular message or function and will call the ComponentFunctionImplemented call to do so. When this is called, the component receives a can do message. This gives clients an easy way to evaluate the capabilities of a particular component. The component must support this request.

```pascal
pascal ComponentResult FatCanDo(short selector)
{
    switch(selector) {

        case kComponentOpenSelect:
        case kComponentCloseSelect:
        case kComponentCanDoSelect:
        case kComponentVersionSelect:
        case kDoBeepSelect:
        case kDoFlashSelect:
            return true;
            break;

        default:
            return false;
            break;
    }
}
```

Our component's can do function simply consists of a switch statement that compares the requested message to the messages we support. If they match, we return true; otherwise, we return false. As we add new messages to our component's arsenal, we need to add them to this function in order to return the proper information for a can do request.

Version Message

What version are you using? That might be a question you hear quite a bit when you deal with many different software programs. The version message is a required message that the component must support in order to return the version number to a client. Clients call the Get-ComponentVersion function in order to obtain the version of a component.

```
enum
{
    interfaceRevision = 0x00010001
};

pascal ComponentResult FatVersion(void)
{
    return interfaceRevision;
}
```

Our component's version function simply returns the version of the component itself. Simple and to the point.

Other Predefined, Unrequired Messages

There are other predefined messages that our component does not handle and that are not required. These messages include the register and unregister messages, which the component can receive when it is registered and unregistered, respectively. Another message is the target message, which allows a component to override another component. These are all advanced messages that you may or may not need, depending on the purpose of your component. Our particular component does not need to handle these messages, so they are not discussed here. The Component Manager chapter in *Inside Macintosh* fully describes these and other messages that can be optionally supported by a component.

Do Beep Message

The first of our component's custom messages is the do beep message. This message accepts the number of times to beep as a parameter and returns the same number as another parameter. Our function, being a component function, is declared as Pascal, as are all other component functions. Otherwise, it is about as standard as any other function you may see. If you like, you can even pass the global instance storage to the function. In our case, we chose not to do this, since it does not require access to any data stored there.

```pascal
pascal ComponentResult FatDoBeep(short inBeepTimes,
                          short *outBeepTimes)
{
    ComponentResult    result = noErr;

    *outBeepTimes = inBeepTimes;
    if (inBeepTimes > 0) {
        short   i;
        for (i=1;i<=inBeepTimes;++i)
            SysBeep(0);
    } else result = kGenericError;

    return result;
}
```

As you can see, the do beep function is quite simple. It sets the outBeepTimes parameter to be the same value as the inBeepTimes parameter. It then loops inBeepTimes times, beeping via SysBeep each iteration. Talk about simple! Mind you, you could do just about anything in this function that you can do in an application—open resource files, load resources, allocate memory, just about anything.

Do Flash Message

The second custom message that our component handles is the do flash message. This function works similarly to the do beep function, but accepts an extra parameter. Not only do we allow the clients to specify how many times to flash the menu bar, but we also allow them to set the delay time (in ticks) between each flash.

```
pascal ComponentResult FatDoFlash(short inFlashTimes,
            long inDelayTime, short *outFlashTimes)
{
    ComponentResult    result = noErr;

    *outFlashTimes = inFlashTimes;
    if (inFlashTimes > 0) {
        short    i;
        long       outTicks;
        for (i=1;i<=inFlashTimes;++i) {
            FlashMenuBar(0);
            Delay(inDelayTime, &outTicks);
            FlashMenuBar(0);
            Delay(inDelayTime, &outTicks);
        }
    } else result = kGenericError;

    return result;
}
```

As you can see, the do flash function is just as simple. It sets the outFlashTimes parameter to be the same value as the inFlashTimes parameter. It then loops inFlashTimes times, flashing via FlashMenuBar and delaying via Delay for each iteration.

You've just had an in-depth look at our component. As you can see, there really are no secrets. It's rather simple to create a component. It looks similar to many other code resources in its structure. As you will see in the rest of this chapter, there are still some interesting tricks you need to pull out of your hat in order to make it all work on the Power Macintosh, but we have outlined it all for you, so it shouldn't be too difficult. Also, look at the code that accompanies this chapter to gain a deeper understanding of the macros introduced at the beginning of this chapter. They may look strange at first, but after they click and you understand them, you will find them extremely useful in your component development. This would be a good place to take a break if you need one.

The thng Resource

Before you can really use a component, you need to have a way to tell the Component Manager a bit about it. Our component file contains a resource of type thng that does just that. This resource contains information that allows the client and the Component Manager to access the component itself easily. The thng resource is normally stored as ID 128 in the component's resource file.

The thng resource has been extended for Component Manager 3.0, which we use in this book. The main changes in version 3.0 include the support of PowerPC native components and components that contain code for multiple platforms—the equivalent of a fat component. Version 3.0 also includes an automatic version control system that ensures that the most recent version of a particular component is always registered. Let's take a look at the structure of the thng resource in the following code.

```
OSType               component type
OSType               component sub type
OSType               component manufacturer
unsigned long        component flags (bits are as follows)
     31.         component wants to be registered at startup
     30.         use fast dispatch when calling component
     24-29.      reserved
     16-23.      type flags
     8-15.       sub type flags
     0-7.        manufacturer flags
unsigned long        component flags mask
OSType               component code resource type
short                component code resource ID
OSType               component name resource type
short                component name resource ID
OSType               component info resource type
short                component info resource ID
OSType               component icon resource type
short                component icon resource ID
long                 component version
long                 component register flags (bits are as follows)
     4-31.       reserved
     3.          component has multiple platforms
     2.          component auto version include flags
     1.          component wants unregister
     0.          component do auto version
short                component icon family resource ID
long                 elements in platform array
ComponentPlatformInfo    platform array []
     long      component flags (bits are as defined above)
     OSType    component code resource type
     short     component code resource ID
     short     platform type
```

Now that you know what it looks like, let's explain it a bit more in detail. As you know, each component is designated by its type, subtype, and manufacturer. These are the first three items in the thng resource. Following this basic information are the component flags. The component wants to be registered at startup bit tells the Component Manager to register the component at computer startup, assuming it is in a file of type thng and can be found in the Extensions folder. The use fast dispatch, when calling component bit, allows for faster dispatching to a component and is mainly used by QuickTime. The component flag's mask field should be set to 0, but allows you to specify which flags are relevant during a component search operation during a call to the Component Manager routines FindNextComponent or CountComponents. The next group of resource types and ID numbers allow you to specify where the 680x0 component code, the component name string, information string, and icon resource are stored.

According to one of the guys who wrote the tech note on how to create PowerPC components, the Fast Dispatch bit exists as a mechanism to replace your entry point (a C switch statement for example) with a jump table that you write in assembly language. This avoids extra copying of stack variables, since you can perform the dispatching with a JMP instruction instead of a JSR. If using fast dispatching, the Component Manager dispatches from the caller with the caller's parameters on the stack by jumping to your component, which then jumps to the method call. Then the component will return directly to the original caller. Otherwise, the caller's parameters on the stack are copied once more by the Component Manager for the JSR to the component. This will dispatch to the method call with a JSR, which finally returns back to the Component Manager. The overall savings is a very small amount of time, but it is important for QuickTime.

Information after this point in the resource is new with version 3.0. Continuing along, we find the component version field, which is used for the new automatic version control option. The component register flags allow us to specify other criteria for our component. If the component supports multiple platforms, the component's Has Multiple Platforms bit should be set. If this bit is not set, then the following component platform information is ignored and it is assumed that the component contains only 680x0 code. The component's Auto Version Include Flags bit tells the Component Manager to use the component flags when searching for other components during an automatic version control search. Normally, the Component Manager only searches by type, subtype, and manufacturer. The component's Wants Unregister bit tells the Component Manager that your component wants to be called when it is unregistered, which is normally not done by default.

The component's Do Auto Version bit specifies if you want automatic version control to be used for your component. If an older version is found during a register, it will be unregistered and the new version will be registered in its place. This ensures that the most recent version is always registered. Next we have the component icon family resource ID. In version 3.0, a component can have an entire icon family for its icon information, as opposed to just a black-and-white ICON resource.

Now the fun stuff. The component platform array begins with a count of how many platform information structures are listed. Each platform information structure contains component flags (as described earlier), the resource type of the platform-specific code, the resource ID of the platform-specific code, and the platform type. By including two platform information structures at the end of your thng—one for 680x0 and one for PowerPC—you essentially end up with a fat component. The nice thing about it is that you can store each piece of code in a separate resource type and can create a 680x0-only or PowerPC-only version simply by changing the thng resource. No recompilation is required.

Component Tester Code

Now that we've created a component and explored the thng resource that is used to identify it, we need some way to call it. We've created a program called Component Tester that allows us to do just that. This little utility application allows us to register, call, and unregister our component (Figure 11-1). We can compile our tester as a 680x0 application or a PowerPC application, and can call either the 680x0 component or the fat component from either one. It will all work fine, assuming you are running Component Manager 3.0 or later. Let's examine the code.

Because the main portion of the application is standard user interface and Dialog Manager-type code, there is no sense in looking at it. (We wouldn't want to waste pages, would we?) So in the following code we will take a look at the main functions that are called when we register, unregister, and call the component to perform its custom work. The first function is called when the user clicks the Register Component Resource... button.

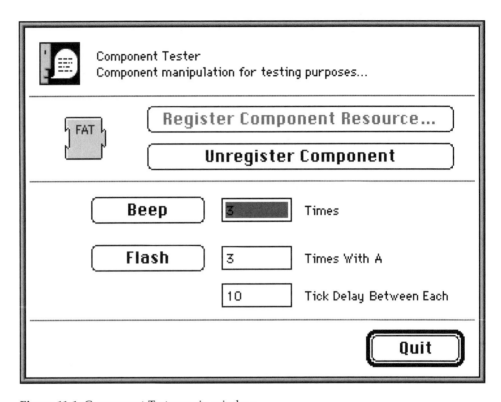

Figure 11-1. Component Tester main window

```
typedef         ComponentInstance FatComponent;
FatComponent    gFatComponent = nil;

OSErr DoRegister(void)
{
    OSErr              err = noErr;
    SFTypeList         typeList = {'thng', '????', '????', '????'};
    StandardFileReply  reply;

    StandardGetFile(nil, 1, typeList, &reply);
    if (reply.sfGood) {

        short fRefNum = FSpOpenResFile(&reply.sfFile, fsRdPerm);

        if (fRefNum != -1) {
            ComponentResourceHandle thngResH =
                (ComponentResourceHandle)
                Get1Resource(kComponentResourceType, 128);
```

```
            if (thngResH) {
                gFatComponent =
                    (FatComponent)RegisterComponentResource
                    (thngResH, registerComponentNoDuplicates);
                ReleaseResource((Handle)thngResH);
                if (gFatComponent == nil)
                    err = -1;
            } else err = ResError() ? ResError() : resNotFound;

            CloseResFile(fRefNum);

        } else err = ResError() ? ResError() : fnfErr;

    } else err = -128;
    return err;
}
```

The DoRegister function allows the user to select a file of type thng that contains our component resource, also of type thng. Once chosen, the thng resource of ID 128 is loaded into memory and is passed to the Component Manager RegisterComponentResource function. After this function has completed successfully, the component is available for clients to open and access it. The component will receive a register message when it is registered, so it can allocate any memory that it may need or prepare itself in any particular way. Some components also check the computing environment when they are registered to make sure they can operate under the current conditions.

Once registered, the Beep and Flash buttons are enabled, since we now have access to the routines within the component. When the user clicks the Beep button, for example, the value from the Beep Times editable text box is read in and passed to the Beep function. The Beep function then opens the component to create a component instance by calling the Component Manager OpenComponent function. The component will receive an open message when OpenComponent is called. Once created, the component is ready to be called. We can then easily call the DoBeep function, which is defined in the header file of our component, in order to make the component beep the chosen number of times. Once complete, we close the component instance by calling the Component Manager CloseComponent function. The component will receive a close message when CloseComponent is called. See the following code.

```
OSErr Beep(short beepTimes)
{
    OSErr              err = noErr;
    ComponentInstance  ci;

    ci = OpenComponent((Component)gFatComponent);
    if (ci) {
        short    outBeepTimes;

        err = DoBeep(ci, beepTimes, &outBeepTimes);
        if (err != noErr) ShowError(err, "\pattempting to DoBeep");

        if (outBeepTimes != beepTimes)
            ShowError(kGenericError,
                "\pcomparing beepTimes to outBeepTimes");

        err = CloseComponent(ci);
        if (err != noErr)
            ShowError(err,
                "\pattempting to CloseComponent");
    } else err = kGenericError;

    return err;
}
```

Before we continue, we should look a bit deeper into the DoBeep function. As mentioned, this function is defined in the header file that is made available to clients of our component. The header file contains information needed in order for the clients to be able to call our components routines, one of which is DoBeep. The header file contains the following definition.

```
enum
{
    kDoBeepSelect = 1,
    kDoFlashSelect
};

pascal ComponentResult DoBeep(FatComponent fatInstance,
    short inBeepTimes, short *outBeepTimes)
    ComponentCallNow(kDoBeepSelect, sizeof(short) + sizeof(short*));
```

The ComponentCallNow macro is defined in the Components.h universal header file as the following code.

```
#define ComponentCallNow(callNumber, paramSize) \
    FIVEWORDINLINE(0x2F3C, paramSize, callNumber, 0x7000, 0xA82A)
```

This function call is what allows the Component Manager to pass the proper parameters to each of the component's unique routines. The macro basically consists of 680x0 assembly code that pushes the proper data on the stack and ultimately calls the function within the component. The callNumber parameter is the identification number of the component routine to call, as defined in the header file of the component itself. The paramSize is the sum of the size of all of the parameters being passed to the component. Note also that the DoBeep function is defined as Pascal in nature.

Calling our component to flash the menu bar, when the user presses the Flash button, is very similar to asking the component to beep. The only differences are the number of parameters passed to the DoFlash function. Examine the similarities in this code.

```
OSErr Flash(short flashTimes, long flashDelay)
{
    OSErr               err = noErr;
    ComponentInstance   ci;

    ci = OpenComponent((Component)gFatComponent);
    if (ci) {
        short outFlashTimes;

        err = DoFlash(ci, flashTimes, flashDelay, &outFlashTimes);
        if (err != noErr) ShowError(err, "\pattempting to DoFlash");

        if (outFlashTimes != flashTimes)
            ShowError(kGenericError,
            "\pcomparing flashTimes to outFlashTimes");

        err = CloseComponent(ci);
        if (err != noErr) ShowError(err,
            "\pattempting to CloseComponent");
    } else err = kGenericError;

    return err;
}
```

For the record, here is the definition of the DoFlash function in the component's header file.

```
pascal ComponentResult DoFlash(FatComponent fatInstance,
    short inFlashTimes, long inDelayTime, short *outFlashTimes)
    ComponentCallNow(kDoFlashSelect, sizeof(short) +
        sizeof(long) + sizeof(short*));
```

Lastly, we must unregister the component when all is done, as in the following code.

```
OSErr DoUnregister(void)
{
    OSErr   err = noErr;

    if (gFatComponent) {
        err = UnregisterComponent((Component)gFatComponent);
        if (err == noErr)
            gFatComponent = nil;
    }

    return err;
}
```

Unregistering the component allows it to deallocate its instance of itself and clean up any messes it may have made before the client puts it away for another day. The Component Manager UnregisterComponent function takes care of sending the component an unregister message if the component's Wants Unregister bit is set in the component's thng resource.

Component Tester PowerPC Changes

A few additions are needed in order to write a native version of our tester application. Basically, the changes consist of adding PowerPC glue code that mimics the 680x0 code that is used to call the component's custom routines DoBeep and DoFlash. You may remember that the way the DoBeep and DoFlash routines are defined, they consist of 680x0 inline code. Obviously, you cannot call this 680x0 code when running in native PowerPC mode on a Power Macintosh. Therefore, we need to do something.

Because of the magic of header files and #ifdef statements, the ComponentCallNow function expands to nothing when compiled for the PowerPC. Therefore, the declaration in the header file that looks like the following code

```
pascal ComponentResult DoBeep(FatComponent fatInstance,
    short inBeepTimes, short *outBeepTimes)
    ComponentCallNow(kDoBeepSelect, sizeof(short) + sizeof(short*));
```

ends up looking like the following code on a PowerPC.

```
pascal ComponentResult DoBeep(FatComponent fatInstance,
    short inBeepTimes, short *outBeepTimes);
```

If you attempted to compile this code for the PowerPC, you would get an error stating that the DoBeep function had a prototype, but it did not exist. Therefore, all we have to do is write a DoBeep function that is only compiled for the PowerPC and that calls the Component Manager in such a way to make it call our component properly. Does that make any sense whatsoever? Let's take a look at the following code, then we will try to explain it. Remember, this code is only used when compiling the PowerPC version of our Component Tester utility.

```
extern UniversalProcPtr CallComponentUPP;

enum {
    uppCallComponentProcInfo = kPascalStackBased
            | RESULT_SIZE(kFourByteCode)
            | STACK_ROUTINE_PARAMETER(1, kFourByteCode)
};

pascal ComponentResult DoBeep
    (FatComponent fatInstance, short inBeepTimes, short *outBeepTimes)
{
    #define kDoBeepParamSize (sizeof(DoBeepParams))

    #ifdef powerc
    #pragma options align=mac68k
    #endif

    struct DoBeepParams {
            short               *outBeepTimes;
            short               inBeepTimes;
    };
     typedef struct DoBeepParams DoBeepParams;

        struct DoBeepGluePB {
                unsigned char       componentFlags;
                unsigned char       componentParamSize;
                short               componentWhat;
                DoBeepParams        params;
                ComponentInstance   instance;
    };
    typedef struct DoBeepGluePB DoBeepGluePB;

#ifdef powerc
#pragma options align=reset
#endif
```

```
DoBeepGluePB     myDoBeepGluePB;
myDoBeepGluePB.componentFlags = 0;
myDoBeepGluePB.componentParamSize = kDoBeepParamSize;
myDoBeepGluePB.componentWhat = kDoBeepSelect;
myDoBeepGluePB.params.outBeepTimes = outBeepTimes;
myDoBeepGluePB.params.inBeepTimes = inBeepTimes;
myDoBeepGluePB.instance = (ComponentInstance)fatInstance;

return CallUniversalProc(
CallComponentUPP, uppCallComponentProcInfo, &myDoBeepGluePB);
}
```

The reason this function exists is because you cannot execute 680x0 inline code while running in PowerPC native mode. Therefore, to copy what the CallComponentNow macro does, we create structures in memory in order to mimic the look of the 680x0 stack for the call. Because the call is defined as being Pascal in nature, our parameters are defined in reverse order in our DoBeepParams structure. Our DoBeep-GluePB structure contains other information that needs to exist on the stack when the call is made, including the component flags, the size of the parameters, and the message. The CallUniversalProc function is then passed the address of the myDoBeepGluePB structure as a parameter to the CallComponentUPP function, which is defined externally in the InterfaceLib PowerPC library. The CallComponentUPP function is called and handles the calling of our component routine.

> Note that the DoBeepParams is a mirror image of the actual parameters. Also note that since the structure mirrors a 680x0 stack alignment, any byte parameters get passed as two bytes, not one. You will need to follow any byte-sized parameters with a pad byte.

The DoFlash component routine uses a similar glue function. The only differences for this routine are in the parameters and the message passed. You can use this function as a template for all of your component routines, but keep an eye out for any copy-and-paste errors, which can happen quite easily in a situation like this.

Compiling Our Code

The code for this chapter contains three code resource projects—one for the PowerPC, which ultimately creates a 680x0-only and a fat component, and two application projects that build a 680x0-only (Figure 11-2) and a PowerPC-only application (Figure 11-3) for testing the calling conventions and the components themselves. By experimenting with the source code, you should have no problem writing your own custom component to perform just about any task you like.

File	Code	Data		
ComponentTester 68k.µ				
▽ **Sources**	0	0	• ▾	⇧
ComponentTester.c	0	0	• ▸	
▽ **Resources**	0	0	▾	
ComponentTester.rsrc	n/a	n/a	▸	
▽ **Libraries**	0	0	▾	
MacOS.lib	0	0	▸	⇩
3 file(s)	0	0		

Figure 11-2. 680x0 Component Tester application project

File	Code	Data		
Component Tester PPC.µ				
▽ **Sources**	0	0	• ▾	⇧
ComponentTester.c	0	0	• ▸	
PPCGlue.c	0	0	• ▸	
▽ **Resources**	0	0	▾	
ComponentTester.rsrc	n/a	n/a	▸	
▽ **Libraries**	0	0	▾	
InterfaceLib	0	0	▸	
MWCRuntime.lib	0	0	▸	
ToolsLib.o	0	0	▸	⇩
6 file(s)	0	0		

Figure 11-3. PowerPC Component Tester application project

68k_FatComponent.π				
File	**Code**	**Data**	📄	🐛
▽ **Main Segment**	**0**	**0**		▾
FatComponent.c	0	0		▸
FatComponentCommon.c	0	0		▸
▽ **Group2**	**0**	**0**		▾
MacOS.lib	0	0		▸
FatComponent.rsrc	n/a	n/a		▸
4 file(s)	**0**	**0**		

Figure 11-4. 680x0 portion of our fat component project

PPC_FatComponent.π				
File	**Code**	**Data**	📄	🐛
▽ **Main Group**	**0**	**0**		▾
FatComponent.c	0	0		▸
FatComponentCommon.c	0	0		▸
▽ **Group2**	**0**	**0**		▾
InterfaceLib	0	0		▸
MathLib	0	0		▸
ToolsLib.o	0	0		▸
5 file(s)	**0**	**0**		

Figure 11-5. PowerPC portion of our fat component project

Component Tips

Writing a component can be a real thrill, especially when you have completed it and others are using it from their own programs. By creating a simple system extension file of type thng and a header file describing the component's routines, you have a completely stand-alone functional entity that can be easy to maintain and use. Here are some tips and ideas to watch for when writing a component.

- Like HyperCard externals, components can be a great way to provide needed functionality while hiding your proprietary algorithms. The nice thing about components is that they work with any application that supports them, not just HyperCard. In fact, you could probably write a HyperCard external that interfaced to other components. Now *that* might be cool.

- Depending on what your component does for a living, you may not have to make it PowerPC native. If it simply opens a file and reads some data from it then displays a quick dialog box, making it native might not be a top priority. Eventually, when all Macintosh computers are Power Macintosh computers, you will want to rethink this. For now … it's up to you.

- When your component is called, it is functioning in someone else's environment. That is, an application is calling you and it may have a limited amount of heap space and stack space available for your use. Prepare for the worst and code defensively. In fact, you should code defensively for all of your code resources. You never can tell how adverse the environment in which you will be running may be.

- The next time you are writing an application, think how you might factor some of the features of your program into a component. This may make your application smaller and allow your users to pick and choose the features they like. You can also re-use the component with your next application, making it smaller as well. Not to mention you may be able to license your component to another company for use in their product. You see, writing a component can make you rich!

- Don't get carried away. If you have a little tiny function that simply displays an error alert and beeps a few times, you might not want to write that in the form of a component. Think about it. If the code you are writing into a component is smaller than the rest of the information in the component file, such as the icon and other resources, it may not be a wise decision. As your mother used to say, "I'm sure you'll make the right decision."

CHAPTER TWELVE

Advanced and Undocumented Techniques

That code is teetering on the edge of compatibility.

—Anonymous

Introduction

Throughout this book you have undoubtedly picked up some useful techniques for working with code resources, source code, and development projects in general. Although these techniques have been scattered throughout the chapters, this chapter in particular caters to discussing some very useful techniques that may not be immediately apparent. The concepts in this chapter vary in subject matter, but all have proven to be time-saving tidbits of information. You should note that some of the items in this chapter are documented no place else—but they deserve to be, so we have done so here.

Warning! Portions of the information in this chapter have been known to make certain Apple DTS engineers itch. Some of the techniques described may not be pretty (but they are fun). Mind you, they are also liable to break as future versions of the operating system come into being. The information in this chapter is not guaranteed to work in the future in any way, shape, or form whatsoever. Take this chapter for what it's worth and walk lightly around the innards of the OS! (How's that for a warning, Jim?)

Building Fat Resources

Throughout this book we have shown you how to take advantage of native speed as well as other features of the PowerPC processor and its implementation on the Power Macintosh. Although it's been mentioned in passing, we've never totally discussed how to create a fat resource out of your code resources.

For those of you that may not know yet, if you are skipping around the book a bit, a fat resource is one that contains both 680x0 and PowerPC code in the same package. It will only run on a Power Macintosh, but gives you the best possible performance by choosing, at runtime, whether to execute the 680x0 code or the PowerPC code. This decision is made by the Mixed Mode Manager and is dependent on the ISA of the calling code. That is, if you create a fat resource and it is placed in an application that contains only 680x0 code, you can have the PowerPC code in the fat resource run no matter what, or you can have the Mixed Mode Manager decide which code should run. When the Mixed Mode Manager makes the decision for you, it basically looks at the ISA of the calling code and then calls the code in the fat resource that will not require a mode switch, as described earlier. This saves time by letting the computer stay in the same ISA as it was before the fat resource was called. There are many options that you can set in the RoutineDescriptor of your fat resource to control decisions such as this one.

In order to create a fat resource, you need to use the Rez tool with either ToolServer or MPW. The Rez tool allows you to execute scripts written in the Rez language. Using the Rez language, you can perform a variety of actions on resources in any type of file. It is also very handy for merging resources together along with other data, such as a RoutineDescriptor.

By executing a simple Rez script, we are able to create a fat resource that contains a RoutineDescriptor with two RoutineRecord structures. We specify the output resource type and ID, as well as the ProcInfo values of the functions in the source resources. We then specify the file name, resource type, and ID of the source resources. Rez finds the template for the type fdes in the file MixedMode.r and knows how to put all the pieces together (see the following code).

```
#include "MixedMode.r"

type 'LDEF' as 'fdes';

resource 'LDEF' (128) {
    $5,     // 68K ProcInfo
    $5,     // PowerPC ProcInfo
    $$Resource("68k LDEF", 'LDEF', 128),
    $$Resource("PPC LDEF No RD", 'LDEF', 128)
};
```

Assuming the script is stored in a file named CreateFatResource.r, we can execute it by having ToolServer or MPW execute a simple command line, as in the following code. Once executed, the target file, (also known as the output file) contains the fat resource. We can then use this fat resource as we see fit.

```
Rez -a CreateFatResource.r -o "Fat LDEF Output File"
```

> Because versions may vary and you may or may not be using ToolServer with CodeWarrior, or THINK C, or may even be using MPW, you should read the documentation that came with your development environment to learn how to execute commands properly. In most cases, you simply type the command line and press the Enter key. After you figure it out once, it should be easy to make changes to suit your specific needs from project to project. You should also read the ToolServer and Rez documentation on the enclosed CD for complete information on using these tools.

Building Safe Fat Resources

Safe fat resources are similar to fat resources except they can be run on both 680x0 machines and the Power Macintosh. In fact, a safe fat resource is exactly the same as a fat resource, except for a short stub of 680x0 code that precedes the RoutineDescriptor. This stub of code is executed the first time the safe fat resource is called and, depending on the type of computer on which it is running (680x0 or Power Macintosh), it modifies itself in a manner that allows it to execute properly on either machine. If you are familiar with assembly language and want to delve deeper into what this code stub actually does, you should look at it in the MixedMode.r file that comes with your development environment. For those of you that really want more control over the safe fat resource, you can easily edit this code stub to suit your specific needs.

In order to create a safe fat resource, you perform the exact same steps as creating a fat resource, except your Rez file is slightly different. Instead of using the template for fdes found in MixedMode.r, you use the template for sdes. The safe fat resource template contains the 680x0 code stub that we discussed earlier and automatically tacks it on to the beginning of the target resource in the output file. (See the following code).

```
#include "MixedMode.r"

type 'LDEF' as 'sdes';

resource 'LDEF' (128) {
    $5,    // 68K ProcInfo
    $5,    // PowerPC ProcInfo
    $$Resource("68k LDEF", 'LDEF', 128),
    $$Resource("PPC LDEF No RD", 'LDEF', 128)
};
```

You will probably want to change the name of your Rez script to CreateSafeFatResource.r in order to keep the versions straight, as in the following code. Otherwise, they are, technically, exactly the same.

```
Rez -a CreateSafeFatResource.r -o "Safe Fat LDEF Output File"
```

Using FatMan to Create Fat and Safe Fat Resources

On the CD that came with this book, you will find a program called FatMan. This program, written by yours truly, allows you to create fat and safe fat resources easily by simply choosing the proper settings and typing in some information (Figure 12-1). FatMan does not require you to learn and use the Rez language or any other tools.

Using FatMan, you can easily select the destination resource type and ID, as well as the type and creator of the file to which the resource will be saved. You can also choose if you want the Use Current ISA bit set in the RoutineDescriptor, which can help to optimize the use of your code in specific circumstances. You can choose to copy the resources from one file to another, as well. When selecting the source resources, you tell FatMan how the 680x0 source is stored and how the PowerPC source is stored. You can then tell FatMan to create either a fat or safe fat resource. FatMan will request the files it needs to create

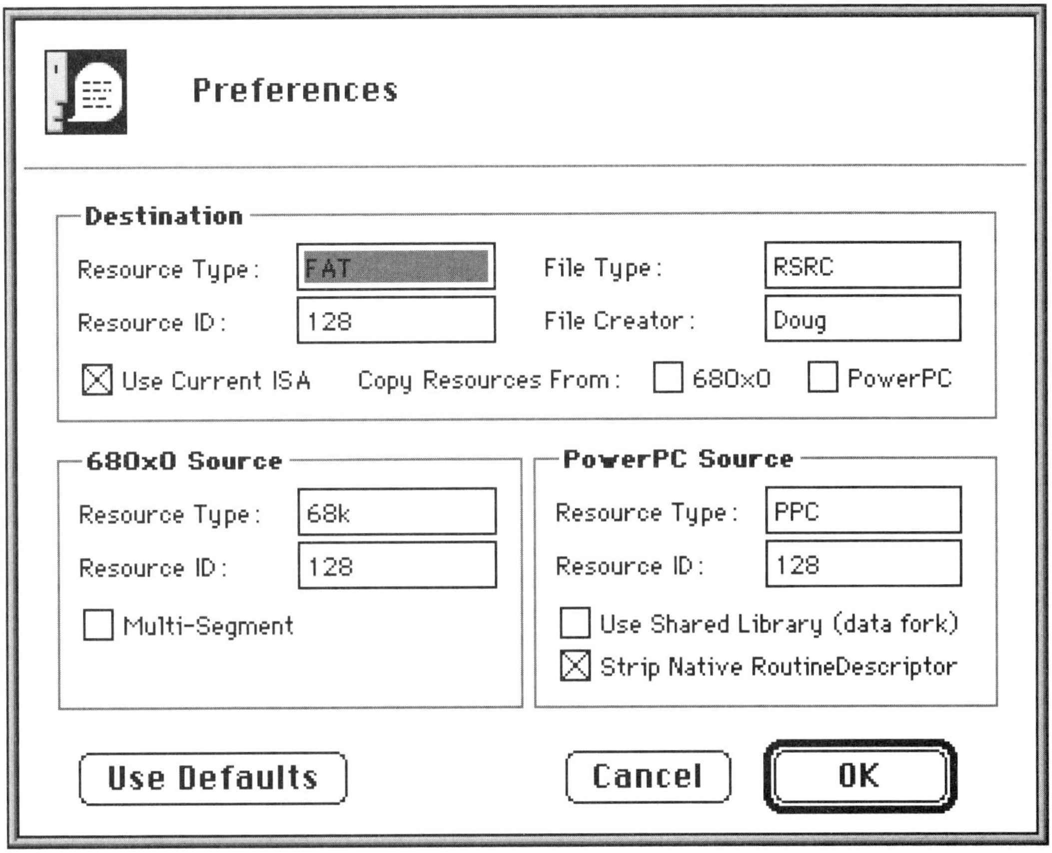

Figure 12-1. FatMan preferences dialog box

the destination resource and ask you to enter the ProcInfo value for the routines. You can use FatMan's ProcInfo Calculator to figure out this value if you do not know it already (Figure 12-2).

After FatMan has done its work, which takes mere seconds, you will have a fat or safe fat resource ready to be used in your program. One thing to note, however, is that FatMan is a development tool that is under development and it may not be perfect. However, in many cases, it can save you valuable time in your programming effort. Use the contact information in the About the Author section of this book to keep up to date with the latest version of FatMan and other source code discussed in this book. Enjoy!

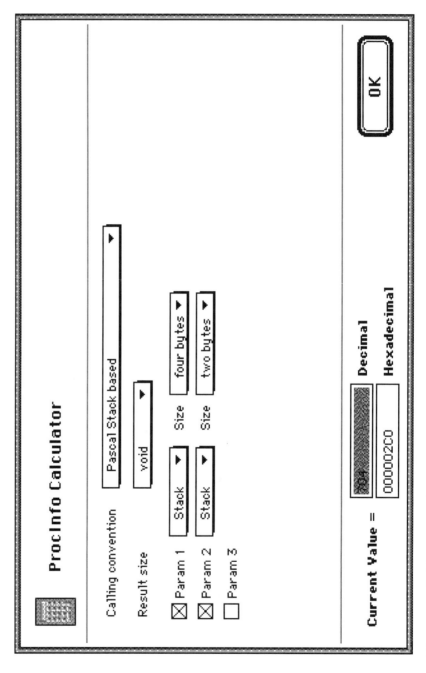

Figure 12-2. FatMan's ProcInfo Calculator dialog box

Multiple Cell Formats in a List

The List Manager is a great thing to have around on the Macintosh. It allows you to create lists of items for users to manipulate. You can even use it to create a spreadsheet-style interface, although you would never want to use it for a real spreadsheet, since it has some pretty serious limitations. Most of the time, you see the List Manager used to display short lists of items, such as possible keyboard layouts as seen in the Keyboard control panel (Figure 12-3).

As we've discussed earlier, the List Manager allows you to customize the look of the data that is displayed in the list by means of a list definition procedure. This function is stored as a resource of type LDEF and is called mainly to draw list cells. The majority of the time, your cells will all look the same. They will all display the same type of data and will draw each cell in a similar manner. However, there may be times when you want certain cells to have the ability to draw items in a way that differs from the others. You could have your list definition know how to draw each type of cell or you could take another, more generic approach.

We've created a list definition that doesn't actually do any drawing whatsoever, yet gives you full customization over the way each individual cell draws itself. (See the following code.) As you know, each cell contains data that is set by using the LSetCell function. Our LDEF assumes that the cell data for a cell consists of a simple structure

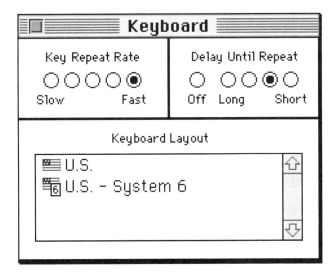

Figure 12-3. A simple list in the Keyboard control panel

containing a universal procedure pointer that ultimately points to a drawing function and a reference constant.

```
typedef void (*RefconLDEFDrawProcType) \
    (Rect *r, Cell cell, ListHandle lh, long refCon);

enum {
    uppRefconLDEFDrawProcInfo = kCStackBased
            | STACK_ROUTINE_PARAMETER(1, SIZE_CODE(sizeof(Rect *)))
            | STACK_ROUTINE_PARAMETER(2, SIZE_CODE(sizeof(Cell)))
            | STACK_ROUTINE_PARAMETER(3, SIZE_CODE(sizeof(ListHandle)))
            | STACK_ROUTINE_PARAMETER(4, SIZE_CODE(sizeof(long)))
};

#if USESROUTINEDESCRIPTORS
typedef UniversalProcPtr RefconLDEFDrawProcUPP;
#else
typedef RefconLDEFDrawProcType RefconLDEFDrawProcUPP;
#endif

typedef struct RefconLDEFCell {
    long                refCon;
    RefconLDEFDrawProcUPP    drawProc;
} RefconLDEFCell, *RefconLDEFCellPtr, **RefconLDEFCellHdl;
```

Whenever a cell is asked to draw itself, the LDEF simply calls the drawing function to do the actual drawing, passing the reference constant as one of its parameters (as in the following code). Other parameters passed to the drawing function include the rectangle, the cell coordinates, and the list handle.

```
void DrawMsg(Boolean fSelect, Rect *r, Cell cell, ListHandle lh)
{
    RefconLDEFCell    cellData;
    short             dataLen;

    // get cell
    dataLen = (short)sizeof(cellData);
    LGetCell((Ptr)(&cellData), &dataLen, cell, lh);

    // call draw proc
    if (cellData.drawProc) {
        EraseRect(r);
        CallRefconLDEFDrawProc(cellData.drawProc, r,
            cell, lh, cellData.refCon);
    }
```

```
        // hilite if selected
    if (fSelect)
          HiliteMsg(fSelect, r);
}
```

Using this mechanism, you can set a different drawing function for every single cell in your list if you so needed. It also lets you use one LDEF for all the lists in your application, since your drawing functions (which are usually the only differing parts of a list definition anyway) are all functions in your program. This makes it much easier to use your source-level debugger to debug your drawing functions and also allows easy access to your application's global variables from within your list. All around, this mechanism works very well and lets you take advantage of the List Manager in a unique and useful way.

To learn more about this technique and see it in action, read Chapter Six, "List Definitions." It uses this technique.

Code Optimization

You may be asking yourself, what is a book on code resources doing talking about code optimization? Well, the answer is, code resources contain code and in order to keep your system running smoothly you want to make sure your code resources are as optimized as possible. The point of the Power Macintosh is speed. But even the fastest processor in the world can't make up for nonoptimized code. This section outlines a few points that you should keep in mind whether you are programming code resources, applications, or any other type of code.

Optimize Inner Loops

Assuming you are writing code that has the equivalent of an inner loop, you should spend most of your time optimizing it, as opposed to code that only executes once in a while. The nature of an inner loop is that the code in that section is executed many times in a row. You should make use of compiler options and processor features, such as the use of registers, to make sure your code is as fast as it can be. Allowing the processor to access certain data from registers, as opposed to memory, saves time that can really speed your loops.

Unroll Loops

Assuming you have a loop that performs some task a specific number of times, you can easily unroll the loop to avoid branching back to the top of the loop. That is, instead of executing one iteration of the loop and then branching back to the beginning of it, you can execute two or four iterations before branching back and starting over. By doing this, you avoid numerous TeST and BRAnch instructions (under 680x0, anyway), and will ultimately save time. This can be especially useful in a time-sensitive loop.

Optimize the Code that Executes the Most

Much like the optimization of inner loops, you should spend time optimizing the code that is executed most often in your program. You can use a tool known as a profiler, which comes with your development environment, to see exactly what code is taking the most time to execute and which functions are executing most frequently. By studying this information, you can choose the code that needs to be optimized first in order to speed up your program the most.

Use Macros Instead of Function Calls

Function calls take time because parameters need to be prepared for the function, the function must then save registers, examine the parameters, do the work, restore the registers, and finally return to the caller. In many cases you may have small utility functions that can be replaced with inline macros instead. When a macro is used, the code that the macro defines is placed inline (i.e., directly in the code itself). No function call is used. If a macro defines ten lines of code, those ten lines will be substituted wherever the macro is used. Although this makes your code larger, it can be a useful technique to provide a burst of speed in time-critical code.

Don't Multiply or Divide

One of the slowest things you can ask your computer to do is to multiply or divide. If you plan on multiplying or dividing by a power of two, you should instead choose to use the shift operator. Instead of multiplying by two, shift the bits one place to the left. Instead of dividing by four, shift the bits two places to the right. The speed increase can be incredible.

Optimize Last

The most important rule regarding optimization is to optimize last (and make sure you leave time for performance tuning if you have a tight schedule). Many people spend too much time optimizing their code early on. This usually makes it less maintainable and often ends up being wasted time since the real bottlenecks of the project aren't exposed early on. You should first make sure your code operates properly with all the functionality you want. Once that is complete, run a profiler over it to figure out where the real bottlenecks are. Finally, optimize those bottlenecks. Very often you will find that you end up optimizing far less code (meaning more of your code stays neat, maintainable, and portable).

Debugging Techniques

There are so many possible causes for errors or crashes in your programs that it would take most of the ink in the world just to list them, much less explain them all. Suffice it to say that this would be close to impossible. After years of programming the Macintosh, you adopt certain techniques that help you through some of the rougher spots. Here are a few of them that I like to use when debugging code resources and other programs.

- Many code resources are called just after they are loaded using GetResource or a similar Resource Manager routine. Use this to your advantage by setting a break point on this routine. When you see your code resource being loaded, you can step right into its code a few steps away, as it is being called.
- Depending on whether a code resource is detached or not, it may appear in memory as a Memory Manager handle or a handle to a resource. Keep this in mind when you are dumping the contents of a heap and looking for your code. It may not appear in the form you assume.
- Code resources may move in memory if they are not locked. You will always want to ensure that while a code resource is being executed, it is locked in memory. If you are experiencing strange crashes at random locations, make sure that your code is locked down during execution. If it is not, you might find it moving out from under itself while it is in the middle of execution. Very bad.
- Many code resources are compiled with a specific header attached to them. This header almost always contains the resource type of the code within it. You can look for this in memory when debug-

ging to make sure you have the right resource. You can also customize your own resource header. See the documentation for your development environment on how to implement this.

If You Have to Support System 6

First of all, try to get out of it in any way you can. Others will agree that System 6 is simply not worth supporting from this point onward. This can be proven by looking at the system requirements of almost all new software coming from Apple. System 6 is no longer a priority.

Because of the fact that some offices still have System 6 machines floating around and many companies like to purchase "complete solutions," some developers are still making their software System 6 compatible. In many cases, this means slipped schedules, especially if you are writing a system extension or similar low-level code. If you keep in mind that System 7 was a major rewrite of the system software, it makes sense why there may be differences between it and previous systems.

If you patch a trap, for example, there may be subtle differences in the original trap under System 6 and System 7. These subtle changes can cause spectacular crashes in strange situations. Most of the time, these crashes will occur on low-end System 6 machines like your trusty Mac Plus. Not that the Mac Plus is a bad machine, but since most developers use Quadras or Power Macintosh computers running System 7, and rarely test on the low-end machines, they tend to have some problems, even in shipping software.

If you are forced to support System 6, you should commit to nothing less than System 6.0.5, which was one of the most stable software versions. System 6.0.7 or 6.0.8 are adequate if you need enhanced sound capabilities. Remember not to depend on Color QuickDraw. Even though it is built in to System 7, it may not exist on a System 6 machine. And don't forget the 68000 chip—it can sometimes exhibit crashes that you will not otherwise catch on your 68030, 68040, or PowerPC. Also, expect to pad your schedule by a few days here and there, because it is almost certain that you will have a crash on a 1MB Mac Plus running System 6.0.5 that will take forever to debug due to the processor speed. Take heed when supporting System 6. It is not an easy task.

Sending AppleEvents from a Code Resource

Believe it or not, you can send AppleEvents from any type of code, including INIT resources. In fact, our MenuScripts project discussed earlier in this book did just that. You should note, however, that even though you can send AppleEvents, don't expect a reply. As you know, AppleEvent replies can be filtered through WaitNextEvent and are handled in the main event loop of an application. Since your INIT resources (or other code resources) do not have a main event loop, they will not be able to receive any replies to an AppleEvent. This is not the end of the world, but it is something of which to be aware when sending AppleEvents from your code resources.

Writing a Daemon Application

A daemon application, also known as a faceless-background application, is a very useful type of program. The daemon application is stored in a file of type appe in most cases. It has absolutely no user interface, including menus, except for it being able to use the Notification Manager to alert the user if needed. It cannot be opened from the Finder, but must be launched programatically via the LaunchApplication function instead. When it is launched, it does not appear in the application menu. The brilliance of the daemon application, however, is that it can send and receive AppleEvents. It is also launched automatically at startup if it is located in the Extensions folder.

The daemon application is written much as a normal application is written. However, there is no need to initialize the WindowManager, MenuManager, and others at application startup. Also, the daemon need only handle null events and AppleEvents in its main event loop. All other user interface-related events are never sent to it.

The fact that the daemon is called with null events indicates that it is given periodic time, just like all applications. If you were planning on writing an INIT that patched SystemTask, for example, simply to obtain periodic time, you can avoid the INIT and the patch by using a daemon application instead. The added benefit is that you can send and receive AppleEvents to and from any other process on the local Macintosh or any Macintosh on the network.

The File Sharing Extension is a daemon application. When you use the Sharing Setup control panel to turn file sharing on and off, it is simply launching and quitting the File Sharing Extension via the Process Manager call LaunchApplication and by sending a Quit AppleEvent. Your daemon application can be used in a similar manner to allow the user to turn it on and off instantly, without having to restart.

Something of which to be aware is that from within a daemon, you cannot make any calls (even ones in the operating system) that cause QuickDraw to be used. You can't even call the Random function. If you attempt to call any standard file routines, for example, your program will crash almost immediately due to the fact that QuickDraw is not initialized in a daemon application. Because of this, all daemon applications also have very little stack space. This can sometimes cause problems and is something for which you should watch.

To summarize, daemon applications

- can call InitGraf
- get only 2K of stack space by default, but can increase this by using SetApplLimit
- should have large variables located in the heap and not locally on the stack
- cannot call other Init_ calls such as InitMenus and InitWindows
- cannot use any QuickDraw routines that draw
- cannot make any other call that may display an alert, including any AppleEvents that may do so
- cannot call ResolveAlias, as it may attempt to display a dialog box if a server needs to be mounted, however, MatchAlias can be used with the KARMNoVI rule

All in all, daemon applications are very useful and offer several advantages to developers and users. They are easier to debug than an INIT and, ultimately, can be more compatible, as they need not patch traps for certain innate functionality. Write a daemon today!

Creating Stand-alones

I'm sure you've seen programs that allow you to create a stand-alone document. HyperCard 2.2 allows you to export a stack as a stand-alone application. That is, once exported in this format, you can double-click the stack and it will run without HyperCard. This is relatively simple to do and is becoming a very popular thing.

Let's assume that you want to create a stand-alone text document reader. First you need to write the program that can display text documents. You should write it in such a way that it gets the data to display from a resource of type TEXT, for example. This is the program that gets created when the user wants a stand-alone reader.

Now you need to write a stand-alone text document maker. This program contains a resource that contains the entire resource fork of the reader. That is, using the FSpOpenRF and FSRead functions, you read the resource fork of the reader as a stream and store it in a re-source in the maker. When the maker wants to create a stand-alone document reader it simply writes the contents of the resource out to a resource fork (using the FSpOpenRF and FSWrite functions), places the text data to be displayed in a resource of the proper type (e.g., TEXT) inside the reader, and then sets the file type to APPL.

You've just created an application that is your original reader program. It can be opened from the Finder and will display the data stored within it. Remember, if you want to create a PowerPC native version of your reader, you may also need to deal with the data fork of the file. We'll leave that as an exercise for the reader. Pun intended.

Patching Traps

You've probably heard of the concept of patching a trap, but what does it mean? A trap is a function that is built in to the operating system. The term trap refers to the fact that the number that represents one of these functions is called a trap word and is stored in a trap table. It is called a word, since it is normally 2 bytes in length. When you patch a trap, you are intercepting the original operating system function and replacing it with a pointer to your own function. When a program attempts to call the original function, it actually, unknow-ingly, executes your function. Your function can then choose to execute the original function if it so desires.

You use the NGetTrapAddress and NSetTrapAddress (or their de-rivatives) to get the original address of a trap and set it to point to your function. You use the original address in order to call through to it if you so choose. Most of the time, you will find that an INIT is what patches traps on a systemwide level. Your code is loaded into the sys-tem heap and the patches are applied. Patches of this nature affect all programs on the computer. You can also patch traps from within an application, which cause only that particular application to be affected by the patches. This is due to the fact that many different copies of the trap tables exist—one systemwide and others for each application.

You should make sure that your patches do as little as possible and execute as fast as possible, because when you patch a trap you be-come a part of the operating system. If your code is slow, you slow the entire computer; every single program running will be effected by your tortoise-like code and your users will become annoyed. Heed this warning.

By patching traps you can alter the functionality of any trap on the Macintosh. For example, you may want to patch the HOpenResFile function in order to look for all files being opened that have the word

"Résumé" in their titles. Whenever a program attempted to open a file containing that name, your patch could choose not to allow the file to be opened. You might even choose to display an alert that tells your employees to work on their résumé at home and not at work. This might be sneaky, but hey, you're paying them, right?

Patching a Register-based Trap

In Chapter Four, "System Extensions," we discussed patching traps that were Pascal in calling convention. However, sometimes you need to patch a trap that is not as simple. Some traps are register-based. That is, these traps take their parameters in registers, as opposed to on the stack, such as the Pascal-style traps. Patching these traps can be a bit difficult on 680x0 Macintosh computers. On Power Macintosh computers, however, it can be quite simple.

For example, let's say you want to patch the File Manager trap Delete (see Traps.h for a list of trap words, including that for Delete). Delete expects that register A0 will contain a pointer to an HFileParam structure. This structure defines the file in question—one that is about to be deleted, in this case. Upon exiting, the Delete trap is supposed to fill register D0 with a word result, (i.e., any error that occurred while trying to delete the file). In order to patch this trap on a 680x0 Macintosh, you will need to write your routine, or at least part of it, in assembly language. This allows you to extract the HFileParam pointer from register A0 and put it in a local variable that you can easily access from your C code.

When you patch a register-based trap, the trap word is in register D1 when your patch gets control. Many operating system traps use bits 9 and 10 (the flag bits) of the trap word to indicate variations of a trap. For example, if you wanted to tell the difference between Delete and HDelete, you need to check bit 9; to tell if a File Manager request was asynchronous or synchronous, you need to check bit 10.

However, patching this trap for the PowerPC is a bit easier, since the use of RoutineDescriptors allows you to write a routine that is passed the parameters "on the stack" from the registers in which they are initially placed. No need for assembly language here. By using the macros provided to create the proper procedure information for your C routine, you can easily access the HFileParam data. If you've made it this far, you probably have what it takes to get this working on your own, so give it a try.

All is not fair in love and war and patching file system traps. You should keep in mind that if you start patching traps like Delete, you should be prepared for the problems that will inevitably arise. There are many idiosyncrasies, beyond the scope of this book, that can happen depending on other software being run on the Macintosh, such as Macintosh File Sharing. For example, Macintosh File Sharing sometimes executes the same file system call twice. That is, it reexecutes a synchronous call as an asynchronous one in order to prevent deadlock conditions. In general, you should do what you can to save and restore all registers before and after execution of your patch to help compatibility. You have been warned, now back to the fun.

System Extension Conflicts

As previously mentioned, most of the time INITs are the programs that patch traps. This can sometimes cause what are known as INIT or system extension conflicts. Because many INITs may be loaded that patch the same traps to do their magic, discrepancies sometimes occur between them. For example, one INIT may assume that a particular trap works in a particular way and only returns one of two possible error codes. If another INIT comes along and also patches that trap, it may decide that it needs to force the original to return yet a third error code. Depending on the order in which the INITs load, which decides the order in which the patches themselves are called, one may not expect the new error code and your code may unexpectedly crash or behave strangely. Issues like this, including many that are much more subtle, are the cause for many problems between system extensions.

Disabling Command-Option-Escape

Under System 7, the system allows you to type Command-Option-Escape simultaneously in order to quit the current application. For most users, this is not a problem and can help get out of sticky situations if your Macintosh freezes up for some reason. However, there may be a case when you do not want a user to be able to quit out of applications in this manner. Network administrators sometimes have this need to ensure security on their machines.

The Command-Option-Escape mechanism makes use of the SysError function. This is the same function that is called to display the "It is now safe to turn off your Macintosh" message after you select Shutdown in the Finder. In order to intercept the Command-Option-Escape sequence, you can simply patch the SysError function and, because SysError is a selector-based trap, watch for selector $4E22 in register D0. If you see this selector, then simply return to the caller, as opposed to jumping to the original SysError. Interception guaranteed.

Getting the Directory ID of the Frontmost Finder Window

It may be useful, at times, for you to be able to get the directory ID of the frontmost window in the Finder. For example, I once wrote a system extension that would create a file in the frontmost Finder window when a specific hot key combination was pressed. In order to do it, I wrote an INIT that first patched PopUpMenuSelect in order to intercept its calls and then had a jGNEFilter to intercept keyboard events for the hot key. When the hot key was pressed, I would use PostEvent to fake a mouse click (with the command key down) over the center of the front window's title bar. You may know that if you normally command-click on the title of a Finder window you see a popup menu that displays the full path to the window (Figure 12-4).

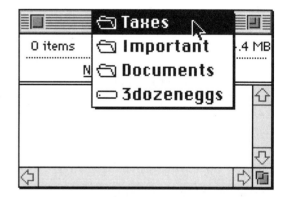

Figure 12-4. Command-clicking on a Finder window's title

My PopUpMenuSelect patch was then called and, instead of actually allowing the menu to be shown, it would simply look at the menu items in reverse order to get the full path and then punt the rest of the call so the popup menu never actually displayed itself. At this point, I had the full path to the window in question. With the full path to the window, I could easily use the PBGetCatInfo function to calculate the vRefNum and directory ID. Armed with this information, creating a file was child's play.

The only shortcoming to this method is that it cannot reliably figure out on which disk a folder on the desktop is located (Figure 12-5). Command-click on the window title of a folder on the desktop and

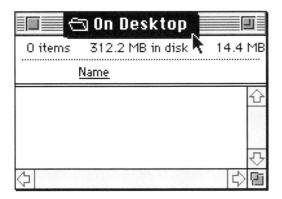

Figure 12-5. Command-clicking on a Finder
window's title that is on the desktop

you will see exactly what I mean. Otherwise, this is an easy, compatible way to get some otherwise hard-to-find information.

Creating Your Own A5 World

You may find it necessary, at some point in your programming endeavors, to draw using QuickDraw at some inopportune time. For instance, let's say you write a system extension that patches HOpenResFile in order to intercept resource files being opened. It is possible that this patch may be called at a time when there is no valid A5 world. Let's say, one step further, that you wanted to draw something on the screen each time your patch was called. If no A5 world existed, you would crash pretty quickly the moment you attempted to draw.

The answer to this dilemma is to create your own A5 world, temporarily, in order to facilitate your need to draw. This is no easy task and the following code may not be the panacea, but it works as of this writing. How's that for a disclaimer? Let's take a look at the code.

```
typedef struct {
    QDGlobals    qd;            // QuickDraw globals
    GrafPtr      thePort;       // a5
    char         stuff[28];     // Misc stuff
    GrafPort     port;          // The color port we open to draw in
} QDWorld;
```

```
typedef struct {
    THz                 oldZone;            // saved heap zone
    UniversalProcPtr    saveDeskHook;       // saved DeskHook
    UniversalProcPtr    saveDragHook;       // saved DragHook
    unsigned char       savedResLoad;       // saved ResLoad
    long                oldA5;              // saved A5
    Ptr                 pFMExist;           // Font Manager initialized flag
    Ptr                 pQDExist;           // QuickDraw initialized flag
    unsigned char       savedFMExist;
            // saved value of Font Manager initialized flag
    unsigned char       savedQDExist;
            // saved value of QuickDraw initialized flag
    QDWorld             qdWorld;            // our QuickDraw world
} A5Params, *A5ParamsPtr;
```

These two structures are used to keep track of the information that we use while we create and use our own A5 world. You will note that we need to save and restore a good number of low-memory globals. This all comes with the territory of hacking QuickDraw, a dangerous task I might add.

The first function we call in the following code is Prepare-A5World. This is the function that takes care of creating and initializing our new A5 world, as well as saving lots of information that we need to restore when we are done. I left the comments in the code, since they really seem to sum up what is being done throughout this function. You should note that this code, in a sense, is balancing on the edge of compatibility and should be used with caution. If you so much as delete one line, you will be asking for problems.

```
void PrepareA5World(A5ParamsPtr pp, Rect *screenBitsBounds)
{
    //
    // save the zone and set to the System zone
    // this may not be needed but we used this code
    // in a system extension that used the system heap
    //

    pp->oldZone = GetZone();
    SetZone(SystemZone());

    //
    // save DeskHook and DragHook, which are low memory proc ptrs
    // then set them to 0 so they are ignored
    //
```

```
    pp->saveDeskHook = LMGetDeskHook();
    pp->saveDragHook = LMGetDragHook();
    LMSetDeskHook((UniversalProcPtr)0L);
    LMSetDragHook((UniversalProcPtr)0L);

    //
    // set ResLoad to true so our resources are loaded
    // may not be needed in your code
    //

    pp->savedResLoad = LMGetResLoad();
    SetResLoad(true);

    //
    // save the values of the Font Manager and QuickDraw init flags
    //

    pp->pFMExist = (Ptr)0x0D42;
    pp->pQDExist = (Ptr)0x08F3;
    pp->savedFMExist = *(pp->pFMExist);
    pp->savedQDExist = *(pp->pQDExist);

    //
    // set our a5 world, initialize it, and init the Font Manager
    //

    pp->oldA5 = SetA5((long)&(pp->qdWorld.thePort));
    InitGraf(&(pp->qdWorld.qd.thePort));
    if ((pp->savedFMExist == 0x00) && (LMGetWidthTabHandle() == nil))
        *(pp->pFMExist) = 0xFF;
    InitFonts();

    //
    // open a color port, requires Color QuickDraw
    //

    OpenCPort((CGrafPtr)(&pp->qdWorld.port));

    //
    // return the bounds of the a5 world we have created
    //

    *screenBitsBounds = pp->qdWorld.qd.screenBits.bounds;
}
```

The RestoreA5World function is called when drawing is complete, as in the following code. This ensures that the previous A5 world, if any, is properly restored.

```
void RestoreA5World(A5ParamsPtr pp)
{
    //
    // close the color port
    //

    CloseCPort((CGrafPtr)(&pp->qdWorld.port));

    //
    // restore the old a5 world
    //

    SetA5(pp->oldA5);

    //
    // restore other saved settings
    //

    *(pp->pQDExist) = pp->savedQDExist;
    *(pp->pFMExist) = pp->savedFMExist;
    LMSetDeskHook(pp->saveDeskHook);
    LMSetDragHook(pp->saveDragHook);
    LMSetResLoad(pp->savedResLoad);
    SetZone(pp->oldZone);
}
```

Let's take a look at how you might use these two routines to actually
do some drawing. (See the following code.) Although you would
never have a need to use these from within an application, this is the
easiest way to test that our routines are working. So, this is what we
did.

```
void main(void)
{
    unsigned long    randSeed;
    A5Params         a5p;
    Rect             screenBitsBounds;

    InitGraf(&qd.thePort);
    InitFonts();
    FlushEvents(everyEvent, 0);
    InitWindows();
    InitMenus();
    TEInit();
    InitDialogs(nil);
    InitCursor();
    GetDateTime((unsigned long *)&randSeed);
    LMSetRndSeed(randSeed);
    DrawMenuBar();
```

```
    PrepareA5World(&a5p, &screenBitsBounds);

    ForeColor(redColor);
    PaintRect(&screenBitsBounds);

    RestoreA5World(&a5p);

    while (!Button()) {}

    UpdateRectangle(&screenBitsBounds);

    FlushEvents(everyEvent, 0);
}
```

This tiny application simply initializes the Macintosh Toolbox, prepares our custom A5 world, draws to it using QuickDraw, then restores the previous A5 world. You will note that after we restore the previous A5 world, we simply wait for the user to click the mouse. At this point, the entire screen is red. After the user clicks, we call a utility function UpdateRectangle that simply updates the entire screen for us to redraw what was there before we messed it all up. The program then flushes any events that may have piled up and returns. To be complete, the following code is our UpdateRectangle routine.

```
void UpdateRectangle(Rect *updateRect)
{
    RgnHandle    thisScreenBoundary = NewRgn();
    GrafPtr      oldPort;
    GrafPtr      theBigPicture;

    if (thisScreenBoundary) {
        RectRgn(thisScreenBoundary, updateRect);
        GetPort(&oldPort);
        GetWMgrPort(&theBigPicture);
        SetPort(theBigPicture);
        DrawMenuBar();
        PaintOne(nil, thisScreenBoundary);
        PaintBehind(LMGetWindowList(), thisScreenBoundary);
        SetPort(oldPort);
        DisposeRgn(thisScreenBoundary);
    }
}
```

Some things to note about using your own A5 world follow. Keep them in mind to make sure you use this technology properly.

- A5 is very volatile. QuickDraw is very precise. If you don't set something up just right, it will crash and burn like you've never seen before. Be careful when using these functions. Ever hear of _Jackson?
- A5 causes you to lose globals. If you were to attempt to access a global variable in the previous code while your temporary A5 world was being used, you would be accessing garbage data. Remember, in an application, global variables are referenced as an offset from register A5. If you change the value in register A5, then you will not know how to get to your globals.

Adding a Rightmost System Menu

At the time I needed to write a program that added a rightmost system menu, I probably wouldn't have succeeded had it not been for Rob Mathews of Tiger Slider fame. A rightmost system menu (Figure 12-6), as I call it, is a menu that is available in all programs and lives on the right side of the menu bar next to the Help and Application menus. Rightmost system menus are installed by system extensions and usually allow quick access to some otherwise boring or lengthy task. For example, the rightmost menu I added allowed the user to choose any available network printer without opening the Chooser. This saved time when switching printers was something you did more than a few times a day.

Adding this menu was easy, after Rob gave me the code. He spent a day or two figuring out the intricacies of the way the system handled these menus and came up with a way to add them reliably. Rob's mechanism required three patches to traps in order to add the custom menu, manipulate it, and receive selections from it. The patches are GetMenu, MenuSelect, and SystemMenu.

Figure 12-6. Two rightmost system menus as added by the system software

GetMenu

When our GetMenu patch is called to insert the Help menu, which has a specific ID number of –16490, we would walk the current menu list to calculate a unique ID number for the menu we wanted to add. When we found one, we would create our menu by calling NewMenu and then InsertMenu to add it to the menu list. Any menus with ID numbers within a specific range (close to –16490) are automatically added to the right side of the menu bar. In order to add the icon as the title of the menu, you simply set the title of the menu to a specific "code," which happens to be a Pascal string with a length bytes of 5, the first character being 0x01, and the remaining four characters (a long) being a handle to an icon family. The menu bar definition then knows to draw this title in a special way.

MenuSelect

MenuSelect is patched so we can watch for menus from which items are being selected. Whenever the user clicks on the menu bar, Menu-Select is called. By patching this trap, we are able to update our menu on the fly, before it is displayed to the user. We can check specific items, disable or enable other items, or do nothing at all.

SystemMenu

Our tail patch to SystemMenu allows us to intercept selections of our items. After the original SystemMenu is called, the long parameter contains the menu ID and menu item number of that selected by the user. Using this information, we can see if the user selected our menu and then act on the specific item appropriately.

Believe it or not, that's all there is to it. Mind you, you need to be careful that you patch these traps properly and handle yourself properly. Remember, you are in a system extension and do not have run of the house in this situation. Luckily, the SystemMenu patch is marked as being one that moves memory already, so you can safely allocate memory, display dialog boxes, and perform other feats from within your patch. Good luck adding your menu!

Conclusion

If you've made it this far, you probably have a good understanding of the Power Macintosh and what it takes to program it effectively. Much of what you've learned throughout this book can also be applied to other types of software components that you may find yourself writing. The sky isn't the limit anymore.

I sincerely hope you enjoyed the information presented here and, most of all, learned something from it. If I help one person become a better programmer, then the months of writing were worth it. Until next time, farewell and happy coding.

Projects to Try on Your Own

Here is a list of projects, not necessarily covered in the book, that you might want to research and try on your own. You can find documentation on some of these topics in various places, but the best place to go is to log on to your favorite online service and download sample source code from other programmers like yourself. You can also post public messages in these areas to ask questions about where to look for information on specific topics.

- Write an AppleScript extension, also known as an osax, to extend the capabilities of AppleScript. By writing an osax, which is basically just an AppleEvent handler in disguise, you can add new functionality to AppleScript that can be used by anyone who installs your osax onto their Macintosh. Think of the possibilities.
- Write a Control Strip module. Control Strip is a utility from Apple that they ship on many new PowerBooks. It puts a small floating palette on your screen that executes modules in order to allow quick access to the time and date, printer switching, speaker volume switching, monitor bit depth switching, and more.
- After Dark modules are a fun thing to take the time to write. After Dark is a screensaver that can be purchased at your local computer store. You can obtain a developer's kit from Berkeley Systems, the makers of After Dark. With their kit you can write your very own screen-saver modules with color animation and sound. Use the GWorld techniques you learned in Chapter Seven and have at it!

- XTND technology allows you to write code that converts one type of document to another. Any program that supports XTND can take advantage of your module to convert from a MacWrite file, for example, to your own file format. Because XTND uses an intermediary file format, you need only know how to convert from your format to this intermediary. You need not know about any other files formats, yet you can convert to and from all of them.
- Photoshop supports a wide variety of plug-ins including those that filter images, import and export data, and more. You can obtain the Photoshop software developer's kit direct from Adobe so you can write all sorts of neat extensions to this tool that is popular with graphic artists. We discussed filters in this book, but you should explore developing others as well.

Suggested Reading

Believe it or not, this book is not the end all of documentation on the subject of code resources. Even though I've gathered a lot of information and put it all in one place, there are many other places to find good articles on this subject. Here is a short list of some of my favorites.

Magazines

MacTech. *MacTech* magazine is a monthly publication that discusses everything having to do with Macintosh programming. Not only does *MacTech* include articles about programming languages, new technologies, new development products, and more, but they also surprise you every so often with a free CD (or two!) filled with cool stuff at no extra cost. *MacTech* is required reading for any serious developer.

d e v e l o p. *d e v e l o p* is a monthly publication that contains some pretty serious articles at times. Many Apple (and ex-Apple) employees write articles for *d e v e l o p*. The articles in *d e v e l o p* can get very deep at times, but can be real lifesavers when you're trying to figure out the latest technology from Apple. Each month, the magazine also includes a CD that contains the text and source code from the current issue and all back issues. Many Apple technical notes and other development information and tools are also on the CD.

Books

Inside Macintosh. *Inside Macintosh* is a collection of books published by Addison-Wesley. Consisting of a number of volumes, *Inside Macintosh* is the definitive place to turn when you have a question about just about anything in the Macintosh environment. Volumes are dedicated to QuickDraw GX, The Macintosh Toolbox, Interapplication Communication, Files, and much more. *Inside Macintosh* is also available on CD, which should be owned by any developer who owns a CD-ROM drive; it's that important.

Macintosh Programming Secrets **(Second Edition).** *Macintosh Programming Secrets*, written by Scott Knaster and Keith Rollin, is one of the bibles that all programmers should own. It discusses the little things that make programs great—like how to teach your ants to march, how to manipulate dialog boxes in advanced ways, how to safely copy files, and more.

How to Write Macintosh Software **(Third Edition).** *How To Write Macintosh Software* is the other bible that all programmers should own. Also written by Scott Knaster, this book delves into the depths of the operating system and explores how it works. Although it only discusses the 680x0 and does not touch on the PowerPC, it is still filled with information that will help all of your programming efforts. And remember, even Power Macintosh programmers need to know a little 680x0 here and there.

XCMDS for HyperCard. Gary Bond wrote this book, which is the only one available that discusses writing external commands and functions for HyperCard. Mind you, it doesn't cover version 2.0 of HyperCard and all the new features that were added with it. Even so, this book is a very good reference and contains lots of code for the HyperCard guru.

PowerPC 601 RISC Microprocessor User's Manual. This book, available directly from Motorola, totally discusses the PowerPC 601 chip in depth. If you plan on programming the Power Macintosh in assembly language, you will need this book. Mind you, one of Apple's hopes was that you would not need to use assembly language much when programming the Power Macintosh, but some of you may be hard core and want that thrill. This book is a good reference to have around in any case, but it is not for the faint of heart.

Other

Technical Notes. From time to time, Apple releases technical notes that explain information that may be confusing to developers or to introduce a new technology. These notes can be found on most developer CDs from Apple.

Online Services. America Online, eWorld, and CompuServe all contain Macintosh developer forums. Join your favorite and visit these areas. You will be blown away at the wealth of information available online.

Internet. Most major online services also allow access to Internet newsgroups. There are many newsgroups that cover Macintosh programming. You can communicate with other developers from all over the world on the Internet.

Your CodeWarrior CD-ROM. The CD that came with this book contains lots of example source code. Not only is all the code from the book on the CD, but there are also many other examples provided by Metrowerks. Check it out!

Appendix

Chapter Three Source Code

main.c

```c
/*
   File Name:   main.c
*/

#include <EPPC.h>
#include <AppleEvents.h>

#include "globs.h"
#include "init.h"
#include "utils.h"
#include "prefs.h"
#include "modules.h"
#include "main.h"

/********************************************************************

     main

********************************************************************/

void main(void)
{
     /* initialize ourselves */
     InitMacintosh();
     InitGlobals();
     UnloadSeg(&InitMacintosh);
```

```
                    /* handle events */
                    HandleEvent();

                    /* get out */
                    CleanUp();
          }

/*******************************************************************

          CleanUp

*******************************************************************/

void CleanUp(void)
{
          ExitToShell();
}

/*******************************************************************

          HandleEvent

*******************************************************************/

void HandleEvent(void)
{
          while (!gDone) {

                    Boolean gotEvent = WaitNextEvent(everyEvent, &gTheEvent,
                              gSleepTime, nil);

                    if (gotEvent) {

                              switch(gTheEvent.what) {

                                        case nullEvent:
                                                  IdleTime();
                                                  break;

                                        case mouseDown:
                                                  DoMouseDown();
                                                  break;

                                        case updateEvt:
                                                  /*
                                                  {
```

```
                                    GrafPtr   savePort;
                                    GetPort(&savePort);
                                    SetPort((WindowPtr)gTheEvent.message);
                                    BeginUpdate((WindowPtr)gTheEvent.message);

                                    EndUpdate((WindowPtr)gTheEvent.message);
                                    SetPort(savePort);
                                }
                                */
                                break;

                        case autoKey:
                        case keyDown:
                                if (gTheEvent.modifiers & cmdKey) {
                                        AdjustMenus();
                                        DoMenuCommand(MenuKey(gTheEvent.message &
                                                charCodeMask));
                                }
                                break;

                        case app4Evt:
                                gInBackground = (!(gTheEvent.message & 0x0001));
                                InitCursor();
                                break;

                        case kHighLevelEvent:
                                {
                                        OSErr err =
                                                AEProcessAppleEvent(&gTheEvent);
                                        if (err != noErr) {
                                                NumToString((long)err, gStr);
                                                ParamText(gStr, "\p", "\p", "\p");
                                                StopAlert(alertAEProcessAEError,
                                                        nil);
                                                ParamText("\p", "\p", "\p", "\p");
                                        }
                                }
                                break;

                        default:
                                break;
                }
            }
        }
}

/*******************************************************************

    DoMouseDown

*******************************************************************/
```

```c
void DoMouseDown(void)
{
    WindowPtr    window;
    short        thePart = FindWindow(gTheEvent.where, &window);

    switch(thePart) {

        case inMenuBar:
            AdjustMenus();
            DoMenuCommand(MenuSelect(gTheEvent.where));
            break;

        case inSysWindow:
            SystemClick(&gTheEvent, window);
            break;

        case inGrow:
            {
                long newSize = GrowWindow(window, gTheEvent.where,
                    &qd.screenBits.bounds);
                if (newSize)
                    SizeWindow(window, LoWord(newSize),
                        HiWord(newSize), true);
            }
            break;

        case inContent:
            if (window != FrontWindow())
                SelectWindow(window);
            break;

        case inDrag:
            DragWindow(window, gTheEvent.where,
                &qd.screenBits.bounds);
            break;

        case inGoAway:
            if (TrackGoAway(window, gTheEvent.where))
                CloseWindow(window);
            break;

        case inZoomIn:
        case inZoomOut:
            if (TrackBox(window, gTheEvent.where, thePart)) {
                SetPort(window);
                EraseRect(&window->portRect);
                ZoomWindow(window, thePart, true);
                InvalRect(&window->portRect);
            }
            break;
    }
}
```

```
/********************************************************************

    DoMenuCommand

********************************************************************/

void DoMenuCommand(long menuResult)
{
    short       menuID;
    short       menuItem;
    short       daRefNum;
    WindowPtr   window;
    OSErr       err = noErr;

    window = FrontWindow();
    menuID = HiWord(menuResult);
    menuItem = LoWord(menuResult);

    switch(menuID) {

        case menuApple:
            switch(menuItem) {
                case itemAbout:
                    Alert(alertAbout, nil);
                    break;

                default:
                    GetItem(GetMHandle(menuApple), menuItem, gStr);
                    daRefNum = OpenDeskAcc(gStr);
                    break;
            }
            break;

        case menuFile:
            switch(menuItem) {
                case itemQuit:
                    gDone = true;
                    break;
                default:
                    SysBeep(0);
                    break;
            }
            break;

        case menuEdit:
            switch(menuItem) {
                case itemSelectAll:
                    break;
```

```
                    case itemPreferences:
                        DoPreferences();
                        break;

                    default:
                        SystemEdit(menuItem-1);
                }
                break;

        case menuCode:
            switch(menuItem) {
                case itemExecuteResource:
                    err = ExecuteResource();
                    if (err != noErr) {
                        NumToString((long)err, gStr);
                        ParamText(gStr, "\p", "\p", "\p");
                        StopAlert(alertExecuteResourceError, nil);
                        ParamText("\p", "\p", "\p", "\p");
                    }
                    break;
            #ifdef __powerc
                case itemExecuteSharedLib: {
                    Str255   errName;
                    err = ExecuteSharedLib(errName);
                    if (err != noErr) {
                        NumToString((long)err, gStr);
                        ParamText(gStr, errName, "\p", "\p");
                        StopAlert(alertExecuteSharedLibError, nil);
                        ParamText("\p", "\p", "\p", "\p");
                    }
                    break;
                }
            #endif
            }
            break;

        default:
            break;
    }

    HiliteMenu(0);
}

/*********************************************************************

    AdjustMenus

*********************************************************************/

void AdjustMenus(void)
{
```

```
        WindowPtr       frontmost;
        MenuHandle      menu;

        frontmost = FrontWindow();

        menu = GetMHandle(menuApple);
        EnableItem(menu, 0);
        menu = GetMHandle(menuFile);
        EnableItem(menu, 0);
        menu = GetMHandle(menuEdit);
        EnableItem(menu, 0);
        DisableItem(menu, itemUndo);
        DisableItem(menu, itemCut);
        DisableItem(menu, itemCopy);
        DisableItem(menu, itemPaste);
        DisableItem(menu, itemClear);
        DisableItem(menu, itemSelectAll);

        menu = GetMHandle(menuCode);
        EnableItem(menu, 0);
        #ifndef __powerc
        DisableItem(menu, itemExecuteSharedLib);
        #endif


/*
        if (IsDAWindow(frontmost)) {
                menu = GetMHandle(menuEdit);
                EnableItem(menu, 0);
        } else {menu = GetMHandle(menuEdit);
                DisableItem(menu, 0);
        }
*/

        DrawMenuBar();
}

/*********************************************************************

        IdleTime

*********************************************************************/

void IdleTime(void)
{
        if (gInIdle == true)
                return;

        gInIdle = true;

        /* do stuff here */
```

```
        gInIdle = false;
}
```

main.h

```
/*
    File Name:      main.h
*/

#pragma once

void main(void);
void CleanUp(void);
void HandleEvent(void);
void DoMouseDown(void);
void DoMenuCommand(long menuResult);
void AdjustMenus(void);
void IdleTime(void);
```

modules.c

```
/*
    File Name:   modules.c
*/

#include <StandardFile.h>
#include <FragLoad.h>
#include <MixedMode.h>
#include <ConditionalMacros.h>
#include "globs.h"
#include "prefs.h"
#include "modules.h"


/**********************************************************************

    ExecuteSharedLib

    This code is only executed from the native application. It loads
    a shared library, looks up an exported symbol (function) name,
    creates a RoutineDescriptor to represent that function, and then
    executes the function. When complete, it closes the connection to
    the shared library.

**********************************************************************/
```

```
#ifdef __powerc
OSErr ExecuteSharedLib(Str255 errName)
{
    OSErr               err = noErr, err2 = noErr;
    ConnectionID    connID = kNoConnectionID;
    Ptr                        mainAddr = nil;

    //
    // attempt to locate and prepare the shared library
    //

    err = GetSharedLibrary("\pShared Library", kPowerPCArch, kLoadNewCopy,
                                    &connID, &mainAddr, errName);
    if (err == noErr) {
            Ptr         symAddr = nil;
            SymClass    symClass;

    //
    // look up the symbol (in this case, a function) that we're interested in
    //

            err = FindSymbol(connID, "\pBeepThreeTimes", &symAddr, &symClass);
            if (err == noErr) {

                    //
                    // create a routine descriptor for the function, call it,
                    // then dispose the routine descriptor.
                    //

                    UniversalProcPtr upp = NewRoutineDescriptor((ProcPtr)symAddr,
                            kCStackBased, GetCurrentISA());
                    if (upp) {
                            SetCursor(*GetCursor(watchCursor));
                            CallUniversalProc(upp, kCStackBased);
                            InitCursor();
                            DisposeRoutineDescriptor(upp);
                    } else err = memFullErr;
            }

    //
    // look up another symbol, just for fun.
    //

    if (err == noErr) {
            err = FindSymbol(connID, "\pShowLibAlert", &symAddr, &symClass);
            if (err == noErr) {

                    //
                    // create a routine descriptor for the function, call it,
                    // then dispose the routine descriptor.
                    //
```

```
                              UniversalProcPtr upp =
                                      NewRoutineDescriptor((ProcPtr)symAddr,
                                      kCStackBased, GetCurrentISA());
                          if (upp) {
                                  CallUniversalProc(upp, kCStackBased);
                                  DisposeRoutineDescriptor(upp);
                          } else err = memFullErr;
              }
          }

          //
          // close the connection
          //

          err2 = CloseConnection(&connID);
          if (err == noErr) err = err2;
      }

      return err;
}
#endif

/***********************************************************************

    ExecuteResource

    This function is called on both platforms in order to execute a
    private resource.

***********************************************************************/

OSErr ExecuteResource(void)
{
    FSSpec          codeSpec;
    Boolean         good;
    OSErr           err = noErr;
    short           saveResFile = CurResFile();
    short           fRefNum;

    // choose a valid file based on our preferences
    good = ChooseCodeContainingFile(&codeSpec);
    if (!good) return noErr;

    fRefNum = FSpOpenResFile(&codeSpec, fsRdPerm);
    if (fRefNum != -1) {
            UseResFile(fRefNum);

            switch(gCodeCallPreference) {
                    case item68kRadio:
                            err = Call68k();
                            break;
```

```
                    case itemPowerPCRadio:
                            err = CallPPC();
                            break;
                    case itemNoModeSwitchRadio:
                            err = CallFat();
                            break;
                    default:
                            DebugStr("\pgCodeCallPreference is invalid!");
                            // should NEVER happen
                            break;
            }

            CloseResFile(fRefNum);
            UseResFile(saveResFile);
    }

    return err;
}


/**********************************************************************

    Call68k

    This function can be called from 68k code or PowerPC code.
    We use our handy macros in order to create the proper RoutineDescriptor
    when needed on the PowerMac. We have a special macro that returns
    a RoutineDescriptor to 68k code. We can then call the code with
    our CallModuleEntryProc function.

**********************************************************************/

OSErr Call68k(void)
{
    long                moduleResult;
    ModuleEntryProcUPP  mepUPP;
    Handle              hCode = Get1Resource(kModule68kResType, kModuleResID);
    OSErr               err = noErr;

    if (hCode) {
            HLockHi(hCode);

            mepUPP = NewModuleEntryProc68k(*hCode);
            moduleResult = CallModuleEntryProc(mepUPP, 0L);
            DisposeRoutineDescriptor(mepUPP);

            HUnlock(hCode);
            ReleaseResource(hCode);
    } else err = ResError();

    return err;
}
```

```
/***********************************************************************

        CallPPC

        This function can be called from 68k code or PowerPC code.
        Since our PowerPC code resource already has a RoutineDescriptor
        tacked onto itself (by the linker) we can simply dereference the
        resource handle and call it.

 ***********************************************************************/

OSErr CallPPC(void)
{
        long            moduleResult;
        Handle          hCode = Get1Resource(kModulePPCResType, kModuleResID);
        OSErr           err = noErr;

        if (hCode) {
                HLockHi(hCode);

                moduleResult = CallModuleEntryProc((ModuleEntryProcUPP)*hCode, 0L);

                HUnlock(hCode);
                ReleaseResource(hCode);
        } else err = ResError();

        return err;
}


/***********************************************************************

        CallFat

        This function can be called from 68k code or PowerPC code.
        Since our fat code resource already has a RoutineDescriptor
        tacked onto itself (by the linker) we can simply dereference the
        resource handle and call it.

 ***********************************************************************/

OSErr CallFat(void)
{
        long            moduleResult;
        Handle          hCode = Get1Resource(kModuleFatResType, kModuleResID);
        OSErr           err = noErr;

        if (hCode) {
                HLockHi(hCode);

                moduleResult = CallModuleEntryProc((ModuleEntryProcUPP)*hCode, 0L);
```

```
            HUnlock(hCode);
            ReleaseResource(hCode);
        } else err = ResError();

        return err;
}


/*********************************************************************


    ChooseCodeContainingFile

    This function merely allows the user to choose which private
    resource they would like to execute.

*********************************************************************/

Boolean ChooseCodeContainingFile(FSSpecPtr fsp)
{
        SFTypeList          typeList = {kModuleFileType};
        short               numTypes = 1;
        StandardFileReply   reply;
        FileFilterUPP       fileFilter;
        Boolean             result = false;

        fileFilter = NewFileFilterProc(MyFileFilter);
        if (fileFilter) {
                StandardGetFile(fileFilter, numTypes, typeList, &reply);
                result = reply.sfGood;
                DisposeRoutineDescriptor(fileFilter);
        }

        *fsp = reply.sfFile;
        return result;
}


/*********************************************************************


    MyFileFilter

    This function filters files in our StandardGetFile dialog box.
    This way, we make sure the user selects a file that contains the
    proper type of code that we are looking for.

*********************************************************************/

pascal Boolean MyFileFilter(CInfoPBPtr cpbp)
{
        FSSpec      fileSpec;
        Boolean     dontDisplayFile = true;
        OSErr       err;
        short       fRefNum;
        short       saveResFile = CurResFile();
        ResType     rType = '????';
```

```
                        err = FSMakeFSSpec(cpbp->hFileInfo.ioVRefNum,
                cpbp->hFileInfo.ioFlParID,
                        cpbp->hFileInfo.ioNamePtr, &fileSpec);
                if (err != noErr) { SysBeep(0); return dontDisplayFile; }

                fRefNum = FSpOpenResFile(&fileSpec, fsRdPerm);
                if (fRefNum != -1) {
                UseResFile(fRefNum);

                switch(gCodeCallPreference) {
                        case item68kRadio:
                                rType = kModule68kResType;
                                break;
                        case itemPowerPCRadio:
                                rType = kModulePPCResType;
                                break;
                        case itemNoModeSwitchRadio:
                                rType = kModuleFatResType;
                                break;
                        default:
                                DebugStr("\pgCodeCallPreference is invalid!");
                                // should NEVER happen
                                break;
                }

                dontDisplayFile = (Count1Resources(rType) == 0);

                CloseResFile(fRefNum);
                UseResFile(saveResFile);
        }

        return dontDisplayFile;
}
```

modules.h

```
/*
  File Name:   modules.h
*/

#pragma once

#ifdef __powerc
OSErr       ExecuteSharedLib(Str255 errName);
#endif
OSErr       ExecuteResource(void);
OSErr       Call68k(void);
OSErr       CallPPC(void);
OSErr       CallFat(void);
Boolean     ChooseCodeContainingFile(FSSpecPtr fsp);
```

```
pascal        Boolean MyFileFilter(CInfoPBPtr cpbp);

// modules are stored in files of a specific type

#define kModuleFileType          'xMOD'

// code is stored in various forms. the data fork of the file also contains the PPC
// only code so it can take advantage of Virtual Memory paging when needed. in your
// application you would not store it in this many forms, but in these examples we
// do in order to show you many of the possibilities.

#define kModule68kResType   '68k '
// resource that contains 68k code only, with no RD
#define kModulePPCResType   'PPC '
// resource that contains PPC code only, with no RD
#define kModuleFatResType   'FAT '
// resource that contains both 68k & PPC code, and has RD

#define kModuleResID              128              // always id 128

typedef long (*ModuleProc)(long inData);

enum {
    uppModuleEntryProcInfo = kCStackBased
            | RESULT_SIZE(SIZE_CODE(sizeof(long)))
            | STACK_ROUTINE_PARAMETER(1, SIZE_CODE(sizeof(long)))
};

#if USESROUTINEDESCRIPTORS
typedef UniversalProcPtr   ModuleEntryProcUPP;
#define CallModuleEntryProc(userRoutine, params)   \
          CallUniversalProc((UniversalProcPtr)(userRoutine),
uppModuleEntryProcInfo, params)
#define NewModuleEntryProc(userRoutine)   \
          (ModuleEntryProcUPP) NewRoutineDescriptor((ProcPtr)(userRoutine),
uppModuleEntryProcInfo, GetCurrentISA())
#define NewModuleEntryProc68k(userRoutine)   \
          (ModuleEntryProcUPP) NewRoutineDescriptor((ProcPtr)(userRoutine),
uppModuleEntryProcInfo, (ISAType) kM68kISA)
#define WTF() DebugStr("\p USESROUTINEDESCRIPTORS");
#else
typedef ModuleProc   ModuleEntryProcUPP;
#define CallModuleEntryProc(userRoutine, params)   \
          (*(userRoutine))(params)
#define NewModuleEntryProc(userRoutine)   \
          (ModuleEntryProcUPP)(userRoutine)
#define NewModuleEntryProc68k(userRoutine)   \
          (ModuleEntryProcUPP)(userRoutine)
#define WTF() DebugStr("\p! USESROUTINEDESCRIPTORS");
#endif
```

globs.c

```
/*
    File Name:   globs.c
*/

#include "globs.h"

EventRecord      gTheEvent;
Boolean          gDone;
Boolean          gInBackground;
Boolean          gInIdle;
long             gSleepTime;
Str255           gStr;
short            gCodeCallPreference;
```

globs.h

```
/*
    File Name:   globs.h
*/

#pragma once


/* constants */

#define kSleepTime      15
#define kMinimumSystem  0x0700



/* alerts */

#define alertNeedSystem7OrLater         128
#define alertMenuBarResourceNotFound    129
#define alertAEProcessAEError           130
#define alertInitAEError                131
#define alertExecuteResourceError       132
#define alertExecuteSharedLibError      133

#define alertAbout                      1000



/* menus */

#define menubarResID      128

#define menuApple         1
```

```
#define   itemAbout                1

#define menuFile              2
#define   itemQuit                 1

#define menuEdit              3
#define   itemUndo                 1
#define   itemCut                  3
#define   itemCopy                 4
#define   itemPaste                5
#define   itemClear                6
#define   itemSelectAll            8
#define   itemPreferences          10

#define menuCode              4
#define   itemExecuteResource    1
#define   itemExecuteSharedLib   2

/* global variables */

extern EventRecord        gTheEvent;
extern Boolean            gDone;
extern Boolean            gInBackground;
extern Boolean            gInIdle;
extern long               gSleepTime;
extern Str255             gStr;
extern short              gCodeCallPreference;
```

ae.c

```
/*
   File Name:   ae.c
*/

#include <EPPC.h>
#include <AppleEvents.h>

#include "globs.h"
#include "ae.h"

struct triplets {
     AEEventClass        theEventClass;
     AEEventID           theEventID;
     AEEventHandlerUPP   theHandler;
};
typedef struct triplets triplets;

static triplets keywordsToInstall[] = {
     { kCoreEventClass,            kAEOpenApplication,
           (AEEventHandlerUPP)DoAEOpenApplication },
```

```
                 { kCoreEventClass,     kAEOpenDocuments,
                       (AEEventHandlerUPP)DoAEOpenDocuments },
                 { kCoreEventClass,     kAEPrintDocuments,
                       (AEEventHandlerUPP)DoAEPrintDocuments },
                 { kCoreEventClass,     kAEQuitApplication,
                       (AEEventHandlerUPP)DoAEQuitApplication }
                       /* The above are the four required AppleEvents. */
          };


/*********************************************************************

          InitAE

*********************************************************************/

OSErr InitAE(void)
{
          OSErr   err = noErr;
          short   i;

          for (i = 0; i < (sizeof(keywordsToInstall) / sizeof(triplets)); ++i) {
                 err = AEInstallEventHandler(keywordsToInstall[i].theEventClass,
          keywordsToInstall[i].theEventID,

          NewAEEventHandlerProc(keywordsToInstall[i].theHandler),
                 0L,              /* unused refcon */
                 false);          /* not system handler */
                 if (err != noErr) return err;
          }
          return err;
}


/*********************************************************************

          DoAEOpenApplication

          Do things here if we are opened with no documents, open new document
          for example.

*********************************************************************/

pascal OSErr DoAEOpenApplication(AppleEvent *message, AppleEvent *reply,
          long refcon)
{
          OSErr err = noErr;

          return err;
}
```

```
/***********************************************************************

    DoAEOpenDocuments

***********************************************************************/

pascal OSErr DoAEOpenDocuments(AppleEvent *message, AppleEvent *reply, long refcon)
{
    OSErr         err = noErr;
    AEDesc        fileListDesc;
    long          numFiles;
    DescType      actualType;
    long          actualSize;
    AEKeyword     actualKeyword;
    FSSpec        oneFile;
    long          index;

    /* extract the list of aliases into fileListDesc */
    err = AEGetKeyDesc(message, keyDirectObject, typeAEList, &fileListDesc);
    if (err != noErr) return err;

    /* count the list elements */
    err = AECountItems(&fileListDesc, &numFiles);
    if (err != noErr) { AEDisposeDesc(&fileListDesc); return err; }

    /* get each from list and process it */
    for (index = 1; index <= numFiles; index ++) {
        err = AEGetNthPtr(&fileListDesc, index, typeFSS, &actualKeyword,
            &actualType, (Ptr)&oneFile, sizeof(oneFile), &actualSize);
        if (err != noErr) {
            AEDisposeDesc(&fileListDesc);
            return err;
        }

        /* oneFile\f>contains\f>FSSpec\f>of\f>file\f>in\f>question\f>*/
        SysBeep(0);
    }
    AEDisposeDesc(&fileListDesc);
    return err;
}

/***********************************************************************

    DoAEPrintDocuments

***********************************************************************/

pascal OSErr DoAEPrintDocuments(AppleEvent *message, AppleEvent *reply, long refcon)
{
```

```
        OSErr          err = noErr;
        AEDesc         fileListDesc;
        long           numFiles;
        DescType       actualType;
        long           actualSize;
        AEKeyword      actualKeyword;
        FSSpec         oneFile;
        long           index;

        /* extract the list of aliases into fileListDesc */
        err = AEGetKeyDesc(message, keyDirectObject, typeAEList, &fileListDesc);
        if (err != noErr) return err;

        /* count the list elements */
        err = AECountItems(&fileListDesc, &numFiles);
        if (err != noErr) { AEDisposeDesc(&fileListDesc); return err; }

        /* get each from list and process it */
        for (index = 1; index <= numFiles; index ++) {
                err = AEGetNthPtr(&fileListDesc, index, typeFSS, &actualKeyword,
                        &actualType, (Ptr)&oneFile, sizeof(oneFile), &actualSize);
                if (err != noErr) {
                        AEDisposeDesc(&fileListDesc);
                        return err;
                }

                /* oneFile contains FSSpec of file in question */
                SysBeep(0);
        }
        AEDisposeDesc(&fileListDesc);
        return err;
}


/*******************************************************************

        DoAEQuitApplication

*******************************************************************/

pascal OSErr DoAEQuitApplication(AppleEvent *message, AppleEvent *reply,
        long refcon)
{
        OSErr   err = noErr;

        // do our stuff here

        gDone = true;
        return err;
}
```

ae.h

```
/*
        File Name:   ae.h
*/

#pragma once

#include <AppleEvents.h>

OSErr InitAE(void);
pascal OSErr DoAEOpenApplication(AppleEvent *message, AppleEvent *reply,
    long refcon);
pascal OSErr DoAEOpenDocuments(AppleEvent *message, AppleEvent *reply,
    long refcon);
pascal OSErr DoAEPrintDocuments(AppleEvent *message, AppleEvent *reply,
    long refcon);
pascal OSErr DoAEQuitApplication(AppleEvent *message, AppleEvent *reply,
    long refcon);
```

dlogutils.c

```
/*
        File Name:   dlogutils.c
*/

#include "dlogutils.h"

/*******************************************************************************

    SetDialogItemState

*******************************************************************************/

void SetDialogItemState(DialogPtr dlg, short controlNumber, short value)
{
    short    iKind;
    Handle   iHandle;
    Rect     iRect;

    GetDItem(dlg, controlNumber, &iKind, &iHandle, &iRect);
    SetCtlValue((ControlHandle) iHandle, value);
}

/*******************************************************************************

    GetDialogItemState

*******************************************************************************/

short GetDialogItemState(DialogPtr dlg, short controlNumber)
{
```

```
        short   iKind;
        Handle  iHandle;
        Rect    iRect;

        GetDItem(dlg, controlNumber, &iKind, &iHandle, &iRect);
        return GetCtlValue((ControlHandle) iHandle);
}

/********************************************************************************

        DoRadioGroup

********************************************************************************/

void DoRadioGroup(DialogPtr dlg, short lo, short hi, short on)
{
        short i;

        for (i=lo;i<=hi;++i)
                SetDialogItemState(dlg, i, 0);
        SetDialogItemState(dlg, on, 1);
}

/********************************************************************************

        DoRadioGroup

********************************************************************************/

short GetRadioFromGroup(DialogPtr dlg, short lo, short hi)
{
        short i;

        for (i=lo;i<=hi;++i) {
                if (GetDialogItemState(dlg, i))
                        return i;
        }
        return 0;
}

/********************************************************************************

        ToggleCheckBox

********************************************************************************/

void ToggleCheckBox(DialogPtr dlg, short buttonNumber)
{
        short newState;
```

```
        if (GetDialogItemState(dlg, buttonNumber) == 0)
                newState = 1;
        else
                newState = 0;
        SetDialogItemState(dlg, buttonNumber, newState);
}


/****************************************************************************

        EnableControl

****************************************************************************/

void EnableControl(DialogPtr dlg, short controlNumber)
{
        short    iKind;
        Handle   iHandle;
        Rect     iRect;

        GetDItem(dlg, controlNumber, &iKind, &iHandle, &iRect);
        HiliteControl((ControlHandle)iHandle, 0);
}


/****************************************************************************

         DisableControl

****************************************************************************/

void DisableControl(DialogPtr dlg, short controlNumber)
{
        short    iKind;
        Handle   iHandle;
        Rect     iRect;

        GetDItem(dlg, controlNumber, &iKind, &iHandle, &iRect);
        HiliteControl((ControlHandle)iHandle, 255);
}
```

dlogutils.h

```
/*
        File Name:   dlogutils.h
*/

#pragma once

void        SetDialogItemState(DialogPtr dlg, short controlNumber, short value);
short       GetDialogItemState(DialogPtr dlg, short controlNumber);
void        DoRadioGroup(DialogPtr dlg, short lo, short hi, short on);
```

```
short        GetRadioFromGroup(DialogPtr dlg, short lo, short hi);
void         ToggleCheckBox(DialogPtr dlg, short buttonNumber);
void         EnableControl(DialogPtr dlg, short controlNumber);
void         DisableControl(DialogPtr dlg, short controlNumber);
```

init.c

```c
/*
    File Name:   init.c
*/

#include <GestaltEqu.h>

#include "globs.h"
#include "ae.h"
#include "prefs.h"
#include "utils.h"
#include "init.h"

/*********************************************************************

    InitMacintosh

*********************************************************************/

void InitMacintosh(void)
{
    unsigned long randSeed;

    InitGraf(&qd.thePort);
    InitFonts();
    FlushEvents(everyEvent, 0);
    InitWindows();
    InitMenus();
    TEInit();
    InitDialogs(nil);
    InitCursor();
    GetDateTime((unsigned long *)&randSeed);
    LMSetRndSeed(randSeed);
    DrawMenuBar();
}

/*********************************************************************

    InitGlobals

*********************************************************************/

void InitGlobals(void)
{
```

```
OSErr   err = noErr;
long    response;

gInIdle = false;
gDone = false;
gInBackground = false;
gSleepTime = kSleepTime;
if (PowerPCPresent())
        gCodeCallPreference = itemPowerPCRadio;
else
        gCodeCallPreference = item68kRadio;
        // only one choice when running on 68k

/* check for proper system version */
err = Gestalt(gestaltSystemVersion, &response);
if ((err != noErr) || (response < kMinimumSystem)) {
        StopAlert(alertNeedSystem7OrLater, nil);
        ExitToShell();
}

/* add menus and configure apple menu */
{
        Handle menuBar = GetNewMBar(menubarResID);
        if (!menuBar) {
                StopAlert(alertMenuBarResourceNotFound, nil);
                ExitToShell();
        }
        SetMenuBar(menuBar);
        DisposHandle(menuBar);
        AddResMenu(GetMHandle(menuApple), 'DRVR');
        DrawMenuBar();
}

/* initialize apple events */
err = InitAE();
if (err != noErr) {
        NumToString((long)err, gStr);
        ParamText(gStr, "\p", "\p", "\p");
        StopAlert(alertInitAEError, nil);
        ParamText("\p", "\p", "\p", "\p");
        ExitToShell();
}
}
```

init.h

```
/*
    File Name:   init.h
*/
```

```
#pragma once

void InitMacintosh(void);
void InitGlobals(void);
```

prefs.c

```
/*
   File Name:   prefs.c
*/

#include "globs.h"
#include "dlogutils.h"
#include "utils.h"
#include "prefs.h"


/********************************************************************

     DoPreferences

********************************************************************/

void DoPreferences(void)
{
     DialogPtr      d;
     Boolean        done = false;
     short          itemHit;

     d = GetNewDialog(dlogPreferencesID, nil, (WindowPtr)-1);
     if (d == nil) return;

     SetDialogDefaultItem(d, ok);
     SetDialogCancelItem(d, cancel);

     DoRadioGroup(d, item68kRadio, itemNoModeSwitchRadio, gCodeCallPreference);

     // if we are running on a 68k, we don't have much choice
     if (!PowerPCPresent()) {
          DisableControl(d, itemPowerPCRadio);
          DisableControl(d, itemNoModeSwitchRadio);
     }

     ShowWindow(d);

     while (!done) {
          ModalDialog(nil, &itemHit);
          switch(itemHit) {
               case ok:
```

```
                                    gCodeCallPreference = GetRadioFromGroup(d, item68kRadio,
                                            itemNoModeSwitchRadio);
                                    // no break
                            case cancel:
                                    done = true;
                                    break;
                            case item68kRadio:
                            case itemPowerPCRadio:
                            case itemNoModeSwitchRadio:
                                    DoRadioGroup(d, item68kRadio, itemNoModeSwitchRadio,
                                            itemHit);
                                    break;
                    }
            }
            DisposeDialog(d);
    }
```

prefs.h

```
    /*
        File Name:   prefs.h
    */

    #pragma once

    #define      dlogPreferencesID       2000
    #define      item68kRadio            6
    #define      itemPowerPCRadio        7
    #define      itemNoModeSwitchRadio   8

    void  DoPreferences(void);
```

utils.c

```
    /*
        File Name:      utils.c
    */

    #include <GestaltEqu.h>
    #include "utils.h"

    /********************************************************************

        PowerPCPresent

    ********************************************************************/

    Boolean PowerPCPresent(void)
    {
```

```
        long    response;
        return   ((Gestalt(gestaltSysArchitecture, &response) == noErr) &&
                        (response == gestaltPowerPC));
}

/*********************************************************************

        CFMPresent

*********************************************************************/

Boolean CFMPresent(void)
{
        long    response;
        return   (Gestalt(gestaltCFMAttr, &response) == noErr &&
                        (response & (1 << gestaltCFMPresent)) != 0);
}

/*********************************************************************

        IsAppWindow

*********************************************************************/

Boolean IsAppWindow(WindowPtr window)
{
        if (window == nil)
                return false;
        else
                return (((WindowPeek) window)->windowKind >= 0);
}

/*********************************************************************

        IsDAWindow

*********************************************************************/

Boolean IsDAWindow(WindowPtr window)
{
        if (window == nil )
                return false;
        else
                return (((WindowPeek) window)->windowKind < 0);
}
```

utils.h

```
/*
  File Name:   utils.h
*/
```

```
#pragma once

Boolean PowerPCPresent(void);
Boolean CFMPresent(void);
Boolean IsAppWindow(WindowPtr window);
Boolean IsDAWindow(WindowPtr window);
```

Shared Library.c

```
/*
    File Name:      Shared Library.c
*/

#include <CodeFragments.h>
#include "Shared Library.h"

short   gFileRefNum;

/***************************************************************************

    __initialize

***************************************************************************/

OSErr __initialize(InitBlockPtr ibp)
{
    OSErr   err = noErr;

    gFileRefNum = -1;

    //
    // we should always be kDataForkCFragLocator when a shared library. Assuming
    // this is is the case, we want to open our resource file so we can access
    // our resources if needed. our termination routine will close the file.
    //

    if (ibp->fragLocator.where == kDataForkCFragLocator) {
            gFileRefNum = FSpOpenResFile(ibp->fragLocator.u.onDisk.fileSpec,
                    fsRdPerm);
            if (gFileRefNum == -1)
                    err = ResError();
    }

    return err;
}

/***************************************************************************

    __terminate

***************************************************************************/
```

```
void __terminate(void)
{
    if (gFileRefNum != -1)
            CloseResFile(gFileRefNum);
}


/***************************************************************************


    BeepThreeTimes


***************************************************************************/

void BeepThreeTimes(void)
{
    short           saveResFile = CurResFile();
    DialogPtr       d;

    UseResFile(gFileRefNum);

    d = GetNewDialog(256, nil, (WindowPtr)-1);
    if (d) {
            ShowWindow(d);
            DrawDialog(d);
    }

    SysBeep(0);
    SysBeep(0);
    SysBeep(0);

    if (d)
            DisposeDialog(d);

    UseResFile(saveResFile);
}


/***************************************************************************


    ShowLibAlert


***************************************************************************/
#define kAlertID   128
void ShowLibAlert(void)
{
    short   saveResFile = CurResFile();
    UseResFile(gFileRefNum);
    NoteAlert(kAlertID, nil);
    UseResFile(saveResFile);
}
```

Shared Library.h

```
/*
    File Name:   Shared Library.h
*/

#pragma once

OSErr       __initialize(InitBlockPtr ibp);
void        __terminate(void);
void        BeepThreeTimes(void);
void        ShowLibAlert(void);
```

xShell.c

```
/*
    File Name:   xShell.c
*/

#include "modules.h"
#include "xShell.h"

#ifndef __powerc
#include <SetUpA4.h>
#include <A4Stuff.h>
#else
ProcInfoType __procinfo = uppModuleEntryProcInfo;
#endif

long main(long inData)
{
#ifndef __powerc
    long oldA4;
    oldA4 = SetCurrentA4();
    RememberA4();
#endif

#ifdef __powerc
    ParamText("\pPowerPC", "\p", "\p", "\p");
#else
    ParamText("\p68k", "\p", "\p", "\p");
#endif

    NoteAlert(128, nil);
    ParamText("\p", "\p", "\p", "\p");

#ifndef __powerc
    SetA4(oldA4);
#endif
```

```
        return 0L;
    }
```

xShell.h

```
/*
   File Name:     xShell.h
*/


#pragma once
```

Chapter Four Source Code
INIT.c

```
/*
   File Name:   INIT.c
*/


#ifdef USESROUTINEDESCRIPTORS
#undef USESROUTINEDESCRIPTORS
#define USESROUTINEDESCRIPTORS 1
#else
#define USESROUTINEDESCRIPTORS 1
#endif

//extern pascal UniversalProcPtr NewFatRoutineDescriptor(ProcPtr theM68kProc,
//   ProcPtr thePowerPCProc, ProcInfoType theProcInfo)
//   THREEWORDINLINE(0x303C, 0x0002, 0xAA59);


/*** includes ***********************************************************/

#include <LowMem.h>
#include <ToolUtils.h>
#include <OSUtils.h>
#include <Dialogs.h>
#include <Files.h>
#include <Menus.h>
#include <Script.h>
#include <Resources.h>
#include <Types.h>
#include <Memory.h>
#include <GestaltEqu.h>
#include <Errors.h>
#include <Folders.h>
#include <FragLoad.h>
#include <MixedMode.h>
//#include <ConditionalMacros.h>
```

```c
#include "INIT.h"
#include "common.h"
#include "A4Stuff.h"#include "SetupA4.h"

/*** definitions ***************************************************/

#define kMinimumSystemVersion       0x00000700   // minimum system version

#define kINITResourceType           'INIT'       // our INIT code resource type
#define kINITResourceID             0            // and ID

#define kPPCResourceType            'PPC '       // our PowerPC code resource type
#define kPPCResourceID              0            // and ID

#define rStringListID               128          // INIT string list resource
#define iMenuScriptsFolderName       1           // MenuScripts folder name
#define iAnyApplicationFolderName    2

/*** typedefs *****************************************************/

typedef pascal long (*MenuSelectProc)(Point pt);
typedef pascal long (*MenuKeyProc)(short ch);
typedef pascal void (*SystemMenuProc)(long menuResult);

/*** global variables *********************************************/

GlobalsPtr     gGlobalsPtr;

/*** function prototypes ******************************************/

OSErr       RememberMe(FSSpecPtr fsp);
pascal      long MenuKey68k(short ch);
pascal      long MenuSelect68k(Point startPt);
pascal      void SystemMenu68k(long menuResult);
void        ApplyPatches(void * menuSelectCode, void * menuKeyCode,
                void * systemMenuCode);
OSErr       PatchPPC(void);

/*************************************************************************

    main

*************************************************************************/

void main(void)
{
    FSSpec   menuScriptsFolderFSSpec;
    FSSpec   anyApplicationFolderFSSpec;
    Str32    menuScriptsFolderName;
    Str32    anyApplicationFolderName;
```

```
Handle   hINIT = nil;
THz      savedZone;
long     oldA4;
long     response;
long     foundDirID;
short    foundVRefNum;
OSErr    err = noErr;

//
// make sure we are in the system heap
//

savedZone = GetZone();
SetZone(SystemZone());

//
// set up our A4 context for this file
//

oldA4 = SetCurrentA4();
RememberA4();

//
// verify minimum system version
//

err = Gestalt(gestaltSystemVersion, &response);
if ((err != noErr) || (response < kMinimumSystemVersion)) goto fail;

//
// allocate our global data
//

gGlobalsPtr = (GlobalsPtr)NewPtrSysClear(sizeof(Globals));
if (gGlobalsPtr == nil) {
      err = MemError() ? MemError() : memFullErr;
      goto fail;
}

//
// find ourselves (it's a Zen thing)
//

err = RememberMe(&gGlobalsPtr->ourFSSpec);
if (err != noErr) goto fail;

//
// find out where our MenuScripts folder is located (in the System folder)
// and figure out it's directory id
//
```

```
// load folder name string from resource string list
GetIndString(menuScriptsFolderName, rStringListID, iMenuScriptsFolderName);
if (menuScriptsFolderName[0] == 0) {
      err = resNotFound;
      goto fail;
}

// locate dirID of system folder
err = FindFolder(kOnSystemDisk, kSystemFolderType, kDontCreateFolder,
      &foundVRefNum, &foundDirID);
if (err != noErr) goto fail;

// make a spec for the MenuScripts folder
err = FSMakeFSSpec(foundVRefNum, foundDirID, menuScriptsFolderName,
      &menuScriptsFolderFSSpec);
if (err == fnfErr) {
       // create it if it doesn't exist and get it's directory id
       err = FSpDirCreate(&menuScriptsFolderFSSpec, smSystemScript,
            &gGlobalsPtr->menuScriptsFolderDirID);
} else if (err == noErr) {
      // otherwise just get it's directory id
      err = GetDirectoryID(&menuScriptsFolderFSSpec,
            &gGlobalsPtr->menuScriptsFolderDirID);
}
if (err != noErr) goto fail;

// load folder name string from resource string list
GetIndString(anyApplicationFolderName, rStringListID,
      iAnyApplicationFolderName);
if (anyApplicationFolderName[0] == 0) {
      err = resNotFound;
      goto fail;
}

// make a spec for the Any Application folder
err = FSMakeFSSpec(foundVRefNum, gGlobalsPtr->menuScriptsFolderDirID,
      anyApplicationFolderName, &anyApplicationFolderFSSpec);
if (err == fnfErr) {
      // create it if it doesn't exist and get it's directory id
      err = FSpDirCreate(&anyApplicationFolderFSSpec, smSystemScript,
            &gGlobalsPtr->anyApplicationFolderDirID);
} else if (err == noErr) {
      // otherwise just get it's directory id
      err = GetDirectoryID(&anyApplicationFolderFSSpec,
            &gGlobalsPtr->anyApplicationFolderDirID);
}
if (err != noErr) goto fail;
```

```
        //
        // get a handle to our INIT resource
        //

        hINIT = Get1Resource(kINITResourceType, kINITResourceID);
        if (hINIT == nil) {
                err = ResError() ? ResError() : resNotFound;
                goto fail;
        }

        //
        // patch traps
        //

        err = Gestalt(gestaltSysArchitecture, &response);
        if (err != noErr) goto fail;

        if (response == gestalt68k)
                ApplyPatches(MenuSelect68k, MenuKey68k, SystemMenu68k);
        else if (response == gestaltPowerPC)
                err = PatchPPC();
        else err = gestaltUnknownErr;          // who knows what might be next?

        if (err != noErr) goto fail;

        //
        // make sure the INIT stays in memory
        //

        DetachResource(hINIT);

        goto exit;

fail:
        // we get here if we fail

        //
        // deallocate our global memory if it exists
        //

        if (gGlobalsPtr) {
                DisposePtr((Ptr)gGlobalsPtr);
                gGlobalsPtr = nil;
        }

        //
        // at this point our INIT is not detached, therefore, when our INIT file is closed
        // the resource will automatically be released.
        //
```

```
      /*
      if (hINIT) {
            ReleaseResource(hINIT);
            hINIT = nil;
       }
      */

      //
      // alert the user to the problem
      //

      if (err != noErr) {
            SysBeep(0);
      }

exit:
      // we get here upon success or failure

      //
      // restore a4
      //

      SetA4(oldA4);

      //
      // restore zone
      //

      SetZone(savedZone);
}

/*********************************************************************

      RememberMe

*********************************************************************/

OSErr RememberMe(FSSpecPtr fsp)
{
      FCBPBRec        pb;
      OSErr           err = noErr;

      pb.ioCompletion = nil;
      pb.ioNamePtr = fsp->name;
      pb.ioVRefNum = 0;
      pb.ioRefNum = CurResFile();
      pb.ioFCBIndx = 0;
```

```
                        err = PBGetFCBInfoSync(&pb);

                        fsp->vRefNum = pb.ioFCBVRefNum;
                        fsp->parID = pb.ioFCBParID;

                        return err;
                }


/****************************************************************************

        MenuKey68k

****************************************************************************/
pascal long MenuKey68k(short ch)
{
        long        result;
        long        oldA4;
        OSErr       err = noErr;

        //
        // to access our globals
        //

        oldA4 = SetUpA4();

        //
        // call the original MenuSelect first to see what was selected
        //

        result = ((MenuKeyProc)gGlobalsPtr->oldMenuKeyAddr)(ch);

        //
        // examine the menu selection
        //

        if (result != 0L) {
                err = DoMenuPatchStuff(result, gGlobalsPtr);
                if (err == noErr)
                        result = 0L;
        }

        //
        // restore a4 and return
        //

        RestoreA4(oldA4);
        return result;
}
```

```
/****************************************************************************

    MenuSelect68k

****************************************************************************/

pascal long MenuSelect68k(Point startPt)
{
     long       result;
     long       oldA4;
     OSErr      err = noErr;

     //
     // to access our globals
     //

     oldA4 = SetUpA4();

     //
     // call the original MenuSelect first to see what was selected
     //

     result = ((MenuSelectProc)gGlobalsPtr->oldMenuSelectAddr)(startPt);

     //
     // examine the menu selection
     //

     if (result != 0L) {
            err = DoMenuPatchStuff(result, gGlobalsPtr);
            if (err == noErr)
                  result = 0L;
     }

     //
     // restore a4 and return
     //

     RestoreA4(oldA4);
     return result;}
}

/****************************************************************************

    SystemMenu68k

****************************************************************************/

pascal   void SystemMenu68k(long menuResult)
{
```

```
    long     oldA4;
    OSErr    err = noErr;

    //
    // to access our globals
    //

    oldA4 = SetUpA4();

    //
    // examine the menu selection
    //

    if (menuResult != 0L) {
            err = DoMenuPatchStuff(menuResult, gGlobalsPtr);
            if (err == noErr)
                    menuResult = 0L;
    }

    //
    // call the original SystemMenu if we didn't handle it
    //

    if (((err == fnfErr) || (err == noErr)) && (menuResult != 0L))
        ((SystemMenuProc)gGlobalsPtr->oldSystemMenuAddr)(menuResult);

    //
    // restore a4 and return
    //

    RestoreA4(oldA4);
}

/****************************************************************************

    ApplyPatches

****************************************************************************/

void ApplyPatches(void * menuSelectCode, void * menuKeyCode, void * systemMenuCode)
{
    gGlobalsPtr->oldMenuSelectAddr = GetToolTrapAddress(_MenuSelect);
    SetToolTrapAddress((UniversalProcPtr)menuSelectCode, _MenuSelect);

    gGlobalsPtr->oldMenuKeyAddr = GetToolTrapAddress(_MenuKey);
    SetToolTrapAddress((UniversalProcPtr)menuKeyCode, _MenuKey);

    gGlobalsPtr->oldSystemMenuAddr = GetToolTrapAddress(_SystemMenu);
    SetToolTrapAddress((UniversalProcPtr)systemMenuCode, _SystemMenu);
}
```

```
/******************************************************************************

     PatchPPC

******************************************************************************/

OSErr PatchPPC(void)
{
     OSErr              err = noErr;
     Handle             ppcCodeH = nil;
     SymClass           symClass;
     Ptr                symAddr;
     ConnectionID       connID = kNoConnectionID;
     Str255             errStr;
     Ptr                mainAddr;
     UniversalProcPtr   menuSelectUPP = nil, menuKeyUPP = nil,
                        systemMenuUPP = nil;

     //
     // load the PPC resource-based code
     //

     ppcCodeH = Get1Resource(kPPCResourceType, kPPCResourceID);
     if (ppcCodeH == nil) return ResError() ? ResError() : resNotFound;
     DetachResource(ppcCodeH);
     HLock(ppcCodeH);

     //
     // open a connection to the code fragment
     //

     errStr[0] = 0;
     err = GetMemFragment(*ppcCodeH, GetHandleSize(ppcCodeH), kPPCFragmentName,
                                      kLoadNewCopy, &connID, &mainAddr, errStr);
     if (err != noErr) goto fail;

     //
     // find global data variable
     //

     err = FindSymbol(connID, kGlobalsSymbolName, &symAddr, &symClass);
     if (err != noErr) goto fail;

     //
     // point the PPC globals to our globals that we have already initialized
     //

     *(Globals**)symAddr = gGlobalsPtr;

     //
     // get MenuSelect address
     //
```

```
        err = FindSymbol(connID, kMenuSelectFunctionName, &symAddr, &symClass);
        if (err != noErr) goto fail;
#if 1
    menuSelectUPP = (UniversalProcPtr)NewRoutineDescriptor((ProcPtr)symAddr,
            kMenuSelectProcInfo, kPowerPCISA);
#else
    menuSelectUPP = (UniversalProcPtr)NewFatRoutineDescriptor(MenuSelect68k,
            symAddr, kMenuKeyProcInfo);
#endif
        if (menuSelectUPP == (UniversalProcPtr)symAddr)
            DebugStr("\p No RoutineDescriptor");
        if (menuSelectUPP == nil) goto fail;


        //
        // get MenuKey address
        //


        err = FindSymbol(connID, kMenuKeyFunctionName, &symAddr, &symClass);
        if (err != noErr) goto fail;
#if 1
    menuKeyUPP = (UniversalProcPtr)NewRoutineDescriptor((ProcPtr)symAddr,
            kMenuKeyProcInfo, kPowerPCISA);
#else
    menuKeyUPP = (UniversalProcPtr)NewFatRoutineDescriptor(MenuKey68k,
symAddr,
            kMenuKeyProcInfo);
#endif
        if (menuKeyUPP == (UniversalProcPtr)symAddr)
            DebugStr("\p No RoutineDescriptor");
        if (menuKeyUPP == nil) goto fail;


        //
        // get SystemMenu address
        //


        err = FindSymbol(connID, kSystemMenuFunctionName, &symAddr, &symClass);
        if (err != noErr) goto fail;
#if 1
    systemMenuUPP = (UniversalProcPtr)NewRoutineDescriptor((ProcPtr)symAddr,
            kSystemMenuProcInfo, kPowerPCISA);
#else
    systemMenuUPP = (UniversalProcPtr)NewFatRoutineDescriptor(SystemMenu68k,
            symAddr, kSystemMenuProcInfo);
#endif
        if (systemMenuUPP == (UniversalProcPtr)symAddr)
            DebugStr("\p No RoutineDescriptor");
        if (systemMenuUPP == nil) goto fail;


        //
        // apply the patches
        //
```

```
        ApplyPatches(menuSelectUPP, menuKeyUPP, systemMenuUPP);

        goto exit;
fail:
        if (menuSelectUPP) {
                DisposeRoutineDescriptor(menuSelectUPP);
                menuSelectUPP = nil;
        }
        if (menuKeyUPP) {
                DisposeRoutineDescriptor(menuKeyUPP);
                menuKeyUPP = nil;
        }
        if (connID != kNoConnectionID) {
                CloseConnection(&connID);
                connID = kNoConnectionID;
        }
        if (ppcCodeH) {
                DisposeHandle(ppcCodeH);
                ppcCodeH = nil;
        }
        if (errStr[0] != 0)
                DebugStr(errStr);
exit:
        return err;
}
```

INIT.h

```
/*
  File Name:   INIT.h
*/

#pragma once
```

PPCPatches.c

```
/*
  File Name:   PPCPatches.c
*/

/*** includes ************************************************/

#include <GestaltEqu.h>
#include <Errors.h>
#include <Folders.h>
#include <FragLoad.h>
#include <MixedMode.h>
#include <ConditionalMacros.h>
```

```
#include "PPCPatches.h"
#include "common.h"

/*** global variables ***************************************************/

GlobalsPtr    gGlobalsPtr = nil;

/**************************************************************************

    MenuSelectPPC

**************************************************************************/

#define CallMenuSelect(pt)   CallUniversalProc(gGlobalsPtr->oldMenuSelectAddr,
                                kMenuSelectProcInfo, pt)

pascal long MenuSelectPPC(Point startPt)
{
    long    result;
    OSErr   err = noErr;

    //
    // call the original MenuSelect first to see what was selected
    //

    result = CallMenuSelect(startPt);

    //
    // examine the menu selection
    //

    if (result != 0L) {
        err = DoMenuPatchStuff(result, gGlobalsPtr);
        if (err == noErr)
            result = 0L;
    }

    return result;
}


/**************************************************************************

    MenuKeyPPC

**************************************************************************/

#define CallMenuKey(ch)   CallUniversalProc(gGlobalsPtr->oldMenuKeyAddr,
                                kMenuKeyProcInfo, ch)
```

```
pascal long MenuKeyPPC(short ch)
{
    long      result;
    OSErr     err = noErr;

    //
    // call the original MenuSelect first to see what was selected
    //

    result = CallMenuKey(ch);

    //
    // examine the menu selection
    //

    if (result != 0L) {
            err = DoMenuPatchStuff(result, gGlobalsPtr);
            if (err == noErr)
                    result = 0L;
    }

    return result;
}

/**************************************************************************

    SystemMenuPPC

**************************************************************************/

#define CallSystemMenu(menuResult)   CallUniversalProc(gGlobalsPtr->oldSystemMenuAddr,
                                           kSystemMenuProcInfo, menuResult)

pascal   void SystemMenuPPC(long menuResult)
{
    OSErr     err = noErr;

    //
    // examine the menu selection
    //

    if (menuResult != 0L) {
            err = DoMenuPatchStuff(menuResult, gGlobalsPtr);
            if (err == noErr)
                    menuResult = 0L;
    }

    //
    // call the original SystemMenu if we didn't handle it
    //
```

```
            if (((err == fnfErr) || (err == noErr)) && (menuResult != 0L)) {
                    long ignore = CallSystemMenu(menuResult);
            }
    }
```

PPCPatches.h

```
/*
    File Name:   PPCPatches.h
*/

#pragma once

pascal      long MenuKeyPPC(short ch);
pascal      long MenuSelectPPC(Point startPt);
pascal      void SystemMenuPPC(long menuResult);
```

common.c

```
/*
  File Name:   common.c
*/

/*** includes ****************************************************/

#include <LowMem.h>
#include <ToolUtils.h>
#include <OSUtils.h>
#include <Dialogs.h>
#include <Files.h>
#include <Menus.h>
#include <Script.h>
#include <Resources.h>
#include <Types.h>
#include <Memory.h>
#include <GestaltEqu.h>
#include <Errors.h>
#include <Folders.h>
#include <Processes.h>
#include <EPPC.h>
#include <AppleEvents.h>
#include <Aliases.h>
#include <AppleEvents.h>
#include <AEObjects.h>
#include <AEPackObject.h>
#include <AERegistry.h>

#include "common.h"
```

```
/*************************************************************************

    DoMenuPatchStuff                                             .

*************************************************************************/

OSErr DoMenuPatchStuff(long menuResult, GlobalsPtr gp)
{
    FSSpec        appFolderSpec;
    OSErr         err = noErr;
    short         menuID = HiWord(menuResult);
    short         menuItem = LoWord(menuResult);
    MenuHandle    hMenu = GetMHandle(menuID);
    FSSpec        menuItemSpec;
    Str255        itemString;

    if (hMenu) {
            GetItem(hMenu, menuItem, itemString);
    } else {
//          ShowErrorAlert(&gp->ourFSpec, aGetMenuHandle, -1);
            return -1;
    }

    //
    // see if a folder exists for the current application
    //

    err = FSMakeFSSpec(-1, gp->menuScriptsFolderDirID,
            (unsigned char *)LMGetCurApName(), &appFolderSpec);
    if (err == noErr) {
            long    appFolderDirID;

            //
            // get directory id of current app's folder
            //

            err = GetDirectoryID(&appFolderSpec, &appFolderDirID);
            if (err == noErr) {

    //
    // make spec for potential item to launch within the current app's folder
    //

                    err = FSMakeFSSpec(-1, appFolderDirID,
                            itemString, &menuItemSpec);
                    if (err == noErr) {
                            err = OpenSelection(&menuItemSpec, kOpenItem);
                            if (err != noErr) {
                                    ShowErrorAlert(&gp->ourFSSpec, aOpenSelection,
```

```
                                                err);
                                        return err;
                                } else goto exit;
                        } // fnfErr
                } else {
                        ShowErrorAlert(&gp->ourFSSpec, aGetAppDirID, err);
                        return err;
                }
        } // fnfErr

        //
        // if we are still here, check the Any Application folder
        //

        err = FSMakeFSSpec(-1, gp->anyApplicationFolderDirID, itemString,
                &menuItemSpec);
        if (err == noErr) {
                err = OpenSelection(&menuItemSpec, kOpenItem);
                if (err != noErr)
                        ShowErrorAlert(&gp->ourFSSpec, aOpenSelection, err);
                else goto exit;
        } // fnfErr

exit:
        return err;
}


/*****************************************************************************

        GetDirectoryID

*****************************************************************************/

OSErr GetDirectoryID(FSSpec *spec, long *dirID)
{
        OSErr           err = noErr;
        CInfoPBRec      pb;

        pb.hFileInfo.ioNamePtr = spec->name;
        pb.hFileInfo.ioVRefNum = spec->vRefNum;
        pb.hFileInfo.ioFDirIndex = 0;
        pb.hFileInfo.ioDirID = spec->parID;

        err = PBGetCatInfoSync(&pb);

        *dirID = pb.hFileInfo.ioDirID;

        return err;
}
```

```
/**************************************************************************

    ShowErrorAlert

***************************************************************************/

#define alrtErrorID   128

void ShowErrorAlert(FSSpecPtr fsp, short action, OSErr err)
{
    Str255   errorString;
    Str32    errorNumStr;
    Str15    emptyString;
    short    fRefNum = -1;

    fRefNum = FSpOpenResFile(fsp, fsRdPerm);
    if (fRefNum != -1) {
            emptyString[0] = 0;
            NumToString((long)err, errorNumStr);
            GetIndString(errorString, rErrorStringListID, action);
            ParamText(errorString, errorNumStr, emptyString, emptyString);
            StopAlert(alrtErrorID, nil);
            ParamText(emptyString, emptyString, emptyString, emptyString);
            CloseResFile(fRefNum);
    } else SysBeep(0);
}


/**************************************************************************

    OpenSelection

    OpenSelection prepares and sends the Finder OpenSelection event
    This is a hacked down version of OpenSelection() from the DTS Sampler "FinderOpenSel
    1.0.1" The original version has several options, I've stripped out the ones I don't
    need and left just the code to tell the finder to open the directory window
    containing the incoming file.

***************************************************************************/

#define aeSelectionKeyword   'fsel'
#define aeOpenSelection      'sope'
#define kFinderSig           'FNDR'
#define kSystemType          'MACS'

OSErr OpenSelection(FSSpecPtr fsp, Boolean openOption)
{
    AppleEvent            aeEvent, aeReply;
    AEDesc                aeDirDesc, listElem, myAddressDesc;
    FSSpec                dirSpec;
    AEDesc                fileList;
    OSErr                 err = noErr;
```

```
ProcessSerialNumber    process;
AliasHandle            dirAlias, fileAlias;

//
// get the process serial number of the Finder
//

err = GetPSN(kSystemType, kFinderSig, &process);

if (err == noErr) {

        //
        // create an address descriptor
        //

        err = AECreateDesc(typeProcessSerialNumber, (Ptr)&process,
                sizeof(process), &myAddressDesc);

                if (err == noErr) {

                //
                // create the apple event
                //

                        err = AECreateAppleEvent(kFinderSig, aeOpenSelection,
                        &myAddressDesc, kAutoGenerateReturnID, kAnyTransactionID,
                        &aeEvent);

                //
                // no need to keep this address desc around anymore
                //

                        AEDisposeDesc(&myAddressDesc);

                if (err == noErr) {

                        //
                        // make a spec to the parent folder
                        //

                        err = FSMakeFSSpec(fsp->vRefNum, fsp->parID,
                            nil, &dirSpec);
                        err = NewAlias(nil, &dirSpec, &dirAlias);

                        //
                        // we are either opening the item or "showing" it
                        //

                        if (openOption == kOpenItem)
                                err = NewAlias(nil, fsp, &fileAlias);
                        else if (openOption == kShowItem)
                        // since we are opening a window,
```

```
        // we just make the file alias the same as the dir alias
             err = NewAlias(nil, &dirSpec, &fileAlias);

      //
      // create list of items to open
      //

if (err == noErr) {
   err = AECreateList(nil, 0, false, &fileList);

                 //
                 // create parent folder descriptor
                 //

     HLock((Handle)dirAlias);
     AECreateDesc(typeAlias, (Ptr)*dirAlias,
          GetHandleSize((Handle)dirAlias), &aeDirDesc);
     HUnlock((Handle)dirAlias);
     if ((err = AEPutParamDesc(&aeEvent, keyDirectObject,
          &aeDirDesc)) == noErr) {

       AEDisposeDesc(&aeDirDesc);

       //
       // create the file descriptor and add to aliasList
       //

       HLock((Handle)fileAlias);
       AECreateDesc(typeAlias, (Ptr)*fileAlias,
         GetHandleSize((Handle)fileAlias), &listElem);
       HLock((Handle)fileAlias);
       err = AEPutDesc(&fileList, 0, &listElem);
     }

     if (err == noErr) {

       AEDisposeDesc(&listElem);

       //
       // add the aliasList to the event
       //

       err = AEPutParamDesc(&aeEvent, aeSelectionKeyword,
        &fileList);
       AEDisposeDesc(&fileList);

       if (err == noErr)
           err = AESend(&aeEvent, &aeReply, kAENoReply +
               kAEAlwaysInteract + kAECanSwitchLayer,
               kAENormalPriority, kAEDefaultTimeout, nil, nil);
     }
   }
```

```
                AEDisposeDesc(&aeEvent);
            }
    }

            if ((Handle)dirAlias)
                DisposHandle((Handle)dirAlias);
            if ((Handle)fileAlias)
                DisposHandle((Handle)fileAlias);
        }

    return err;
}

/************************************************************************


    GetPSN

    returns the process serial number of the file that is currently
    running with given creator and type. if the returns PSN is all
    zeros then it was not found.

    ************************************************************************/

OSErr GetPSN(OSType creator, OSType type, ProcessSerialNumber *process)
{
    ProcessSerialNumber    processSerNum;
    ProcessSerialNumber    returnProcessSerNum;
    ProcessInfoRec    processInfo;
    Str32        processName;
    FSSpec        fsSpec;

    returnProcessSerNum.highLongOfPSN = 0L;
    returnProcessSerNum.lowLongOfPSN = 0L;

    /* start from the beginning */
    processSerNum.highLongOfPSN = 0L;
    processSerNum.lowLongOfPSN = kNoProcess;

    processInfo.processInfoLength = sizeof(ProcessInfoRec);
    processInfo.processName = (StringPtr)&processName;
    processInfo.processAppSpec = &fsSpec;

    while (GetNextProcess(&processSerNum) == noErr) {
            if (GetProcessInformation(&processSerNum, &processInfo) == noErr) {
                    if ((processInfo.processType == (long)type) &&
                            (processInfo.processSignature == creator)) {
                            BlockMove(&processSerNum, process,
                                    sizeof(ProcessSerialNumber));
                            return noErr;
                    }
            }
    }
```

```
        return -1;
    }
```

common.h

```
/*
    File Name:   common.h
*/

#pragma once

/*** includes **********************************************************/

#include <Processes.h>

/*** definitions *******************************************************/

#define kPPCFragmentName          "\pMenuScript Fragment"
#define kMenuSelectFunctionName    "\pMenuSelectPPC"
#define kMenuKeyFunctionName       "\pMenuKeyPPC"
#define kSystemMenuFunctionName    "\pSystemMenuPPC"
#define kGlobalsSymbolName         "\pgGlobalsPtr"

#define rErrorStringListID         129
#define aGetAppDirID               1
#define aGetMenuHandle             2
#define aOpenSelection             3

/*** typedefs **********************************************************/

#ifdef powerc
    #pragma options align=mac68k
#endif

typedef struct {
    long             menuScriptsFolderDirID;
    long             anyApplicationFolderDirID;
    UniversalProcPtr oldMenuSelectAddr;
    UniversalProcPtr oldMenuKeyAddr;
    UniversalProcPtr oldSystemMenuAddr;
    FSSpec           ourFSSpec;
} Globals, *GlobalsPtr, **GlobalsHdl;

#ifdef powerc
    #pragma options align=reset
#endif

enum
```

```
{
    kMenuSelectProcInfo = kPascalStackBased
                        | RESULT_SIZE(SIZE_CODE(sizeof(long)))
                        | REGISTER_RESULT_LOCATION(kRegisterD0)
                        | STACK_ROUTINE_PARAMETER(1,SIZE_CODE(sizeof(Point))),
    kMenuKeyProcInfo = kPascalStackBased
                        | RESULT_SIZE(SIZE_CODE(sizeof(long)))
                        | REGISTER_RESULT_LOCATION(kRegisterD0)
                        | STACK_ROUTINE_PARAMETER(1,SIZE_CODE(sizeof(short))),
    kSystemMenuProcInfo = kPascalStackBased
                        | STACK_ROUTINE_PARAMETER(1,SIZE_CODE(sizeof(long)))
};

/*** function prototypes **************************************************/

    OSErr    DoMenuPatchStuff(long menuResult, GlobalsPtr gp);
    #define  kOpenItem   true
    #define  kShowItem   false
    OSErr    OpenSelection(FSSpecPtr fsp, Boolean openOption);
    OSErr    GetPSN(OSType creator, OSType type, ProcessSerialNumber *process);
    OSErr    GetDirectoryID(FSSpecPtr fsp, long *dirID);
    void     ShowErrorAlert(FSSpecPtr fsp, short action, OSErr err);
```

Chapter Five Source Code

cdev.c

```
/*
  File Name:   cdev.c
*/

#include "cdev.h"
#include "dlogutils.h"
#include "allcommon.h"
#include <GestaltEqu.h>
#include <Processes.h>
#include <Icons.h>

#ifndef __powerc
#include "A4Stuff.h"
#include "SetupA4.h"
#endif

/*********************************************************************

    main

    procInfo = 1043120 decimal

*********************************************************************/
```

```
pascal long main(   short        message,
                    short        item,
                    short        numItems,
                    short        CPanelID,
                    EventRecord  *theEvent,
                    Handle       cdevStorage,   // private storage
                    DialogPtr    CPDialog)
{
    long    result = 0L;

#ifndef __powerc
    long    oldA4;
    oldA4 = SetCurrentA4();
    RememberA4();
#endif

    if (message == macDev) {     /* check our configuration */
            result = CanRun();
            goto exit;
} else if (cdevStorage != nil) {

            switch(message) {

            /* init ourselves */
            case initDev:
                    cdevStorage = InitControlPanel(CPDialog, numItems);
                    if (cdevStorage == nil) {
                            result = (long)cdevMemErr;
                            goto exit;
                    }
                    break;

            /* close ourselves down - can't depend on the item list here! */
            case closeDev:
                    if (cdevStorage != nil) {
                            CloseControlPanel(cdevStorage);
                            cdevStorage = nil;
                    }
                    break;

            /* handle hit on item & update cdevStorage each time since
               we can not trust the item list during a closeDev msg */
            case hitDev:
                    HitControlPanel(CPDialog, item, numItems, cdevStorage);
                    break;

            case macDev:
                    /* check our configuration, ignore it in here though */
                    break;

            case nulDev:    /* null event */
                    break;
```

```
                 case cursorDev:    /* adjust our cursor */
                       break;

                 case updateDev:    /* handle any update drawing */
                       UpdatePanel(CPDialog, cdevStorage, numItems);
                       break;

                 case activDev:     /* activate any needed items */
                 case deactivDev:   /* deactivate any needed items */
                 case keyEvtDev:    /* respond to keydown */
                       break;

                 case undoDev:      /* undo event */
                 case cutDev:       /* cut event */
                 case copyDev:      /* copy event */
                 case pasteDev:     /* paste event */
                 case clearDev:     /* clear event */
                       break;
            }

         result = (long)cdevStorage;
         goto exit;

    } else {

         /*
         **   if cdevStorage = NIL then ControlPanel
         ** will put up memory error
         */

         result = nil; /* cdevStorage == nil */
         goto exit;
    }

exit:

#ifndef __powerc
    SetA4(oldA4);
#endif

    return result;
}

/************************************************************************

   HitControlPanel

*************************************************************************/

void HitControlPanel(DialogPtr d, short item, short numItems, Handle cdevStorage)
```

```
{
    short myItem = item - numItems;
    switch (myItem) {
            case itemIcon:
                    Alert(129, nil);
                    break;
            case itemOnRadio:
            case itemOffRadio:
                    DoRadioGroup(d, itemOnRadio + numItems, itemOffRadio + numItems,
                            item);
                    (*(PreferencesHdl)cdevStorage)->fEnabled = (GetRadioFromGroup(d,
                            itemOnRadio + numItems, itemOffRadio + numItems) ==
                            (itemOnRadio + numItems));
                    UpdateINIT((PreferencesHdl)cdevStorage);
                    break;
    }
}

/**********************************************************************

    CloseControlPanel

**********************************************************************/

void CloseControlPanel(Handle cdevStorage)
{
    ChangedResource(cdevStorage);
    WriteResource(cdevStorage);
    ReleaseResource(cdevStorage);
}

/**********************************************************************

    InitControlPanel

**********************************************************************/

Handle InitControlPanel(DialogPtr d, short numItems)
{
    Handle  cdevStorage = nil;
    short   iType;
    Rect    iRect;
    Handle  iHandle;

    cdevStorage = Get1Resource(kPreferencesResType, kPreferencesResID);
    if (cdevStorage != nil) {
            DoRadioGroup(d, itemOnRadio + numItems, itemOffRadio + numItems,
                    (*(PreferencesHdl)cdevStorage)->fEnabled ?
                    itemOnRadio : itemOffRadio + numItems);
            GetDItem(d, numItems + itemStaticText, &iType, &iHandle, &iRect);
    #ifdef __powerc
```

```
                    SetIText(iHandle, "\pThis cdev is native PowerPC code.");
            #else
                    SetIText(iHandle, "\pThis cdev is 680x0 code.");
            #endif
            }

        return cdevStorage;
    }

    /************************************************************************

        CanRun

    ************************************************************************/

    long CanRun(void)
    {
        long    response;
        OSErr   err = noErr;

        err = Gestalt(gestaltSystemVersion, &response);
        if ((err != noErr) || (response <\f>0x00000700)) {
                return (long)false;
        } else {
                return (long)true;
        }
    }

    /************************************************************************

        UpdatePanel

    ************************************************************************/

    void UpdatePanel(DialogPtr d, Handle prefs, short numItems)
    {
        GrafPtr     savePort;

        /* set up port to draw */
        GetPort(&savePort);
        SetPort(d);

        /* draw here */

        /* restore port */
        SetPort(savePort);
    }
```

```
/*********************************************************************

    UpdateINIT

*********************************************************************/

void UpdateINIT(PreferencesHdl ph)
{
    OSErr              err = noErr;
    PreferencesPtr     pp;

    err = Gestalt(kGestaltSelector, (long*)&pp);
    if (err == noErr) {
            pp->fEnabled = (*ph)->fEnabled;
    } else SysBeep(0);   // INIT is not loaded, most likely
}
```

cdev.h

```
/*
    File Name:    cdev.h
*/

#pragma once

#include "allcommon.h"

#define    itemIcon              1
#define    itemStaticText        4
#define    itemOnRadio           6
#define    itemOffRadio          7

void       HitControlPanel(DialogPtr d, short item, short numItems,
                 Handle cdevStorage);
void       CloseControlPanel(Handle cdevStorage);
Handle     InitControlPanel(DialogPtr d, short numItems);
long       CanRun(void);
void       UpdatePanel(DialogPtr d, Handle prefs, short numItems);
void       UpdateINIT(PreferencesHdl ph);
```

INIT.c

```
/*
    File Name:    INIT.c
*/

#ifdef USESROUTINEDESCRIPTORS
```

```
#undef USESROUTINEDESCRIPTORS
#define USESROUTINEDESCRIPTORS 1
#else
#define USESROUTINEDESCRIPTORS 1
#endif

//extern pascal UniversalProcPtr NewFatRoutineDescriptor(ProcPtr theM68kProc,
//    ProcPtr thePowerPCProc, ProcInfoType theProcInfo)
//    THREEWORDINLINE(0x303C, 0x0002, 0xAA59);


/*** includes *************************************************/

#include <LowMem.h>
#include <ToolUtils.h>
#include <OSUtils.h>
#include <Dialogs.h>
#include <Files.h>
#include <Menus.h>
#include <Script.h>
#include <Resources.h>
#include <Types.h>
#include <Memory.h>
#include <GestaltEqu.h>
#include <Errors.h>
#include <Folders.h>
#include <FragLoad.h>
#include <MixedMode.h>
//#include <ConditionalMacros.h>

#include "INIT.h"
#include "common.h"
#include "allcommon.h"
#include "A4Stuff.h"
#include "SetupA4.h"

/*** definitions *************************************************/

#define kMinimumSystemVersion     0x00000700    // minimum system version

#define kINITResourceType         'INIT'        // our INIT code resource type
#define kINITResourceID           0             // and ID

#define kPPCResourceType          'PPC '        // our PowerPC code resource type
#define kPPCResourceID            0             // and ID

#define rStringListID             128           // INIT string list resource
```

```
#define iMenuScriptsFolderName      1                  // MenuScripts folder name
#define iAnyApplicationFolderName    2


/*** typedefs ***********************************************************/

typedef pascal long (*MenuSelectProc)(Point pt);
typedef pascal long (*MenuKeyProc)(short ch);
typedef pascal void (*SystemMenuProc)(long menuResult);


/*** global variables ***************************************************/

GlobalsPtr      gGlobalsPtr;

/*** function prototypes ************************************************/

OSErr     RememberMe(FSSpecPtr fsp);
pascal    long MenuKey68k(short ch);
pascal    long MenuSelect68k(Point startPt);
pascal    void SystemMenu68k(long menuResult);
void      ApplyPatches(void * menuSelectCode, void * menuKeyCode,
                void * systemMenuCode);
OSErr     PatchPPC(void);
pascal    OSErr GestaltGetGlobals(OSType selector, long *response);


/*************************************************************************

    main

*************************************************************************/

void main(void)
{
    FSSpec    menuScriptsFolderFSSpec;
    FSSpec    anyApplicationFolderFSSpec;
    Str32     menuScriptsFolderName;
    Str32     anyApplicationFolderName;
    Handle    hINIT = nil;
    PreferencesHdl  ph = nil;
    THz       savedZone;
    long      oldA4;
    long      response;
    long      foundDirID;
    short     foundVRefNum;
    OSErr     err = noErr;

    //
    // make sure we are in the system heap
    //

    savedZone = GetZone();
    SetZone(SystemZone());
```

```
//
// set up our A4 context for this file
//

oldA4 = SetCurrentA4();
RememberA4();

//
// verify minimum system version
//

err = Gestalt(gestaltSystemVersion, &response);
if ((err != noErr) || (response <kMinimumSystemVersion)) goto fail;

//
// allocate our global data
//

gGlobalsPtr = (GlobalsPtr)NewPtrSysClear(sizeof(Globals));
if (gGlobalsPtr == nil) {
        err = MemError() ? MemError() : memFullErr;
        goto fail;
}

//
// find ourselves (it's a Zen thing)
//

err = RememberMe(&gGlobalsPtr->ourFSSpec);
if (err != noErr) goto fail;

//
// find out where our MenuScripts folder is located (in the System folder)
// and figure out its directory id
//

// load folder name string from resource string list
GetIndString(menuScriptsFolderName, rStringListID, iMenuScriptsFolderName);
if (menuScriptsFolderName[0] == 0) {
        err = resNotFound;
        goto fail;
}

// locate dirID of system folder
err = FindFolder(kOnSystemDisk, kSystemFolderType, kDontCreateFolder,
        &foundVRefNum, &foundDirID);
if (err != noErr) goto fail;

// make a spec for the MenuScripts folder
err = FSMakeFSSpec(foundVRefNum, foundDirID, menuScriptsFolderName,
```

```
            &menuScriptsFolderFSSpec);
    if (err == fnfErr) {
            // create it if it doesn't exist and get its directory id
            err = FSpDirCreate(&menuScriptsFolderFSSpec, smSystemScript,
                    &gGlobalsPtr->menuScriptsFolderDirID);
    } else if (err == noErr) {
            // otherwise just get its directory id
            err = GetDirectoryID(&menuScriptsFolderFSSpec,
                    &gGlobalsPtr->menuScriptsFolderDirID);
    }
    if (err != noErr) goto fail;

    // load folder name string from resource string list
    GetIndString(anyApplicationFolderName, rStringListID,
            iAnyApplicationFolderName);
    if (anyApplicationFolderName[0] == 0) {
            err = resNotFound;
            goto fail;
    }

    // make a spec for the Any Application folder
    err = FSMakeFSSpec(foundVRefNum, gGlobalsPtr->menuScriptsFolderDirID,
            anyApplicationFolderName, &anyApplicationFolderFSSpec);
    if (err == fnfErr) {
            // create it if it doesn't exist and get its directory id
            err = FSpDirCreate(&anyApplicationFolderFSSpec, smSystemScript,
                    &gGlobalsPtr->anyApplicationFolderDirID);
    } else if (err == noErr) {
            // otherwise just get its directory id
            err = GetDirectoryID(&anyApplicationFolderFSSpec,
                    &gGlobalsPtr->anyApplicationFolderDirID);
    }
    if (err != noErr) goto fail;

    //
    // get a handle to our INIT resource
    //

    hINIT = Get1Resource(kINITResourceType, kINITResourceID);
    if (hINIT == nil) {
            err = ResError() ? ResError() : resNotFound;
            goto fail;
    }

    //
    // load preferences and copy into our global data, then release resource
    //

    ph = (PreferencesHdl)Get1Resource(kPreferencesResType, kPreferencesResID);
    if (ph == nil) {
            err = ResError() ? ResError() : resNotFound;
            goto fail;
```

```
    }
    BlockMove(*ph, &(gGlobalsPtr->preferences), sizeof(Preferences));
    ReleaseResource((Handle)ph);

    //
    // patch traps
    //

    err = Gestalt(gestaltSysArchitecture, &response);
    if (err != noErr) goto fail;

    if (response == gestalt68k)
            ApplyPatches(MenuSelect68k, MenuKey68k, SystemMenu68k);
    else if (response == gestaltPowerPC)
            err = PatchPPC();
    else err = gestaltUnknownErr;      // who knows what might be next?

    if (err != noErr) goto fail;

    //
    // install our gestalt selector
    //

    err = NewGestalt(kGestaltSelector, (SelectorFunctionUPP)&GestaltGetGlobals);
    if (err != noErr) goto fail;

    //
    // make sure the INIT stays in memory
    //

    DetachResource(hINIT);

    goto exit;

fail:
    // we get here if we fail

    //
    // deallocate our global memory if it exists
    //

    if (gGlobalsPtr) {
            DisposePtr((Ptr)gGlobalsPtr);
            gGlobalsPtr = nil;
    }

    //
    // Our INIT will be released automatically when the file is closed
    //
```

```
/*
    if (hINIT) {
            ReleaseResource(hINIT);
            hINIT = nil;
    }
*/

    //
    // alert the user to the problem
    //

    if (err != noErr) {
            SysBeep(0);
    }

exit:
    // we get here upon success or failure

    //
    // restore a4
    //

    SetA4(oldA4);

    //
    // restore zone
    //

    SetZone(savedZone);
}

/************************************************************************

    RememberMe

*************************************************************************/

OSErr RememberMe(FSSpecPtr fsp)
{
    FCBPBRec    pb;
    OSErr       err = noErr;

    pb.ioCompletion = nil;
    pb.ioNamePtr = fsp->name;
    pb.ioVRefNum = 0;
    pb.ioRefNum = CurResFile();
    pb.ioFCBIndx = 0;

    err = PBGetFCBInfoSync(&pb);

    fsp->vRefNum = pb.ioFCBVRefNum;
    fsp->parID = pb.ioFCBParID;
```

```
        return err;
    }

/************************************************************************

    MenuKey68k

************************************************************************/

pascal long MenuKey68k(short ch)
{
    long        result;
    long        oldA4;
    OSErr       err = noErr;

    //
    // to access our globals
    //

    oldA4 = SetUpA4();

    //
    // call the original MenuSelect first to see what was selected
    //

    result = ((MenuKeyProc)gGlobalsPtr->oldMenuKeyAddr)(ch);

    //
    // examine the menu selection
    //

    if ((result != 0L) && (gGlobalsPtr->preferences.fEnabled)) {
            err = DoMenuPatchStuff(result, gGlobalsPtr);
            if (err == noErr)
                    result = 0L;
    }

    //
    // restore a4 and return
    //

    RestoreA4(oldA4);
    return result;
}

/************************************************************************

    MenuSelect68k

************************************************************************/
```

```
pascal long MenuSelect68k(Point startPt)
{
    long      result;
    long      oldA4;
    OSErr     err = noErr;

    //
    // to access our globals
    //

    oldA4 = SetUpA4();

    //
    // call the original MenuSelect first to see what was selected
    //

    result = ((MenuSelectProc)gGlobalsPtr->oldMenuSelectAddr)(startPt);

    //
    // examine the menu selection
    //

    if ((result != 0L) && (gGlobalsPtr->preferences.fEnabled)) {
            err = DoMenuPatchStuff(result, gGlobalsPtr);
            if (err == noErr)
                  result = 0L;
    }

    //
    // restore a4 and return
    //

    RestoreA4(oldA4);
    return result;
}

/***********************************************************************

    SystemMenu68k

***********************************************************************/

pascal    void SystemMenu68k(long menuResult)
{
    long      oldA4;
    OSErr     err = noErr;

    //
    // to access our globals
    //

    oldA4 = SetUpA4();
```

```
        //
        // examine the menu selection
        //

        if ((menuResult != 0L) && (gGlobalsPtr->preferences.fEnabled)) {
                err = DoMenuPatchStuff(menuResult, gGlobalsPtr);
                if (err == noErr)
                        menuResult = 0L;
        }

        //
        // call the original SystemMenu if we didn't handle it
        //

        if (((err == fnfErr) || (err == noErr)) && (menuResult != 0L))
                ((SystemMenuProc)gGlobalsPtr->oldSystemMenuAddr)(menuResult);

        //
        // restore a4 and return
        //

        RestoreA4(oldA4);
}

/***************************************************************************

    ApplyPatches

***************************************************************************/

void ApplyPatches(void * menuSelectCode, void * menuKeyCode, void * systemMenuCode)
{
        gGlobalsPtr->oldMenuSelectAddr = GetToolTrapAddress(_MenuSelect);
        SetToolTrapAddress((UniversalProcPtr)menuSelectCode, _MenuSelect);

        gGlobalsPtr->oldMenuKeyAddr = GetToolTrapAddress(_MenuKey);
        SetToolTrapAddress((UniversalProcPtr)menuKeyCode, _MenuKey);

        gGlobalsPtr->oldSystemMenuAddr = GetToolTrapAddress(_SystemMenu);
        SetToolTrapAddress((UniversalProcPtr)systemMenuCode, _SystemMenu);
}

/***************************************************************************

    PatchPPC

***************************************************************************/

OSErr PatchPPC(void)
{
```

```
    OSErr              err = noErr;
    Handle             ppcCodeH = nil;
    SymClass           symClass;
    Ptr                symAddr;
    ConnectionID       connID = kNoConnectionID;
    Str255             errStr;
    Ptr                mainAddr;
    UniversalProcPtr   menuSelectUPP = nil, menuKeyUPP = nil,
                       systemMenuUPP = nil;

  //
  // load the PPC resource-based code
  //

  ppcCodeH = Get1Resource(kPPCResourceType, kPPCResourceID);
  if (ppcCodeH == nil) return ResError() ? ResError() : resNotFound;
  DetachResource(ppcCodeH);
  HLock(ppcCodeH);

  //
  // open a connection to the code fragment
  //

  errStr[0] = 0;
  err = GetMemFragment(*ppcCodeH, GetHandleSize(ppcCodeH), kPPCFragmentName,
                                  kLoadNewCopy, &connID, &mainAddr, errStr);
  if (err != noErr) goto fail;

  //
  // find global data variable
  //

  err = FindSymbol(connID, kGlobalsSymbolName, &symAddr, &symClass);
  if (err != noErr) goto fail;

  //
  // point the PPC globals to our globals that we have already initialized
  //

  *(Globals**)symAddr = gGlobalsPtr;

  //
  // get MenuSelect address
  //

  err = FindSymbol(connID, kMenuSelectFunctionName, &symAddr, &symClass);
  if (err != noErr) goto fail;
#if 1
  menuSelectUPP = (UniversalProcPtr)NewRoutineDescriptor((ProcPtr)symAddr,
        kMenuSelectProcInfo, kPowerPCISA);
#else
```

```
    menuSelectUPP = (UniversalProcPtr)NewFatRoutineDescriptor(MenuSelect68k,
        symAddr, kMenuKeyProcInfo);
#endif
    if (menuSelectUPP == (UniversalProcPtr)symAddr)
        DebugStr("\p No RoutineDescriptor");
    if (menuSelectUPP == nil) goto fail;


    //
    // get MenuKey address
    //

    err = FindSymbol(connID, kMenuKeyFunctionName, &symAddr, &symClass);
    if (err != noErr) goto fail;
#if 1
    menuKeyUPP = (UniversalProcPtr)NewRoutineDescriptor((ProcPtr)symAddr,
        kMenuKeyProcInfo, kPowerPCISA);
#else
    menuKeyUPP = (UniversalProcPtr)NewFatRoutineDescriptor(MenuKey68k, symAddr,
        kMenuKeyProcInfo);
#endif
    if (menuKeyUPP == (UniversalProcPtr)symAddr)
        DebugStr("\p No RoutineDescriptor");
    if (menuKeyUPP == nil) goto fail;


    //
    // get SystemMenu address
    //

    err = FindSymbol(connID, kSystemMenuFunctionName, &symAddr, &symClass);
    if (err != noErr) goto fail;
#if 1
    systemMenuUPP = (UniversalProcPtr)NewRoutineDescriptor((ProcPtr)symAddr,
        kSystemMenuProcInfo, kPowerPCISA);
#else
    systemMenuUPP = (UniversalProcPtr)NewFatRoutineDescriptor(SystemMenu68k,
        symAddr, kSystemMenuProcInfo);
#endif
    if (systemMenuUPP == (UniversalProcPtr)symAddr)
        DebugStr("\p No RoutineDescriptor");
    if (systemMenuUPP == nil) goto fail;


    //
    // apply the patches
    //

    ApplyPatches(menuSelectUPP, menuKeyUPP, systemMenuUPP);

    goto exit;
fail:
    if (menuSelectUPP) {
        DisposeRoutineDescriptor(menuSelectUPP);
        menuSelectUPP = nil;
```

```
        }
        if (menuKeyUPP) {
                DisposeRoutineDescriptor(menuKeyUPP);
                menuKeyUPP = nil;
        }
        if (connID != kNoConnectionID) {
                CloseConnection(&connID);
                connID = kNoConnectionID;
        }
        if (ppcCodeH) {
                DisposeHandle(ppcCodeH);
                ppcCodeH = nil;
        }
        if (errStr[0] != 0)
                DebugStr(errStr);
exit:
    return err;
}


/***************************************************************************


    GestaltGetGlobals

    This Gestalt function returns a ptr to the INITs preferences so they
    can be changed on the fly.

    **************************************************************************/

pascal OSErr GestaltGetGlobals(OSType selector, long *response)
{
    long oldA4 = SetUpA4();
    *response = (long)&(gGlobalsPtr->preferences);
    RestoreA4(oldA4);
    return noErr;
}
```

INIT.h

```
/*
  File Name:   INIT.h
*/

#pragma once
```

PPCPatches. c

```
/*
  File Name:   PPCPatches.c
*/

/*** includes *********************************************************/
```

```
#include <GestaltEqu.h>
#include <Errors.h>
#include <Folders.h>
#include <FragLoad.h>
#include <MixedMode.h>
#include <ConditionalMacros.h>

#include "PPCPatches.h"
#include "common.h"

/*** global variables ***************************************************/

GlobalsPtr     gGlobalsPtr = nil;

/***********************************************************************

    MenuSelectPPC

***********************************************************************/

#define CallMenuSelect(pt)    CallUniversalProc(gGlobalsPtr->oldMenuSelectAddr,
                                  kMenuSelectProcInfo, pt)

pascal long MenuSelectPPC(Point startPt)
{
    long      result;
    OSErr     err = noErr;

    //
    // call the original MenuSelect first to see what was selected
    //

    result = CallMenuSelect(startPt);
    //
    // examine the menu selection
    //

    if ((result != 0L) && (gGlobalsPtr->preferences.fEnabled)) {
        err = DoMenuPatchStuff(result, gGlobalsPtr);
        if (err == noErr)
            result = 0L;
    }

    return result;
}


/***********************************************************************

    MenuKeyPPC

***********************************************************************/
```

```
#define CallMenuKey(ch)    CallUniversalProc(gGlobalsPtr->oldMenuKeyAddr,
                                  kMenuKeyProcInfo, ch)

pascal long MenuKeyPPC(short ch)
{
    long      result;
    OSErr     err = noErr;

    //
    // call the original MenuSelect first to see what was selected
    //

    result = CallMenuKey(ch);

    //
    // examine the menu selection
    //

    if ((result != 0L) && (gGlobalsPtr->preferences.fEnabled)) {
            err = DoMenuPatchStuff(result, gGlobalsPtr);
            if (err == noErr)
                    result = 0L;
    }

    return result;
}

/***************************************************************************

    SystemMenuPPC

***************************************************************************/

#define CallSystemMenu(menuResult)    CallUniversalProc(gGlobalsPtr->oldSystemMenuAddr,
                                          kSystemMenuProcInfo, menuResult)

pascal   void SystemMenuPPC(long menuResult)
{
    OSErr     err = noErr;

    //
    // examine the menu selection
    //

    if ((menuResult != 0L) && (gGlobalsPtr->preferences.fEnabled)) {
            err = DoMenuPatchStuff(menuResult, gGlobalsPtr);
            if (err == noErr)
                    menuResult = 0L;
    }
```

```
                    //
                    // call the original SystemMenu if we didn't handle it
                    //

                    if (((err == fnfErr) || (err == noErr)) && (menuResult != 0L))
                            CallSystemMenu(menuResult);
            }
```

PPCPatches.h

```
            /*
               File Name:    PPCPatches.h
            */

            #pragma once

            pascal    long MenuKeyPPC(short ch);
            pascal    long MenuSelectPPC(Point startPt);
            pascal    void SystemMenuPPC(long menuResult);
```

common.c

```
            /*
               File Name:    common.c
            */

            /*** includes ***********************************************************/

            #include <LowMem.h>
            #include <ToolUtils.h>
            #include <OSUtils.h>
            #include <Dialogs.h>
            #include <Files.h>
            #include <Menus.h>
            #include <Script.h>
            #include <Resources.h>
            #include <Types.h>
            #include <Memory.h>
            #include <GestaltEqu.h>
            #include <Errors.h>
            #include <Folders.h>
            #include <Processes.h>
            #include <EPPC.h>
            #include <AppleEvents.h>
            #include <Aliases.h>
            #include <AppleEvents.h>
            #include <AEObjects.h>
            #include <AEPackObject.h>
            #include <AERegistry.h>

            #include "common.h"
```

```
/*************************************************************************

    DoMenuPatchStuff

*************************************************************************/

OSErr DoMenuPatchStuff(long menuResult, GlobalsPtr gp)
{
    FSSpec        appFolderSpec;
    OSErr         err = noErr;
    short         menuID = HiWord(menuResult);
    short         menuItem = LoWord(menuResult);
    MenuHandle    hMenu = GetMHandle(menuID);
    FSSpec        menuItemSpec;
    Str255        itemString;

    if (hMenu) {
            GetItem(hMenu, menuItem, itemString);
    } else {
//        ShowErrorAlert(&gp->ourFSpec, aGetMenuHandle, -1);
            return -1;
    }

    //
    // see if a folder exists for the current application
    //

    err = FSMakeFSSpec(-1, gp->menuScriptsFolderDirID,
            (unsigned char *)LMGetCurApName(), &appFolderSpec);
    if (err == noErr) {
            long    appFolderDirID;

            //
            // get directory id of current app's folder
            //

            err = GetDirectoryID(&appFolderSpec, &appFolderDirID);
            if (err == noErr) {

            //
            // make spec for potential item to launch within the current app's folder
            //

                    err = FSMakeFSSpec(-1, appFolderDirID, itemString,
                            &menuItemSpec);
                    if (err == noErr) {
                            err = OpenSelection(&menuItemSpec, kOpenItem);
                            if (err != noErr) {
                                    ShowErrorAlert(&gp->ourFSpec,
                                            aOpenSelection, err);
                                    return err;
```

```
                                        } else goto exit;
                        } // fnfErr
                } else {
                        ShowErrorAlert(&gp->ourFSSpec, aGetAppDirID, err);
                        return err;
                }
        } // fnfErr

        //
        // if we are still here, check the Any Application folder
        //

        err = FSMakeFSSpec(-1, gp->anyApplicationFolderDirID, itemString,
                &menuItemSpec);
        if (err == noErr) {
                err = OpenSelection(&menuItemSpec, kOpenItem);
                if (err != noErr)
                        ShowErrorAlert(&gp->ourFSSpec, aOpenSelection, err);
                else goto exit;
        } // fnfErr

exit:
    return err;
}

/****************************************************************************
*

    GetDirectoryID

****************************************************************************
/

OSErr GetDirectoryID(FSSpec *spec, long *dirID)
{
    OSErr        err = noErr;
    CInfoPBRec   pb;

    pb.hFileInfo.ioNamePtr = spec->name;
    pb.hFileInfo.ioVRefNum = spec->vRefNum;
    pb.hFileInfo.ioFDirIndex = 0;
    pb.hFileInfo.ioDirID = spec->parID;

    err = PBGetCatInfoSync(&pb);

    *dirID = pb.hFileInfo.ioDirID;

    return err;
}
```

```
/***************************************************************************

   ShowErrorAlert

***************************************************************************/

#define alrtErrorID   128

void ShowErrorAlert(FSSpecPtr fsp, short action, OSErr err)
{
    Str255  errorString;
    Str32   errorNumStr;
    Str15   emptyString;
    short   fRefNum = -1;

    fRefNum = FSpOpenResFile(fsp, fsRdPerm);
    if (fRefNum != -1) {
            emptyString[0] = 0;
            NumToString((long)err, errorNumStr);
            GetIndString(errorString, rErrorStringListID, action);
            ParamText(errorString, errorNumStr, emptyString, emptyString);
            StopAlert(alrtErrorID, nil);
            ParamText(emptyString, emptyString, emptyString, emptyString);
            CloseResFile(fRefNum);
    } else SysBeep(0);
}


/***************************************************************************

   OpenSelection

   OpenSelection prepares and sends the Finder OpenSelection event.
   This is a hacked down version of OpenSelection() from the DTS Sampler
   "FinderOpenSel 1.0.1" The original version has several options, I've
   stripped out the ones I don't need and left just the code to tell the
   finder to open the directory window containing the incoming file.

***************************************************************************/

#define aeSelectionKeyword   'fsel'
#define aeOpenSelection      'sope'
#define kFinderSig           'FNDR'
#define kSystemType          'MACS'

OSErr OpenSelection(FSSpecPtr fsp, Boolean openOption)
{
    AppleEvent            aeEvent, aeReply;
    AEDesc                aeDirDesc, listElem, myAddressDesc;
    FSSpec                dirSpec;
    AEDesc                fileList;
    OSErr                 err = noErr;
```

```
ProcessSerialNumber   process;
AliasHandle           dirAlias, fileAlias;

//
// get the process serial number of the Finder
//

err = GetPSN(kSystemType, kFinderSig, &process);

if (err == noErr) {

        //
        // create an address descriptor
        //

        err = AECreateDesc(typeProcessSerialNumber, (Ptr)&process,
                sizeof(process), &myAddressDesc);

                if (err == noErr) {

        //
        // create the apple event
        //

                err = AECreateAppleEvent(kFinderSig, aeOpenSelection,
                &myAddressDesc, kAutoGenerateReturnID, kAnyTransactionID,
                &aeEvent);

        //
        // no need to keep this address desc around anymore
        //

                        AEDisposeDesc(&myAddressDesc);

                if (err == noErr) {

                        //
                        // make a spec to the parent folder
                        //

                        err = FSMakeFSSpec(fsp->vRefNum, fsp->parID,
                        nil, &dirSpec);
                                err = NewAlias(nil, &dirSpec, &dirAlias);

                        //
                        // we are either opening the item or "showing" it
                        //

                        if (openOption == kOpenItem)
                                err = NewAlias(nil, fsp, &fileAlias);
                        else if (openOption == kShowItem)
                        // since we are opening a window,
```

```
                            // we just make the file alias the same as the dir alias
                                err = NewAlias(nil, &dirSpec, &fileAlias);

                    //
                    // create list of items to open
                    //

if (err == noErr) {
    err = AECreateList(nil, 0, false, &fileList);

                //
                // create parent folder descriptor
                //

    HLock((Handle)dirAlias);
    AECreateDesc(typeAlias, (Ptr)*dirAlias,
        GetHandleSize((Handle)dirAlias), &aeDirDesc);
    HUnlock((Handle)dirAlias);
    if ((err = AEPutParamDesc(&aeEvent, keyDirectObject,
        &aeDirDesc)) == noErr) {

        AEDisposeDesc(&aeDirDesc);

        //
         // create the file descriptor and add to aliasList
        //

        HLock((Handle)fileAlias);
        AECreateDesc(typeAlias, (Ptr)*fileAlias,
          GetHandleSize((Handle)fileAlias), &listElem);
        HLock((Handle)fileAlias);
        err = AEPutDesc(&fileList, 0, &listElem);
}

if (err == noErr) {

    AEDisposeDesc(&listElem);

    //
     // add the aliasList to the event
    //

    err = AEPutParamDesc(&aeEvent, aeSelectionKeyword,
     &fileList);
    AEDisposeDesc(&fileList);

    if (err == noErr)
        err = AESend(&aeEvent, &aeReply, kAENoReply +
            kAEAlwaysInteract + kAECanSwitchLayer,
            kAENormalPriority, kAEDefaultTimeout, nil, nil);
  }
}
```

```
        AEDisposeDesc(&aeEvent);
    }
}

    if ((Handle)dirAlias)
        DisposHandle((Handle)dirAlias);
    if ((Handle)fileAlias)
        DisposHandle((Handle)fileAlias);
    }

    return err;
}

/*********************************************************************

    GetPSN

    returns the process serial number of the file that is currently
    running with given creator and type. if the returns PSN is all
    zeros then it was not found.

*********************************************************************/

OSErr GetPSN(OSType creator, OSType type, ProcessSerialNumber *process)
{
    ProcessSerialNumber    processSerNum;
    ProcessSerialNumber    returnProcessSerNum;
    ProcessInfoRec         processInfo;
    Str32                  processName;
    FSSpec                 fsSpec;

    returnProcessSerNum.highLongOfPSN = 0L;
    returnProcessSerNum.lowLongOfPSN = 0L;

    /* start from the beginning */
    processSerNum.highLongOfPSN = 0L;
    processSerNum.lowLongOfPSN = kNoProcess;

    processInfo.processInfoLength = sizeof(ProcessInfoRec);
    processInfo.processName = (StringPtr)&processName;
    processInfo.processAppSpec = &fsSpec;

    while (GetNextProcess(&processSerNum) == noErr) {
            if (GetProcessInformation(&processSerNum, &processInfo) == noErr) {
                    if ((processInfo.processType == (long)type) &&
                            (processInfo.processSignature == creator)) {
                            BlockMove(&processSerNum, process,
                                    sizeof(ProcessSerialNumber));
                            return noErr;
                    }
            }
    }
```

```
    return -1;
}
```

common.h

```
/*
    File Name:    common.h
*/

#pragma once

/*** includes ***********************************************************/

#include <Processes.h>
#include "allcommon.h"

/*** definitions ********************************************************/

#define kPPCFragmentName            "\pMenuScript Fragment"
#define kMenuSelectFunctionName     "\pMenuSelectPPC"
#define kMenuKeyFunctionName        "\pMenuKeyPPC"
#define kSystemMenuFunctionName     "\pSystemMenuPPC"
#define kGlobalsSymbolName          "\pgGlobalsPtr"

#define rErrorStringListID     129
#define aGetAppDirID           1
#define aGetMenuHandle         2
#define aOpenSelection         3

/*** typedefs ***********************************************************/

#ifdef powerc
    #pragma options align=mac68k
#endif

typedef struct {
    long              menuScriptsFolderDirID;
    long              anyApplicationFolderDirID;
    UniversalProcPtr  oldMenuSelectAddr;
    UniversalProcPtr  oldMenuKeyAddr;
    UniversalProcPtr  oldSystemMenuAddr;
    FSSpec            ourFSSpec;
    Preferences       preferences;
} Globals, *GlobalsPtr, **GlobalsHdl;

#ifdef powerc
    #pragma options align=reset
#endif

enum
{
```

```
        kMenuSelectProcInfo = kPascalStackBased
                            | RESULT_SIZE(SIZE_CODE(sizeof(long)))
                            | REGISTER_RESULT_LOCATION(kRegisterD0)
                            | STACK_ROUTINE_PARAMETER(1,SIZE_CODE(sizeof(Point))),
        kMenuKeyProcInfo = kPascalStackBased
                            | RESULT_SIZE(SIZE_CODE(sizeof(long)))
                            | REGISTER_RESULT_LOCATION(kRegisterD0)
                            | STACK_ROUTINE_PARAMETER(1,SIZE_CODE(sizeof(short))),
        kSystemMenuProcInfo = kPascalStackBased
                            | STACK_ROUTINE_PARAMETER(1,SIZE_CODE(sizeof(long)))
};


/*** function prototypes ************************************************/

OSErr    DoMenuPatchStuff(long menuResult, GlobalsPtr gp);
#define  kOpenItem   true
#define  kShowItem   false
OSErr    OpenSelection(FSSpecPtr fsp, Boolean openOption);
OSErr    GetPSN(OSType creator, OSType type, ProcessSerialNumber *process);
OSErr    GetDirectoryID(FSSpecPtr fsp, long *dirID);
void     ShowErrorAlert(FSSpecPtr fsp, short action, OSErr err);
```

dlogutils.c

```
/*
    File Name:   dlogutils.c
*/

#include "dlogutils.h"

/*******************************************************************************

    SetDialogItemState

*******************************************************************************/

void SetDialogItemState(DialogPtr dlg, short controlNumber, short value)
{
    short    iKind;
    Handle   iHandle;
    Rect     iRect;

    GetDItem(dlg, controlNumber, &iKind, &iHandle, &iRect);
    SetCtlValue((ControlHandle) iHandle, value);
}

/*******************************************************************************

    GetDialogItemState

*******************************************************************************/
```

```
short GetDialogItemState(DialogPtr dlg, short controlNumber)
{
     short    iKind;
     Handle   iHandle;
     Rect     iRect;

     GetDItem(dlg, controlNumber, &iKind, &iHandle, &iRect);
     return GetCtlValue((ControlHandle) iHandle);
}

/*******************************************************************************

     DoRadioGroup

*******************************************************************************/

void DoRadioGroup(DialogPtr dlg, short lo, short hi, short on)
{
     short i;

     for (i=lo;i<=hi;++i)
           SetDialogItemState(dlg, i, 0);
     SetDialogItemState(dlg, on, 1);
}

/*******************************************************************************

     GetRadioFromGroup

*******************************************************************************/

short GetRadioFromGroup(DialogPtr dlg, short lo, short hi)
{
     short i;

     for (i=lo;i<=hi;++i) {
           if (GetDialogItemState(dlg, i))
                 return i;
     }
     return 0;
}

/*******************************************************************************

     ToggleCheckBox

*******************************************************************************/

void ToggleCheckBox(DialogPtr dlg, short buttonNumber){short newState;
{
     short newState;
```

```
        if (GetDialogItemState(dlg, buttonNumber) == 0)
               newState = 1;
        else
               newState = 0;
        SetDialogItemState(dlg, buttonNumber, newState);
}


/**************************************************************************


        SetDItemType


**************************************************************************/

void SetDItemType(DialogPtr dlg, short itemNumber, short newType)
{
        short    iKind;
        Handle   iHandle;
        Rect     iRect;

        GetDItem(dlg, itemNumber, &iKind, &iHandle, &iRect);
        SetDItem(dlg, itemNumber, newType, iHandle, &iRect);
}


/**************************************************************************


        EnableControl


**************************************************************************/

void EnableControl(DialogPtr dlg, short controlNumber)
{
        short    iKind;
        Handle   iHandle;
        Rect     iRect;

        GetDItem(dlg, controlNumber, &iKind, &iHandle, &iRect);
        HiliteControl((ControlHandle)iHandle, 0);
}


/**************************************************************************


        DisableControl


**************************************************************************/

void DisableControl(DialogPtr dlg, short controlNumber)
{
        short    iKind;
        Handle   iHandle;
        Rect     iRect;
```

```
    GetDItem(dlg, controlNumber, &iKind, &iHandle, &iRect);
    HiliteControl((ControlHandle)iHandle, 255);
}


/*******************************************************************************

    NumberCharacters

*******************************************************************************/

short NumberCharacters(DialogPtr dlg, short itemNumber)
{
    Str255   textStr;
    short    result;

    GetItemText(dlg, itemNumber, textStr);
    result = textStr[0];
    return result;
}


/*******************************************************************************

    GetItemText

*******************************************************************************/

void GetItemText(DialogPtr dlg, short itemNumber, unsigned char* textStr)
{
    short    iKind;
    Handle   iHandle;
    Rect     iRect;

    GetDItem(dlg, itemNumber, &iKind, &iHandle, &iRect);
    GetIText(iHandle, textStr);
}


/*******************************************************************************

    SetItemText

*******************************************************************************/

void SetItemText(DialogPtr dlg, short itemNumber, unsigned char* textStr)
{
    short    iKind;
    Handle   iHandle;
    Rect     iRect;

    GetDItem(dlg, itemNumber, &iKind, &iHandle, &iRect);
    SetIText(iHandle, textStr);
}
```

```
/****************************************************************************

    GetItemOSType

****************************************************************************/

OSType GetItemOSType(DialogPtr dlg, short itemNumber)
{
    short    iKind;
    Handle   iHandle;
    Rect     iRect;
    Str255   textStr;
    OSType   osType;

    GetDItem(dlg, itemNumber, &iKind, &iHandle, &iRect);
    GetIText(iHandle, textStr);

    BlockMove(&textStr[1], &osType, sizeof(OSType));
    return osType;
}

/****************************************************************************

    SetItemOSType

****************************************************************************/

void SetItemOSType(DialogPtr dlg, short itemNumber, OSType osType)
{
    short    iKind;
    Handle   iHandle;
    Rect     iRect;
    Str255   textStr;

    BlockMove(&osType, &textStr[1], sizeof(OSType));
    textStr[0] = sizeof(OSType);
    GetDItem(dlg, itemNumber, &iKind, &iHandle, &iRect);
    SetIText(iHandle, textStr);
}

/****************************************************************************

    GetItemNumber

****************************************************************************/
unsigned long GetItemNumber(DialogPtr dlg, short itemNumber)
{
    short    iKind;
    Handle   iHandle;
    Rect     iRect;
    Str255   textStr;
    long     result;
```

```
        GetDItem(dlg, itemNumber, &iKind, &iHandle, &iRect);
        GetIText(iHandle, textStr);
        StringToNum(textStr, &result);
        return result;
}

/******************************************************************************

        SetItemNumber

******************************************************************************/

void SetItemNumber(DialogPtr dlg, short itemNumber, unsigned long number)
{
        short    iKind;
        Handle   iHandle;
        Rect     iRect;
        Str255   textStr;

        NumToString(number, textStr);
        GetDItem(dlg, itemNumber, &iKind, &iHandle, &iRect);
        SetIText(iHandle, textStr);
}

/******************************************************************************

        SetWindowFont

******************************************************************************/

void SetWindowFont(DialogPtr d, short fontNum, short fontSize, Style fontStyle, short fontMode)
{
        FontInfo    fInfo;
        GrafPtr     savePort;

        GetPort(&savePort);
        SetPort(d);

        TextFont(fontNum);
        TextSize(fontSize);
        TextFace(fontStyle);
        TextMode(fontMode);

        GetFontInfo(&fInfo);

        (*((DialogPeek)d)->textH)->fontAscent = fInfo.ascent;
        (*((DialogPeek)d)->textH)->lineHeight = fInfo.ascent +
                fInfo.descent + fInfo.leading;
        (*((DialogPeek)d)->textH)->txFont = fontNum;
        (*((DialogPeek)d)->textH)->txFace = fontStyle;
        (*((DialogPeek)d)->textH)->txMode = fontMode;
```

```
        (*((DialogPeek)d)->textH)->txSize = fontSize;

        SetPort(savePort);
}
```

dlogutils.h

```
/*
    File Name:   dlogutils.h
*/

#pragma once

void       SetDialogItemState(DialogPtr dlg, short controlNumber, short value);
short      GetDialogItemState(DialogPtr dlg, short controlNumber);
void       DoRadioGroup(DialogPtr dlg, short lo, short hi, short on);
short      GetRadioFromGroup(DialogPtr dlg, short lo, short hi);
void       ToggleCheckBox(DialogPtr dlg, short buttonNumber);
void       SetDItemType(DialogPtr dlg, short itemNumber, short newType);
void       EnableControl(DialogPtr dlg, short controlNumber);
void       DisableControl(DialogPtr dlg, short controlNumber);
short      NumberCharacters(DialogPtr dlg, short itemNumber);
void       GetItemText(DialogPtr dlg, short itemNumber, unsigned char* textStr);
void       SetItemText(DialogPtr dlg, short itemNumber, unsigned char* textStr);
OSType     GetItemOSType(DialogPtr dlg, short itemNumber);
void       SetItemOSType(DialogPtr dlg, short itemNumber, OSType osType);
unsigned   long GetItemNumber(DialogPtr dlg, short itemNumber);
void       SetItemNumber(DialogPtr dlg, short itemNumber, unsigned long number);
void       SetWindowFont(DialogPtr d, short fontNum, short fontSize,
                 Style fontStyle, short fontMode);
```

allcommon.h

```
/*
    File Name:   allcommon.h
*/

#pragma once

#define kGestaltSelector          'Menu'
// you should make sure you register yours with Apple before
// using a Gestalt Selector. Because this is just an example,
// I chose not to.

#define kPreferencesResType       'PREF'
#define kPreferencesResID         128

typedef struct {
    short   fEnabled;
} Preferences, *PreferencesPtr, **PreferencesHdl;
```

Chapter Six Source Code

ViewByNameLDEF.c

```c
/*
    File Name:   ViewByNameLDEF.c
*/

#include <Icons.h>

#include "ViewByNameLDEF.h"
#include "RefConLDEF.h"

RefconLDEFDrawProcUPP   gListElementProcUPP = nil;
DialogPtr               gd = nil;
ListHandle              glh = nil;

void main(void)
{
    unsigned long   randSeed;
    Boolean         fDone = false;
    GrafPtr         savePort;
    Rect            rView, rDataBnds = {0, 0, kNumRows, kNumColumns};
    Point           cellSize = {kCellHeight, 0};
    UserItemUPP     drawFrameUPP = nil;

    // initialize the Mac
    InitGraf(&qd.thePort);
    InitFonts();
    FlushEvents(everyEvent, 0);
    InitWindows();
    InitMenus();
    TEInit();
    InitDialogs(nil);
    InitCursor();
    GetDateTime(&randSeed);
    LMSetRndSeed(randSeed);
    DrawMenuBar();

    // allocate global UPP for our draw proc
    gListElementProcUPP = NewRefconLDEFDrawProc(ListElementProc);
    if (gListElementProcUPP == nil) goto exit;

    // allocate local UPP to fra    me our list user item
    drawFrameUPP = NewUserItemProc(DrawFrame);
    if (drawFrameUPP == nil) goto exit;

    // get our main dialog box
    gd = GetNewDialog(dlogMainID, nil, (WindowPtr)-1);
    if (gd == nil) goto exit;
```

```
        // set the port, font, and user item proc
        GetPort(&savePort);
        SetPort(gd);
        SetWindowFont(gd, geneva, 9, 0, srcCopy);
        SetUserItemProc(gd, itemList, (ProcPtr)drawFrameUPP);

        // create the list with one column
        GetDialogItemRect(gd, itemList, &rView);
        rView.right -= kScrollBarWidth;
        glh = LNew(&rView, &rDataBnds, cellSize, kRefConLDEFID, gd, true,
                false, false, true);
        if (glh == nil) goto exit;

        // show the window
        ShowWindow(gd);

        // fill the list with the contents of the root directory
        FillList(-1, fsRtDirID, glh, kAddToEnd, 0);
        LUpdate(gd->visRgn, glh);

        // loop until done
        while (!fDone) {
                short   itemHit;
                ModalDialog(nil, &itemHit);
                switch(itemHit) {

                        case itemQuit:
                                fDone = true;
                                break;

                        case itemList:
                                HandleClickOnList(gd, glh);
                                break;

                        default:
                                break;
                }
        }

exit:
    // clean up
    if (glh) LDispose(glh);
    if (gd) DisposeDialog(gd);
    if (gListElementProcUPP) DisposeRoutineDescriptor(gListElementProcUPP);
    if (drawFrameUPP) DisposeRoutineDescriptor(drawFrameUPP);
    SetPort(savePort);
}
```

```
/***************************************************************************

     FillList

***************************************************************************/

void FillList(short vRefNum, long dirID, ListHandle theList, short beforeThisRow, short indentLevel)
{
     short              index;
     OSErr              err = noErr;
     CInfoPBRec         pb;
     ListItemHdl        lih = nil;
     RefconLDEFCell     cellData;
     Cell               cell = {0,0};
     short              maxItems = 32000 / sizeof(RefconLDEFCell);
                        // roughly approximate the max items in the list
     // turn off list drawing
     LDoDraw(false, theList);

     // loop through the items in the directory we want to add
     index = 0;
     do {

          // allocate a list element
          lih = (ListItemHdl)NewHandleClear(sizeof(ListItem));
          if (lih == nil) goto exit;
          HLock((Handle)lih);

          // get the file information for the next item in the directory
          ++index;
          pb.hFileInfo.ioNamePtr = (*lih)->spec.name;
          pb.hFileInfo.ioVRefNum = vRefNum;
          pb.hFileInfo.ioFDirIndex = index;
          pb.hFileInfo.ioDirID = dirID;
          err = PBGetCatInfoSync(&pb);

          if (err == noErr) {
               if (pb.hFileInfo.ioFlAttrib & ioDirMask)   // we have a folder
                    (*lih)->iconID = rFolderIcon;         // use folder icon
               else                                       // get custom icon id
                    (*lih)->iconID =
                         GetIconID(pb.hFileInfo.ioFlFndrInfo.fdType);

               // add a row
               cell.v = LAddRow(1, beforeThisRow++, theList);

               // set up the cell data
               (*lih)->spec.parID = dirID;
               (*lih)->spec.vRefNum = vRefNum;
               (*lih)->indentLevel = indentLevel;
               (*lih)->isOpen = false;
```

```
                    cellData.refCon = (long)lih;
                    cellData.drawProc = gListElementProcUPP;

                    // set the cell data
                    LSetCell(&cellData, sizeof(RefconLDEFCell), cell, theList);
            }

        HUnlock((Handle)lih);
        if (err != noErr) DisposeHandle((Handle)lih);

    } while ((err == noErr) && ((**theList).dataBounds.bottom <= maxItems));

exit:
    LDoDraw(true, theList);
}

/***************************************************************************

    HandleClickOnList

***************************************************************************/

void HandleClickOnList(DialogPtr d, ListHandle theList)
{
        Point                   localPt = {0,0};
        Boolean                 doubleClick = false;
        Rect                    cellRect = {0,0,0,0};
        ListItemHdl             lih = nil;
        RefconLDEFCell          cellData;
        short                   dataLen = sizeof(RefconLDEFCell);
        Cell                    theCell = {0,0};
        Rect                    iconRect, trackRect;
        Boolean                 found = false;

        // get the location of the mouse click in local coordinates
        GetMouse(&localPt);

        // if we are clicking in area of the folder flag icons...
        if (localPt.h < (**theList).rView.left + 20) {

                // see if we clicked in any cell in particular
                theCell.h = theCell.v = 0;
                do {

                        LRect(&cellRect, theCell, theList);
                        if (PtInRect(localPt, &cellRect))
                                found = true;
                } while (!found && LNextCell(false, true, &theCell, theList));

                // if we did, then see if the cell is a folder by checking the iconID
                if (found) {
```

```
                LGetCell(&cellData, &dataLen, theCell, theList);
                lih = (ListItemHdl)cellData.refCon;
                if ((*lih)->iconID == rFolderIcon) {
                        iconRect = cellRect;
                        iconRect.left += 4;
                        iconRect.right = iconRect.left + 16;
                        iconRect.top += 1;
                        iconRect.bottom = iconRect.top + 16;
                        trackRect = cellRect;
                        trackRect.right = trackRect.left + 20;

                        // track the flag icon
                        doubleClick = TrackIconByRect(&iconRect, &trackRect,
                        (*lih)->isOpen ? rArrowOpenedIcon : rArrowClosedIcon);

                        // if the user released within the flag then
                        // we do the same as a double click
                        if (doubleClick) {
                                Cell theTCell;

                        // we also select the cell that we are about to "open"
                                if (AnyCellsSelected(theList, &theTCell))
                                        LSetSelect(false, theTCell, theList);
                                LSetSelect(true, theCell, theList);
                        }
                } else {
                // otherwise let LClick tell us if the user double-clicked
                // on a non-folder item and do whatever you like.
                        doubleClick = LClick(localPt, 0, theList);
                }
        }
} else {
        // otherwise let LClick tell us if the user double-clicked on an item.
        doubleClick = LClick(localPt, 0, theList);
}

// if the user double-clicked on something...
if (doubleClick) {
        // find out what
        if (AnyCellsSelected(theList, &theCell)) {
                LGetCell(&cellData, &dataLen, theCell, theList);
                lih = (ListItemHdl)cellData.refCon;

                // if it's a folder...
                if ((*lih)->iconID == rFolderIcon) {
                        // and it's not opened...
                        if ((*lih)->isOpen == false) {
                                // get the directory id of it
                                long dirID = GetDirectoryID(&((*lih)->spec));
                                if (dirID != 0L) {
                // and fill the list with its contents then redraw the list
```

```
                              FillList((*lih)->spec.vRefNum, dirID,
                                      theList, theCell.v + 1,
                                      (*lih)->indentLevel + 1);
                              (*lih)->isOpen = true;
                              LSetCell(&cellData, sizeof(RefconLDEFCell),
                                      theCell, theList);
                              LUpdate(gd->visRgn, glh);
                      }
              } else {
// close the folder by deleting list rows below it until we reach the
// same indentation level as the folder we are closing.
                      short   indentLevelToDelete =
                              (*lih)->indentLevel + 1;
                      short   numRowsToDelete = 0;
                      short   firstRowToDelete = theCell.v + 1;

                      (*lih)->isOpen = false;
                      LSetCell(&cellData, sizeof(RefconLDEFCell),
                              theCell, theList);

                      // loop checking each cells indentation level
              checkNextCell:
                      theCell.v++;
                      if (theCell.v < (**theList).dataBounds.bottom) {
                              dataLen = sizeof(RefconLDEFCell);
                              LGetCell(&cellData, &dataLen, theCell,
                                      theList);
                              lih = (ListItemHdl)cellData.refCon;
                              if ((*lih)->indentLevel >=
                              indentLevelToDelete) {
                                      numRowsToDelete++;
                                      DisposeHandle((Handle)lih);
                                      lih = nil;
                                      goto checkNextCell;
                              }
                      }

              // once we count how many rows to delete, nuke them all at once
                      if (numRowsToDelete > 0L)
                              LDelRow(numRowsToDelete, firstRowToDelete,
                                      theList);
              }
          }
      }
   }
}
```

```
/*************************************************************************

     ListElementProc

     This function is called for each cell to draw its contents. By using
     the RefConLDEF we allow the ability to have a different drawing
     procedure for each cell if we need it. In this case however, we
     decide to simply use one simple function to draw each cell.
*************************************************************************/

void ListElementProc(Rect *cellRect, Cell lCell, ListHandle theList, long refCon)
{
     ListItemHdl     lih;
     GrafPtr         savePort;
     Rect            iconRect;
     short           width;
     FInfo           fndrInfo;

     // typecast our refCon
     lih = (ListItemHdl)refCon;

     // set up the port
     GetPort(&savePort);
     SetPort((**theList).port);
     PenNormal();

     // draw the file/folder name, in italics if it is an alias
     MoveTo(cellRect->left + (44 + (20 * (*lih)->indentLevel)),
           cellRect->bottom - 4);
     if (FSpGetFInfo(&((*lih)->spec), &fndrInfo) == noErr) {
           if (fndrInfo.fdFlags & 0x8000)
                 TextFace(italic);
           DrawString((*lih)->spec.name);
           TextFace(0);
     } else
           DrawString((*lih)->spec.name);
     width = StringWidth((*lih)->spec.name);

     // draw the folder flag icon if need be
     if ((*lih)->iconID == rFolderIcon) {
           iconRect = *cellRect;
           iconRect.left += 4;
           iconRect.right = iconRect.left + 16;
           iconRect.top += 1;
           iconRect.bottom = iconRect.top + 16;
           PlotIconID(&iconRect, atNone, ttNone,
                 (*lih)->isOpen ? rArrowOpenedIcon : rArrowClosedIcon);
     }

     // draw the folder icon or file icon. if the real icon for the file can not be
     // grabbed from the desktop database then we draw the generic version as
```

```
            // stored in the iconID field of the cells data
            iconRect = *cellRect;
            iconRect.left += (24 + (20 * (*lih)->indentLevel));
            iconRect.right = iconRect.left + 16;
            iconRect.top += 1;
            iconRect.bottom = iconRect.top + 16;

            if ((*lih)->iconID == rFolderIcon) {
                    PlotIconID(&iconRect, atNone, ttNone, (*lih)->iconID);
            } else {
                    if (DrawFileIcon(&((*lih)->spec), &iconRect) != noErr)
                            PlotIconID(&iconRect, atNone, ttNone, (*lih)->iconID);
            }

        SetPort(savePort);
}

#pragma mark -

/*****************************************************************************

    DrawFrame

*****************************************************************************/

pascal void DrawFrame(DialogPtr d, short theItem)
{
    Rect    r;
    GrafPtr    savePort;

    GetPort(&savePort);
    SetPort(d);
    GetDialogItemRect(d, theItem, &r);
    InsetRect(&r, -1, -1);
    FrameRect(&r);
    SetPort(savePort);
}

/*****************************************************************************

    GetDialogItemRect

*****************************************************************************/

void GetDialogItemRect(DialogPtr dlg, short itemNumber, Rect *r)
{
    short    iKind;
    Handle    iHandle;
    GetDItem(dlg, itemNumber, &iKind, &iHandle, r);
}
```

```
/************************************************************************

     SetWindowFont

*************************************************************************/

void SetWindowFont(DialogPtr d, short fontNum, short fontSize, Style fontStyle, short fontMode)
{
     FontInfo    fInfo;
     GrafPtr     savePort;

     GetPort(&savePort);
     SetPort(d);

     TextFont(fontNum);
     TextSize(fontSize);
     TextFace(fontStyle);
     TextMode(fontMode);

     GetFontInfo(&fInfo);

     (*((DialogPeek)d)->textH)->fontAscent = fInfo.ascent;
     (*((DialogPeek)d)->textH)->lineHeight = fInfo.ascent +
             fInfo.descent + fInfo.leading;
     (*((DialogPeek)d)->textH)->txFont = fontNum;
     (*((DialogPeek)d)->textH)->txFace = fontStyle;
     (*((DialogPeek)d)->textH)->txMode = fontMode;
     (*((DialogPeek)d)->textH)->txSize = fontSize;

     SetPort(savePort);
}


/*************************************************************************

     SetUserItemProc

*************************************************************************/

void SetUserItemProc(DialogPtr dlg, short userItem, ProcPtr userProc)
{
     short   iKind;
     Handle  iHandle;
     Rect    iRect;

     GetDItem(dlg, userItem, &iKind, &iHandle, &iRect);
     SetDItem(dlg, userItem, iKind, (Handle)userProc, &iRect);
}
```

```
/*******************************************************************************

     ShowError

*******************************************************************************/

void ShowError(OSErr errorCode, unsigned char * errorStr)
{
     Str32   errorCodeStr;
     NumToString((long)errorCode, errorCodeStr);
     ParamText(errorCodeStr, errorStr, "\p", "\p");
     StopAlert(256, nil);
     ParamText("\p", "\p", "\p", "\p");
}

/*******************************************************************************

     GetDirectoryID

*******************************************************************************/

long GetDirectoryID(FSSpec *spec)
{
     OSErr        err;
     CInfoPBRec   pb;

     pb.hFileInfo.ioNamePtr = spec->name;
     pb.hFileInfo.ioVRefNum = spec->vRefNum;
     pb.hFileInfo.ioFDirIndex = 0;
     pb.hFileInfo.ioDirID = spec->parID;
     err = PBGetCatInfoSync(&pb);
     if (err == noErr)
            return pb.hFileInfo.ioDirID;
     else
            return 0L;
}

/*************************************************************************

     TrackIconByRect

*************************************************************************/

Boolean TrackIconByRect(Rect *drawRect, Rect *trackRect, short iconID)
{
     Boolean     mouseReleasedWithin = false;
     Point       oldPt, newPt;

     oldPt.h = oldPt.v = -1;
```

```
        if (StillDown()) {
              while (WaitMouseUp()) {
                    GetMouse(&newPt);
                    if (DeltaPoint(oldPt, newPt)) {
                          if (PtInRect(newPt, trackRect)) {
                                if (!mouseReleasedWithin)
                                      PlotIconID(drawRect, atNone,
                                            ttSelected, iconID);   /* in */
                                mouseReleasedWithin = true;
                          } else {
                                if (mouseReleasedWithin)
                                      PlotIconID(drawRect, atNone,
                                            ttNone, iconID);   /* out */
                                mouseReleasedWithin = false;
                          }
                          oldPt = newPt;
                    }
              }
        }
        if (mouseReleasedWithin)
              PlotIconID(drawRect, atNone, ttNone, iconID);
              /* draw "out" as last thing */
        return mouseReleasedWithin;
}

/**************************************************************************

      GetIconID

**************************************************************************/

#define rINITIcon             133
#define rApplicationIcon      134
#define rDocumentIcon         135
#define rTEXTIcon             136
#define rcdevIcon             137
#define rttroIcon             138
#define rdfilIcon             139
#define rsfilIcon             140

short GetIconID(OSType fileType)
{
      switch(fileType) {
            case 'APPL':
                  return rApplicationIcon;
                  break;
            case 'TEXT':
                  return rTEXTIcon;
                  break;
            case 'cdev':
                  return rcdevIcon;
                  break;
```

```
                    case 'INIT':
                            return rINITIcon;
                            break;
                    case 'ttro':
                            return rttroIcon;
                            break;
                    case 'dfil':
                            return rdfilIcon;
                            break;
                    case 'sfil':
                            return rsfilIcon;
                            break;
                    default:
                            return rDocumentIcon;
            }
    }


    /**************************************************************************

        AnyCellsSelected

    **************************************************************************/

    Boolean AnyCellsSelected(ListHandle lh, Cell *theCell)
    {
        theCell->v = theCell->h = 0;
        return LGetSelect(true, theCell, lh);
    }


    /**************************************************************************

        DrawFileIcon

    **************************************************************************/

    OSErr DrawFileIcon(FSSpec *spec, Rect *drawRect)
    {
        OSErr   err = noErr;
        Handle  theSuite = NULL;
        DTPBRec pb;
        short   ioDTRefNum;
        FInfo   fndrInfo;
        Handle  theIconData = NULL;

        /* get desktop database reference number */
        pb.ioNamePtr = NULL;
        pb.ioVRefNum = -1; // spec->vRefNum;
        err = PBDTGetPath(&pb);
        if (err != noErr) goto exit;
        ioDTRefNum = pb.ioDTRefNum;
```

```
/* create an icon suite to store icons in */
err = NewIconSuite(&theSuite);
if (err != noErr) goto exit;

/* get file type/creator */
err = FSpGetFInfo(spec, &fndrInfo);
if (err != noErr) goto exit;

/* get small bw icon */
theIconData = NewHandle(kSmallIconSize);
if (theIconData) {
      HLock(theIconData);
      pb.ioCompletion = NULL;
      pb.ioDTRefNum = ioDTRefNum;
      pb.ioDTBuffer = *theIconData;
      pb.ioDTReqCount = kSmallIconSize;
      pb.ioIconType = kSmallIcon;
      pb.ioFileCreator = fndrInfo.fdCreator;
      pb.ioFileType = fndrInfo.fdType;
      err = PBDTGetIconSync(&pb);
      if (err == noErr) {
             HUnlock(theIconData);
             err = AddIconToSuite(theIconData, theSuite, small1BitMask);
       } else {
             DisposeHandle(theIconData);
             theIconData = NULL;
      }
      if (err != noErr) goto exit;
}

/* get small 4 bit icon */
theIconData = NewHandle(kSmall4BitIconSize);
if (theIconData) {
      HLock(theIconData);
      pb.ioCompletion = NULL;
      pb.ioDTRefNum = ioDTRefNum;
      pb.ioDTBuffer = *theIconData;
      pb.ioDTReqCount = kSmall4BitIconSize;
      pb.ioIconType = kSmall4BitIcon;
      pb.ioFileCreator = fndrInfo.fdCreator;
      pb.ioFileType = fndrInfo.fdType;
      err = PBDTGetIconSync(&pb);
      if (err == noErr) {
             HUnlock(theIconData);
             err = AddIconToSuite(theIconData, theSuite, small4BitData);
       } else {
             DisposeHandle(theIconData);
             theIconData = NULL;
      }
      if (err != noErr) goto exit;
}
```

```
        /* get small 8 bit icon */
        theIconData = NewHandle(kSmall8BitIconSize);
        if (theIconData) {
                HLock(theIconData);
                pb.ioCompletion = NULL;
                pb.ioDTRefNum = ioDTRefNum;
                pb.ioDTBuffer = *theIconData;
                pb.ioDTReqCount = kSmall8BitIconSize;
                pb.ioIconType = kSmall8BitIcon;
                pb.ioFileCreator = fndrInfo.fdCreator;
                pb.ioFileType = fndrInfo.fdType;
                err = PBDTGetIconSync(&pb);
                if (err == noErr) {
                        HUnlock(theIconData);
                        err = AddIconToSuite(theIconData, theSuite, small8BitData);
                } else {
                        DisposeHandle(theIconData);
                        theIconData = NULL;
                }
                if (err != noErr) goto exit;
        }

        /* plot the icons */
        err = PlotIconSuite(drawRect, atNone, ttNone, theSuite);
        if (err != noErr) goto exit;

exit:
        /* dispose the suite if need be */
        if (theSuite != NULL)
                DisposeIconSuite(theSuite, true);
        return err;
}
```

ViewByNameLDEF.h

```
/*
    File Name:   ViewByNameLDEF.h
*/

#pragma once

#define dlogMainID          128
#define itemQuit            1
#define itemList            3

#define rFolderIcon         128
#define rArrowOpenedIcon    129
#define rArrowClosedIcon    130

#define kCellHeight         18
```

```
#define kNumColumns          1
#define kNumRows             0

#define kScrollBarWidth      15

typedef struct ListItem {
    FSSpec         spec;             // file/folder specification
    short          iconID;          // id of icon to draw for it
    unsigned char  indentLevel;     // level of indentation
    unsigned char  isOpen;          // if a folder, whether it is open or closed
} ListItem, *ListItemPtr, **ListItemHdl;

#define kAddToEnd 32767

void        FillList(short vRefNum, long dirID, ListHandle theList,
                 short beforeThisRow, short indentLevel);
void        HandleClickOnList(DialogPtr d, ListHandle theList);
void        ListElementProc(Rect *cellRect, Cell lCell, ListHandle theList,
                 long refCon);
pascal void DrawFrame(DialogPtr d, short theItem);
void        GetDialogItemRect(DialogPtr dlg, short itemNumber, Rect *r);
void        SetWindowFont(DialogPtr d, short fontNum, short fontSize,
                 Style fontStyle, short fontMode);
void        SetUserItemProc(DialogPtr dlg, short userItem, ProcPtr userProc);
void        ShowError(OSErr errorCode, unsigned char * errorStr);
long        GetDirectoryID(FSSpec *spec);
Boolean     TrackIconByRect(Rect *drawRect, Rect *trackRect, short iconID);
short       GetIconID(OSType fileType);
Boolean     AnyCellsSelected(ListHandle lh, Cell *theCell);
OSErr       DrawFileIcon(FSSpec *spec, Rect *drawRect);
```

Chapter Seven Source Code

Icon Family CDEF.c

```
/*
    File Name:   Icon Family CDEF.c
*/

/*
    Icon Family CDEF

    Variation codes:

    0 :   MIN = id of icon
          MAX = id of pressed icon
    1:    MIN = id of icon, uses ttSelected when pressed
*/
```

```
#include <Icons.h>
#include <Controls.h>

#ifdef __powerc
    ProcInfoType __procInfo = uppControlDefProcInfo;
#endif

void   Draw(short varCode, ControlHandle control, long param);
long   Test(ControlHandle control, long param);
void   CalcRegions(ControlHandle control, long param);

/*************************************************************************

    main

*************************************************************************/

pascal long   main(short varCode, ControlHandle control, short message, long param)
{
    long result = 0L;

    switch(message) {

            case drawCntl:
                    Draw(varCode, control, param);
                    break;
            case testCntl:
                    result = Test(control, param);
                    break;

            case calcCntlRgn:
                    CalcRegions(control, param);
                    break;

            case initCntl:
            case dispCntl:
            case calcThumbRgn:
            case posCntl:
            case thumbCntl:
            case dragCntl:
            case autoTrack:
            default:
                    break;
    }

    return result;
}
```

```
/*************************************************************************

    Draw

*************************************************************************/

void Draw(short varCode, ControlHandle control, long param)
{
    Rect    r = (*control)->contrlRect;
    short   id, transform = ttNone;
    OSErr   whoCares = noErr;

    if ((*control)->contrlVis == 0xFF) {
            id = (*control)->contrlMin;
            if ((*control)->contrlHilite == 255) {
                    transform = ttDisabled;
            } else {
                    if ((*control)->contrlHilite == 0) {
                            id = (*control)->contrlMin;
                    } else {
                            if (varCode == 0) {
                                    id = (*control)->contrlMax;
                            } else {
                                    id = (*control)->contrlMin;
                                    transform = ttSelected;
                            }
                    }
            }
            whoCares = PlotIconID(&r, atAbsoluteCenter, transform, id);
    }
}

/*************************************************************************

    Test

*************************************************************************/

long Test(ControlHandle control, long param)
{
    Rect    r = (*control)->contrlRect;
    Point   hitPt;
    long    result;

    hitPt.h = LoWord(param);
    hitPt.v = HiWord(param);
    if ((*control)->contrlHilite == 255) {
            result = 0L;
    } else {
            if (PtInRect(hitPt, &r))
                    result = inButton;
```

```
                else
                        result = 0L;
        }

        return result;
}

/****************************************************************************

    CalcRegions

****************************************************************************/

void CalcRegions(ControlHandle control, long param)
{
    Rect r = (*control)->contrlRect;
    param = param & 0x7FFFFFFF;
    RectRgn((RgnHandle)param, &r);
}
```

TigerSlider.cp

```
/*
    File Name:        Tiger Slider.cp
*/

#include    "Tiger Slider.h"
#include    <QDOffscreen.h>
#include    <Controls.h>

#ifdef powerc
ProcInfoType __procinfo = uppControlDefProcInfo;
#endif

/****************************************************************************

    main - this is the entry point called by the system whenever our routine should take some action.

****************************************************************************/
pascal long main (short /*varCode*/, ControlHandle theControl, short theMessage, long theParam)
{
    long result = 0;

    switch (theMessage)
    {
            case        initCntl:
                        InitTheControl (theControl);
                        break;
```

```
        case    dispCntl:
                DisposeTheControl (theControl);
                break;

        case    drawCntl:
                DrawTheControl (theControl);
                break;

        case    testCntl:
                if (PtInRect ((*(Point*) &theParam),
                &(*theControl) -> contrlRect))
                {
                // tell the Control Manager that a click occurred in some
                // part of the control, and that dragCntl should be called -
                // the number 130 is not particularly special, except that it
                // indicates that the click area is a custom part of ours
                        result = 130;
                }
                break;

        case    dragCntl:
                if (theParam)
                {
                        DragTheControl (theControl);
                        result = 1;
                // signals that we handled the dragging all by ourselves
                }
                break;

    case calcCntlRgn:
    case calcThumbRgn:
                // these messages are received if we are in 32-bit mode
                RectRgn ((RgnHandle) (theParam), &(*theControl) -> contrlRect);
                break;

    case calcCRgns:
                // this message is only received in 24 bit mode; we have to be sure
                // that we clear the high byte (we do so using StripAddress)
                RgnHandle tempRgn = (RgnHandle) StripAddress ((Ptr) theParam);
                RectRgn (tempRgn, &(*theControl) -> contrlRect);
        break;
    }

    return (result);
}
```

```
/******************************************************************************

    InitTheControl - used to allocate the GWorlds and prepare the backgrounds by filling them in with
    pictures.

******************************************************************************/
void InitTheControl (ControlHandle theControl)
{
    OSErr              err;
    SliderInfoH        resHandle;

// The info about this slider is stored in a resource of type 'Sinf' that has the same
// ID as the refcon of this control. Note that the refcon is only used during the
// creation of the control; the application may use it in any way after that (i.e., after
// GetNewControl or NewControl has returned). The CDEF, however, does use the contrlData
// field all the time to keep track of the 'Sinf' handle, so don't mess with contrlData
// in your application!

    (*theControl) -> contrlData = nil;
    resHandle = (SliderInfoH) GetResource (kSliderInfoType, (*theControl) -> contrlRfCon);
    if (!resHandle)
    {
// the resource was not found - set contrlData to nil so that other functions know that
// initialization failed! If this happens, no crash will occur, but the CDEF won't do anything.
        (*theControl) -> contrlData = nil;
    }
    else
    {
        (*theControl) -> contrlData = (Handle) resHandle;

        // make a non-purgeable, non-resource copy of the 'Sinf' handle - from now on,
        // "contrlData" always refers to a copy of the 'Sinf'.
        HNoPurge ((*theControl) -> contrlData);
        DetachResource ((*theControl) -> contrlData);

        HLock ((*theControl) -> contrlData);                    // temporary for this function

        Rect compositeRect = (*theControl) -> contrlRect;
        OffsetRect (&compositeRect, -compositeRect.left, -compositeRect.top);

// allocate the GWorlds - note that we use the bit depth specified in the 'Sinf' resource, rather than
// matching the depth of the screen. An improvement that can be made here would be to match the depth
// of the screen that the majority of the control appears on, and use that screen's color table-however
// if this change is made, it introduces the necessity of checking to make sure that the user hasn't
// moved the control to another screen each time it's drawn, and dealing with it (by reallocating the
// GWorlds and reloading the picture) if so. This task is left as an exercise to the reader - have fun!
// also note that we don't do anything useful here if the GWorld cannot be allocated, but we check that
// allocation was successful everywhere else before we use it, so that no crash will occur. You might see
// some funny things on screen, though! Fortunately, you know how much memory your slider needs (based
// on the bit depth, as described above) so your program can check for it before creating the control.
```

```
err = NewGWorld (&(*resHandle) -> indicatorWorld, (*resHandle) -> bitDepth,
        &(*resHandle) -> indicatorRect, nil, nil, 0);
if (err)
{
        // not enough memory in the application heap! Try it in temporary memory.
        err = NewGWorld (&(*resHandle) -> indicatorWorld, (*resHandle) -> bitDepth,
                &(*resHandle) -> indicatorRect, nil, nil, useTempMem);
}

if (!err)
{
        GWorldPtr                               currPort;
        GDHandle                    currDev;

        GetGWorld (&currPort, &currDev);                // save the current GWorld
        SetGWorld ((*resHandle) -> indicatorWorld, nil);
        // set to the new one, so that any drawing takes place there
        PixMapHandle pixMap = GetGWorldPixMap ((*resHandle) -> indicatorWorld);
        LockPixels (pixMap);

        PicHandle picture = GetPicture ((*resHandle) -> indicatorPictResID);
        if (picture)
        {
                DrawPicture (picture, &(*resHandle) -> indicatorWorld->portRect);
        }

        UnlockPixels (pixMap);
        SetGWorld (currPort, currDev);                  // restore the original GWorld
}

err = NewGWorld (&(*resHandle) -> backgroundWorld, (*resHandle) -> bitDepth,
        &compositeRect, nil, nil, 0);
if (err)
{
        // not enough memory in the application heap! Try it in temporary memory.
        err = NewGWorld (&(*resHandle) -> backgroundWorld, (*resHandle) -> bitDepth,
                &compositeRect, nil, nil, useTempMem);
}

if (!err)
{
        GWorldPtr                               currPort;
        GDHandle                    currDev;

        GetGWorld (&currPort, &currDev);                // save the current GWorld
        SetGWorld ((*resHandle) -> backgroundWorld, nil);
        // set to the new one, so that any drawing takes place there
        PixMapHandle pixMap = GetGWorldPixMap ((*resHandle) -> backgroundWorld);
        LockPixels (pixMap);

        PicHandle picture = GetPicture ((*resHandle) -> backgroundPictResID);
        if (picture)
```

```
                              {
                                    DrawPicture (picture, &compositeRect);
                              }

                              UnlockPixels (pixMap);
                              SetGWorld (currPort, currDev);                    // restore the original GWorld
                        }

                  err = NewGWorld (&(*resHandle) -> compositeWorld, (*resHandle) -> bitDepth,
                        &compositeRect, nil, nil, 0);
                  if (err)
                  {
                        // not enough memory in the application heap! Try it in temporary memory.
                        NewGWorld (&(*resHandle) -> compositeWorld, (*resHandle) -> bitDepth,
                              &compositeRect, nil, nil, useTempMem);
                  }

                  HUnlock ((*theControl) -> contrlData);
      }
}

/*******************************************************************************

      DisposeTheControl - used to deallocate the GWorlds.

*******************************************************************************/
void DisposeTheControl (ControlHandle theControl)
{
      SliderInfoH                   sHandle = (SliderInfoH) (*theControl) -> contrlData;

      if (sHandle)
      {
            if ((*sHandle) -> indicatorWorld)
            {
                  DisposeGWorld ((*sHandle) -> indicatorWorld);
            }

            if ((*sHandle) -> backgroundWorld)
            {
                  DisposeGWorld ((*sHandle) -> backgroundWorld);
            }

            if ((*sHandle) -> compositeWorld)
            {
                  DisposeGWorld ((*sHandle) -> compositeWorld);
            }

            DisposeHandle ((Handle) sHandle);
      }
}
```

```
/*****************************************************************************

    DrawTheControl - technically it's possible to determine whether we need to draw the
    entire control or just the indicator, but it's simpler just to draw the entire
    thing - "just drawing the indicator" doesn't really make much sense under our
    offscreen buffering mechanism.

*****************************************************************************/
void DrawTheControl (ControlHandle theControl)
{
    if ((*theControl) -> contrlData)
    {
        HLock ((*theControl) -> contrlData);
        SliderInfoP      infoPtr = (*(SliderInfoH) (*theControl) -> contrlData);

        if ((*theControl) -> contrlVis && infoPtr -> indicatorWorld && infoPtr -> backgroundWorld
            && infoPtr -> compositeWorld)
        {
            GWorldPtr                        currPort;
            GDHandle             currDev;

            GetGWorld (&currPort, &currDev);            // save the current GWorld
            SetGWorld (infoPtr -> compositeWorld, nil);
            // set to the new one, so that any drawing takes place there
            PixMapHandle compositePixMap = GetGWorldPixMap (infoPtr -> compositeWorld);
            LockPixels (compositePixMap);

            // first, copy the background to the composite
            PixMapHandle backgroundPixMap = GetGWorldPixMap (infoPtr -> backgroundWorld);
            LockPixels (backgroundPixMap);

            CopyBits ((BitMap*) *backgroundPixMap, (BitMap*) *compositePixMap,
                    &infoPtr -> backgroundWorld -> portRect,
                    &infoPtr -> compositeWorld -> portRect, srcCopy, nil);

            UnlockPixels (backgroundPixMap);

            // now draw the indicator on top of the background image that's in the composite
            PixMapHandle indicatorPixMap = GetGWorldPixMap (infoPtr -> indicatorWorld);
            LockPixels (indicatorPixMap);

            // calulate where the indicator should appear
            Rect    destinationRect = infoPtr -> indicatorRect;
            short   offsetUnits = (*theControl) -> contrlValue - (*theControl) -> contrlMin;
            OffsetRect (&destinationRect, (infoPtr -> pixelsPerValue * offsetUnits), 0);

            CopyBits ((BitMap*) *indicatorPixMap, (BitMap*) *compositePixMap,
                    &infoPtr -> indicatorWorld -> portRect, &destinationRect,
                    srcCopy, nil);

            UnlockPixels (indicatorPixMap);
```

```
                        // now copy the composite to the screen
                        SetGWorld (currPort, currDev);
                        // restore the original GWorld

                        ForeColor (blackColor);
                        // avoid unwanted coloring by CopyBits - you have to do this to
                        BackColor (whiteColor);
                        // prevent CopyBits from changing the color of the pixels being copied!

                        CopyBits ((BitMap*) *compositePixMap,
                                  &((GrafPtr) (*theControl) -> contrlOwner) -> portBits,
                                  &infoPtr -> compositeWorld -> portRect, &(*theControl) -> contrlRect,
                                  srcCopy, nil);

                        UnlockPixels (compositePixMap);
                }
                HUnlock ((*theControl) -> contrlData);
        }
}

/********************************************************************************

        DragTheControl

********************************************************************************/
void DragTheControl (ControlHandle theControl)
{
        if ((*theControl) -> contrlData)
        {
                HLock ((*theControl) -> contrlData);
                SliderInfoP     infoPtr = (*(SliderInfoH) (*theControl) -> contrlData);
                Point           mousePt,             // where the mouse is right now
                                topLeftPt;           // where the top left of the control
                                                     // is in local coords
                short           leftEdgeOffset,      // the distance between the mousePt and where
                                                     // the left edge of the indicator should be
                                leftLoc,             // ignore mouse coords to the left of this position
                                rightLoc,            // ignore mouse coords to the right of this position
                                oldMouseHoriz,       // where the mouse was horizontally last time through
                                                     // the loop
                                oldValue,            // original value of the control
                                newValue;            // new value of the control
                GWorldPtr       currPort;
                GDHandle        currDev;
                Rect            oldThumb,            // only the union of the old and new positions needs
                                                     // to be drawn each time the slider moves,
                                                     // and this rectangle stores the old one
                                newThumb,            // the new rectangle for the indicator
                                unionOfRects,
                                tempRect;
```

```
GetGWorld (&currPort, &currDev);                    // save the current GWorld
PixMapHandle compositePixMap = GetGWorldPixMap (infoPtr -> compositeWorld);
LockPixels (compositePixMap);

PixMapHandle backgroundPixMap = GetGWorldPixMap (infoPtr -> backgroundWorld);
LockPixels (backgroundPixMap);

PixMapHandle indicatorPixMap = GetGWorldPixMap (infoPtr -> indicatorWorld);
LockPixels (indicatorPixMap);

ForeColor (blackColor);                // avoid unwanted coloring by CopyBits
BackColor (whiteColor);

// calulate where the indicator is to start with
oldThumb = infoPtr -> indicatorRect;
short offsetUnits = (*theControl) -> contrlValue - (*theControl) -> contrlMin;
OffsetRect (&oldThumb, (infoPtr -> pixelsPerValue * offsetUnits), 0);

SetPt (&topLeftPt, (*theControl) -> contrlRect.left, (*theControl) -> contrlRect.top);
oldMouseHoriz = -1;                    // ensure we always draw at least once

leftEdgeOffset = (infoPtr -> indicatorRect.right - infoPtr -> indicatorRect.left) / 2;
leftLoc = infoPtr -> indicatorRect.left + leftEdgeOffset;
rightLoc = leftLoc + (infoPtr -> pixelsPerValue * ((*theControl) -> contrlMax -
        (*theControl) -> contrlMin));

oldValue = (*theControl) -> contrlValue,
newValue = oldValue;

// always at least once - otherwise the user might click and
// release the mouse before we started tracking;
// we want to be sure we jump to the new value if this happens

do
{
            GetMouse (&mousePt);
            mousePt.h -= topLeftPt.h;
            mousePt.v -= topLeftPt.v;

            mousePt.h = min (mousePt.h, rightLoc);
            mousePt.h = max (mousePt.h, leftLoc);

            if (mousePt.h != oldMouseHoriz)
            {
                    newThumb = oldThumb;
                    newThumb.left = mousePt.h - leftEdgeOffset;
                    newThumb.right = newThumb.left + (infoPtr -> indicatorRect.right
                            infoPtr -> indicatorRect.left);

                    UnionRect (&oldThumb, &newThumb, &unionOfRects);
                    SetGWorld (infoPtr -> compositeWorld, nil);
```

```
                              CopyBits ((BitMap*) *backgroundPixMap, (BitMap*) *compositePixMap,
                                        &unionOfRects, &unionOfRects, srcCopy, nil);

                              CopyBits ((BitMap*) *indicatorPixMap, (BitMap*) *compositePixMap,
                                        infoPtr -> indicatorWorld -> portRect, &newThumb,
                                        srcCopy, nil);

                              SetGWorld (currPort, currDev);  // restore the original GWorld
                              tempRect = unionOfRects;
                              OffsetRect (&tempRect, topLeftPt.h, topLeftPt.v);
                              CopyBits ((BitMap*) *compositePixMap,
                                        &((GrafPtr) (*theControl) -> contrlOwner) -> portBits,
                                        unionOfRects, &tempRect, srcCopy, nil);

                              oldThumb = newThumb;
                              oldMouseHoriz = mousePt.h;

                              short rawValue = newThumb.left - infoPtr -> indicatorRect.left;
                              newValue = rawValue / infoPtr -> pixelsPerValue;
                              if ((rawValue % infoPtr -> pixelsPerValue) >
                                        (infoPtr -> pixelsPerValue / 2))
                              {
                                        // it's more than halfway to the next "stop"
                                        newValue ++;
                              }
                    }
          }                   while (StillDown ());

     UnlockPixels (indicatorPixMap);
     UnlockPixels (backgroundPixMap);
     UnlockPixels (compositePixMap);
     SetGWorld (currPort, currDev);  // restore the original GWorld

     HUnlock ((*theControl) -> contrlData);

     // note that we redraw it even if the actual control value has not changed as a result of
     // the drag - this ensures that the indicator snaps into a position representing an exact
     // value.
     (*theControl) -> contrlValue = newValue;
     DrawTheControl (theControl);
     }
}
```

Tiger Slider.h

```c
/*
     File Name:          Tiger Slider.h
*/

#pragma once

#include   <QDOffscreen.h>

#define   min(a,b) ((a) > (b) ? (b) : (a))
#define   max(a,b) ((a) > (b) ? (a) : (b))


#if defined(powerc) || defined (__powerc)
#pragma options align=mac68k
#endif

typedef struct SliderInfo
{
     short          backgroundPictResID,
                    indicatorPictResID,
                    bitDepth,
                    pixelsPerValue;
// how many pixels to the right does each control value represent?

     Rect           indicatorRect;
// where does the indicator appear when the control value is minimum?

     GWorldPtr      indicatorWorld,
                    backgroundWorld,
                    compositeWorld;
} SliderInfo, *SliderInfoP, **SliderInfoH;

#if defined(powerc) || defined(__powerc)
#pragma options align=reset
#endif

#define   kSliderInfoType     'Sinf'

pascal   long   main (short varCode, ControlHandle theControl,
                      short theMessage, long theParam);
void           InitTheControl (ControlHandle theControl);
void           DisposeTheControl (ControlHandle theControl);
void           DrawTheControl (ControlHandle theControl);
void           DragTheControl (ControlHandle theControl);
```

Chapter Eight Source Code

InfinityWindoid.c

```c
// ****************************************************************************
//
//   InfinityWindoid.c
//
// ----------------------------------------------------------------------------
//   Copyright © 1991-94 Infinity Systems. All rights reserved.
// ----------------------------------------------------------------------------
//   DESCRIPTION:
//          This file contains the main source for a WDEF (Window Definition)
//          resource. It provides a 'windoid' appearance for use on floating
//          windows.
//
//          See the file 'About Infinity Windoid' for more information and a list
//          of features this WDEF supports.
// ----------------------------------------------------------------------------
//   WRITTEN BY:
//          Troy Gaul, Infinity Systems
//
//   HOW TO CONTACT THE AUTHOR:
//          Send e-mail to: tgaul@halcyon.com
//                                 or: tgaul@aol.com
//                                 or: tgaul@eworld.com
// ****************************************************************************

#include "WindoidDefines.h"
     // Must be included before Apple interfaces.

#include <Memory.h>
#include <ToolUtils.h>
#include <Types.h>

#include "WindoidDraw.h"
#include "WindoidTypes.h"
#include "WindoidUtil.h"


// ----------------------------------------------------------------------------
//
//   Function Prototypes    for main
//
// ----------------------------------------------------------------------------
void DoWInit(WindowPeek window, long param, short varCode);
void DoWDispose(WindowPeek window, long param);
long DoWHit(WindowPeek window, long param);
```

```
void DoWDraw(WindowPeek window, long param);
void DoWCalcRgns(WindowPeek window, long param);
void DoWGrow(WindowPeek window, long param);
void DoWDrawGIcon(WindowPeek window, long param);



// -------------------------------------------------------------------------
//
//   Windoid Main Function
//
// -------------------------------------------------------------------------
//    This is the main entry point for all calls to this code resource. It
//    dispatches to routines that correspond to the message it is given.
// -------------------------------------------------------------------------
pascal long
main(short varCode, WindowPeek window, short message, long param)
{
      long result = 0;
      GrafPtr  savePort;
      Boolean  needSyncPorts;

      // This sets up the appropriate drawing environment, but only for those
      // messages for which we actually need to draw.
      needSyncPorts = (message == wDraw
                                || message == wHit
                                || message == wGrow
                                || message == wDrawGIcon) && HasCQDraw();
      if (needSyncPorts) {
            GetPort(&savePort);
            SyncPorts();
      }

        switch (message) {
              case wNew:           DoWInit(window, param, varCode);
                                              break;

              case wDispose:       DoWDispose(window, param);
                                              break;

              case wDraw:          DoWDraw(window, param & 0xFFFF);
                                              break;
                        // There's a tech note that says that for the draw message, only
                        // the low-order word of param is set correctly, so we should do
                        // this (& 0xFFFF) to be sure we're looking at the correct value.

              case wHit:           result = DoWHit(window, param);
                                              break;

              case wCalcRgns:      DoWCalcRgns(window, param);
                                              break;
```

```
                    case wGrow:          DoWGrow(window, param);
                                                      break;

                    case wDrawGIcon:   DoWDrawGIcon(window, param);
                                                      break;
            }

        if (needSyncPorts)
            SetPort(savePort);

        return result;
}




// --------------------------------------------------------------------------------
//
//   SetZoomRects
//
// --------------------------------------------------------------------------------
//       Fills out the zoom rectangles that are stored in our data record that
//       hangs off of the dataHandle of the Window. These define the normal
//       user state (the current position and size that the user has made the
//       window) and standard state (the state the application determines is
//       the position and size for the window when it is zoomed out to "full
//       size").
//
//       The standard state is initialized to be equal to the initial position
//       and size of the window. The WDEF doesn't modify this state after that;
//       the application should set it to an appropriate rectangle (either after
//       making the window or whenever the zoom box is hit, whichever is
//       appropriate for the application's use of the zoom box.
// --------------------------------------------------------------------------------
static void
SetZoomRects(WindowPeek window)
{
    if (window->spareFlag) {
        Rect contRect;
        GetGlobalContentRect(window, &contRect);

        WindData.wState.stdState = contRect;
        WindData.wState.userState = contRect;
    }
}




// --------------------------------------------------------------------------------
//
//   GetZoomHitType
//
// --------------------------------------------------------------------------------
```

```
static long
GetZoomHitType(WindowPeek window)
{
    Rect contentRect = (**window->contRgn).rgnBBox;
    Rect standardStateRect = WindData.wState.stdState;

    long result = EqualRect(&contentRect, &standardStateRect) ? wInZoomIn
            : wInZoomOut;

    // Calculate offset for zoom rects (make sure they are up to date).
    if (result == wInZoomOut)
            WindData.wState.userState = contentRect;

    return result;
}



// ***************************************************************************
//
//   DoWInit -- Windoid initialization.
//
// ***************************************************************************


// ---------------------------------------------------------------------------
//
//   DoWInit
//
// ---------------------------------------------------------------------------
//      This routine initializes the WDEF's information in the window record
//      by allocating a handle that will hang from the WindowRecord's dataHandle
//      field. This handle contains the zoom rects at the beginning (just like
//      Apple's System WDEFs). This is followed by a set of flags that the
//      Infinity Windoid uses to determine features in use by a window.
//
//      The set of variation codes that the Infinity Windoid uses is the same
//      set that is used by the new Apple System 7.5 floating window WDEF. They
//      are as follows:
//      1 - Set to allow the window's appearance reflect the hilite flag.
//      2 - Set to allow drawing of a grow box.
//      4 - Set to put a zoom box in the titlebar.
//      8 - Set to put the titlebar down the side of the window.
//
//      To use a variation code, add the number corresponding to the flag(s) you
//      want to the procID that you use when creating the window. For example,
//      to use all of the options, pass NewWindow or give a WIND resource a
//      procID of (128 * 16) + 1 + 2 + 4 + 8.
//
//      I suggest you always set the first flag (without it, the WDEF will
//      always draw with the pattern in the titlebar and it will never
//      dim -- dimming is necessary for the proper appearance when a modal
//      window is displayed above a floater, however).
// ---------------------------------------------------------------------------
```

```
void
DoWInit(WindowPeek window, long param, short varCode)
{
      Handle zoomDataHndl = NewHandleClear(sizeof(WindoidData));

      if (zoomDataHndl != nil) {
            WindoidDataPtr wdata = (WindoidDataPtr) *zoomDataHndl;
                  // Make it easier to access.

            wdata->closeToggle   = 0;
            wdata->zoomToggle    = 0;

            wdata->ignoreHilite  = (varCode & kSystem75_toggleTBar) == 0;
            wdata->hasGrow       = (varCode & kSystem75_hasGrow)    != 0;
            window->spareFlag    = (varCode & kSystem75_hasZoom)    != 0;
            wdata->isHoriz       = (varCode & kSystem75_vertTBar)   == 0;

            window->dataHandle   = zoomDataHndl;
            SetZoomRects(window);
      }
}



// ****************************************************************************
//
//   DoWDispose -- Windoid disposal.
//
// ****************************************************************************
void
DoWDispose(WindowPeek window, long param)
{
    if (window->dataHandle)
          DisposeHandle(window->dataHandle);
}
```

WindoidDraw.c

```
// ****************************************************************************
//
//   WindoidDraw.c
//
// ----------------------------------------------------------------------------
//   Copyright © 1991-94 Infinity Systems. All rights reserved.
// ----------------------------------------------------------------------------
//   DESCRIPTION:
//          This file contains the code that the WDEF uses to get the locations
//          and sizes of parts, and to draw them.
// ----------------------------------------------------------------------------
//   WRITTEN BY:
//          Troy Gaul
//          Infinity Systems
// ****************************************************************************
```

```
#include "WindoidDraw.h"

#include <Memory.h>

#include "WindoidTypes.h"
#include "WindoidUtil.h"


// ***************************************************************************
//
//   Routines to get Rects for title bar parts
//
// ***************************************************************************


// --------------------------------------------------------------------------
//
//   GetTitleBarRect
//
// --------------------------------------------------------------------------
void
GetTitleBarRect(WindowPeek window, Rect *titleBar)
{
     *titleBar = (**window->strucRgn).rgnBBox;

     if (WindData.isHoriz) {
          // Titlebar on top.
          titleBar->bottom = titleBar->top + kTitleHeight;
          titleBar->right -= 1;     // Shadow compensation.

     } else {
          // Titlebar on left.
          titleBar->right = titleBar->left + kTitleHeight;
          titleBar->bottom -= 1;     // Shadow compensation.
     }
}



// --------------------------------------------------------------------------
//
//   GetCloseBox
//
// --------------------------------------------------------------------------
void
GetCloseBox(WindowPeek window, Rect *theRect)
{
     GetTitleBarRect(window, theRect);

     if (WindData.isHoriz)
             InsetRect(theRect, kGadgetMargin, kGadgetInset);   // Titlebar on top.
     else
             InsetRect(theRect, kGadgetInset, kGadgetMargin);   // Titlebar on left.
```

```
        theRect->bottom = theRect->top + kGadgetSize;
        theRect->right = theRect->left + kGadgetSize;
}



// --------------------------------------------------------------------------
//
//   GetZoomBox
//
// --------------------------------------------------------------------------
void
GetZoomBox(WindowPeek window, Rect *theRect)
{
    GetTitleBarRect(window, theRect);

    if (WindData.isHoriz) {
            // Align zoom box with titlebar pattern.
            if (IsEven(theRect->right - theRect->left))
                    OffsetRect(theRect, -1, 0);
            InsetRect(theRect, kGadgetMargin, kGadgetInset);   // Titlebar on top.

    } else {
            // Align zoom box with titlebar pattern.
            if (IsEven(theRect->bottom - theRect->top))
                    OffsetRect(theRect, 0, -1);

            InsetRect(theRect, kGadgetInset, kGadgetMargin);   // Titlebar on left.
    }

    theRect->top = theRect->bottom - kGadgetSize;
    theRect->left = theRect->right - kGadgetSize;
}



// --------------------------------------------------------------------------
//
//   GetGrowBox
//
// --------------------------------------------------------------------------
void
GetGrowBox(WindowPeek window, Rect *theRect)
{
    GetGlobalContentRect(window, theRect);

    theRect->left = ++theRect->right - kScrollBarPixels;
    theRect->top = ++theRect->bottom - kScrollBarPixels;
}
```

```
// ****************************************************************************
//
//   Color Setup routines
//
// ****************************************************************************
// ---------------------------------------------------------------------------
//
//   SetWFrameColor
//
// ---------------------------------------------------------------------------
void
SetWFrameColor(WindowPeek window, Boolean isColor)
{
    Boolean isActive = window->hilited || WindData.ignoreHilite;

    if (isColor) {
        if (isActive)
            WctbForeColor(window, wFrameColor);
        else
            AvgWctbForeColor(window, wHiliteColorLight, wHiliteColorDark,
                                        wInactiveFramePct);

    } else {
        ForeColor(blackColor);
    }
}


// ---------------------------------------------------------------------------
//
//   SetWTitleColor
//
// ---------------------------------------------------------------------------
void
SetWTitleColor(WindowPeek window, Boolean isColor)
{
    Boolean isActive = window->hilited || WindData.ignoreHilite;

    if (isColor) {
        if (isActive)
            WctbForeColor(window, wTextColor);
        else            // Set the color for inactive titlebar text.
            AvgWctbForeColor(window, wHiliteColorLight, wHiliteColorDark,
                                        wInactiveTextPct);

    } else {
        ForeColor(blackColor);
    }
}
```

```
//  -------------------------------------------------------------------------
//
//   SetWTitleBarColors
//
//  -------------------------------------------------------------------------
//         Set the foreground and background for the drawing of the
//         titlebar pattern.
//  -------------------------------------------------------------------------
void
SetWTitleBarColors(WindowPeek window, Boolean isColor)
{
     Boolean isActive = window->hilited || WindData.ignoreHilite;

     if (isColor) {
           if (isActive) {
                 AvgWctbForeColor(window, wHiliteColorLight, wHiliteColorDark,
                                              wTitleBarDarkPct);
                 AvgWctbBackColor(window, wHiliteColorLight, wHiliteColorDark,
                                              wTitleBarLightPct);

           } else {
                 WctbForeColor(window, wContentColor);
                 WctbBackColor(window, wContentColor);
            }

     } else {
           ColorsNormal();
     }
}


//  -------------------------------------------------------------------------
//
//   SetGadgetFrameEraseColors
//
//  -------------------------------------------------------------------------
//         Set the foreground and background for the drawing of the
//         titlebar pattern, in inverse so we can erase some of the
//         background by using normal drawing routines.
//  -------------------------------------------------------------------------
void
SetGadgetFrameEraseColors(WindowPeek window, Boolean isColor)
{
     if (isColor) {
           AvgWctbBackColor(window, wHiliteColorLight, wHiliteColorDark,
                                       wTitleBarDarkPct);
           AvgWctbForeColor(window, wHiliteColorLight, wHiliteColorDark,
                                       wTitleBarLightPct);

     } else {
           ForeColor(whiteColor);
```

```
                    BackColor(blackColor);
        }
}



// *****************************************************************************
//
//    Drawing routines
//
// *****************************************************************************
// ---------------------------------------------------------------------------
//
//    DrawTitlebarTinges
//
// ---------------------------------------------------------------------------
static void
DrawTitlebarTinges(WindowPeek window, Boolean isColor, const Rect *bounds)
{
        Rect tempRect = *bounds;
        InsetRect(&tempRect, 1, 1);

        if (isColor) {
                AvgWctbForeColor(window, wTingeLight, wTingeDark,
                                            wTitleBarTingeDarkPct);
                FrameBottomRightShading(tempRect);

                WctbForeColor(window, wTingeLight);
                tempRect.right--;
                tempRect.bottom--;
                FrameTopLeftShading(tempRect);

        } else {
                ForeColor(whiteColor);
                BackColor(blackColor);
                FrameRect(&tempRect);
        }
}



// ---------------------------------------------------------------------------
//
//    DrawCloseBox
//
// ---------------------------------------------------------------------------
void
DrawCloseBox(WindowPeek window, Boolean isColor, const Rect *theRect)
{
        Rect tempRect;

        // Paint the area on the edges out with the background color.
        SetGadgetFrameEraseColors(window, isColor);
```

```
        tempRect = *theRect;
        InsetRect(&tempRect, -kTingeInset, -kTingeInset);
        FrameRect(&tempRect);

        if (isColor) {
                WctbForeColor(window, wTingeDark);
                BackColor(whiteColor);
                FrameTopLeftShading(*theRect);

                tempRect = *theRect;
                tempRect.top++;
                tempRect.left++;
                WctbForeColor(window, wTingeLight);
                FrameRect(&tempRect);

                InsetRect(&tempRect, 1, 1);
                WctbForeColor(window, wTingeDark);
                FrameBottomRightShading(tempRect);

                tempRect.right--;
                tempRect.bottom--;
                AvgWctbForeColor(window, wTitleBarLight, wTitleBarDark,
                                          wCloseBoxColor);
                PaintRect(&tempRect);

        } else {
                ColorsNormal();
                FrameBox(theRect);
        }
}

// ---------------------------------------------------------------------------
//
//   DrawZoomBox
//
// ---------------------------------------------------------------------------
void
DrawZoomBox(WindowPeek window, Boolean isColor, const Rect *theRect)
{
    Rect tempRect;

    DrawCloseBox(window, isColor, theRect);
    tempRect = *theRect;

    tempRect.bottom -= kGadgetSize / 2;
    tempRect.right -= kGadgetSize / 2;
            // This should handle gadgets of various sizes elegantly.

    if (isColor) {
            WctbForeColor(window, wTingeDark);
            tempRect.left += 2;     // Inset past the tinge.
```

```
                tempRect.top += 2;
                FrameBottomRightShading(tempRect);

        } else {
                FrameRect(&tempRect);
        }
}



// ---------------------------------------------------------------------------
//
//   DrawXedBox
//
// ---------------------------------------------------------------------------
//       Draw close or zoom box with an X in it (or inverted in B&W).
// ---------------------------------------------------------------------------
void
DrawXedBox(WindowPeek window, Boolean isColor, const Rect *theRect)
{
        if (isColor) {
                AvgWctbForeColor(window, wTingeLight, wTingeDark, wXedBoxPct);
                PaintRect(theRect);

                WctbForeColor(window, wTitleBarDark);
                FrameRect(theRect);

                // Draw the 'X'.
                MoveTo(theRect->left,      theRect->top   );
                LineTo(theRect->right - 1, theRect->bottom - 1);
                MoveTo(theRect->right - 1, theRect->top   );
                LineTo(theRect->left,      theRect->bottom - 1);

        } else {
                PaintRect(theRect);
        }
}



// ---------------------------------------------------------------------------
//
//   DrawGrow3DBox
//
// ---------------------------------------------------------------------------
static void
DrawGrow3DBox(WindowPeek window, Rect *theRect, Boolean isLight)
{
        Rect tempRect = *theRect;

        WctbForeColor(window, wTingeDark);
        FrameRect(theRect);
```

```
    // Add the top light outer border on the top-left edge.
    tempRect.left++;
    tempRect.top++;
    WctbForeColor(window, wTingeLight);
    FrameTopLeftShading(tempRect);

    // Finally, fill in the center.
    AvgWctbForeColor(window, wTitleBarLight, wTitleBarDark,
                              isLight ? wGrowBoxColorLt : wGrowBoxColorDk);

    InsetRect(&tempRect, 1, 1);
    PaintRect(&tempRect);
}



// ---------------------------------------------------------------------------
//
//   DrawGrowBox
//
// ---------------------------------------------------------------------------
void
DrawGrowBox(WindowPeek window, Boolean isColor)
{
    Boolean isActive = window->hilited || WindData.ignoreHilite;
    Rect theRect;
    GetGrowBox(window, &theRect);

    if (!isActive) {
        if (isColor) {
            WctbForeColor(window, wFrameColor);
            WctbBackColor(window, wContentColor);
        }
        FrameBox(&theRect);

    } else {
        Rect smallRect;
        Rect largeRect;

        // Add the size box chevrons.
        SetRect(&smallRect, theRect.left + 3, theRect.top + 3,
                                    theRect.left + 10, theRect.top + 10);
        SetRect(&largeRect, smallRect.left + 2, smallRect.top + 2,
                                    theRect.right - 2, theRect.bottom - 2);

        if (isColor) {
            WctbForeColor(window, wFrameColor);
            AvgWctbBackColor(window, wHiliteColorLight, wHiliteColorDark,
                                        wGrowBoxBackground);
            FrameBox(&theRect);

            // Draw the dark border parts for the bottom rectangle.
```

```
                     OffsetRect(&largeRect, -1, -1);
                     DrawGrow3DBox(window, &largeRect, false);

                     // Draw the dark border parts for the top rectangle.
                     smallRect.right--;
                     smallRect.bottom--;
                     DrawGrow3DBox(window, &smallRect, true);

            } else {
                     ColorsNormal();
                     FrameBox(&theRect);

                     FrameRect(&largeRect);
                     FrameBox(&smallRect);
            }
     }
}


// -------------------------------------------------------------------------
//
//   ToggleCloseBox
//
// -------------------------------------------------------------------------
void
ToggleCloseBox(WindowPeek window, Boolean isColor)
{
     Rect tempRect;
     GetCloseBox(window, &tempRect);

     if (WindData.closeToggle)
             DrawCloseBox(window, isColor, &tempRect);
     else
             DrawXedBox(window, isColor, &tempRect);
}


// -------------------------------------------------------------------------
//
//   ToggleZoomBox
//
// -------------------------------------------------------------------------
void
ToggleZoomBox(WindowPeek window, Boolean isColor)
{
     Rect tempRect;
     GetZoomBox(window, &tempRect);

     if (WindData.zoomToggle)
             DrawZoomBox(window, isColor, &tempRect);
     else
             DrawXedBox(window, isColor, &tempRect);
}
```

```
// -------------------------------------------------------------------------
//
//   GetTitlebarPat
//
// -------------------------------------------------------------------------
//           Choose correct pattern, depending on position of window in global
//           coordinates. (Concept of new (2.3) version taken from _Macintosh
//           Programming Secrets_, Second Edition, by Scott Knaster and Keith
//           Rollin, page 423.)
// -------------------------------------------------------------------------
static void
GetTitlebarPat(Boolean isActive, Point *corner, Pattern *titlePat)
{
     long seed = isActive ? 0x00550055 : 0x00000000;

     if (IsOdd(corner->h))
           seed <= 1;
     if (IsOdd(corner->v))
           seed <= 8;

     *((long*) titlePat + 1) = *((long*) titlePat) = seed;
}



// -------------------------------------------------------------------------
//
//   SubtractGadgetRect
//
// -------------------------------------------------------------------------
static void
SubtractGadgetRect(RgnHandle theRgn, const Rect *theRect)
{
     Rect subRect = *theRect;
     RgnHandle subRgn = NewRgn();

     InsetRect(&subRect, -kTingeInset, -kTingeInset);
           // To give the correct visual appearance.

     RectRgn(subRgn, &subRect);
     DiffRgn(theRgn, subRgn, theRgn);

     DisposeRgn(subRgn);
}



// -------------------------------------------------------------------------
//
//   DrawTitleString
//
// -------------------------------------------------------------------------
//           When this routine is called, the background color will already be set
//           to the color of the background of the titlebar.
// -------------------------------------------------------------------------
```

```
static void
DrawTitleString(WindowPeek window, Boolean isColor, const Rect *titleRect,
                        Rect *stringRect)
{
    Boolean isActive = window->hilited || WindData.ignoreHilite;
    short maxWidth;
    short titleWidth;
    short inset;
    short strAreaLeft;
    Rect titleStrBounds;
    RGBColor saveFore;

    if (window->titleHandle != nil && (*window->titleHandle)[0] != 0
            && WindData.isHoriz)
    {
        maxWidth = titleRect->right - titleRect->left - 2 * kGadgetMargin;
        strAreaLeft = titleRect->left + kGadgetMargin;
        if (window->goAwayFlag || window->spareFlag) {
            maxWidth -= 2 * (kGadgetSize + kGadgetMargin);
            strAreaLeft += kGadgetSize + kGadgetMargin;
        }

        if (maxWidth > 0) {
            char saveTitleHandleState;

            // Set up fonts, colors for text drawing.
            TextFont(kTitleFont);
            TextSize(kTitleSize);
            TextFace(kTitleStyle);
            TextMode(srcOr);

            saveTitleHandleState = HGetState((Handle) window->titleHandle);
            HLock((Handle) window->titleHandle);
                // StringWidth and DrawString may move memory.

            if (isColor)
                GetForeColor(&saveFore);
            SetWTitleColor(window, isColor);

            // Calculate the width of the title string.
            titleWidth = StringWidth(*window->titleHandle) + 2 *
                kTitleMargin;

            // Limit its size to maxWidth.
            titleWidth = (titleWidth > maxWidth) ? maxWidth : titleWidth;

            // Determine where to position it.
            inset = (short) (maxWidth * titleWidth) / 2;

            // Make the title appear centered.
            if (IsEven(titleWidth))              // We need an odd width or
                titleWidth--;                    // the overlap is wrong.
```

```
            inset -= IsEven(inset);
                // This is done so that the title doesn't
                // shift as the windowUs width changes.

            // Set up the Rect to enclose the title within the titlebar.
            SetRect(&titleStrBounds, strAreaLeft + inset,
                titleRect->top + 1,
                strAreaLeft + inset + titleWidth,
                titleRect->bottom - 1);

            // Inset the bounds so as not to erase part of the tinges.
            if (isActive)
                InsetRect(&titleStrBounds, 0, kTingeInset);

            // Return the title string areaUs boundry.
            *stringRect = titleStrBounds;

    // Make sure this area is cleared to the titlebar background color.
            EraseRect(&titleStrBounds);

            // Inset past the empty sides.
            InsetRect(&titleStrBounds, kTitleMargin, 0);

            // Outset it so decenders may overwrite the bottom tinge.
            if (isActive)
                InsetRect(&titleStrBounds, 0, -kTingeInset);
            // Clip the drawing to the string's area.
            {
                RgnHandle saveClip = NewRgn();
                RgnHandle clipRgn = NewRgn();

                GetClip(saveClip);

            // Get the region the title string should go into.
            RectRgn(clipRgn, &titleStrBounds);

            // Make sure we don't clobber other windows.
            SectRgn(saveClip, clipRgn, clipRgn);
            if (!EmptyRgn(clipRgn)) {
                SetClip(clipRgn);

                // Draw the title.
                MoveTo(titleStrBounds.left,
                    titleStrBounds.bottom - kTitleVDelta);
                DrawString(*window->titleHandle);

                // Clean up.
                SetClip(saveClip);
            }
```

```
                    DisposeRgn(saveClip);
                    DisposeRgn(clipRgn);
            }

        if (isColor)
                RGBForeColor(&saveFore);

        HSetState((Handle) window->titleHandle, saveTitleHandleState);

        TextFont(systemFont);
        TextSize(0);
        TextFace(0);
    }
  }
}


// ---------------------------------------------------------------------------
//
//   DrawAndSubtractTitle
//
// ---------------------------------------------------------------------------
//        Draws the title in the titlebar (by calling DrawTitleString) and
//        subtracts it from the titlebar region (by making the rect returned
//        into a region and using DiffRgn).
// ---------------------------------------------------------------------------
static void
DrawAndSubtractTitle(WindowPeek window, const Rect *titleRect, Boolean isColor,
                                    RgnHandle titleRgn)
{
    Rect strRect;
    strRect.top = strRect.left = strRect.bottom = strRect.right = 0;

    // Draw the titlebar string (if any).
    DrawTitleString(window, isColor, titleRect, &strRect);
            // Since the area affected by the title string is returned in
            // strRect, we can use its left and right to draw the pattern.

    if (!EmptyRect(&strRect)) {
            RgnHandle tempRgn = NewRgn();

            RectRgn(tempRgn, &strRect);
            DiffRgn(titleRgn, tempRgn, titleRgn);

            DisposeRgn(tempRgn);
    }
}
```

```
// --------------------------------------------------------------------------
//
//   DrawTitleBar
//
// --------------------------------------------------------------------------
//      This routine actually draws the pattern into the titlebar. Note: it
//      takes a Rect as a parameter (not by address) because it goes ahead and
//      modifies it. I figured this was no worse than needing to copy it into
//      a local variable, so I went ahead and did it this way.
// --------------------------------------------------------------------------
void
DrawTitleBar(WindowPeek window, Boolean isColor)
{
    Boolean isHoriz = WindData.isHoriz;
    Boolean isActive = window->hilited || WindData.ignoreHilite;
    RgnHandle titleRgn = NewRgn();

    Rect titleRect;
    GetTitleBarRect(window, &titleRect);

    // Draw the frame.
    SetWFrameColor(window, isColor);
    FrameRect(&titleRect);

    // Set up the titleRgn region to be the whole titlebar,
    // parts will then be 'punched out' of it.
    {
        Rect insetTitleRect = titleRect;
        InsetRect(&insetTitleRect, 1 + (isActive ? kTingeInset : 0),
                1 + (isActive ? kTingeInset : 0));
                // Make room for the tinge, if any (which was already drawn).
        RectRgn(titleRgn, &insetTitleRect);
    }

    // Draw the tinges and gadgets.
    if (isActive) {
        Rect tempRect;

        // Draw the tinges.
        DrawTitlebarTinges(window, isColor, &titleRect);

        // Draw and subtract the close box.
        if (window->goAwayFlag) {
            GetCloseBox(window, &tempRect);
            DrawCloseBox(window, isColor, &tempRect);
            SubtractGadgetRect(titleRgn, &tempRect);
        }

        // Draw and subtract the zoom box.
        if (window->spareFlag) {
            GetZoomBox(window, &tempRect);
```

```
                    DrawZoomBox(window, isColor, &tempRect);
                    SubtractGadgetRect(titleRgn, &tempRect);
            }
    }

    // Get the colors to draw the rest.
    SetWTitleBarColors(window, isColor);

    // Draw the title.
    DrawAndSubtractTitle(window, &titleRect, isColor, titleRgn);

    // Draw the pattern.
    {
            Pattern pat;
            GetTitlebarPat(isActive, (Point*) &titleRect.top, &pat);
            FillRgn(titleRgn, &pat);
    }

    DisposeRgn(titleRgn);
}




// -------------------------------------------------------------------------
//
//  DrawWindowFrame
//
// -------------------------------------------------------------------------
void
DrawWindowFrame(WindowPeek window, Boolean isColor)
{
    Rect tempRect = (**window->strucRgn).rgnBBox;

    // Draw content frame and shadow.
    tempRect.bottom--;
    tempRect.right--;

    SetWFrameColor(window, isColor);
    FrameRect(&tempRect);

    // Draw Shadow.
    if (isColor)
            WctbForeColor(window, wFrameColor); // This got messed up in 2.6.
    OffsetRect(&tempRect, 1, 1);
    FrameBottomRightShading(tempRect);
}



// -------------------------------------------------------------------------
```

WindoidDraw.h

```
// *****************************************************************************
//
//    WindoidDraw.h
//
// -----------------------------------------------------------------------------
//    Copyright © 1991-94 Infinity Systems. All rights reserved.
// -----------------------------------------------------------------------------
#ifndef Infinity_WINDOIDDRAW
#define Infinity_WINDOIDDRAW

#include "WindoidDefines.h"

#include <Fonts.h>
#include <Types.h>
#include <Windows.h>


// *****************************************************************************
//
//    Constants
//
// *****************************************************************************


// -----------------------------------------------------------------------------
//
//    Titlebar and gadget sizes and offsets
//
// -----------------------------------------------------------------------------
enum {
    kTingeInset       = 1,
    kTitleHeight      = 13,
    kTitleVDelta      = 2,
    kGadgetMargin     = 8,
    kGadgetHitFudge   = 1
};

#define kGadgetInset (2 + kTingeInset)    // Inset from top/bottom of titlebar.
#define kGadgetSize (kTitleHeight - (2 * kGadgetInset))


// -----------------------------------------------------------------------------
//
//    Scroll Bar width
//
// -----------------------------------------------------------------------------
enum {
    kScrollBarPixels = 16
};
```

```
// ----------------------------------------------------------------------------
//
//   Font information for titlebar title
//
// ----------------------------------------------------------------------------
enum {
    kTitleFont      = applFont,
    kTitleSize      = 9,
    kTitleStyle     = bold,
    kTitleMargin    = 5         // Space between pattern and edges of text.
};




// ----------------------------------------------------------------------------
//
//   Color table tinge percentage constants
//
// ----------------------------------------------------------------------------
enum {
    wTitleBarLightPct       = 0x1,
    wTitleBarTingeDarkPct   = 0x4,

    wCloseBoxColor          = 0x5,
    wTitleBarDarkPct        = 0x8,
    wXedBoxPct              = 0x8,

    wGrowBoxBackground      = 0x1,
    wGrowBoxColorLt         = 0x4,
    wGrowBoxColorDk         = 0x5,

    wInactiveFramePct       = 0xA,
    wInactiveTextPct        = 0x7
};




// ----------------------------------------------------------------------------
//
//   Color table constants
//
// ----------------------------------------------------------------------------
//        These are the constants defined in the Apple technical note regarding
//        Color, Windows, and System 7. Last I checked, they weren't in an Apple
//        header file. (But the ones < 5 are, from the previous, pre-System 7
//        coloring scheme.)
// ----------------------------------------------------------------------------
enum {
    wHiliteColorLight = 5,
    wHiliteColorDark,
    wTitleBarLight,
```

```
        wTitleBarDark,
        wDialogLight,
        wDialogDark,
        wTingeLight,
        wTingeDark
};


// ****************************************************************************
//
//   Prototypes
//
// ****************************************************************************


// ----------------------------------------------------------------------------
//
//   Part rectangles
//
// ----------------------------------------------------------------------------
void GetTitleBarRect(WindowPeek window, Rect *titleBar);

void GetCloseBox(WindowPeek window, Rect *theRect);

void GetZoomBox(WindowPeek window, Rect *theRect);

void GetGrowBox(WindowPeek window, Rect *theRect);


// ----------------------------------------------------------------------------
//
//   Coloring
//
// ----------------------------------------------------------------------------
void SetWFrameColor(WindowPeek window, Boolean isColor);

void SetWTitleColor(WindowPeek window, Boolean isColor);

void SetWTitleBarColors(WindowPeek window, Boolean isColor);

void SetGadgetFrameEraseColors(WindowPeek window, Boolean isColor);


// ----------------------------------------------------------------------------
//
//   Part drawing
//
// ----------------------------------------------------------------------------
void DrawCloseBox(WindowPeek window, Boolean isColor, const Rect *theRect);

void DrawZoomBox(WindowPeek window, Boolean isColor, const Rect *theRect);
```

```
void DrawXedBox(WindowPeek window, Boolean isColor, const Rect *theRect);

void DrawGrowBox(WindowPeek window, Boolean isColor);

void ToggleCloseBox(WindowPeek window, Boolean isColor);

void ToggleZoomBox(WindowPeek window, Boolean isColor);

void DrawTitleBar(WindowPeek window, Boolean isColor);

void DrawWindowFrame(WindowPeek window, Boolean isColor);


// -------------------------------------------------------------------------
#endif
```

WindoidUtil.c

```
// *************************************************************************
//
//   WindoidUtil.c
//
// -------------------------------------------------------------------------
//   Copyright © 1991-94 Infinity Systems. All rights reserved.
// -------------------------------------------------------------------------
//   DESCRIPTION:
//          This file contains various utility routines that the Infinity Windoid
//          WDEF uses in order to get its job done.
// -------------------------------------------------------------------------
//   WRITTEN BY:
//          Troy Gaul (tgaul@halcyon.com)
//          Infinity Systems
// *************************************************************************

#include "WindoidUtil.h"

#include <GestaltEqu.h>
#include <Memory.h>

#include "WindoidDraw.h"
#include "WindoidTypes.h"



// *************************************************************************
//
//   Environment-determining Routines
//
// -------------------------------------------------------------------------
//          These use SysEnvirons by default so we don't have to rely on Gestalt
//          being available and so MPW won't include that code in our resource.
//          This can be changed by defining qUseGestalt to be 1.
// *************************************************************************
```

```
// -----------------------------------------------------------------------
//
//   HasSystem7
//
// -----------------------------------------------------------------------
Boolean
HasSystem7()
{
#if SystemSevenOrLater
    long vers = 0;

    return (Gestalt(gestaltSystemVersion, &vers) == noErr
                && ((vers & 0xFFFF) >= 0x0700));
#else
    SysEnvRec theWorld;

    return (SysEnvirons(1, &theWorld) == noErr
                && theWorld.systemVersion >= 0x0700);
#endif
}


// -----------------------------------------------------------------------
//
//   HasCQDraw
//
// -----------------------------------------------------------------------
Boolean
HasCQDraw()
{
#if SystemSevenOrLater
    long vers = 0;

    return (Gestalt(gestaltQuickdrawVersion, &vers) == noErr
                && (vers & 0xFF00));
#else
    SysEnvRec theWorld;

    return ((SysEnvirons(1, &theWorld) == noErr) &&
                theWorld.hasColorQD);
#endif
}


// -----------------------------------------------------------------------
//
//   SyncPorts
//
// -----------------------------------------------------------------------
```

```
//          Straight from the pages of _Macintosh Programming Secrets_, Second
//          Edition by Scott Knaster and Keith Rollin (page 425). (except that this
//          version doesn't check Gestalt, it will only be called if CQD is running)
//          This routines was added to 2.3. It makes sure the drawing environment
//          is set correctly if the system has color. This is not needed for the
//          code in this WDEF as it is, but if a DoWDrawGIcon handler is implemented,
//          this is needed to make sure the drawing environment is set as Apple
//          tells us it will be for drawing the gray, xor'ed border.
// --------------------------------------------------------------------------
void
SyncPorts()
{
    GrafPtr bwPort;
    CGrafPtr colorPort;

    GetWMgrPort(&bwPort);
    GetCWMgrPort(&colorPort);
    SetPort((GrafPtr) colorPort);

    BlockMoveData(&bwPort->pnLoc, &colorPort->pnLoc, 10);
    BlockMoveData(&bwPort->pnVis, &colorPort->pnVis, 14);
    PenPat((ConstPatternParam) &bwPort->pnPat);
    BackPat((ConstPatternParam) &bwPort->bkPat);
}



// ****************************************************************************
//
//   Color Mixing Routines
//
// ****************************************************************************


// --------------------------------------------------------------------------
//
//   UseDefaultColor
//
// --------------------------------------------------------------------------
//          This routine will return some defaults in case neither the window's
//          color table nor the System's is long enough to contain the color
//          requested. It was provided by Jim Petrick as part of a fix for a bug
//          in version 2.3 of the Infinity Windoid. This problem would be seen if
//          a custom WCTB was being used that was not as long as the default
//          System one (or if the System one had been changed to a shorter size).
//          The rest of Jim's fix can be found in GetWctbColor.
// --------------------------------------------------------------------------
static void
UseDefaultColor(short index, RGBColor *theColor)
{
    switch (index) {
            case wContentColor:
            case wTitleBarColor:
```

```
                case wHiliteColorLight:
                case wTitleBarLight:
                        theColor->red = theColor->green = theColor->blue = 0xFFFF;
                        break;

                case wDialogLight:
                case wTingeLight:
                        theColor->red = theColor->green = 0xCCCC;
                        theColor->blue = 0xFFFF;
                        break;

                case wTingeDark:
                        theColor->red = theColor->green = 0x3333;
                        theColor->blue = 0x6666;
                        break;

                default:
                        theColor->red = theColor->green = theColor->blue = 0;
                        break;
        }
}


// --------------------------------------------------------------------------
//
//   GetWctbColor
//
// --------------------------------------------------------------------------
//          Given a partCode, return the RGBColor associated with it. (Using the
//          default window color table.)
// --------------------------------------------------------------------------
static void
GetWctbColor(WindowPeek window, short partCode, RGBColor *theColor)
{
    AuxWinHandle awHndl;
    short count;

    // Get the Color table for the window if it has one.
    (void) GetAuxWin((WindowPtr) window, &awHndl);
    count = (**(WCTabHandle) (**awHndl).awCTable).ctSize;

    // If the table didn't contain the entry of interest, look to the
    // default table.
    if (count < partCode) {
            (void) GetAuxWin(nil, &awHndl);
            count = (**(WCTabHandle) (**awHndl).awCTable).ctSize;
    }

    // If the entry is there, use it, if not make a best guess at a default value.
    if (count < partCode)
            UseDefaultColor(partCode, theColor);
```

```
    else
            *theColor = (**(WCTabHandle) (**awHndl).awCTable).ctTable[partCode].rgb;
}




// --------------------------------------------------------------------------
//
//   WctbForeColor
//
// --------------------------------------------------------------------------
void
WctbForeColor(WindowPeek window, short partCode)
{
    RGBColor theColor;

    GetWctbColor(window, partCode, &theColor);
    RGBForeColor(&theColor);
}




// --------------------------------------------------------------------------
//
//   WctbBackColor
//
// --------------------------------------------------------------------------
void
WctbBackColor(WindowPeek window, short partCode)
{
    RGBColor theColor;

    GetWctbColor(window, partCode, &theColor);
    RGBBackColor(&theColor);
}




// --------------------------------------------------------------------------
//
//   MixColor
//
// --------------------------------------------------------------------------
//          Note: MixColor uses pragma processor 68020 to reduce code size with
//          MPW. This is okay because MixColor will only be called if we are
//          doing System 7 color, which requires Color Quickdraw, which is only
//          available on systems with 68020's or better. If it isn't compiled this
//          way, several glue routines will be added to the code WDEF resource to
//          handle the long integer arithmetic.
// --------------------------------------------------------------------------
#pragma processor 68020

static void
MixColor(const RGBColor *light, const RGBColor *dark, short shade,
```

```
                        RGBColor *result)
{
    shade = 0x0F - shade;
            // This is necessary because we give shades between light and
            // dark (0% is light), but for colors, $0000 is black and $FFFF
            // is dark.

    result->red   = (long) (light->red   - dark->red)   - shade / 15 + dark->red;
    result->green = (long) (light->green - dark->green) - shade / 15 + dark->green;
    result->blue  = (long) (light->blue  - dark->blue)  - shade / 15 + dark->blue;
}


#pragma processor 68000
// ----------------------------------------------------------------------------
//
//   AvgWctbColor
//
// ----------------------------------------------------------------------------
//       Mix two parts by the given shade, which is actually a value
//       between 0 (0%) and 15 (100%), return the RGBColor.
// ----------------------------------------------------------------------------
static void
AvgWctbColor(WindowPeek window, short light, short dark, short shade,
                    RGBColor *theColor)
{
    RGBColor lightColor;
    RGBColor darkColor;

    GetWctbColor(window, light, &lightColor);
    GetWctbColor(window, dark, &darkColor);
    MixColor(&lightColor, &darkColor, shade, theColor);
}


// ----------------------------------------------------------------------------
//
//   AvgWctbForeColor
//
// ----------------------------------------------------------------------------
void
AvgWctbForeColor(WindowPeek window, short light, short dark, short shade)
{
    RGBColor theColor;

    AvgWctbColor(window, light, dark, shade, &theColor);
    RGBForeColor(&theColor);
}
```

```
// ------------------------------------------------------------------------
//
//   AvgWctbBackColor
//
// ------------------------------------------------------------------------
void
AvgWctbBackColor(WindowPeek window, short light, short dark, short shade)
{
    RGBColor theColor;

    AvgWctbColor(window, light, dark, shade, &theColor);
    RGBBackColor(&theColor);
}



// ************************************************************************
//
//   CheckDisplay -- Check to see if we are using color title bars
//
// ************************************************************************


// ------------------------------------------------------------------------
//
//   CheckAvailable
//
// ------------------------------------------------------------------------
//    Given a light and dark index value, a count, and an array of
//    'percentage' values (0x0 to 0xF, or 0 to 15), see if each of the
//    values in the ramp maps to a different color on the screen. If not,
//    we need to use black-and-white.
// ------------------------------------------------------------------------
static Boolean
CheckAvailable(WindowPeek window, short light, short dark, short count,
                    short *ramp)
{
    RGBColor theColor;
    short i;
    short colorIndex = 0;
    short lastIndex;

    for (i = 0 ; i < count ; i++) {
            AvgWctbColor(window, light, dark, ramp[i], &theColor);

            lastIndex = colorIndex;
            colorIndex = Color2Index(&theColor);

            if (i > 0 && colorIndex == lastIndex)   // return false if two entries
                    return false;                    // have the same index value
    }
```

```
        return true;
}


// ---------------------------------------------------------------------------
//
//   CheckDisplay
//
// ---------------------------------------------------------------------------
//         This routine checks to see if the device in question is color, if
//         System 7 is running, and if there are 'enough' colors to draw the
//         title bar in color under System 7. This might not be the case if
//         the application is using a custom window palette.
//
//         It does so in the same way that Apple's system WDEF does. I essentially
//         took the assembly code that Apple released and made this use the same
//         algorithm.
// ---------------------------------------------------------------------------
Boolean
CheckDisplay(short theDepth, short deviceFlags, GDHandle targetDevice,
                    WindowPeek window)
{
        Boolean inColor;
        Boolean use7Color = false;                      // Assume Black and White.

        if (theDepth >= 4 && (**targetDevice).gdType != fixedType && HasSystem7()) {
                // A passive matrix screen on a PowerBook is a fixed device type.
                // This seems to be how the Apple WDEF determines when to use black
                // and white on those displays.

                RGBColor testColor;
                GetWctbColor(window, wTingeLight, &testColor);

                // Check for B&W control panel setting.
                if (testColor.red != 0 || testColor.green != 0 || testColor.blue != 0)
                        use7Color = true;               // System 7.0 Color.
        }
        // Note: Since I didn't find another way to see if the user had changed
        // the settings in the Color control panel to the Black-and-white setting,
        // I actually check to see if the rgb components of the light tinge color
        // are non-zero (which seemed to be the case with that setting).

        // Check to see if there are 'enough' colors to draw in color.
        inColor = HasCQDraw() && (deviceFlags & (0x0001 < gdDevType));

        if (use7Color && inColor && theDepth <= 8) {
                GDHandle saveDevice = GetGDevice();
                short ramp[5];
                        // Make this array big enough for the largest ramp.

                use7Color = false;
```

```
        SetGDevice(targetDevice);

        ramp[0] = 0x00;
        ramp[1] = 0x07;
        ramp[2] = 0x08;
        ramp[3] = 0x0A;
        ramp[4] = 0x0D;
        if (CheckAvailable(window, wHiliteColorLight, wHiliteColorDark, 5, ramp)) {
            ramp[0] = 0x00;
            ramp[1] = 0x01;
            ramp[2] = 0x04;
            if (CheckAvailable(window, wTitleBarLight, wTitleBarDark, 3, ramp)) {
                ramp[0] = 0x00;
                ramp[1] = 0x04;
                ramp[2] = 0x0F;
                if (CheckAvailable(window, wTingeLight, wTingeDark, 3,
                    ramp))
                    use7Color = true;
            }
        }
        SetGDevice(saveDevice);
    }

    return use7Color;
}


// *****************************************************************************
//
//   General Helper Functions
//
// *****************************************************************************


// ----------------------------------------------------------------------------
//
//   ColorsNormal
//
// ----------------------------------------------------------------------------
void
ColorsNormal()
{
    ForeColor(blackColor);
    BackColor(whiteColor);
}


// ----------------------------------------------------------------------------
//
//   MoveRectTo
//
// ----------------------------------------------------------------------------
void
MoveRectTo(Rect *theRect, short left, short top)
```

```
    {
        theRect->right   += left - theRect->left;
        theRect->bottom  += top - theRect->top;
        theRect->left  = left;
        theRect->top   = top;
    }



// ----------------------------------------------------------------------------
//
//   FrameBox
//
// ----------------------------------------------------------------------------
void
FrameBox(const Rect *theRect)
{
    Rect tempRect = *theRect;

    FrameRect(theRect);
    InsetRect(&tempRect, 1, 1);
    EraseRect(&tempRect);
}



// ----------------------------------------------------------------------------
//
//   FrameTopLeftShading
//
// ----------------------------------------------------------------------------
void
FrameTopLeftShading(Rect theRect)
{
    theRect.right--;                 // Compensate for the way the rectangle hangs.
    theRect.bottom--;

    MoveTo(theRect.left, theRect.bottom);     // •••••
    LineTo(theRect.left, theRect.top  );      // •
    LineTo(theRect.right, theRect.top );      // •
}



// ----------------------------------------------------------------------------
//
//   FrameBottomRightShading
//
// ----------------------------------------------------------------------------
void
FrameBottomRightShading(Rect theRect)
{
    theRect.right--;    // Compensate for the way the rectangle hangs.
    theRect.bottom--;
```

```
    MoveTo(theRect.left, theRect.bottom);        //              •
    LineTo(theRect.right, theRect.bottom);       //              •
    LineTo(theRect.right, theRect.top );         //       • • • • •
}


// ---------------------------------------------------------------------------
//
//   GetGlobalMappingPoint
//
// ---------------------------------------------------------------------------
//        This routine returns a point that gives the horizontal and vertical
//   offsets needed to map something into global coordinates.
// ---------------------------------------------------------------------------
void
GetGlobalMappingPoint(WindowPeek window, Point *thePoint)
{
    GrafPtr savePort;

    GetPort(&savePort);
    SetPort((GrafPtr) window);

    SetPt(thePoint, 0, 0);
    LocalToGlobal(thePoint);

    SetPort(savePort);
}


// ---------------------------------------------------------------------------
//
//   GetGlobalContentRect
//
// ---------------------------------------------------------------------------
void
GetGlobalContentRect(WindowPeek window, Rect *contentRect)
{
    Point mappingPoint;

    *contentRect = window*>port.portRect;
    GetGlobalMappingPoint(window, &mappingPoint);
    OffsetRect(contentRect, mappingPoint.h, mappingPoint.v);
}


// ---------------------------------------------------------------------------
```

WindowidUtil.h

```
// ***************************************************************************
//
//   WindoidUtil.h
//
// ---------------------------------------------------------------------------
//   Copyright © 1991-94 Infinity Systems. All rights reserved.
// ---------------------------------------------------------------------------
#ifndef Infinity_WINDOIDUTIL
#define Infinity_WINDOIDUTIL

#include "WindoidDefines.h"

#include <QuickDraw.h>
#include <Types.h>
#include <Windows.h>


// ---------------------------------------------------------------------------
//
//   Macros to make code cleaner
//
// ---------------------------------------------------------------------------
#define IsOdd(value) ((value) & 1)
#define IsEven(value) (!IsOdd(value))


// ---------------------------------------------------------------------------
//
//   Generally useful routines
//
// ---------------------------------------------------------------------------
Boolean HasSystem7();

Boolean HasCQDraw();

void SyncPorts();


// ---------------------------------------------------------------------------
//
//   Window Color Table color access
//
// ---------------------------------------------------------------------------
void WctbForeColor(WindowPeek window, short partCode);

void WctbBackColor(WindowPeek window, short partCode);

void AvgWctbForeColor(WindowPeek window, short light, short dark, short shade);
```

```
void AvgWctbBackColor(WindowPeek window, short light, short dark, short shade);

void ColorsNormal();


// ----------------------------------------------------------------------------
//
//   CheckDisplay
//
// ----------------------------------------------------------------------------
//    Determine if the device is adequate for drawing in color with System 7.
// ----------------------------------------------------------------------------
Boolean CheckDisplay(short theDepth, short deviceFlags, GDHandle targetDevice,
                               WindowPeek window);


// ----------------------------------------------------------------------------
//
//   General utility drawing routines
//
// ----------------------------------------------------------------------------
void MoveRectTo(Rect *theRect, short left, short top);

void FrameBox(const Rect *theRect);

void FrameTopLeftShading(Rect theRect);

void FrameBottomRightShading(Rect theRect);


// ----------------------------------------------------------------------------
//
//   Window position/size access
//
// ----------------------------------------------------------------------------
void GetGlobalMappingPoint(WindowPeek window, Point *thePoint);

void GetGlobalContentRect(WindowPeek window, Rect *contentRect);


// ----------------------------------------------------------------------------
#endif
```

WindoidDefines.h

```
// ****************************************************************************
//
//   WindoidDefines.h
//
// ----------------------------------------------------------------------------
//   Copyright © 1991-94 Infinity Systems. All rights reserved.
```

```
// -------------------------------------------------------------------------
//     This file contains only the #defines used to determine how to compile
//     the Infinity Windoid WDEF. By modifying only this file, you can choose
//     what capabilities will be included when the WDEF is compiled.
// *************************************************************************
#ifndef Infinity_WINDOIDDEFINES
#define Infinity_WINDOIDDEFINES



// -------------------------------------------------------------------------
//
//    System version define
//
// -------------------------------------------------------------------------
#if __powerc       // Since PowerPCs donUt run System 6...
     #undef SystemSevenOrLater
     #define SystemSevenOrLater 1
#endif

#if !SystemSevenOrLater
     #define SystemSixOrLater 1
          // This is used so that we can cut down on the code size in MPW. If
          // support for earlier systems is important, get rid of this.
          // Note: for this define to work, precompiled headers cannot be used.
#endif


// -------------------------------------------------------------------------
endif
// *************************************************************************
//
//    DoWHit — Windoid hit routine.
//
// *************************************************************************
long
DoWHit(WindowPeek window, long param)
{
     Rect theRect;
     Point hitPt;
     long result = wNoHit;

     hitPt.v = HiWord(param);
     hitPt.h = LoWord(param);

     if (PtInRgn(hitPt, window->strucRgn)) {
          result = wInContent;

          if (PtInRgn(hitPt, window->contRgn)) {
               // Look for a hit in the grow box.
               if (WindData.hasGrow) {
                    GetGrowBox(window, &theRect);
```

```
                            InsetRect(&theRect, -1, -1);
                            if (PtInRect(hitPt, &theRect))
                                    result = wInGrow;

                    }

            } else {
                    // Look for a hit in the titlebar.
                    Rect titleRect;
                    GetTitleBarRect(window, &titleRect);

                    if (PtInRect(hitPt, &titleRect))
                    {
                            Boolean isActive = window->hilited ||
                                    WindData.ignoreHilite;
                            result = wInDrag;

                            if (isActive) {
                                    if (window->goAwayFlag) {
                                        GetCloseBox(window, &theRect);
                                        InsetRect(&theRect, -kGadgetHitFudge, -
                                                kGadgetHitFudge);
                                        if (PtInRect(hitPt, &theRect))
                                                result = wInGoAway;
                                    }

                                    if (window->spareFlag) {
                                        GetZoomBox(window, &theRect);
                                        InsetRect(&theRect, -kGadgetHitFudge, -
                                                kGadgetHitFudge);
                                        if (PtInRect(hitPt, &theRect))
                                                result = GetZoomHitType(window);
                                    }
                            }
                    }
            }
    }

    return result;
}


// **************************************************************************
//
//    DoWDraw — Windoid drawing routines.
//
// **************************************************************************
typedef struct {
    WindowPeek    wdlWindow;
    long          wdlParam;
} WDLDataRec;
    // This information is used to communicate with DeviceLoop callback routine.
```

```
// -------------------------------------------------------------------------
//
//   WindoidDrawLoop
//
// -------------------------------------------------------------------------
//             This routine actually does the real work of the drawing of stuff into
//             the window.
// -------------------------------------------------------------------------
static pascal void
WindoidDrawLoop(short depth, short deviceFlags, GDHandle targetDevice,
                         WDLDataRec *userData)
{
     WindowPeek window = userData->wdlWindow;        // Make sure our macros work.
     Boolean isColor = CheckDisplay(depth, deviceFlags, targetDevice, window);

     switch (userData->wdlParam) {
             case wNoHit:
                     DrawTitleBar(window, isColor);
                     DrawWindowFrame(window, isColor);
                     break;

             case wInGoAway:
                     ToggleCloseBox(window, isColor);
                     break;

             case wInZoomIn:
             case wInZoomOut:
                     if (window->spareFlag)
                             ToggleZoomBox(window, isColor);
                     break;
     }
     ColorsNormal();
}


// -------------------------------------------------------------------------
//
//   DoWDraw
//
// -------------------------------------------------------------------------
void
DoWDraw(WindowPeek window, long param)
{
     WDLDataRec userData;

     if (window->visible) {
             userData.wdlWindow = window;
             userData.wdlParam = param;

             if (SystemSevenOrLater || HasSystem7()) {
#if USESROUTINEDESCRIPTORS
                     RoutineDescriptor drawProcRD =
```

```
                            BUILD_ROUTINE_DESCRIPTOR(uppDeviceLoopDrawingProcInfo,
                            WindoidDrawLoop);
                    DeviceLoopDrawingUPP uppDrawProc = &drawProcRD;
                    // This is done to avoid allocating the RoutineDescriptor in
                    // the heap (with NewDeviceLoopDrawingProc) and then needing
                    // to dispose of it right away.
#else
                    DeviceLoopDrawingUPP uppDrawProc
                                = (DeviceLoopDrawingUPP) &WindoidDrawLoop;
#endif

                    DeviceLoop(window->strucRgn, uppDrawProc,
                                    (long) &userData, (DeviceLoopFlags) 0);
            } else {
                    WindoidDrawLoop(1, 0, nil, &userData);
                    // Since System 6 always draws in black-and-white, we don't need
                    // a device loop (otherwise we'd have to make one of our own.)
            }

            switch (param) {
                    case wInGoAway:         // Toggle go-away flag.
                            WindData.closeToggle = !WindData.closeToggle;
                            break;

                    case wInZoomIn:
                    case wInZoomOut:
                            WindData.zoomToggle = !WindData.zoomToggle;
                            break;
            }
    }
}


// *******************************************************************************
//
//    DoWCalcRgns — Windoid region calculating routine
//
// *******************************************************************************


// ------------------------------------------------------------------------
//
//    DoWCalcRgns
//
// ------------------------------------------------------------------------
void
DoWCalcRgns(WindowPeek window, long param)
{
    Rect theRect;

    // Calculate the content Rect in global coordinates.
    GetGlobalContentRect(window, &theRect);
```

```
        RectRgn(window->contRgn, &theRect);

        // Start off with the structure equal to the content
        // and make it include the window frame and titlebar.
        InsetRect(&theRect, -1, -1);
        if (WindData.isHoriz)
                theRect.top -= kTitleHeight - 1;
        else
                theRect.left -= kTitleHeight - 1;

        RectRgn(window->strucRgn, &theRect);

        // Add the shadow to the structure.
        {
                RgnHandle tempRgn = NewRgn();

                OffsetRect(&theRect, 1, 1);
                RectRgn(tempRgn, &theRect);
                UnionRgn(tempRgn, window->strucRgn, window->strucRgn);

                DisposeRgn(tempRgn);
        }
}


// *****************************************************************************
//
//    DoWGrow — Draw the growing outline.
//
// *****************************************************************************

// ---------------------------------------------------------------------------
//
//    DoWGrow
//
// ---------------------------------------------------------------------------
void
DoWGrow(WindowPeek window, long param)
{
    Rect growingRect = *(Rect*) param;

    if (WindData.isHoriz)
            growingRect.top  -= kTitleHeight - 1; // Add room for the titlebar.
    else
            growingRect.left -= kTitleHeight - 1; // Add room for the titlebar.
    InsetRect(&growingRect, -1, -1);

    // Draw the window frame.
    FrameRect(&growingRect);

    if (WindData.isHoriz)
```

```
                growingRect.top  += kTitleHeight - 1;
        else
                growingRect.left += kTitleHeight - 1;

        // Now mark the titlebar area.
        MoveTo(growingRect.left, growingRect.top);
        if (WindData.isHoriz)
                LineTo(growingRect.right - 2, growingRect.top);
        else
                LineTo(growingRect.left, growingRect.bottom - 2);

        // Mark the scroll bars too.
        MoveTo(growingRect.right - kScrollBarPixels, growingRect.top + 1);
        LineTo(growingRect.right - kScrollBarPixels, growingRect.bottom - 2);

        MoveTo(growingRect.left, growingRect.bottom - kScrollBarPixels);
        LineTo(growingRect.right - 2, growingRect.bottom - kScrollBarPixels);
}


// ****************************************************************************
//
//    DoWDrawGIcon — Draw the grow icon and scroll frame in the lower right.
//
// ****************************************************************************

// ----------------------------------------------------------------------------
//
//    GrowBoxDrawLoop
//
// ----------------------------------------------------------------------------
static pascal void
GrowBoxDrawLoop(short depth, short deviceFlags, GDHandle targetDevice,
                            WDLDataRec *userData)
{
        WindowPeek window = userData->wdlWindow;
        Boolean isColor = CheckDisplay(depth, deviceFlags, targetDevice, window);

        DrawGrowBox(window, isColor);
        ColorsNormal();
}


// ----------------------------------------------------------------------------
//
//    DoWDrawGIcon
//
// ----------------------------------------------------------------------------
void
DoWDrawGIcon(WindowPeek window, long param)
{
```

```
        if (window->visible && WindData.hasGrow) {
                WDLDataRec userData;
                RgnHandle saveClip = NewRgn();
                RgnHandle tempRgn = NewRgn();
                Point mappingPoint;

                SectRgn(window->port.visRgn, window->port.clipRgn, tempRgn);

                GetClip(saveClip);

                GetGlobalMappingPoint(window, &mappingPoint);
                OffsetRgn(tempRgn, mappingPoint.h, mappingPoint.v);

                SetClip(tempRgn);

                userData.wdlWindow = window;

                if (SystemSevenOrLater || HasSystem7()) {
#if USESROUTINEDESCRIPTORS
                        RoutineDescriptor drawProcRD =
                                BUILD_ROUTINE_DESCRIPTOR(uppDeviceLoopDrawingProcInfo,
                                GrowBoxDrawLoop);
                        DeviceLoopDrawingUPP uppDrawProc = &drawProcRD;
                        // This is done to avoid allocating the RoutineDescriptor
                        // in the heap, allocate it on the stack instead.
#else
                        DeviceLoopDrawingUPP uppDrawProc
                                        = (DeviceLoopDrawingUPP) &GrowBoxDrawLoop;
#endif

                        DeviceLoop(window->strucRgn, uppDrawProc,
                                        (long) &userData, (DeviceLoopFlags) 0);
                } else {
                        GrowBoxDrawLoop(1, 0, nil, &userData);
                        // Since System 6 always draws in black-and-white, we don't need
                        // a device loop (otherwise we'd have to make one of our own.)
                }

                SetClip(saveClip);

                DisposeRgn(saveClip);
                DisposeRgn(tempRgn);
        }
}


// -------------------------------------------------------------------------
```

```
// **************************************************************************
//
//    WindoidTypes.h
//
// --------------------------------------------------------------------------
//    Copyright © 1991-94 Infinity Systems.  All rights reserved.
// --------------------------------------------------------------------------
#ifndef Infinity_WINDOIDTYPES
#define Infinity_WINDOIDTYPES

#include "WindoidDefines.h"

#include <Types.h>
#include <Windows.h>



// **************************************************************************
//
//    Constants
//
// **************************************************************************


// --------------------------------------------------------------------------
//
//    Apple System 7.5 style variations
//
// --------------------------------------------------------------------------
enum {
    kSystem75_toggleTBar = 1,    // Bit 0 tells us whether to hilite/unhilite
                                 //     the title bar.
    kSystem75_hasGrow    = 2,    // Bit 1 is the grow bit.
    kSystem75_hasZoom    = 4,    // Bit 2 is the zoom bit.
    kSystem75_vertTBar   = 8     // Bit 3 set if titlebar is vertical.
};



// **************************************************************************
//
//    Structures
//
// **************************************************************************
typedef struct {
    WStateData          wState;
    unsigned char closeToggle;
    unsigned char zoomToggle;
    unsigned char isHoriz;
    unsigned char ignoreHilite;
    unsigned char hasGrow;
} WindoidData, *WindoidDataPtr, **WindoidDataHandle;
```

```
// -------------------------------------------------------------------------
//
//    Accessor Macro
//
// -------------------------------------------------------------------------
#define WindData (**(WindoidDataHandle) window->dataHandle)
    // This macro is used so I can access the 'globals' easily. Note: the
    // variable containing the window must be named 'window', and it must be in
    // scope at the time of the usage of this macro.  Also, they aren't REALLY
    // globals, because they're kept for EACH window.


// -------------------------------------------------------------------------
#endif
```

Chapter Nine Source Code

PlayFromDisk XCMD.c

```
/*
File Name:   PlayFromDisk XCMD.c
*/

/*************************************************************************


     PlayFromDisk XCMD

     by Joe Zobkiw

     Plays asynchronous sound from a disk-based AIFF file in HyperCard.

     Form: PlayFromDisk [fullPathName]

*************************************************************************/

#include <Sound.h>
#include <SoundInput.h>
#include <Script.h>
#include <HyperXCmd.h>
#include <string.h>
#include "A4Stuff.h"
#include "SetupA4.h"


/*************************************************************************

     #defines

*************************************************************************/

#define kMinParamCount       0
#define kMaxParamCount       1
#define kErrorFlag          (short)-1
```

```
#define kDefaultBufferSize  (1024*100L)   // try to allocate 100K buffer
#define kBufferDecrement    (1024*5L)     // decrement buffer size by 5K
#define kSmallestBuffer     (1024*20L)    // but not below 20K

#define kGlobalIsPlayingFlag    "\pZobkiwIsPlaying"
#define kWindowName             "\pZobkiw"
#define kIdleTime               15      /* every x ticks */

/**********************************************************************

    function prototypes

**********************************************************************/

pascal      void main(XCmdPtr xp);
pascal      void MyCompletionRoutine(SndChannelPtr chan);
void        HandleWindowMessage(XCmdPtr xp);
void        HandleXCMDMessage(XCmdPtr xp);
Handle      ConcatErrorStr(XCmdPtr xp, char *ch, OSErr err);
void        SetError(XCmdPtr xp, char *ch, OSErr err);
Handle      CopyStrToHand(char *ch);
long        HandleToNum(XCmdPtr xp, Handle h);
void        HandleToPStr(Str255 str, Handle h);
char*       ToCStr(char *ch);
char*       ToPStr(char *ch);

/**********************************************************************

    globals

**********************************************************************/

Boolean                 gCloseFile;
short                   gFileRefNum;
long                    gSoundChannel;
FilePlayCompletionUPP   gFPCupp;

/**********************************************************************

    main

**********************************************************************/

pascal void main(XCmdPtr xp)
{
#ifndef powerc
    long    oldA4 = SetCurrentA4();
    RememberA4();
#endif

    if (xp->paramCount == -1) {
```

```
                HandleWindowMessage(xp);
        } else {
                HandleXCMDMessage(xp);
        }

#ifndef powerc
        SetA4(oldA4);
#endif
}

/******************************************************************

        MyCompletionRoutine

        This tells us that the sound is done playing so we can close the
        audio file the next chance we get.

******************************************************************/

pascal void MyCompletionRoutine(SndChannelPtr chan)
{
#ifndef powerc
        long oldA4 = SetUpA4();
#endif

        gCloseFile = true;

#ifndef powerc
        RestoreA4(oldA4);
#endif
}

/******************************************************************

        HandleWindowMessage

        This function is called when our window gets a message. It will be called
        repeatedly with idle events while our sound is playing, since we created
        an invisible window during that time. During these calls we simply check
        to see if the gCloseFile flag is set to true, which means our completion
        routine has been called which means the sound is done playing. When this
        occurs, we tell HyperCard to close the window.

        This in turn calls this function again with an xCloseEvt message. This
        is where we take care of disposing the sound channel, and resetting
        some of the flags that we used to tell HyperCard that we had interrupt
        code, we wanted idle time, and we were playing a sound.

******************************************************************/

void HandleWindowMessage(XCmdPtr xp)
```

```
{
    XWEventInfoPtr          xw = (XWEventInfoPtr)(xp->params[0]);
    WindowPtr               w = xw->eventWindow;
    OSErr                   err = noErr;

    if (xw->event.what == xOpenEvt) {
            ;        // ignore this message
    } else if (xw->event.what == xCloseEvt) {
            // close the sound file
            if (gFileRefNum != -1) {
                FSClose(gFileRefNum);
                gFileRefNum = -1;
            }
            // dispose the sound channel
            if (gSoundChannel != nil) {
                err = SndDisposeChannel((SndChannelPtr)gSoundChannel, true);
                if (err != noErr)
                        SetError(xp, "Error: Disposing sound channel. ", err);
                gSoundChannel = 0L;
            }

            // reset some flags and clean up globals
            SetXWIdleTime(xp, w, 0);
            XWHasInterruptCode(xp, w, false);
            EndXSound(xp);
            SetGlobal(xp, kGlobalIsPlayingFlag, CopyStrToHand("false"));
            xp->passFlag = true;

            if (gFPCupp) {
                DisposeRoutineDescriptor(gFPCupp);
                gFPCupp = nil;
            }

    } else if ((gCloseFile == true) && (gSoundChannel != nil)) {
            // the sound is done playing, tell the window to close
            gCloseFile = false;
            CloseXWindow(xp, w);
    }
}

/***************************************************************************

    HandleXCMDMessage

    This function basically exists to begin the playing of a sound.

***************************************************************************/

void HandleXCMDMessage(XCmdPtr xp)
{
    Str255                  fileName;
```

```
Str32                         tempStr;
StandardFileReply             reply;
FSSpec                        fileSpec;
SFTypeList                    typeList;
long                          bufferSize = kDefaultBufferSize;
OSErr                         err = noErr;
short                         refNum = -1;
WindowPtr                     w = nil;
Rect                          boundsRect = {0,0,33,33};
SndChannelPtr                 chan = nil;

// tell HyperCard that we have interrupt code in this XCMD
XWHasInterruptCode(xp, w, true);

// check parameter count
if ((xp->paramCount != kMinParamCount) && (xp->paramCount != kMaxParamCount)) {
        SetError(xp, "Error: Form = PlayFromDisk [fullPathName]. ", 0);
        goto fail;
}

// check global variable to see if we are already playing,
// if so, stop the current sound, then do nothing.
{
        Handle  hGlob;
        Str32 tempStr;
        hGlob = GetGlobal(xp, kGlobalIsPlayingFlag);
        HandleToPStr(tempStr, hGlob);
        if (StrToBool(xp, tempStr)) {
                MyCompletionRoutine((SndChannelPtr)gSoundChannel);
                return;
        }
}

// initialize globals
gCloseFile = false;
gFileRefNum = -1;
gSoundChannel = 0L;
gFPCupp = NewFilePlayCompletionProc(MyCompletionRoutine);

if (xp->paramCount == 0) {
        // first ask the user to select the file if no parameter
        typeList[0] = 'AIFF';
        typeList[1] = 'AIFC';
        StandardGetFile(nil, 2, typeList, &reply);
        if (!reply.sfGood) {
                SetError(xp, "cancel", 0);
                goto fail;
        }

        fileSpec = reply.sfFile;
```

```
                // attempt to update the screen
                ZeroToPas(xp, "Go to this card", tempStr);
                SendHCMessage(xp, tempStr);
        } else {
                // if the scripter passed in a file name, use it as a full path
                HandleToPStr(fileName, xp->params[0]);
                err = FSMakeFSSpec(0, 0, fileName, &fileSpec);
                if (err != noErr) {
                        SetError(xp, "Error: Couldn't locate file. ", err);
                        goto fail;
                }
        }

        // attempt to create a window with a unique name
        w = NewXWindow(xp, &boundsRect, kWindowName, false, documentProc,
                false, false);
        if (w == nil) {
                SetError(xp, "Error: Couldn't create window. ", 0);
                goto fail;
        }

        // open the file to play
        err = FSpOpenDF(&fileSpec, fsRdPerm, &refNum);
        if ((err != noErr) || (refNum == -1)) {
                SetError(xp, "Error: Couldn't open sound file. ", err);
                goto fail;
        }

        SetCursor(*GetCursor(watchCursor));

        // tell HyperCard that our window wants idle time every 1 tick
        SetXWIdleTime(xp, w, kIdleTime);

        // tell HyperCard that we are about to being playing a sound
        // (ie: using a sound channel
        BeginXSound(xp, nil);

        // allocate our sound channel
        err = SndNewChannel(&chan, sampledSynth, 0, nil);
        if (err != noErr) {
                SetError(xp, "Error: Couldn't allocate sound channel. ", err);
                goto fail;
        }

        // remember refnum & snd chan
        gFileRefNum = refNum;
        gSoundChannel = (long)chan;

tryAgain:
        // play the sound file
        err = SndStartFilePlay(chan, refNum, 0, bufferSize, nil, nil, gFPCupp, true);
```

```
        if ((err == notEnoughBufferSpace) && (bufferSize > kSmallestBuffer)) {
                bufferSize -= kBufferDecrement;
                goto tryAgain;
        }

        if (err != noErr) {
                SetError(xp, "Error: Couldn't play the sound file. ", err);
                goto fail;
        }

        // set a unique global variable to tell that we are now playing
        SetGlobal(xp, kGlobalIsPlayingFlag, CopyStrToHand("true"));

        goto exit;
fail:
        // clean up if fail
        gCloseFile = false;
        gFileRefNum = -1;
        gSoundChannel = 0L;
        if (gFPCupp) {
                DisposeRoutineDescriptor(gFPCupp);
                gFPCupp = nil;
        }
        SetXWIdleTime(xp, w, 0);
        XWHasInterruptCode(xp, w, false);
        EndXSound(xp);
        if (w)
                CloseXWindow(xp, w);
exit:
        InitCursor();
        return;
}

/*************************************************************************



*************************************************************************/

Handle      ConcatErrorStr(XCmdPtr xp, char *ch, OSErr err)
{
        Str255  str1;
        Str32   str2;

        if (err == noErr) {
                return((Handle)CopyStrToHand(ch));
        } else {
                strcpy((char*)str1, ch);
                NumToString((long)err, (StringPtr)&str2);
                ToCStr((char*)str2);
                strcat((char*)str1, (char*)str2);
```

```
                    return((Handle)CopyStrToHand((char*)str1));
        }
}

/*************************************************************************



**************************************************************************/

void SetError(XCmdPtr xp, char *ch, OSErr err)
{
        xp->returnValue = (Handle)ConcatErrorStr(xp, ch, err);
}

/*************************************************************************



**************************************************************************/

Handle      CopyStrToHand(char *ch)
{
        Handle  h;

        h = NewHandleClear((long)strlen(ch) + 1);
        if (h)
                strcpy((char*)*h, ch);
        return h;
}

/*************************************************************************



**************************************************************************/

long HandleToNum(XCmdPtr xp, Handle h)
{
        char    str[32];
        long    num;

        strcpy(str, *h);
        num = StrToLong(xp, (StringPtr)ToPStr(str));
        return num;
}

/*************************************************************************
```

```
**************************************************************************/

void HandleToPStr(Str255 str, Handle h)
{
     strcpy((char*)str, *h);
     ToPStr((char*)str);
}

/**************************************************************************



**************************************************************************/

char*ToCStr(char *ch)
{
     unsigned char len, i;

     len = ch[0];
     for (i=0;i<len;++i)
             ch[i] = ch[i+1];
     ch[len] = 0;
     return ch;
}

/**************************************************************************



**************************************************************************/

char*ToPStr(char *ch)
{
     unsigned char len, i;

     for (i=0,len=0;ch[i]!=0;++i)
             ++len;
     while (i--)
             ch[i+1] = ch[i];
     ch[0] = len;
     return ch;
}
```

RecordToDisk XCMD.c

```
/*
     File Name:    RecordToDisk XCMD.c
*/
```

```
/************************************************************************

    RecordToDisk

    by Joe Zobkiw

    Records to a disk-based AIFF file in HyperCard.

    Form: RecordToDisk [horizontal_loc_of_record_dlog, vertical_loc_of_record_dlog]

*************************************************************************/

#include <Sound.h>
#include <SoundInput.h>
#include <Script.h>
#include <HyperXCmd.h>
#include <string.h>
#include "A4Stuff.h"
#include "SetupA4.h"

/************************************************************************

    #defines

*************************************************************************/

#define kMinParamCount      0
#define kMaxParamCount      2
#define kErrorFlag          (short)-1

/************************************************************************

    function prototypes

*************************************************************************/

pascal      void main(XCmdPtr xp);
Handle      ConcatErrorStr(XCmdPtr xp, char *ch, OSErr err);
void        SetError(XCmdPtr xp, char *ch, OSErr err);
OSErr       GetLocOfCardWindow(XCmdPtr xp, Point *pt);
Handle      CopyStrToHand(char *ch);
long        HandleToNum(XCmdPtr xp, Handle h);
char*       ToCStr(char *ch);
char*       ToPStr(char *ch);

/************************************************************************

    main

*************************************************************************/
```

```
pascal void main(XCmdPtr xp)
{
    StandardFileReply      reply;
    Point                  corner;
    OSErr                  err = noErr;
    short                  refNum = -1;
    Boolean                cancelled = false;
    Boolean                fileCreated = false;
    Str32                  tempStr;

#ifndef powerc
    long    oldA4 = SetCurrentA4();
    RememberA4();
#endif

    // check parameter count
    if ((xp->paramCount != kMinParamCount) && (xp->paramCount != kMaxParamCount)) {
            SetError(xp, "Error: Form = RecordToDisk [h, v]. ", 0);
            goto fail;
    }

    if (xp->paramCount == 2) {
            // use location as passed by scripter
            corner.h = (short)HandleToNum(xp, xp->params[0]);
            corner.v = (short)HandleToNum(xp, xp->params[1]);
    } else {
            // try to get the card window location to align dialog in relation to it
            err = GetLocOfCardWindow(xp, &corner);
            if (err == kErrorFlag) {
                SetError(xp, "Error: Couldn't get location of card window. "
                , 0);
                goto fail;
            }
    }

    // first ask the user to save the file
    StandardPutFile("\pSave AIFF file as:", "\pAIFF Audio", &reply);
    if (!reply.sfGood) {
            SetError(xp, "cancel", 0);
            goto exit;
    }

    // attempt to update the screen
    ZeroToPas(xp, "Go to this card", tempStr);
    SendHCMessage(xp, tempStr);

    // if we are replacing a file, do so
    if (reply.sfReplacing) {
            err = FSpDelete(&reply.sfFile);
```

```
            if (err != noErr) {
                    SetError(xp, "Error: Couldn't replace file. ", err);
                    goto fail;
            }
      }

      // create the new file
      err = FSpCreate(&reply.sfFile, '????', 'AIFF', smRoman);
      if (err != noErr) {
            SetError(xp, "Error: Couldn't create sound file. ", err);
            goto fail;
      }
      fileCreated = true;

      // open the file
      err = FSpOpenDF(&reply.sfFile, fsRdWrPerm, &refNum);
      if ((err != noErr) || (refNum == -1)) {
            SetError(xp, "Error: Couldn't open sound file. ", err);
            goto fail;
      }

      // record to the file, first tell HyperCard we are about to do
      // something with sound.
      BeginXSound(xp, nil);
      err = SndRecordToFile(nil, corner, siBestQuality, refNum);
      EndXSound(xp);
      cancelled = (err == userCanceledErr);
      if (cancelled) {
            SetError(xp, "cancel", 0);
            goto fail;
      }
      if (err != noErr) {
            SetError(xp, "Error: Couldn't record to sound file. ", err);
            goto fail;
      }

      goto exit;
fail:
      // clean up
      if (refNum != -1)
            FSClose(refNum);
      refNum = -1;
      if (fileCreated)
            FSpDelete(&reply.sfFile);
exit:

      if (refNum != -1) {
            // close the file
            FSClose(refNum);
            // flush the volume
            FlushVol(nil, reply.sfFile.vRefNum);
```

```
                  if (cancelled)
                      FSpDelete(&reply.sfFile);
       }

#ifndef powerc
       SetA4(oldA4);
#endif

       return;
}

/***********************************************************************



 ***********************************************************************/

Handle       ConcatErrorStr(XCmdPtr xp, char *ch, OSErr err)
{
       Str255  str1;
       Str32   str2;

       if (err == noErr) {
               return((Handle)CopyStrToHand(ch));
       } else {
               strcpy((char*)str1, ch);
               NumToString((long)err, str2);
               ToCStr((char*)str2);
               strcat((char*)str1, (char*)str2);
               return((Handle)CopyStrToHand((char*)str1));
       }
}

/***********************************************************************



 ***********************************************************************/

void SetError(XCmdPtr xp, char *ch, OSErr err)
{
       xp->returnValue = (Handle)ConcatErrorStr(xp, ch, err);
}

/***********************************************************************



 ***********************************************************************/

OSErrGetLocOfCardWindow(XCmdPtr xp, Point *pt)
```

```
{
     Handle  h;
     char    str[256];

     strcpy(str, "item 1 of rect of card window");
     h = EvalExpr(xp, (StringPtr)ToPStr(str));
     if (xp->result == noErr) {
             pt->h = HandleToNum(xp, h);
             DisposeHandle(h);

             strcpy(str, "item 2 of rect of card window");
             h = EvalExpr(xp, (StringPtr)ToPStr(str));
             if (xp->result == noErr) {
                 pt->v = HandleToNum(xp, h);
                 DisposeHandle(h);
                 return noErr;
             }
     }
     return(kErrorFlag);
}

/**************************************************************************


***************************************************************************/

Handle      CopyStrToHand(char *ch)
{
     Handle  h;

     h = NewHandleClear((long)strlen(ch) + 1);
     if (h)
             strcpy((char*)*h, ch);
     return h;
}

/**************************************************************************


***************************************************************************/

long HandleToNum(XCmdPtr xp, Handle h)
{
     char    str[32];
     long    num;

     strcpy(str, *h);
     num = StrToLong(xp, (StringPtr)ToPStr(str));
     return num;
```

```
    }
    /*************************************************************************



     **********************************************************************/

    char*ToCStr(char *ch)
    {
        unsigned char len, i;

        len = ch[0];
        for (i=0;i<len;++i)
                ch[i] = ch[i+1];
        ch[len] = 0;
        return ch;
    }

    /*************************************************************************



     **********************************************************************/

    char*ToPStr(char *ch)
    {
        unsigned char len, i;

        for (i=0,len=0;ch[i]!=0;++i)
                ++len;
        while (i--)
                ch[i+1] = ch[i];
        ch[0] = len;
        return ch;
    }
```

Chapter Ten Source Code

ColorFill.c

```
    /*
        File Name:              ColorFill.c
    */

    /***********************************************************************

        Fade

     **********************************************************************/
```

```
#include "Photoshop.h"

#ifdef __powerc
enum {
    uppPhotoshopFilterProcInfo = kPascalStackBased
            | STACK_ROUTINE_PARAMETER(1, SIZE_CODE(sizeof(short)))
            | STACK_ROUTINE_PARAMETER(2, SIZE_CODE(sizeof(Ptr)))
            | STACK_ROUTINE_PARAMETER(3, SIZE_CODE(sizeof(Ptr)))
            | STACK_ROUTINE_PARAMETER(4, SIZE_CODE(sizeof(Ptr)))
};
ProcInfoType __procinfo = uppPhotoshopFilterProcInfo;
#endif

/* typedefs */

#define itemForegroundColor     3
#define itemBackgroundColor     4
#define itemShowTimer           6

typedef struct TParameters {
    short               whichColor;
    Boolean             fShowTimer;
    unsigned long       startTicks;
    unsigned long       endTicks;
} TParameters, *PParameters, **HParameters;

typedef struct Globals {
    short       result;
    FilterRecord *stuff;
} Globals, *GPtr, **GHdl;

#define gResult ((*globals).result)
#define gStuff  ((*globals).stuff)

/* function prototypes */

void InitGlobals(GPtr globals);
void DoAbout(GPtr globals);
void DoParameters(GPtr globals);
void DoPrepare(GPtr globals);
void DoStart(GPtr globals);
void DoContinue(GPtr globals);
void DoFinish(GPtr globals);

void DoFilterRect(GPtr globals);

/*****************************************************************************

    main

*****************************************************************************/
```

```
pascal void main (short selector, FilterRecord *stuff, long *data, short *result)
{
      Globals        globalValues;
      GPtr           globals = &globalValues;

      if (!*data) {
             InitGlobals(globals);
             *data = (long)NewHandle(sizeof(Globals));
             if (!*data) {
                    *result = memFullErr;
                    return;
             }
             **(GHdl)*data = globalValues;
      }

      globalValues = **(GHdl)*data;

      gStuff = stuff;
      gResult = noErr;

      switch(selector) {

             case filterSelectorAbout:
                    DoAbout(globals);
                    break;

             case filterSelectorParameters:
                    DoParameters(globals);
                    break;

             case filterSelectorPrepare:
                    DoPrepare(globals);
                    break;

             case filterSelectorStart:
                    DoStart(globals);
                    break;

             case filterSelectorContinue:
                    DoContinue(globals);
                    break;

             case filterSelectorFinish:
                    DoFinish(globals);
                    break;

             default:
                    gResult = filterBadParameters;

      }
```

```
        *result = gResult;
        **(GHdl)*data = globalValues;
}


/***************************************************************************

        InitGlobals

        Initialize any globals that may need it.

***************************************************************************/

void InitGlobals(GPtr globals)
{

}


/***************************************************************************

        DoAbout

***************************************************************************/

void DoAbout(GPtr globals)
{
        ShowAbout(16000);
}


/***************************************************************************

        DoParameters

        Asks the user for the plug-in filter module's parameters. Note that
        the image size information is not yet defined at this point. Also, do
        not assume that the calling program will call this routine every time the
        filter is run (it may save the data held by the parameters handle) and pass
        them in through this call.

***************************************************************************/

#define kOptionsDialogID 16001

void DoParameters(GPtr globals)
{
        short          item, whichColor;
        DialogPtr      dp;
        DialogTHndl    dt;
        Boolean        done = false, fShowTimer;

        // if our parameters have not been saved and passed in by the host program
        // we can allocate new ones and initialize them.
```

```
if (!gStuff->parameters) {
        gStuff->parameters = NewHandle((long)sizeof(TParameters));
        if (!gStuff->parameters) {
                gResult = memFullErr;
                return;
        }
        ((PParameters)*gStuff->parameters)->whichColor = itemForegroundColor;
        ((PParameters)*gStuff->parameters)->fShowTimer = false;
}

// load our DLOG resource in order to allow Photoshop to
// prepare for movable modalness
dt = (DialogTHndl)GetResource('DLOG', kOptionsDialogID);
HNoPurge((Handle)dt);
CenterDialog(dt);
SetUpMoveableModal(dt, gStuff->hostSig);

// load our dialog
dp = GetNewDialog(kOptionsDialogID, nil, (WindowPtr) -1);

// prepare the dialog
SetDialogDefaultItem(dp, ok);
SetDialogCancelItem(dp, cancel);
SetDialogTracksCursor(dp, true);
SetRadioGroupState(dp, itemForegroundColor, itemBackgroundColor,
        ((PParameters)*gStuff->parameters)->whichColor);
SetCheckBoxState(dp, itemShowTimer,
        ((PParameters)*gStuff->parameters)->fShowTimer);
SetArrowCursor();

// be movable and modal and perform the standard dialog item handling
// since we don't have any special items that need special handling
while (!done) {
        MoveableModalDialog(dp, gStuff->processEvent, nil, &item);
        switch (item) {
                case ok:
                        whichColor = GetRadioGroupState(dp, itemForegroundColor,
                                itemBackgroundColor);
                        ((PParameters)*gStuff->parameters)->whichColor =
                                whichColor;
                        fShowTimer = GetCheckBoxState(dp, itemShowTimer);
                        ((PParameters)*gStuff->parameters)->fShowTimer =
                                fShowTimer;
                        done = true;
                        break;

                case cancel:
                        done = true;
                        gResult = 1;
                        break;
```

```
                        case itemForegroundColor:
                        case itemBackgroundColor:
                        case itemShowTimer:
                                PerformStandardDialogItemHandling(dp, item);
                                break;

                        default:
                                break;
                }
        }

        // nuke the dialog
        DisposDialog(dp);
        HPurge((Handle) dt);
}

/********************************************************************************

        DoPrepare

        Prepare to filter an image.   If the plug-in filter needs a large amount
        of buffer memory, this routine should set the bufferSpace field to the
        number of bytes required. You can also set the bufferSpace field to 0 and
        use the buffer and handle suites to allocate memory later.

********************************************************************************/

void DoPrepare(GPtr globals)
{
        gStuff->bufferSpace = 0;
}

/********************************************************************************

        DoStart

********************************************************************************/

void DoStart(GPtr globals)
{
        int16   row;
        int32   totalLines = gStuff->filterRect.bottom - gStuff->filterRect.top;

        // insure that the advance state is available
        if (!WarnAdvanceStateAvailable()) {
                gResult = 1;
                goto done;
        }

        // make sure things are still a go
        if (gResult != noErr)448
                goto done;
```

```
    // request first & last planes to process next
    gStuff->inLoPlane = gStuff->outLoPlane = 0;
    gStuff->inHiPlane = gStuff->outHiPlane = gStuff->planes - 1;

    // request area of image to work on, first fill in left/right bounds
    gStuff->inRect.left = gStuff->outRect.left = gStuff->filterRect.left;
    gStuff->inRect.right = gStuff->outRect.right = gStuff->filterRect.right;

    // start the timer
    if (((PParameters)*gStuff->parameters)->fShowTimer)
            ((PParameters)*gStuff->parameters)->startTicks = TickCount();

    // for each row of the image, filter it
    for (row = gStuff->filterRect.top; row < gStuff->filterRect.bottom; ++row) {

            // update the progress if needed
            UpdateProgress(row - gStuff->filterRect.top, totalLines);

            // check for a cancellation by the user
            if (TestAbort()) {
                gResult = userCanceledErr;
                    goto done;
            }

            // set the rectangle to point to the row we are about to work on
            gStuff->inRect.top = gStuff->outRect.top = row;
            gStuff->inRect.bottom = gStuff->outRect.bottom = row + 1;

            // call the advance state procedure
            gResult = AdvanceState();

            // check for errors
            if (gResult != noErr)
                    goto done;

            // filter the row
            DoFilterRect(globals);
    }

done:
    // finish timing
    if (((PParameters)*gStuff->parameters)->fShowTimer)
            ((PParameters)*gStuff->parameters)->endTicks = TickCount();

    // set these rects to be 0 in size since we are done
    SetRect(&gStuff->inRect, 0, 0, 0, 0);
    SetRect(&gStuff->outRect, 0, 0, 0, 0);
}
```

```
/**************************************************************************

    DoContinue

    This function is called repeatedly while inRect or outRect are non-empty.
    Since we do all of our work in the DoStart function, we never get here.
**************************************************************************/

void DoContinue(GPtr globals)
{
    SetRect(&gStuff->inRect, 0, 0, 0, 0);
    SetRect(&gStuff->outRect, 0, 0, 0, 0);
}


/**************************************************************************

    DoFinish

    Called only if DoStart returns noErr. This allows the filter to clean up.
    This routine is also called if the user cancels.

**************************************************************************/

void DoFinish(GPtr globals)
{
    // display timer results if requested
    if (((PParameters)*gStuff->parameters)->fShowTimer) {
        unsigned long totalTicks;
        Str32         totalTicksStr;

        totalTicks = ((PParameters)*gStuff->parameters)->endTicks -
                        ((PParameters)*gStuff->parameters)->startTicks;
        NumToString(totalTicks, totalTicksStr);
        ParamText(totalTicksStr, "\p", "\p", "\p");
        InitCursor();
        NoteAlert(16500, nil);
        ParamText("\p", "\p", "\p", "\p");
    }
}


/**************************************************************************

    DoFilterRect

    This function is called for each section of an image that we need to edit.
    In our case, we pass this function a row of the image at a time.
**************************************************************************/

void DoFilterRect(GPtr globals)
{
```

```
        register    short   width = gStuff->filterRect.right -
                                gStuff->filterRect.left;
        register    short   whichColor =
                                ((PParameters)*gStuff->parameters)->whichColor;
        register    unsigned8    *srcPtr = (unsigned8 *)gStuff->inData;
        register    unsigned8    *dstPtr = (unsigned8 *)gStuff->outData;
        register    short       plane;

        // for each pixel in the row, do something to it
        while (--width >= 0) {

                // for each plane above 4, do nothing to each pixel
                for (plane = gStuff->planes - 1; plane >= 4; -plane)
                        ;

                // for the rest of the planes, edit the pixel value
                for (; plane >= 0; --plane)
                        dstPtr[plane] = (whichColor == itemForegroundColor) ?
                                gStuff->foreColor[plane] : gStuff->backColor[plane];

                // increment to the next pixel
                srcPtr += gStuff->inHiPlane - gStuff->inLoPlane + 1;
                dstPtr += gStuff->planes; // one unsigned8 per plane
        }
}
```

TVTube.c

```
/*
    File Name:              TVTube.c
*/

// *****************************************************************************
//
//   TVTube.c
//
// ----------------------------------------------------------------------------
//   C source file for TV Tube Effect filter plug-in for Photoshop.
// ----------------------------------------------------------------------------
//   Original code from Dissolve.c:
//          Copyright 1990 by Thomas Knoll.
//          Copyright 1991-95 by Adobe Systems, Inc. All rights reserved.
//          Converted to work with Metrowerks CodeWarrior by Joe Zobkiw. (3/2/95)
//   Copyright 1995 by Troy Gaul.
// ----------------------------------------------------------------------------
//   CHANGE HISTORY: (most recent first)
//              3/5/95 - TG - Moved parameters dialog into GetParameters function.
//                              Now calls GetParameters from DoContinue instead of
//                              DoParameters (to facilitate a possible preview area).
//              3/4/95 - TG - Started from Dissolve sample.
```

```
// **************************************************************************

#include "Photoshop.h"

// ---------------------------------------------------------------------------
//
//    Constants
//
// ---------------------------------------------------------------------------
enum {
    kAboutBoxDialogID = 16000,
    kSettingsDialogID = 16001,

    kCommentStringListID = 16000
};

enum {
    kOddFieldsItem = 4,
    kEvenFieldsItem
};



// ---------------------------------------------------------------------------
//
//    __procinfo
//
// ---------------------------------------------------------------------------
#ifdef __powerc

enum {
    uppPhotoshopFilterProcInfo = kPascalStackBased
                | STACK_ROUTINE_PARAMETER(1, SIZE_CODE(sizeof(short)))
                | STACK_ROUTINE_PARAMETER(2, SIZE_CODE(sizeof(Ptr)))
                | STACK_ROUTINE_PARAMETER(3, SIZE_CODE(sizeof(Ptr)))
                | STACK_ROUTINE_PARAMETER(4, SIZE_CODE(sizeof(Ptr)))
};

ProcInfoType __procinfo = uppPhotoshopFilterProcInfo;



#endif
// ---------------------------------------------------------------------------
//
//    TParameters
//
// ---------------------------------------------------------------------------
typedef struct TParameters {
    short oddDelta;
    short evenDelta;
} TParameters, *PParameters, **HParameters;
```

```
// ---------------------------------------------------------------------------
//
//    Globals
//
// ---------------------------------------------------------------------------
typedef struct Globals {
    short result;
    FilterRecord *stuff;

    short wantsParameters;
    short inParameterStage;

    short row;
} Globals, *GPtr, **GHdl;


// Accessor macros.
#define gResult             (globals->result)
#define gStuff              (globals->stuff)

#define gWantsParameters    (globals->wantsParameters)
#define gInParameterStage   (globals->inParameterStage)

#define gRow                (globals->row)



// ---------------------------------------------------------------------------
//
//    Prototypes
//
// ---------------------------------------------------------------------------
void DoAbout(GPtr globals);
void DoParameters(GPtr globals);
void DoPrepare(GPtr globals);
void DoStart(GPtr globals);
void DoContinue(GPtr globals);
void DoFinish(GPtr globals);
void InitGlobals(GPtr globals);



// ---------------------------------------------------------------------------
//
//    Utility macros
//
// ---------------------------------------------------------------------------
#define ClipInRange(x, min, max) \
    (((x) < (min)) ? (min) : (((x) > (max)) ? (max) : (x)))
```

```
// ------------------------------------------------------------------------
//
//    main
//
// ------------------------------------------------------------------------
//              All calls to the plug-in module come through this routine. It must be
//              placed first in the resource. To achieve this, most development systems
//              require that this be the first routine in the source.
// ------------------------------------------------------------------------
pascal void
main(short selector, FilterRecord *stuff, long *data, short *result)
{
     Globals globalValues;
     GPtr globals = &globalValues;

     if (!*data) {
             InitGlobals(globals);

             *data = (long) NewHandle(sizeof(Globals));

             if (!*data) {
                   *result = memFullErr;
                   return;
             }

             **((GHdl) *data) = globalValues;
     }

     globalValues = **((GHdl) *data);

     gStuff = stuff;
     gResult = noErr;

     switch (selector) {

             case filterSelectorAbout:
                   DoAbout(globals);
                   break;

             case filterSelectorParameters:
                   DoParameters(globals);
                   break;

             case filterSelectorPrepare:
                   DoPrepare(globals);
                   break;

             case filterSelectorStart:
                   DoStart(globals);
                   break;
```

```
                case filterSelectorContinue:
                    DoContinue(globals);
                    break;

                case filterSelectorFinish:
                    DoFinish(globals);
                    break;

                default:
                    gResult = filterBadParameters;
                    break;

        }

        *result = gResult;

        **((GHdl) *data) = globalValues;
    }


    // ---------------------------------------------------------------------------
    //
    //    InitGlobals
    //
    // ---------------------------------------------------------------------------
    void
    InitGlobals(GPtr globals)
    {
        gWantsParameters = false;
        gInParameterStage = false;

        gRow = 0;
    }


    // ---------------------------------------------------------------------------
    //
    //    SetupNextFilterStrip
    //
    // ---------------------------------------------------------------------------
    //          Set the inRect and outRect for the image strip indicated by gRow.
    // ---------------------------------------------------------------------------
    static void
    SetupNextFilterStrip(GPtr globals)
    {
        gStuff->inRect.top    = gStuff->outRect.top    = gRow;
        gStuff->inRect.bottom = gStuff->outRect.bottom = gRow + 1;
    }
```

```
// ---------------------------------------------------------------------------
//
//   SetupFirstFilterStrip
//
// ---------------------------------------------------------------------------
static void
SetupFirstFilterStrip(GPtr globals)
{
     // Get all the planes.
     gStuff->inLoPlane = gStuff->outLoPlane = 0;
     gStuff->inHiPlane = gStuff->outHiPlane = gStuff->planes - 1;

     // Get the entire width of the filter rect each time.
     gStuff->inRect.left  = gStuff->outRect.left  = gStuff->filterRect.left;
     gStuff->inRect.right = gStuff->outRect.right = gStuff->filterRect.right;

     // Start with the first scanline.
     gRow = gStuff->filterRect.top;
     SetupNextFilterStrip(globals);
}



// ---------------------------------------------------------------------------
//
//   GetParameters
//
// ---------------------------------------------------------------------------
//           Display the parameters dialog for the user to enter values.  Returns
//           true when it is done.
// ---------------------------------------------------------------------------
static Boolean
GetParameters(GPtr globals)
{
     long odd, even;
     short item;
     DialogPtr dp;
     DialogTHndl dt;
     PParameters params = (PParameters) *gStuff->parameters;

     // Prepare the DLOG resource for use.
     dt = (DialogTHndl) GetResource('DLOG', kSettingsDialogID);
     if (!dt) {
             gResult = ResError() ? ResError() : resNotFound;
             return true;
     }

     HNoPurge((Handle) dt);

     CenterDialog(dt);
     SetUpMoveableModal(dt, gStuff->hostSig);
```

```
// Create the dialog.
dp = GetNewDialog(kSettingsDialogID, nil, (WindowPtr) -1);
if (!dp) {
        gResult = memFullErr;
        return true;
}

// Set the dialog up.
(void) SetDialogDefaultItem(dp, ok);
(void) SetDialogCancelItem(dp, cancel);
(void) SetDialogTracksCursor(dp, true);

StuffNumber(dp, kOddFieldsItem,  params->oddDelta);
StuffNumber(dp, kEvenFieldsItem, params->evenDelta);

SetArrowCursor();

SelectTextItem(dp, kOddFieldsItem);

// Loop to handle the dialog items.
do {
        MoveableModalDialog(dp, gStuff->processEvent, nil, &item);

        if (item == ok) {
            // Validate the input.
            if (!FetchNumber(dp, kOddFieldsItem, -255, 255, &odd))
                    item = 0;
            else if (!FetchNumber(dp, kEvenFieldsItem, -255, 255, &even))
                    item = 0;
        }

} while (item != ok && item != cancel);

DisposeDialog(dp);
HPurge((Handle) dt);

// Handle the dismissal of the dialog.
if (item == ok) {
        params->oddDelta  = odd;
        params->evenDelta = even;
} else {
        gResult = userCanceledErr;
}

return true;
        // Return true because we don't want to be called again.
}
```

```
// -------------------------------------------------------------------------
//
//   FilterRect
//
// -------------------------------------------------------------------------
//           Filter part of the area.
// -------------------------------------------------------------------------
static void
FilterRect(GPtr globals)
{
     Byte *srcPtr = (unsigned8*) gStuff->inData;
     Byte *dstPtr = (unsigned8*) gStuff->outData;

     Boolean isOdd = (gStuff->inRect.top & 0x0001);
     short delta = isOdd ? ((PParameters) *gStuff->parameters)->oddDelta
                         : ((PParameters) *gStuff->parameters)->evenDelta;

     short srcColBytes = gStuff->inHiPlane - gStuff->inLoPlane + 1;
     short dstColBytes = gStuff->planes;
     short count = gStuff->filterRect.right - gStuff->filterRect.left;

     while (count--) {
               short plane;

#if 1
               // All planes.
               for (plane = gStuff->planes - 1; plane >= 0; --plane) {
                       short value = srcPtr[plane] + delta;
                       dstPtr[plane] = ClipInRange(value, 0, 255);
               }
#elif 0
               // Only some planes
               for (plane = gStuff->planes - 1; plane >= 4; --plane)
          //         dstPtr[plane] = 255;
                       ;

               for (; plane >= 0; --plane) {
                       short value = srcPtr[plane] + delta;
                       dstPtr[plane] = ClipInRange(value, 0, 255);
               }
#endif

          srcPtr += srcColBytes;
          dstPtr += dstColBytes;
     }
}
```

```
// ----------------------------------------------------------------------------
//
//     DoAbout
//
// ----------------------------------------------------------------------------
//              Displays the about dialog box for the plug-in module.
// ----------------------------------------------------------------------------
void DoAbout(GPtr globals)
{
     ShowAbout(kAboutBoxDialogID);
}




// ----------------------------------------------------------------------------
//
//     DoParameters
//
// ----------------------------------------------------------------------------
//              Asks the user for the plug-in filter module's parameters. Note that
//              the image size information is not yet defined at this point. Also, do
//              not assume that the calling program will call this routine every time
//              the filter is run (it may save the data held by the parameters handle
//              in a macro file).
// ----------------------------------------------------------------------------
void
DoParameters(GPtr globals)
{
     // Create a parameter block and fill it out with defaults.
     if (!gStuff->parameters) {
          gStuff->parameters = NewHandle(sizeof(TParameters));

          if (!gStuff->parameters) {
               gResult = memFullErr;
               return;
          }

          {
               PParameters params = (PParameters) *gStuff->parameters;

               params->oddDelta  =  50;
               params->evenDelta = -50;
          }

     // Make sure the incoming parameters are valid.
     } else {
          PParameters params = (PParameters) *gStuff->parameters;
```

```
                   params->oddDelta  = ClipInRange(params->oddDelta,  -255, 255);
                   params->evenDelta = ClipInRange(params->evenDelta, -255, 255);
                         // Just in case the param block got messed up (it may have been
                         // stored somewhere by the host application).
            }

      gWantsParameters = true;
            // Set the flag to indicate that a call to DoParameters has been
            // received.
}



// ----------------------------------------------------------------------------
//
//    DoPrepare
//
// ----------------------------------------------------------------------------
//             Prepare to filter an image.  If the plug-in filter needs a large amount
//             of buffer memory, this routine should set the bufferSpace field to the
//             number of bytes required.
// ----------------------------------------------------------------------------
void
DoPrepare(GPtr globals)
{
      gStuff->bufferSpace = 0;
}



// ----------------------------------------------------------------------------
//
//    DoStart
//
// ----------------------------------------------------------------------------
//             Sets up filtering and grabs the first scan line of the filterRect for
//             the first call to DoContinue.
// ----------------------------------------------------------------------------
void
DoStart(GPtr globals)
{
      SetupFirstFilterStrip(globals);

      // Inform DoContinue that we are in the GetParameter stage if we need to.
      if (gWantsParameters) {
            gInParameterStage = true;
            gWantsParameters = false;
      }
}
```

```
// ---------------------------------------------------------------------------
//
//    DoContinue
//
// ---------------------------------------------------------------------------
//              In order for a plug-in to be able to work with versions of Photoshop
//              earlier than 3.0 (and other host applications as well), we need to
//              actually implement the filtering in DoContinue.  Otherwise we could
//              just use the nifty new AdvanceState callback routine and do all the
//              filtering in DoStart.
// ---------------------------------------------------------------------------
void
DoContinue(GPtr globals)
{
    if (gInParameterStage) {
            Boolean done = GetParameters(globals);
            // By bring up the parameters dialog here, we can add code to it
            // that would allow it to support a preview area by having it
            // request parts of the image and get called back.  This mechanism
            // is even simpler with Photoshop 3.0 and later by using the
            // AdvanceState callback function.

            if (done) {
                    gInParameterStage = false;
                    SetupFirstFilterStrip(globals);
            }

    } else {
            // Show the current progress state.
            int32 total = gStuff->filterRect.bottom - gStuff->filterRect.top;
            UpdateProgress(gRow - gStuff->filterRect.top, total);

            // Check for command-period or cancel.
            if (TestAbort()) {
                    gResult = userCanceledErr;

            } else {
                    // Filter the current strip.
                    FilterRect(globals);

                    // Setup for next call to DoContinue.
                    gRow++;
                    if (gRow < gStuff->filterRect.bottom) {
                            SetupNextFilterStrip(globals);
```

```
                        // We're done, so signal this fact to the host.
                    } else {
                            SetRect(&gStuff->inRect,  0, 0, 0, 0);
                            SetRect(&gStuff->outRect, 0, 0, 0, 0);
                    }
                }
            }
        }
    }


    // -------------------------------------------------------------------------
    //
    //    DoFinish
    //
    // -------------------------------------------------------------------------
    //           Do any necessary clean-up.
    // -------------------------------------------------------------------------
    void
    DoFinish(GPtr globals)
    {
    }


    // -------------------------------------------------------------------------
```

Chapter Eleven Source Code

ComponentTester.c

```
  /*
      File Name:              ComponentTester.c
  */

  /*
      Assumes Component Manager 3.0 or later.
  */

#include <GestaltEqu.h>
#include <Components.h>
#include <Icons.h>

#include "FatComponent.h"
#include "FatComponentPrivate.h"
#include "ComponentTester.h"

FatComponent       gFatComponent = nil;
Handle             gIconSuite = nil;

void main(void)
{
```

```
unsigned long       randSeed;
DialogPtr           d = nil;
Boolean             fDone = false;
OSErr               err = noErr;
GrafPtr             savePort;
UserItemUPP         drawComponentIconUPP;

// initialize the Mac
InitGraf(&qd.thePort);
InitFonts();
FlushEvents(everyEvent, 0);
InitWindows();
InitMenus();
TEInit();
InitDialogs(nil);
InitCursor();
GetDateTime((unsigned long *)&randSeed);
LMSetRndSeed(randSeed);
DrawMenuBar();

// get our main dialog box
d = GetNewDialog(dlogMainID, nil, (WindowPtr)-1);
if (d == nil) ExitToShell();

// set it up properly
GetPort(&savePort);
SetPort(d);
SetWindowFont(d, geneva, 9, 0, srcCopy);
drawComponentIconUPP = NewUserItemProc(DrawComponentIcon);
SetUserItemProc(d, itemComponentIcon, (ProcPtr)drawComponentIconUPP);
DisableControl(d, itemUnregister);
DisableControl(d, itemBeep);
DisableControl(d, itemFlash);
SelIText(d, itemBeepTimes, 0, 32767);
ShowWindow(d);

// loop until done
while (!fDone) {
        short itemHit;
        ModalDialog(nil, &itemHit);
        switch(itemHit) {

                // Component Manager will automatically unregister
                // a component here, if one is registered.
                case itemQuit:
                        fDone = true;
                        break;

                // allow the user to choose a component file to register
```

```
case itemRegister:
        err = DoRegister();
        if (err == noErr) {
                DisableControl(d, itemRegister);
                EnableControl(d, itemUnregister);
                EnableControl(d, itemBeep);
                EnableControl(d, itemFlash);

// get the icon suite of the component in order to draw it
// in our dialog
                err = GetComponentIconSuite(
                    (Component)gFatComponent, &gIconSuite);
                if (err != noErr) {
                        ShowError(err,
                        "\pgetting the component's icon suite");
                        err = noErr;
                }
        } else {
                ShowError(err, "\pregistering the component");
                err = noErr;
        }
        break;

// unregister any registered component
case itemUnregister:
        err = DoUnregister();
        if (err == noErr) {
                EnableControl(d, itemRegister);
                DisableControl(d, itemUnregister);
                DisableControl(d, itemBeep);
                DisableControl(d, itemFlash);

                // dispose of the icon suite if any
                if (gIconSuite) {
                        err = DisposeIconSuite(gIconSuite, true);
                        if (err != noErr) {
                                ShowError(err,
                        "\pdisposing the component's icon suite");
                                err = noErr;
                        } else gIconSuite = nil;
                }
                CallUserItemProc(drawComponentIconUPP, d,
                        itemComponentIcon); // update icon
        } else {
                ShowError(err, "\punregistering the component");
                err = noErr;
        }
        break;

// call the current component to beep x number of times
case itemBeep:
```

```
                    {
                            Str255 strBeepTimes;
                            long   beepTimes;

                            GetItemText(d, itemBeepTimes, strBeepTimes);
                            StringToNum(strBeepTimes, &beepTimes);

                            err = Beep((short)beepTimes);
                            if (err != noErr) {
                                    ShowError(err, "\pattempting to beep");
                                    err = noErr;
                            }
                    }
                    break;

            // call the current component to flash the menubar x number of times
                case itemFlash:
                    {
                            Str255 tempStr;
                            long   flashTimes, flashDelay;

                            GetItemText(d, itemFlashTimes, tempStr);
                            StringToNum(tempStr, &flashTimes);
                            GetItemText(d, itemFlashDelay, tempStr);
                            StringToNum(tempStr, &flashDelay);

                            err = Flash((short)flashTimes, flashDelay);
                            if (err != noErr) {
                                    ShowError(err, "\pattempting to flash");
                                    err = noErr;
                            }
                    }
                    break;

                default:
                    break;
            }
    }

    // clean up
    DisposeDialog(d);
    DisposeRoutineDescriptor(drawComponentIconUPP);
    SetPort(savePort);
}
```

```
/ ******************************************************************************

     DoRegister

     Allow the user to pick a file of type 'thng', open it, get the 'thng' resource
     of ID 128 and then call RegisterComponentResource on it. Once the component
     is registered we close the resource file and continue.

****************************************************************************** /

OSErr DoRegister(void)
{
     OSErr                         err = noErr;
     SFTypeList                    typeList = {'thng', '????', '????', '????'};
     StandardFileReply     reply;

     StandardGetFile(nil, 1, typeList, &reply);
     if (reply.sfGood) {

             short fRefNum = FSpOpenResFile(&reply.sfFile, fsRdPerm);

             if (fRefNum != -1) {
                 ComponentResourceHandle thngResH = (ComponentResourceHandle)
                         Get1Resource(kComponentResourceType, 128);

                 if (thngResH) {
                         gFatComponent = (FatComponent)
                                 RegisterComponentResource(thngResH,
                                 registerComponentNoDuplicates);
                         ReleaseResource((Handle)thngResH);
                         if (gFatComponent == nil)
                                 err = -1;
                 } else err = ResError() ? ResError() : resNotFound;

                 CloseResFile(fRefNum);

             } else err = ResError() ? ResError() : fnfErr;

     } else err = -128;
     return err;
}

/ ******************************************************************************

     DoUnregister

     Simply call UnregisterComponent on the current registered component.

****************************************************************************** /

OSErr DoUnregister(void)
```

```
{
     OSErr   err = noErr;

     if (gFatComponent) {
             err = UnregisterComponent((Component)gFatComponent);
             if (err == noErr)
                   gFatComponent = nil;
     }

     return err;
}

/*****************************************************************************

     Beep

     Call the current registered component to beep beepTimes.

*****************************************************************************/

OSErr Beep(short beepTimes)
{
     OSErr                      err = noErr;
     ComponentInstance          ci;

     ci = OpenComponent((Component)gFatComponent);
     if (ci) {
             short outBeepTimes;

             err = DoBeep(ci, beepTimes, &outBeepTimes);
             if (err != noErr) ShowError(err, "\pattempting to DoBeep");

             if (outBeepTimes != beepTimes) ShowError(kGenericError,
                   "\pcomparing beepTimes to outBeepTimes");

             err = CloseComponent(ci);
             if (err != noErr) ShowError(err, "\pattempting to CloseComponent");
     } else err = kGenericError;

     return err;
}

/*****************************************************************************

     Flash

     Call the current registered component to flash flashTimes.

*****************************************************************************/

OSErr Flash(short flashTimes, long flashDelay)
```

```
{
    OSErr                       err = noErr;
    ComponentInstance           ci;

    ci = OpenComponent((Component)gFatComponent);
    if (ci) {
            short outFlashTimes;

            err = DoFlash(ci, flashTimes, flashDelay, &outFlashTimes);
            if (err != noErr) ShowError(err, "\pattempting to DoFlash");

            if (outFlashTimes != flashTimes)
                    ShowError(kGenericError,
                    "\pcomparing flashTimes to outFlashTimes");

            err = CloseComponent(ci);
            if (err != noErr) ShowError(err, "\pattempting to CloseComponent");
    } else err = kGenericError;

    return err;
}

/***********************************************************************

    DrawComponentIcon

    User item proc to draw the components icon.

***********************************************************************/

pascal void DrawComponentIcon(DialogPtr d, short theItem)
{
    Rect    r;
    GrafPtr savePort;

    GetPort(&savePort);
    SetPort(d);

    GetDialogItemRect(d, theItem, &r);
    if (gIconSuite) {
            OSErr err = PlotIconSuite(&r, atNone, ttNone, gIconSuite);
    } else {
            FillRect(&r, &qd.ltGray);
            FrameRect(&r);
    }

    SetPort(savePort);
}
```

```
/*****************************************************************************

     GetItemText

*****************************************************************************/

void GetItemText(DialogPtr dlg, short itemNumber, unsigned char* textStr)
{
     short   iKind;
     Handle  iHandle;
     Rect    iRect;

     GetDItem(dlg, itemNumber, &iKind, &iHandle, &iRect);
     GetIText(iHandle, textStr);
}

/*****************************************************************************

     GetDialogItemRect

*****************************************************************************/

void GetDialogItemRect(DialogPtr dlg, short itemNumber, Rect *r)
{
     short   iKind;
     Handle  iHandle;

     GetDItem(dlg, itemNumber, &iKind, &iHandle, r);
}

/*****************************************************************************

     SetUserItemProc

*****************************************************************************/

void SetUserItemProc(DialogPtr dlg, short userItem, ProcPtr userProc)
{
     short   iKind;
     Handle  iHandle;
     Rect    iRect;

     GetDItem(dlg, userItem, &iKind, &iHandle, &iRect);
     SetDItem(dlg, userItem, iKind, (Handle)userProc, &iRect);
}

/*****************************************************************************

     EnableControl

*****************************************************************************/
```

```
void EnableControl(DialogPtr dlg, short controlNumber)
{
    short   iKind;
    Handle  iHandle;
    Rect    iRect;

    GetDItem(dlg, controlNumber, &iKind, &iHandle, &iRect);
    HiliteControl((ControlHandle)iHandle, 0);
}

/******************************************************************************

    DisableControl

******************************************************************************/

void DisableControl(DialogPtr dlg, short controlNumber)
{
    short   iKind;
    Handle  iHandle;
    Rect    iRect;

    GetDItem(dlg, controlNumber, &iKind, &iHandle, &iRect);
    HiliteControl((ControlHandle)iHandle, 255);
}

/****************************************************************************

    SetWindowFont

****************************************************************************/

void SetWindowFont(DialogPtr d, short fontNum, short fontSize, Style fontStyle, short
fontMode)
{
    FontInfo    fInfo;
    GrafPtr     savePort;

    GetPort(&savePort);
    SetPort(d);

    TextFont(fontNum);
    TextSize(fontSize);
    TextFace(fontStyle);
    TextMode(fontMode);

    GetFontInfo(&fInfo);

    (*((DialogPeek)d)->textH)->fontAscent = fInfo.ascent;
    (*((DialogPeek)d)->textH)->lineHeight = fInfo.ascent +
            fInfo.descent + fInfo.leading;
```

```
        (*((DialogPeek)d)->textH)->txFont = fontNum;
        (*((DialogPeek)d)->textH)->txFace = fontStyle;
        (*((DialogPeek)d)->textH)->txMode = fontMode;
        (*((DialogPeek)d)->textH)->txSize = fontSize;

    SetPort(savePort);
}

/****************************************************************************

    ShowError

****************************************************************************/

void ShowError(OSErr errorCode, unsigned char * errorStr)
{
    Str32    errorCodeStr;
    NumToString((long)errorCode, errorCodeStr);
    ParamText(errorCodeStr, errorStr, "\p", "\p");
    StopAlert(256, nil);
    ParamText("\p", "\p", "\p", "\p");
}
```

ComponentTester.h

```
 /*
    File Name:            ComponentTester.h
 */

#pragma once

#define        dlogMainID            128
#define        itemQuit              1
#define        itemRegister          5
#define        itemUnregister        6
#define        itemBeep              7
#define        itemFlash             8
#define        itemBeepTimes         9
#define        itemFlashTimes        10
#define        itemFlashDelay        11
#define        itemComponentIcon     17

OSErr DoRegister(void);
OSErr DoUnregister(void);
OSErr Beep(short beepTimes);
OSErr Flash(short flashTimes, long flashDelay);
pascal void DrawComponentIcon(DialogPtr d, short theItem);

void GetItemText(DialogPtr dlg, short itemNumber, unsigned char* textStr);
```

```
void GetDialogItemRect(DialogPtr dlg, short itemNumber, Rect *r);
void SetUserItemProc(DialogPtr dlg, short userItem, ProcPtr userProc);
void EnableControl(DialogPtr dlg, short controlNumber);
void DisableControl(DialogPtr dlg, short controlNumber);
void SetWindowFont(DialogPtr d, short fontNum, short fontSize,
     Style fontStyle, short fontMode);
void ShowError(OSErr errorCode, unsigned char * errorStr);
```

FatComponent.c

```
/*
    File Name:              FatComponent.c
*/

/*
    Assumes QuickTime 2.0 or later and Component Manager 3.0 or later.
*/

#include "FatComponent.h"
#include "FatComponentPrivate.h"
#include "FatComponentCommon.h"
#include <Errors.h>
#ifndef __powerc
    #include <A4Stuff.h>
#endif

pascal ComponentResult main (ComponentParameters *params, Handle storage);

#ifdef __powerc
    INSTANTIATE_ROUTINE_DESCRIPTOR(FatCanDo);
    INSTANTIATE_ROUTINE_DESCRIPTOR(FatOpen);
    INSTANTIATE_ROUTINE_DESCRIPTOR(FatClose);
    INSTANTIATE_ROUTINE_DESCRIPTOR(FatVersion);

    INSTANTIATE_ROUTINE_DESCRIPTOR(FatDoBeep);
    INSTANTIATE_ROUTINE_DESCRIPTOR(FatDoFlash);

    RoutineDescriptor MainRD =
BUILD_ROUTINE_DESCRIPTOR(uppComponentRoutineProcInfo, main);
    ProcInfoType __procinfo = uppComponentRoutineProcInfo;
#endif

pascal ComponentResult main (ComponentParameters *params, Handle storage)
{
    ComponentResult      result = noErr;

#ifndef __powerc
    long oldA4;
```

```
        oldA4 = SetCurrentA4();
#endif

        // Did we get a Component Manager request code (< 0)?
        if (params->what < 0) {
                switch (params->what) {
                        case kComponentOpenSelect:
                                result = CallComponentFunctionUniv(params, FatOpen);
                                break;

                        case kComponentCloseSelect:
                                result = CallComponentFunctionWithStorageUniv(storage,
                                        params, FatClose);
                                break;

                        case kComponentCanDoSelect:
                                result = CallComponentFunctionUniv(params, FatCanDo);
                                break;

                        case kComponentVersionSelect:
                                result = CallComponentFunctionUniv(params, FatVersion);
                                break;

                        case kComponentRegisterSelect:     // not supported
                        default:                           // unknown
                                result = paramErr;
                                break;
                }
        } else {                                                        // one of ours
                switch (params->what) {
                        case kDoBeepSelect:
                                result = CallComponentFunctionUniv(params, FatDoBeep);
                                break;

                        case kDoFlashSelect:
                                result = CallComponentFunctionUniv(params, FatDoFlash);
                                break;

                        default:                                        // unknown
                                result = paramErr;
                                break;
                }
        }

#ifndef __powerc
        SetA4(oldA4);
#endif

        return result;
}
```

FatComponent.h

```
/*
     File Name:                FatComponent.h
*/

#pragma once

#include <QuickTimeComponents.h>

#define        fatComponentType 'PHAT'

// Math component request codes
enum
{
     kDoBeepSelect = 1,
     kDoFlashSelect
};

typedef        ComponentInstance FatComponent;

#ifdef __cplusplus
extern "C" {
#endif __cplusplus

pascal ComponentResult DoBeep(FatComponent fatInstance, short inBeepTimes,
              short *outBeepTimes)
     ComponentCallNow(kDoBeepSelect, sizeof(short) + sizeof(short*));

pascal ComponentResult DoFlash(FatComponent fatInstance, short inFlashTimes,
              long inDelayTime, short *outFlashTimes)
     ComponentCallNow(kDoFlashSelect, sizeof(short) + sizeof(long) +
              sizeof(short*));

#ifdef __powerc
#define CallComponentFunctionWithStorageUniv(storage, params, funcName) \
   CallComponentFunctionWithStorage(storage, params, &funcName##RD)
#define CallComponentFunctionUniv(params, funcName) \
   CallComponentFunction(params, &funcName##RD)
#define INSTANTIATE_ROUTINE_DESCRIPTOR(funcName) RoutineDescriptor funcName##RD = \
   BUILD_ROUTINE_DESCRIPTOR (upp##funcName##ProcInfo, funcName)
#else
#define CallComponentFunctionWithStorageUniv(storage, params, funcName) \
   CallComponentFunctionWithStorage(storage, params, (ComponentFunctionUPP)funcName)
#define CallComponentFunctionUniv(params, funcName) \
   CallComponentFunction(params, (ComponentFunctionUPP)funcName)
#endif

enum {
     uppFatOpenProcInfo = kPascalStackBased
              | RESULT_SIZE(SIZE_CODE(sizeof(ComponentResult)))
```

```
                | STACK_ROUTINE_PARAMETER(1, SIZE_CODE(sizeof(ComponentInstance)))
};

enum {
    uppFatCloseProcInfo = kPascalStackBased
                | RESULT_SIZE(SIZE_CODE(sizeof(ComponentResult)))
                | STACK_ROUTINE_PARAMETER(1, SIZE_CODE(sizeof(Handle)))
                | STACK_ROUTINE_PARAMETER(2, SIZE_CODE(sizeof(ComponentInstance)))
};

enum {
    uppFatCanDoProcInfo = kPascalStackBased
                | RESULT_SIZE(SIZE_CODE(sizeof(ComponentResult)))
                | STACK_ROUTINE_PARAMETER(1, SIZE_CODE(sizeof(short)))
};

enum {
    uppFatVersionProcInfo = kPascalStackBased
                | RESULT_SIZE(SIZE_CODE(sizeof(ComponentResult)))
};

enum {
    uppFatTargetProcInfo = kPascalStackBased
                | RESULT_SIZE(SIZE_CODE(sizeof(ComponentResult)))
                | STACK_ROUTINE_PARAMETER(1, SIZE_CODE(sizeof(Handle)))
                | STACK_ROUTINE_PARAMETER(2, SIZE_CODE(sizeof(ComponentInstance)))
};

enum {
    uppFatDoBeepProcInfo = kPascalStackBased
                | RESULT_SIZE(SIZE_CODE(sizeof(ComponentResult)))
                | STACK_ROUTINE_PARAMETER(1, SIZE_CODE(sizeof(short)))
                | STACK_ROUTINE_PARAMETER(2, SIZE_CODE(sizeof(short*)))
};

enum {
    uppFatDoFlashProcInfo = kPascalStackBased
                | RESULT_SIZE(SIZE_CODE(sizeof(ComponentResult)))
                | STACK_ROUTINE_PARAMETER(1, SIZE_CODE(sizeof(short)))
                | STACK_ROUTINE_PARAMETER(2, SIZE_CODE(sizeof(long)))
                | STACK_ROUTINE_PARAMETER(3, SIZE_CODE(sizeof(short*)))
};

#ifdef __cplusplus
}
#endif __cplusplus
```

FatComponentCommon.c

```c
/*
    File Name:              FatComponentCommon.c
*/

#include "FatComponent.h"
#include "FatComponentCommon.h"
#include "FatComponentPrivate.h"
#include <OSUtils.h>

pascal ComponentResult FatOpen(ComponentInstance self)
{
    ComponentResult        result = noErr;
    PrivateGlobals**       globals;

    globals = (PrivateGlobals**)NewHandleClear(sizeof(PrivateGlobals));
    if (globals != nil) {

            // remember ourselves
            (*globals)->self = (Component)self;

            // tell the component manager that we have global storage
            SetComponentInstanceStorage(self, (Handle)globals);
    } else result = MemError() ? MemError() : memFullErr;// NewHandleClear failed

    return result;
}

pascal ComponentResult FatClose(Handle storage, ComponentInstance self)
{
    ComponentResult        result = noErr;
    PrivateGlobals**       globals = (PrivateGlobals**) storage;

    if (globals != nil) {
            DisposeHandle((Handle)globals);
            globals = nil;
    }
    return result;
}

pascal ComponentResult FatCanDo(short selector)
{
    switch(selector) {

            // component Manager request codes
            case kComponentOpenSelect:
            case kComponentCloseSelect:
            case kComponentCanDoSelect:
            case kComponentVersionSelect:
```

```
                // our component request codes
                case kDoBeepSelect:
                case kDoFlashSelect:
                        return true;
                        break;

                case kComponentRegisterSelect:  // not supported
                default:                         // unknown request
                        return false;
                        break;
        }
}

pascal ComponentResult FatVersion(void)
{
        return interfaceRevision;
}

pascal ComponentResult FatDoBeep(short inBeepTimes, short *outBeepTimes)
{
        ComponentResult result = noErr;

        *outBeepTimes = inBeepTimes;
        if (inBeepTimes > 0) {
                short   i;
                for (i=1;i<=inBeepTimes;++i)
                        SysBeep(0);
        } else result = kGenericError;

        return result;
}

pascal ComponentResult FatDoFlash(short inFlashTimes, long inDelayTime, short *outFlashTimes)
{
        ComponentResult result = noErr;

        *outFlashTimes = inFlashTimes;
        if (inFlashTimes > 0) {
                short   i;
                long    outTicks;
                for (i=1;i<=inFlashTimes;++i) {
                        FlashMenuBar(0);
                        Delay(inDelayTime, &outTicks);
                        FlashMenuBar(0);
                        Delay(inDelayTime, &outTicks);
                }
        } else result = kGenericError;

        return result;
}
```

FatComponentCommon.h

```
/*
     File Name:              FatComponentCommon.h
*/

#pragma once

#include <QuickTimeComponents.h>

pascal ComponentResult        FatOpen(ComponentInstance self);
pascal ComponentResult        FatClose(Handle storage, ComponentInstance self);
pascal ComponentResult        FatCanDo(short selector);
pascal ComponentResult        FatVersion(void);
pascal ComponentResult        FatDoBeep(short inBeepTimes, short *outBeepTimes);
pascal ComponentResult        FatDoFlash(short inFlashTimes, long inDelayTime,
                                    short *outFlashTimes);
```

PPCGlue.c

```
/*
     File Name:              PPCGlue.c
*/

/*
     The information in this file is straight from
     Technical Note QT 05 - Component Manager version 3.0
*/

#include "FatComponent.h"
#include "FatComponentPrivate.h"
#include <Menus.h>
#include <Windows.h>
#include <QuickDraw.h>
#include <OSEvents.h>
#include <Resources.h>
#include <Desk.h>
#include <Fonts.h>
#include <ToolUtils.h>
#include <Components.h>
#include <QuickTimeComponents.h>

// in InterfaceLib but was left out of headers
extern UniversalProcPtr CallComponentUPP;

// this lets us call our component from PowerPC code
enum {
   uppCallComponentProcInfo = kPascalStackBased
             | RESULT_SIZE(kFourByteCode)
```

```
                | STACK_ROUTINE_PARAMETER(1, kFourByteCode)
};

// we must have this glue in order to call our component from PowerPC code since
// the Component Manager allows you to create your own routines. we must mimic the
// 68k inline code that our 680x0 tester uses so we create one of these glue
// routines for each of our custom functions.
pascal ComponentResult DoBeep(FatComponent fatInstance,
      short inBeepTimes, short *outBeepTimes)
{
#define kDoBeepParamSize (sizeof(DoBeepParams))

#ifdef powerc
#pragma options align=mac68k
#endif

   struct DoBeepParams {
            short                   *outBeepTimes;
            short                   inBeepTimes;
   };
   typedef struct DoBeepParams DoBeepParams;

   struct DoBeepGluePB {
            unsigned char    componentFlags;          /* Flags - set to zero */
            unsigned char    componentParamSize;      /* Size of the params struct */
            short            componentWhat;           /* The component request selector */
            DoBeepParams     params;                  /* The parameters, see above */
            ComponentInstanceinstance;               /* This component instance */
   };
   typedef struct DoBeepGluePB DoBeepGluePB;

#ifdef powerc
#pragma options align=reset
#endif

   DoBeepGluePB        myDoBeepGluePB;
   myDoBeepGluePB.componentFlags = 0;
   myDoBeepGluePB.componentParamSize = kDoBeepParamSize;
   myDoBeepGluePB.componentWhat = kDoBeepSelect;
   myDoBeepGluePB.params.outBeepTimes = outBeepTimes;
   myDoBeepGluePB.params.inBeepTimes = inBeepTimes;
   myDoBeepGluePB.instance = (ComponentInstance)fatInstance;

   return CallUniversalProc(CallComponentUPP, uppCallComponentProcInfo, &myDoBeepGluePB);
}

pascal ComponentResult DoFlash(FatComponent fatInstance, short inFlashTimes, long inDelayTime, short
*outFlashTimes)
{
#define kDoFlashParamSize (sizeof(DoFlashParams))

#ifdef powerc
```

```
#pragma options align=mac68k
#endif

  struct DoFlashParams {
          short                   *outFlashTimes;
          long                    inDelayTime;
          short                   inFlashTimes;
  };
  typedef struct DoFlashParams DoFlashParams;

  struct DoFlashGluePB {
          unsigned char    componentFlags;          /* Flags - set to zero */
          unsigned char    componentParamSize;      /* Size of the params struct */
          short            componentWhat;           /* The component request selector */
          DoFlashParams    params;                  /* The parameters, see above */
          ComponentInstance instance;               /* This component instance */
  };
  typedef struct DoFlashGluePB DoFlashGluePB;

#ifdef powerc
#pragma options align=reset
#endif

  DoFlashGluePB      myDoFlashGluePB;
  myDoFlashGluePB.componentFlags = 0;
  myDoFlashGluePB.componentParamSize = kDoFlashParamSize;
  myDoFlashGluePB.componentWhat = kDoFlashSelect;
  myDoFlashGluePB.params.outFlashTimes = outFlashTimes;
  myDoFlashGluePB.params.inDelayTime = inDelayTime;
  myDoFlashGluePB.params.inFlashTimes = inFlashTimes;
  myDoFlashGluePB.instance = (ComponentInstance)fatInstance;

  return CallUniversalProc(CallComponentUPP, uppCallComponentProcInfo,
          &myDoFlashGluePB);
}
```

FatComponentPrivate.h

```
/*
    File Name:               FatComponentPrivate.h
*/

#pragma once

#include <QuickTimeComponents.h>

// Component and interface revision levels
enum
{
    interfaceRevision = 0x00010001
```

```
};

enum
{
    kGenericError = -1L
};

typedef        struct PrivateGlobals
{
    Component        self;              // Our component ID
}
PrivateGlobals, *PrivateGlobalsPtr, **PrivateGlobalsHdl;
```

Chapter Twelve Source Code
RefConLDEF.c

```
/*
    File Name:                RefConLDEF.c
*/

#include "RefConLDEF.h"

/**************************************************************************

    function prototypes

**************************************************************************/

void DrawMsg(Boolean fSelect, Rect *r, Cell cell, ListHandle lh);
void HiliteMsg(Boolean fSelect, Rect *r);

/**************************************************************************

    main

**************************************************************************/

pascal void main(short message, Boolean fSelect, Rect *r, Cell cell,
                        short dataOffset, short dataLen, ListHandle lh)
{

    switch(message) {
            case lInitMsg:
                    break;

            case lDrawMsg:
                    DrawMsg(fSelect, r, cell, lh);
                    break;
```

```
            case lHiliteMsg:
                    HiliteMsg(fSelect, r);
                    break;

            case lCloseMsg:
                    break;

            default:
                    break;
      }
}

/***************************************************************************

      DrawMsg

***************************************************************************/

void DrawMsg(Boolean fSelect, Rect *r, Cell cell, ListHandle lh)
{
      RefconLDEFCell  cellData;
      short           dataLen;

      // get cell
      dataLen = (short)sizeof(cellData);
      LGetCell((Ptr)(&cellData), &dataLen, cell, lh);

      // call draw proc
      if (cellData.drawProc) {
              EraseRect(r);
              CallRefconLDEFDrawProc(cellData.drawProc, r, cell, lh, cellData.refCon);
      }

      // hilite if selected
      if (fSelect)
              HiliteMsg(fSelect, r);
}

/***************************************************************************

      HiliteMsg

***************************************************************************/

void HiliteMsg(Boolean fSelect, Rect *r)
{
      unsigned char   hMode;

      hMode = LMGetHiliteMode();
      BitClr((Ptr)(&hMode),(long)pHiliteBit);
```

```
        LMSetHiliteMode(hMode);
        InvertRect(r);
    }
```

RefConLDEF.h

```
    /*
    File Name:          RefConLDEF.h
    */

    #pragma once

    #define kRefConLDEFID 128   // resource id of our LDEF resource

    typedef void (*RefconLDEFDrawProcType)(Rect *r, Cell cell, ListHandle lh, long refCon);

    enum {
        uppRefconLDEFDrawProcInfo = kCStackBased
                | STACK_ROUTINE_PARAMETER(1, SIZE_CODE(sizeof(Rect *)))
                | STACK_ROUTINE_PARAMETER(2, SIZE_CODE(sizeof(Cell)))
                | STACK_ROUTINE_PARAMETER(3, SIZE_CODE(sizeof(ListHandle)))
                | STACK_ROUTINE_PARAMETER(4, SIZE_CODE(sizeof(long)))
    };

    #if USESROUTINEDESCRIPTORS
    typedef UniversalProcPtr RefconLDEFDrawProcUPP;

    #define CallRefconLDEFDrawProc(userRoutine, r, cell, lh, refCon)              \
                CallUniversalProc((UniversalProcPtr)(userRoutine),
    uppRefconLDEFDrawProcInfo, r, cell, lh, refCon)
    #define NewRefconLDEFDrawProc(userRoutine)                \
                (RefconLDEFDrawProcUPP) NewRoutineDescriptor((ProcPtr)(userRoutine),
    uppRefconLDEFDrawProcInfo, GetCurrentISA())
    #else
    typedef RefconLDEFDrawProcType RefconLDEFDrawProcUPP;

    #define CallRefconLDEFDrawProc(userRoutine, r, cell, lh, refCon)              \
                (*(userRoutine))(r, cell, lh, refCon)
    #define NewRefconLDEFDrawProc(userRoutine)                \
                (RefconLDEFDrawProcUPP)(userRoutine)
    #endif

    typedef struct RefconLDEFCell {
        long                            refCon;
        RefconLDEFDrawProcUPP drawProc;
    } RefconLDEFCell, *RefconLDEFCellPtr, **RefconLDEFCellHdl;
```

a5World.c

```c
/*
    File Name:              a5World.c
*/

#include "a5 World.h"

void main(void)
{
    unsigned long randSeed;
    A5Params      a5p;
    Rect          screenBitsBounds;

    // initialize the Mac
    InitGraf(&qd.thePort);
    InitFonts();
    FlushEvents(everyEvent, 0);
    InitWindows();
    InitMenus();
    TEInit();
    InitDialogs(nil);
    InitCursor();
    GetDateTime((unsigned long *)&randSeed);
    LMSetRndSeed(randSeed);
    DrawMenuBar();

    // create our own a5 world
    PrepareA5World(&a5p, &screenBitsBounds);

    // draw within it
    ForeColor(redColor);
    PaintRect(&screenBitsBounds);

    // restore the old a5 world
    RestoreA5World(&a5p);

    // wait for a mouse click
    while (!Button()) {}

    // update the screen
    UpdateRectangle(&screenBitsBounds);

    // flush any stray events
    FlushEvents(everyEvent, 0);
}

//
// Call this function before you want to draw when a5 may be invalid
//
```

```
void PrepareA5World(A5ParamsPtr pp, Rect *screenBitsBounds)
{
    //
    // save the zone and set to the System zone
    // this may not be needed but we used this code
    // in a system extension that used the system heap
    //

    pp->oldZone = GetZone();
    SetZone(SystemZone());

    //
    // save DeskHook and DragHook, which are low memory proc ptrs
    // then set them to 0 so they are ignored
    //

    pp->saveDeskHook = LMGetDeskHook();
    pp->saveDragHook = LMGetDragHook();
    LMSetDeskHook((UniversalProcPtr)0L);
    LMSetDragHook((UniversalProcPtr)0L);

    //
    // set ResLoad to true so our resources are loaded
    // may not be needed in your code
    //

    pp->savedResLoad = LMGetResLoad();
    SetResLoad(true);

    //
    // save the values of the Font Manager and QuickDraw init flags
    //

    pp->pFMExist = (Ptr)0x0D42;
    pp->pQDExist = (Ptr)0x08F3;
    pp->savedFMExist = *(pp->pFMExist);
    pp->savedQDExist = *(pp->pQDExist);

    //
    // set our a5 world, initialize it, and init the Font Manager
    //

    pp->oldA5 = SetA5((long)&(pp->qdWorld.thePort));
    InitGraf(&(pp->qdWorld.qd.thePort));
    if ((pp->savedFMExist == 0x00) && (LMGetWidthTabHandle() == nil))
            *(pp->pFMExist) = 0xFF;
    InitFonts();

    //
    // open a color port, requires Color QuickDraw
    //
```

```
    OpenCPort((CGrafPtr)(&pp->qdWorld.port));

    //
    // return the bounds of the a5 world we have created
    //

    *screenBitsBounds = pp->qdWorld.qd.screenBits.bounds;
}

//
// Call this function when you are through drawing into your a5 world
//

void RestoreA5World(A5ParamsPtr pp)
{
    //
    // close the color port
    //

    CloseCPort((CGrafPtr)(&pp->qdWorld.port));

    //
    // restore the old a5 world
    //

    SetA5(pp->oldA5);

    //
    // restore other saved settings
    //

    *(pp->pQDExist) = pp->savedQDExist;
    *(pp->pFMExist) = pp->savedFMExist;
    LMSetDeskHook(pp->saveDeskHook);
    LMSetDragHook(pp->saveDragHook);
    LMSetResLoad(pp->savedResLoad);
    SetZone(pp->oldZone);
}

//
// Call this function to update the entire screen
//

void UpdateRectangle(Rect *updateRect)
{
    RgnHandle    thisScreenBoundary = NewRgn();
    GrafPtr      oldPort;
    GrafPtr      theBigPicture;

    if (thisScreenBoundary) {
        RectRgn(thisScreenBoundary, updateRect);
```

```
                    GetPort(&oldPort);
                    GetWMgrPort(&theBigPicture);
                    SetPort(theBigPicture);
                    DrawMenuBar();
                    PaintOne(nil, thisScreenBoundary);
                    PaintBehind(LMGetWindowList(), thisScreenBoundary);
                    SetPort(oldPort);
                    DisposeRgn(thisScreenBoundary);
            }
    }
```

a5World.h

```
    /*
        File Name:              a5World.h
    */

    #pragma once

    typedef struct {
        QDGlobals       qd;                     // QuickDraw globals
        GrafPtr         thePort;                // a5
        char            stuff[28];              // Misc stuff
        GrafPortport;                           // The color port we open to draw in
    } QDWorld;

    typedef struct {
        THz                 oldZone;            // saved heap zone
        UniversalProcPtr    saveDeskHook;       // saved DeskHook
        UniversalProcPtr    saveDragHook;       // saved DragHook
        unsigned char       savedResLoad;       // saved ResLoad
        long                oldA5;              // saved A5
        Ptr                 pFMExist;           // Font Manager initialized flag
        Ptr                 pQDExist;           // QuickDraw initialized flag
        unsigned char       savedFMExist;       // saved value of Font Manager init flag
        unsigned char       savedQDExist;       // saved value of QuickDraw init flag
        QDWorld             qdWorld;            // our QuickDraw world
    } A5Params, *A5ParamsPtr;

    void PrepareA5World(A5ParamsPtr pp, Rect *screenBitsBounds);
    void RestoreA5World(A5ParamsPtr pp);
    void UpdateRectangle(Rect *updateRect);
```

Glossary

680x0 Any of the family of 68000 microprocessors made by Motorola. See PowerPC.

680x0 code Code that executes on any of the family of 68000 microprocessors made by Motorola. See PowerPC code.

accelerated resource A resource that contains a RoutineDescriptor and PowerPC code that otherwise functions just as a 680x0 code resource. Examples include native list definitions, native control definitions, native control panels, etc. See private resource.

application extension A fragment containing code and data used to extend the functionality of an application. See system extension.

calling conventions Conventions used to describe the specific way in which a routine is executed. Calling conventions specify how parameters are passed to the routine and how values are returned to the caller.

Code Fragment Manager The system software manager that handles the loading and preparation of code fragments.

code resource A resource containing executable code. Most of the time this refers to a resource containing 680x0 code.

connection A link between any two fragments.

connection ID   The reference number used to identify a connection. See connection.

container   The storage used for a fragment. A container may store more than one fragment. A container may be the data fork of a file or a resource.

emulation   The process by which system software running on a PowerPC mimics a 680x0 in order to execute 680x0 code.

executable code   The instructions necessary to make a microprocessor do something.

executable resource   Any resource that contains executable code.

exported symbol   A symbol in a fragment that is accessible by name to other fragments. See symbol.

fat application   An application that contains 680x0 and PowerPC code. The PowerPC code is stored in the data fork. The resource fork contains a cfrg resource in order to tell the Code Fragment Manager how to access the PowerPC code.

fat   Contains executable code from more than one instruction set, usually in reference to 680x0 code and PowerPC code.

fat resource   A resource that contains 680x0 and PowerPC code. Fat resources are preceded by a routine descriptor that tells where each type of code is located and describes the calling conventions needed to access each type.

fragment   Executable PowerPC code and its associated data. Sometimes called a code fragment.

head patch   A patch to a trap that executes code before executing the original trap. See tail patch.

import library   A shared library that is automatically loaded at runtime by the Code Fragment Manager. See shared library.

initialization routine   A function in a code fragment that is executed immediately after the fragment has been loaded and prepared. See termination routine.

instruction set architecture (ISA)   The set of instructions used in a particular processor or family of processors.

main entry point   The function in a fragment or code resource that is executed whenever the code is called.

main symbol   The main routine of a fragment. Depending on the type of fragment, this may be considered the main entry point. See main entry point.

Mixed Mode Manager   The system software manager that handles the mixed mode architecture of 680x0 code running on the PowerPC microprocessor.

mode switch   The process of switching from the PowerPC processor's native environment to that of the 680x0 emulator or vice versa.

native application   An application that is compiled explicitly for the processor on the machine on which it is executing. In many cases, this is used incorrectly to mean a PowerPC application.

Power Macintosh   The name of Apple's PowerPC computers.

PowerPC   Any of the family of PowerPC microprocessors made by Motorola. See 680x0.

PowerPC code   Code that executes in native mode on any of the family of PowerPC microprocessors made by Motorola. See 680x0 code.

prepare   To resolve imports in a fragment to exports from another fragment. A fragment must be prepared before it can be used.

private resource   Any resource containing executable code whose behavior is defined by your application. Examples include HyperCard XCMDs, Photoshop Plug-ins, etc. See accelerated resource.

procedure pointer   The address of a routine.

RoutineDescriptor   A data structure used by the Mixed Mode Manager that describes the the routines to which it refers. Routine descriptors contain one or more routine records. See RoutineRecord.

RoutineRecord   A data structure that describes a particular routine. This structure contains calling convention information, the location of the routine in memory, and more. See RoutineDescriptor.

safe fat resource   A fat resource that contains and is preceded by a short stub of 680x0 code that helps to identify certain characteristics of the hardware before execution of the main resource code. The safe fat resource allows you to run a fat resource on a machine that does not have the Mixed Mode Manager available. See fat resource.

shared library   A fragment that exports symbols to other fragments and can be accessed during linking and loading of other fragments. See import library.

symbol   The specific name of a code or data element within a fragment. See exported symbol.

system extension   A fragment containing code and data used to extend the functionality of the system software. See application extension.

table of contents (TOC)   An area of static data within a fragment that contains pointers to code and data within the fragment, as well as to imported symbols from other fragments.

tail patch   A patch to a trap that executes code after executing the original trap. See head patch.

termination routine   A function in a code fragment that is executed just before the fragment is unloaded. See initialization routine.

universal header files   A set of header files that can be used to compile code for both 680x0 and PowerPC platforms.

universal procedure pointer   A procedure pointer in the 680x0 environment. In the PowerPC environment, a universal procedure pointer is a pointer to a RoutineDescriptor. See RoutineDescriptor, procedure pointer.

virtual memory   Memory available beyond the standard limits of RAM. In most cases, virtual memory extends this available memory to disk-based storage devices.

Index

About the Author

Joe Zobkiw (pronounced **Zob-**Q) has been a Macintosh software engineer since the mid-'80s. Since that time, he has worked on antivirus software, communications software, and just about everything in between. He really got hooked on programming during his stint as a music synthesis major at Berklee College of Music in Boston. Working on MIDI software while at Berklee got him the jump start he needed to make a career out of commercial Macintosh programming. Today, Joe writes more C than English and keeps busy via his Macintosh software development firm, TripleSoft. When he isn't surfing the net or programming, Joe enjoys listening to tunes, playing with his synthesizers, and counting down the payments of his mortgage.

You can reach Joe at any of the following electronic mail addresses.

America Online:	TripleSoft
eWorld:	TripleSoft
CompuServe:	74631, 1700
Internet:	TripleSoft@aol.com
	TripleSoft@eWorld.com
	74631.1700@compuserve.com

Source code updates for this book will be posted on many major online services including the following services.

America Online:	Use Keyword TripleSoft
eWorld:	Use Shortcut TripleSoft

Metrowerks CodeWarrior Order Form

Please Print Clearly

_____

Name

_____

Company or Educational Institution

_____

Address

_____

Address

_____

City   State/Province   Zip/Postal Code

_____

Telephone Number

_____

Fax Number

_____

E-mail Address

	Qty	Cost Each	Total
CodeWarrior Gold		$399.00	
CodeWarrior Bronze		$99.00	
CodeWarrior Magic		$299.00	
CodeWarrior Academic		$99.00	
Academic Lab Pack 10		$650.00	
Academic Lab Pack 25		$1450.00	
Inside CodeWarrior Doc.		$34.95	
		Total	
		Sales Tax (As May Apply)	
		Shipping & Handling	
		Total Payment	

☐ Visa   ☐ Master Card   ☐ American Express

Credit Card Number   Expiry Date (MM/YY)

Cardholder's Signature

To Order:

Voice: (800) 377-5416
International: (419) 281-1802
Fax: (419) 281-6883

For site license and general sales information:
Please call Metrowerks at (512) 305-0400 or send email to sales@metrowerks.com

Addison-Wesley warrants the enclosed disc to be free of defects in materials and faulty workmanship under normal use for a period of ninety days after purchase. If a defect is discovered in the disc during the warranty period, a replacement disc can be obtained at no charge by sending the defective disc, postage prepaid, with proof of purchase to:

Addison-Wesley Publishing Company
Editorial Department
Trade Computer Books Division
One Jacob Way
Reading, MA 01867

After the ninety-day period, a replacement will be sent upon receipt of the defective disc and a check or money order for $10.00, payable to Addison-Wesley Publishing Company.

Addison-Wesley makes no warranty or representation, either express or implied, with respect to this software, its quality, performance, merchantability, or fitness for a particular purpose. In no event will Addison-Wesley, its distributors, or dealers be liable for direct, indirect, special, incidental, or consequential damages arising out of the use or inability to use the software. The exclusion of implied warranties is not permitted in some states. Therefore, the above exclusion may not apply to you. This warranty provides you with specific legal rights. There may be other rights that you may have that vary from state to state.

Software License

PLEASE READ THIS LICENSE CAREFULLY BEFORE USING THE SOFTWARE. BY USING THE SOFTWARE, YOU ARE AGREEING TO BE BOUND BY THE TERMS OF THIS LICENSE. IF YOU DO NOT AGREE TO THE TERMS OF THIS LICENSE RETURN THE SOFTWARE TO THE PLACE WHERE YOU OBTAINED IT AND YOUR MONEY WILL BE REFUNDED.

1. License: The application, demonstration, system, and other software accompanying this License, whether on disk, in read-only memory, or on any other media (the "Software") the related documentation, and fonts are licensed to you by Metrowerks. You own the disk on which the Software and fonts are recorded but Metrowerks and/or Metrowerks' Licensor retain title to the Software, related documentation, and fonts. This License allows you to use the Software and fonts on a single Apple computer. You may use a copy of the software on a home or portable computer, as long as the extra copy is never loaded at the same time the software is loaded on the primary computer on which you use the Software.

You may make one copy of the Software and fonts in machine-readable form for backup purposes. You must reproduce on such copy the Metrowerks copyright notice and any other proprietary legends that were on the original copy of the Software and fonts. You may also transfer all your license rights in the Software and fonts, the backup copy of the Software and fonts, the related documentation, and a copy of this License to another party, provided the other party reads and agrees to accept the terms and conditions of this License.

2. Restrictions: The Software contains copyrighted material, trade secrets, and other proprietary material. In order to protect them, and except as permitted by applicable legislation, you may not decompile, reverse engineer, disassemble, or otherwise reduce the Software to a human-perceivable form. You may not modify, network, rent, lease, loan, distribute, or create derivative works based upon the Software in whole or in part. You may not electronically transmit the Software from one computer to another or over a network. If the Software was licensed to you for academic use, you may not use the Software for commercial product development.

3. Software Redistribution: The following list describes the Software and Materials that licensees of CodeWarrior may incorporate into their own programs and distribute (in object code form only), solely with their own programs, pursuant to the terms of the CodeWarrior Software License as part of a linked binary:

> All libraries in ":Metrowerks C/C++ f:Libraries f"
> All libraries in ":Metrowerks Pascal f:Libraries f"
> All libraries in ":Metrowerks MPW Tools f:MWPPCLibraries" folder
> All libraries in ":Metrowerks MPW Tools f:MW68KLibraries" folder

The following list describes the Software and Materials that licensees of CodeWarrior may incorporate into their own programs and distribute (in object code form only), solely with their own programs, pursuant to the terms of the CodeWarrior Software License:

> ColorSync system extension, ColorSync System Profile control panel, an related profiles
> Macintosh Drag and Drop, Dragging Enabler, and Clipping Extension system extensions
> PowerTalk Extension and PowerTalk Manager extensions
> QuickTime, QuickTime Power Plug, and QuickTime Musical Instruments system extensions
> Speech Manager system extension
> StdCLibInit system extension
> Thread Manager system extension
> AppleScriptLib and ObjectSupportLib shared libraries
> DragLib shared library
> MathLib shared library
> XTND Interface and XTND Power Enabler shared libraries

In order to protect Metrowerks and Metrowerks' Licensors intellectual property rights in the Software and Materials herein, you must reproduce on each copy a copyright notice that clearly states "Copyright © by Metrowerks and its Licensors,"and distribute such Software and Materials pursuant to a valid agreement that is at least as protective of Metrowerks and Metrowerks' Licensors rights in the Software and Materials as this License.

4. Termination: This License is effective until terminated. You may terminate this License at any time by destroying the Software, related documentation, and fonts and all copies thereof. This License will terminate immediately without notice from Metrowerks if you fail to comply with any provision of this License. Upon termination you must destroy the Software, related documentation, and fonts, and all copies thereof.

5. Export Law Assurances: You agree and certify that neither the Software nor any other technical data received from Metrowerks, nor the direct product thereof, will be exported outside the United States except as authorized and as permitted by the laws and regulations of the United States. If the Software has been rightfully obtained by you outside of the United States, you agree that you will not re-export the Software nor any other technical data received from Metrowerks, nor the direct product thereof, except as permitted by the laws and regulations of the United States and the laws and regulations of the jurisdiction in which you obtained the Software.

6. Government End Users: If you are acquiring the Software and fonts on behalf of any unit or agency of the United States Government, the following provisions apply. The Government agrees: (i) if the Software and fonts are supplied to the Department of Defense (DoD), the Software and fonts are classified as "Commercial Computer Software" and the Government is acquiring only "restricted rights" in the Software, its documentation, and fonts as that term is defined in Clause 252.227-7013(c)(1) of the DFARS; and (ii) if the Software and fonts are supplied to any unit or agency of the United States Government other than DoD, the Government's rights in the Software, its documentation and fonts will be as defined in Clause 52.227-19(c)(2) of the FAR or, in the case of NASA, in Clause 18-52.227-86(d) of the NASA Supplement to the FAR.

7. Limited Warranty on Media: Metrowerks warrants the diskettes and/or compact disc on which the Software and fonts are recorded to be free from defects in materials and workmanship under normal use for a period of ninety (90) days from the date of purchase as evidenced by a copy of the receipt. Metrowerks' entire liability and your exclusive remedy will be replacement of the diskettes and/or compact disc not meeting Metrowerks' limited warranty and which is returned to Metrowerks or a Metrowerks authorized representative with a copy of the receipt. Metrowerks will have no responsibility to replace a disk/disc damaged by accident, abuse, or misapplication. ANY IMPLIED WARRANTIES ON THE DISKETTES AND/OR COMPACT DISC, INCLUDING THE IMPLIED WARRANTIES OF MERCHANTABILITY AND FITNESS FOR A PARTICULAR PURPOSE, ARE LIMITED IN DURATION TO NINETY (90) DAYS FROM THE DATE OF DELIVERY. THIS WARRANTY GIVES YOU SPECIFIC LEGAL RIGHTS, AND YOU MAY ALSO HAVE OTHER RIGHTS WHICH VARY BY JURISDICTION.

8. Disclaimer of Warranty on Metrowerks Software: You expressly acknowledge and agree that use of the Software and fonts is at your sole risk. Except as is stated above, the Software, related documentation, and fonts are provided "AS IS" and without warranty of any kind and Metrowerks and Metrowerks' Licensor(s) (for the purposes of provisions 8 and 9, Metrowerks and Metrowerks' Licensor(s) shall be collectively referred to as "Metrowerks") EXPRESSLY DISCLAIM ALL OTHER WARRANTIES, EXPRESS OR IMPLIED, INCLUDING, BUT NOT LIMITED TO, THE IMPLIED WARRANTIES OF MERCHANTABILITY AND FITNESS FOR A PARTICULAR PURPOSE. METROWERKS DOES NOT WARRANT THAT THE FUNCTIONS CONTAINED IN THE SOFTWARE WILL MEET YOUR REQUIREMENTS, OR THAT THE OPERATION OF THE SOFTWARE WILL BE UNINTERRUPTED OR ERROR-FREE, OR THAT DEFECTS IN THE SOFTWARE AND THE FONTS WILL BE CORRECTED. FURTHERMORE, METROWERKS DOES NOT WARRANT OR MAKE ANY REPRESENTATIONS REGARDING THE USE OR THE RESULTS OF THE USE OF THE SOFTWARE AND FONTS OR RELATED DOCUMENTATION IN TERMS OF THEIR CORRECTNESS, ACCURACY, RELIABILITY, OR OTHERWISE. NO ORAL OR WRITTEN INFORMATION OR ADVICE GIVEN BY METROWERKS OR A METROWERKS AUTHORIZED REPRESENTATIVE SHALL CREATE A WARRANTY OR IN ANY WAY INCREASE THE SCOPE OF THIS WARRANTY. SHOULD THE SOFTWARE PROVE DEFECTIVE, YOU (AND NOT METROWERKS OR A METROWERKS AUTHORIZED REPRESENTATIVE) ASSUME THE ENTIRE COST OF ALL NECESSARY SERVICING, REPAIR, OR CORRECTION. SOME JURISDICTIONS DO NOT ALLOW THE EXCLUSION OF IMPLIED WARRANTIES, SO THE ABOVE EXCLUSION MAY NOT APPLY TO YOU.

9. Limitation of Liability: UNDER NO CIRCUMSTANCES, INCLUDING NEGLIGENCE, SHALL METROWERKS BE LIABLE FOR ANY INCIDENTAL, SPECIAL, OR CONSEQUENTIAL DAMAGES THAT RESULT FROM THE USE OR INABILITY TO USE THE SOFTWARE OR RELATE DOCUMENTATION, EVEN IF METROWERKS OR A METROWERKS AUTHORIZED REPRESENTATIVE HAS BEEN ADVISED OF THE POSSIBILITY OF SUCH DAMAGES. SOME JURISDICTIONS DO NOT ALLOW THE LIMITATION OR EXCLUSION OF LIABILITY FOR INCIDENTAL OR CONSEQUENTIAL DAMAGES SO THE ABOVE LIMITATION OR EXCLUSION MAY NOT APPLY TO YOU.

In no event shall Metrowerks' total liability to you for all damages, losses, and causes of action (whether in contract, tort [including negligence] or otherwise) exceed that portion of the amount paid by you which is fairly attributable to the Software and fonts.

10. Controlling Law and Severability: This License shall be governed by and construed in accordance with the laws of the United States and the State of California, as applied to agreements entered into and to be performed entirely within California between California residents. If for any reason a court of competent jurisdiction finds any provision of this License, or portion thereof, to be unenforceable, that provision of the License shall be enforced to the maximum extent permissible so as to effect the intent of the parties, and the remainder of this License shall continue in full force and effect.

11. Complete Agreement: This License constitutes the entire agreement between the parties with respect to the use of the Software, the related documentation, and fonts, and supersedes all prior or contemporaneous understandings or agreements, written or oral, regarding such subject matter. No amendment to or modification of this License will be binding unless in writing and signed by a duly authorized representative of Metrowerks.

   Should you have any questions or comments concerning this license, please do not hesitate to call Metrowerks, (514) 747-5999, or to write to 1500 du College, suite 300, St-Laurent QC H4L 5G6 Canada. Attention: Warranty Information.